The Classical Utilitarians

Bentham and Mill

The Classical Utilitarians
Bentham and Mill

Edited, with Introduction, by

JOHN TROYER

Hackett Publishing Company, Inc.
Indianapolis/Cambridge

09 08 07 06 05 04   2 3 4 5 6 7

For further information, please address:

Hackett Publishing Company, Inc.
P.O. Box 44937
Indianapolis, IN 46244-0937

www.hackettpublishing.com

Cover design by Jean Whitman
Interior design by Jennifer Plumley
Composition by Professional Book Compositors, Inc.
Printed at Edwards Brothers, Inc.

Library of Congress Cataloging-in-Publication Data

The classical utilitarians Bentham and Mill / edited, with introduction,
by John Troyer.
        p. cm.
    Includes bibliographical references.
    ISBN 0-87220-650-5 (cloth) — ISBN 0-87220-649-1 (paper)
    1. Mill, John Stuart, 1806–1873.   2. Classical school of econom-
ics.   3. Utilitarianism.   4. Bentham, Jeremy, 1748–1832.   5. Mill,
John Stuart, 1806–1873.   I. Troyer, John.

HB94.C428 2003
330.15'3'0922—dc21   2002191279

Contents

Introduction

Jeremy Bentham (1748–1832) was an exceptionally able and influential philosopher, but he was also, in some ways, a rather strange man. He died in 1832, but he can still be seen, ensconced within a glass case, at University College, London. Bentham donated his cadaver for instructive dissection by T. Southwood Smith, a leading advocate for the legalization of such donations, but directed that his skeleton should be preserved. Bentham further requested that the skeleton be stuffed out to fit his clothing and preserved as what he dubbed an "auto-icon." Technology being what it was, his executors had to settle for a wax model of his head, but the original remains and is kept separately, "preserved after the manner of South American head hunters."[1]

Bentham hoped that the preservation of his body, and its periodic display, would remind later generations of "the Founder of the greatest happiness system of morals and legislation" and draw their attention to the virtues of that system. Bentham's hope has undoubtedly been realized, at least to some degree, but today his remains attract many fewer visitors than do the "auto-icons" of Lenin and Chairman Mao. Despite this, the greatest happiness system, as expounded in the writings of Bentham and Mill, is still widely influential, while the systems of Lenin and Mao are moribund.

The continuing vitality of the greatest happiness system is not difficult to understand—it embodies a very natural and compelling model of rationality. This model, which dominates much of contemporary economics (as well as decision theory, "cost-benefit analysis," and "public choice theory") sees rational action as an attempt to maximize net utility (i.e., the result of summing the benefits and costs and subtracting the latter from the former). This view, which is frequently called "means-end" rationality, goes back (at least) to Aristotle. In the *Nicomachean Ethics* Aristotle asserts that "we cannot deliberate about ends but only about the means by which ends can be attained."[2] If we assume, with Aristotle, that happiness is "the highest good attainable by action," and hence the aim of politics, we get something very like Bentham's view.[3] Indeed it is tempting, and not implausible, to interpret philosophers as different as Adam Smith and Chairman Mao as agreeing that the goal of social institutions is the maximization of net happiness and disagreeing only on the most efficient means of realizing that end.

Of course philosophers who share this vision of the proper function of social institutions like law and morality may differ on more than the best methods to attain it; as Aristotle noted, there is widespread agreement that happiness is the goal, but considerable disagreement as to what constitutes happiness.[4] For Bentham the answer is simple: happiness is just pleasure and the absence of pain. The value (or disvalue) of a pleasure (or pain) depends only on its intensity and duration, and can (at least in principle) be quantified precisely. Given this, we can reconstruct one line of Bentham's argument for the principle of utility as something like the following:

i)   The good of a society is the sum of the happiness of the individuals in that society.

ii) The purpose of morality is promotion of the good of society.

iii) A moral principle is ideal if and only if universal conformity to it would maximize the good of society.

iv) Universal conformity to the principle of utility ("Act always so as to maximize total net balance of pleasures and pains") would maximize the good of society.

Therefore the principle of utility is the ideal moral principle.

This line of argument, which will be explored more carefully later (see below, pp. xix–xx), has considerable cogency. Indeed Bentham seems to have thought the premises were self-evident, or at least so obvious as to need no argument. He suggests, at the beginning of Chapter III of *The Principles of Morals and Legislation*, that he *has* given an argument for the first premise, writing that:

> It has been shown that the happiness of the individuals, of whom a community is composed, that is their pleasures and security, is the end and the sole end which the legislator ought to have in view.

But when one looks in prior chapters for this demonstration, one finds only the claim that the interest of the community is "the sum of the interests of the several members who compose it," plus the suggestion that this follows from the (unsupported) assertion that "the community is a fictitious *body*." (See below, p. 9)

Bentham also asserts Premise Four as if it were a truism:

> The principle of utility is capable of being consistently pursued, and it is but tautology to say, that the more consistently it is pursued, the better it must ever be for humankind. (See below, p. 16.)

The second and third premises, which constitute a version of what might be called the "functional" account of morality, are particularly congenial to philosophers who, like Bentham, model morality on the law. Bentham was trained in the law, though he never practiced, and his interest in legal reform was his ruling passion. His earliest writings were stimulated by the dissatisfactions he felt with English law, and the *Principles of Morals and Legislation* was intended as the introduction to a (never completed) model penal code.

The line of argument sketched above was not, of course, *all* that recommended Utilitarianism to Bentham. The theory also fit nicely with many of the legal and social reforms that Bentham favored (e.g., reform of the law, universal suffrage, and educational reform). Its chief alternative, what Bentham calls the "principle of sympathy and antipathy," makes the rightness or wrongness of an action depend on the feelings of approbation or disapprobation it elicits in those individuals who judge it. This is, according to Bentham, a principle "in name" but not "in reality." It offers no consistent guidance, and where it seems to it is likely to mislead. In the case of the law, for example, it frequently suggests penalties that are, by Utilitarian standards, overly harsh. Only Utilitarianism can offer a systematic and coherent guide to legal and social reform—or so Bentham claimed.

His claim attracted a number of particularly able and energetic followers, including several members of Parliament, eager to put the theory into practice. Bentham himself, though at one point (1790) quite eager to gain a seat in Parliament, came to realize that his gifts were for thought and writing rather than active political participation. His inherited income, however, allowed him to indirectly influence political action. In 1824 he funded *The Westminster Review*, which became the organ of the "Philosophical Radicals" or "Benthamites." One of the chief Benthamites, though his high office in the East India Company prohibited active political involvement, was James Mill (1773–1836). James Mill, despite his demanding administrative position, managed to contribute articles to *The Westminster*, wrote an important series of articles for the *Encyclopedia Britannica* in which he applied Benthamite principles to practical issues ranging from freedom of the press to colonial administration, and in 1829 published his influential *Analysis of the Phenomena of the Human Mind*. He also took charge of the education of his nine children, the oldest of whom was John Stuart Mill (1806–1873).

James Mill was a cold and distant father, and an unpleasant and condescending husband, but he knew the value of education and he knew that children were capable of learning a great deal at an early age. With Bentham as his guide (and, after 1814, his neighbor in Queen Park Square, London), James set about giving John Stuart what he hoped would be the best education an effective Utilitarian could have. James was lucky in the choice of a pupil in this educational experiment, for John Stuart was exceptionally gifted. He began Greek at three and by eight had read all of Herodotus, much of Xenophon, and six of Plato's dialogues. John Stuart's account of this education in his *Autobiography* is both fascinating and frightening. His education gave him, at age 20, the knowledge of a political theorist twice his age; it also led to what he called "a crisis" in his mental history. Although brought up on Utilitarian teachings, he had not read the works of Bentham himself until 1821, when his father gave him Dumont's edition of Bentham's *Traités de Législation*. This book gave John Stuart a mission: he would devote his life to making certain that social institutions lived up to Benthamite standards. This mission directed and energized the next five years of his life, but in 1826, in "one of those moods when what is pleasure at other times, becomes insipid or indifferent," he lost his calling:

> In this frame of mind it occurred to me to put the question directly to myself, "Suppose that all your objects in life were realized; that all the changes in institutions and opinions which you are looking forward to, could be completely effected at this very instant; would this be a great joy and happiness to you?" And an irrepressible self-consciousness distinctly answered, "No!" At this my heart sank within me: the whole foundation on which my life was constructed fell down. All my happiness was to have been found in the continual pursuit of this end. The end had ceased to charm, and how could there ever again be any interest in the means? I seemed to have nothing left to live for.[5]

Mill hoped this depression would pass with a night's sleep, but it persisted for months, and only began to lift when he read, in the *Memoirs* of Marmontel, an account of the death of Marmontel's father, and Marmontel's resolve, though "then a mere boy," to help his distressed family. Mill was moved to tears, and reports that "from that moment my burthen grew lighter."[6]

Mill attributed his crisis, at least in part, to an education that placed so much stress on intellectual cultivation that it ignored emotional development. Although he never wavered in his belief that happiness was the *summum bonum,* he changed his views on the relative importance of social engineering and personal development. This shift in emphasis can be seen in his later criticisms of Bentham, his increasing admiration for Coleridge, and his growing appreciation of the arts. This change was strongly reinforced by Mill's romantic involvement with Harriet Taylor, the wife of a prosperous London merchant. Falling in love with anyone would doubtless have increased Mill's appreciation of the value of the emotions, but falling in love with a woman who gave aesthetic appreciation a very high priority was bound to reinforce the importance he attributed to the arts. Their unusually intense and intimate relationship began in 1830 and lasted until Harriet's death in 1858. Harriet's husband, John Taylor, was remarkably tolerant of the situation, and managed to ignore the gossip and retain his joviality until his death in 1846. Five years after John Taylor's death, John Stuart Mill married Harriet Taylor, but their earlier relationship prevented an easy acceptance into society as a married couple. Both John Stuart and Harriet were willing, at times it seems almost eager, to live estranged from friends and family, but their isolation must have had costs as well as benefits. Mill's almost pathological sensitivity to anything that might be construed as a slight to Harriet, as well as his remarkably overblown descriptions of her virtues, were surely due in part to discomfort about their deportment from 1830 to 1849. It is also likely that their unorthodox relationship influenced the doctrines of *On Liberty*, the work most clearly their joint effort.

Whatever its social liabilities, Mill's relationship with Harriet helped enormously with his work. It is not clear that his writings owe as much to her thought as Mill sometimes suggests, but her opinions and criticisms certainly helped to shape much of what he published. Her influence is particularly clear in those parts of Mill's writings on Utilitarianism in which he criticizes or diverges from Bentham's teachings. But before turning to Mill's amendments to his mentor's views, Bentham's own position needs to be examined more carefully.

The premises of the line of argument sketched above (p. viii) may have seemed obvious to Bentham, but each of them raises difficulties. The first premise, i.e., the claim that the good of a society is simply the sum of the happiness of the individuals composing it, raises at least two problems. One concerns the *distribution* of happiness in a society, the other the *measurement* of that happiness. Since these are problems that continue to worry contemporary Utilitarians, they are worth discussing in some detail.

Bentham's claim about what constitutes the good of a society entails that one social arrangement, call it *A*, is better than an alternative, call it *B*, if and only if the sum of the happiness of the individuals in the society under *A* is greater than it is under *B*. How the happiness is *distributed* among the individuals is, according to this standard, irrelevant. If arrangement *A* has 1,000 people at happiness level 10, while *B* has 501 at level 20 and 499 at level 0, *B* will be ranked higher than *A*. This indifference to distribution worried early Utilitarians, and it remains a worry for contemporary supporters of the theory.

Some early Utilitarians responded to this worry by claiming that their theory was, in fact, sensitive to distribution, and that Bentham's slogan "The Greatest Happiness of the Greatest Number" showed this. Ben-

tham writes that he learned this "happy phrase" from Priestley, or perhaps Beccaria, but he came to dislike and disown it. In 1829, in an article
on Utilitarianism composed as an aid to James Mill in Mill's controversy
with Macaulay, Bentham writes:

> Greatest happiness *of the greatest number.* Some years have now elapsed
> since, upon a closer scrutiny, reason, altogether incontestable, was found for
> discarding this appendage. On the surface, additional clearness and correct-
> ness given to the idea: at bottom the opposite qualities. (See below, p. 92.)

What bothered Bentham was that "The Greatest Happiness of the Greatest Number," at least as he interpreted it, was an injunction to prefer distributions that have the majority of the population at the highest level of
happiness, even when this conflicts with "the greatest happiness principle." Bentham's worry was the possibility that a dominant majority might
have the power to raise its level of happiness by treating the minority very
badly: he cites, as one example of such a possibility, an imagined enslave-
ment of the Roman Catholics by the Protestants in Great Britain (see
below, p. 93). If we assume that the alternative to this policy of enslave-
ment is one of roughly equal treatment for all, then we might be faced
with a choice between a situation in which everyone enjoys a reasonably
high level of happiness, call it level 600, and a distribution in which the
majority is raised to a significantly higher level, say level 700, while the
happiness of the minority is lowered to level 10. If we assume that there
are 4,000 people in the society, with the minority numbering 1,000, the
choice facing us will be one between the following:

D1	D2
4,000 people at level 600	3,000 people at level 700
	1,000 people at level 10

The "Greatest Happiness Principle" will rank *D1* higher than *D2*,
since *D1* contains a total utility of 2,400,000, while *D2* contains only
2,110,000. [To get these totals, multiply each level of happiness by the
number of people experiencing it.] But "The Greatest Happiness of the
Greatest Number," as Bentham reads it, will rank *D2* higher than *D1*,
since the majority in *D2* is happier than the majority in *D1*.

Of course Bentham's reading of "The Greatest Happiness of the
Greatest Number" is not the only possible interpretation of this slogan.
But under the most plausible alternatives, the slogan provides no guidance at all in many cases. Consider, for example, the choice between the
following:

<u>D3</u>   <u>D4</u>

800 people at level 799   850 people at level 750
200 people at level 10   150 people at level 10

The greatest happiness occurs in *D3*, but more people enjoy the top happiness in *D4*. The basic problem is that "The Greatest Happiness of the Greatest Number" asks us to maximize *both* of two values that can vary independently.[7] Given this, it is hard to disagree with Francis Ysidro Edgeworth, the brilliant 19th-century Utilitarian economist, when he writes that the slogan has no "intelligible or tenable meaning."[8]

Of course appeal to slogans is not the only way to make Utilitarianism sensitive to distribution. Another approach is to add equality to the list of intrinsic goods that must be considered when computing utilitarian sums. This strategy of expanding the roster of intrinsic goods to avoid counter-intuitive implications has a long history among Utilitarians.[9] Indeed Judith Thomson attributes the fact that Utilitarianism "keeps on reappearing, every spring, like a weed with a long root" to its willingness to embrace increasingly ecumenical accounts of the good:

> ...the sophisticated modern utilitarian does not for a moment believe that the good is exhausted by the pleasant.... The sophisticated modern utilitarian may have a theory of the good according to which the good includes the pleasant. If so, he is very likely to think it includes other things too, such as, for example, distributive equality.[10]

This approach requires that we find a measure of total happiness and a measure of degree of equality and then construe Utilitarianism as a theory demanding the maximization of some function of these two measures. There are at least two problems facing this move. The first is developing a measure for degree of inequality. Perfect equality is clear enough, but departures from perfection need to be ranked in a way that assigns an appropriate number to every possible distribution. This is a difficult task, but economists have developed a number of measures that might provide help.[11] One of the more attractive is the so-called "Gini coefficient," which assigns a number from 0 (representing absolute equality) to 1 (representing maximum *in*equality) for every possible distribution. The Gini coefficient is sensitive to distributional data that are ignored by measures that consider only information about deviation from the mean. It also turns out that any transfer of happiness from a more happy person to a less happy one reduces the Gini coefficient. Given all this, we might, as Utilitarians, decide to adopt the Gini coefficient as our measure of degree of inequality. But having adopted it, how are we to *use* it? If we take a measure of total happiness that makes most societies have a lot of it, then simply adding the inverse of the coefficient won't make much difference. Multiplying by it will make more, but pretty clearly neither simple addition nor multiplication is going to work. But rather than looking for more complicated ways of combining equality and total happiness, let's look briefly at a second problem facing this approach—one that calls into question its basic assumption.

There is a very good reason for holding that equality is *not*, in fact, an intrinsic good. It seems to most philosophers and economists that any distributional change that makes at least one person better off and no one worse off is an improvement; conversely, any change that makes at least one person worse off and no one better off is a worsening. But if equality is an intrinsic good, then "downward leveling" will always be at least a presumptive improvement, and it will be an absolute improvement if it involves no loss in total net utility. But consider a situation in which nine people are at happiness level 5 and a tenth person is at level 15: it doesn't seem even a presumptive improvement, from a utilitarian point of view, to reduce the tenth person's happiness level to 5.[12]

Up to this point we have been considering distributions of *happiness*. If we look instead at alternative distributions of *economic goods*, things are different. There is a strong *prima facie* Utilitarian argument for downward redistribution of unequally distributed economic goods, given what economists call "the decreasing marginal utility" of such goods, i.e., the tendency for people to get less utility per unit of economic good as the amount of that good they have increases. Suppose that nine people have 5 apples each and a tenth person has 15 apples, and that each wants all the apples she can get. It seems likely that taking nine of the tenth person's apples and giving one to each of the others will in fact increase total net utility. This is doubtless what Jim Dixon, the protagonist of Kingsley Amis's *Lucky Jim*, is alluding to in the following exchange:

> Bertrand looked quickly round the group, then went on "But their home policy…soak the rich…I mean…Well, it is that, pure and simple, isn't it?"
> Pretending not to notice Margaret's warning frown and Carol's expectant grin, Dixon said quietly: "Well, what's wrong with it, even if it is that and no more? If one man's got ten buns and another's got two, and a bun has to be given up by one of them, then surely you take it from the man with ten buns." [13]

A similarly "instrumental" argument for the equal distribution of social benefits can be derived from the fact that *un*equal distribution of these benefits tends to produce resentment and social unrest. But there is nothing in classical Utilitarianism that favors equality *in itself.* If a person believes that an equal distribution of *happiness* is sometimes better than an unequal one, even though the unequal distribution has a greater sum, the classical Utilitarian must contend that this is an illusion. But the Utilitarian need not claim that the illusion is *ungrounded;* indeed it rests securely on the generally accepted assumption that equal distributions of economic goods and other social benefits tend to maximize total happiness.

I turn now to difficulties concerning the *measurement* of happiness. In discussing the distribution of happiness, *numbers* were assigned to various "levels of happiness" without any mention of how they might be derived, or whether in fact it makes any sense to assign numbers *at all.* Generous readers with doubts about the intelligibility of quantifying happiness may have simply ignored the numbers in the sample distributions, taking them to be heuristic fictions of some sort. But Utilitarians need to take the sort of quantification illustrated by the sample distributions seriously. If it makes no sense to say that one "lot" of happiness (to use Bentham's phrase) is twice as great as another, then it will make no sense to say things like "Giving a bun to a man with 9 buns produces less happiness than giving a bun to a man with only 1 bun."

Bentham himself had no qualms about assigning numbers to "lots" of happiness—indeed he gloried in it. Chapter IV of *Principles of Morals and Legislation* contains what is often called "Bentham's Hedonic Calculus," complete with its "memoriter verses":

> *Intense, long, certain, speedy, fruitful, pure—*
> Such marks in *pleasures* and in *pains* endure.
> Such pleasures seek if *private* be thy end:
> If it be *public,* wide let them *extend.*
> Such *pains* avoid, whichever be thy view:
> If pains *must* come, let them *extend* to few.
> (See below, p. 71.)

These verses raise even more questions than the prose account they summarize, but most of the qualities of pleasures and pains that Bentham mentions have to do with the epistemic and causal properties of the sensations rather than their measurement proper.[14] Fruitfulness, for example, is just the tendency of a pleasure or pain to give rise to similar sensations, while certainty is just the probability it is reasonable to assign to a possible outcome. For individual pleasures and pains, considered in themselves, their value is given by the product of their duration and their intensity.

This isn't entirely clear in Chapter IV, which asserts only that the value of a single pain or pleasure is *some* function of its intensity and duration, but Bentham makes his view explicit in the following passage:

> It is in respect to the aggregate of these its three dimensions that body is said to be great or small: it is of them that its magnitude is composed: its magnitude is the product of all of them together. Of pleasure the same may be said in respect of its two dimensions. Its magnitude is the product of one of them by the other.[15]

It may seem quibbling to question Bentham's choice of multiplication as the appropriate function, but it raises a real problem. Even if we agree that pains and pleasures differ only in two respects, and that their relative values must be a function of these two respects, it is not at all clear how we are to decide which function is the *right* one. Bentham's choice of multiplication appears to be based solely on the analogy with the determination of geometric area. But there are other analogies at hand, should we decide on, say, addition. If we want to determine Jones' total wealth we don't *multiply* his saving account balance by his checking account balance, we *add* them. And of course Bentham himself computes the total net utility of a society by summing rather than multiplying.[16]

But whatever function the Utilitarian decides to use, numbers need to be assigned to intensity levels. Bentham simply assumes that this can be done, and provides no clue about *how* it is to be accomplished. One way of attempting this is suggested, strangely enough, by Mill's claim that pleasures differ in *quality* as well as *quantity*. This claim, which some Utilitarians view as an indispensable insight and others see as a disastrous mistake, seems at first only to complicate the measurement problem. Mill's primary motivation for this claim was a desire to free Utilitarianism from the criticism that it was a doctrine fit only for swine, and gave no value to anything but the satisfaction of "animal appetites." (See below, p. 100.) The Epicureans had countered similar criticisms by pointing out that people, unlike pigs, could get pleasure from intellectual activity. They then went on to note that while the pleasures of the senses tend to be more intense than those of the intellect, the latter are more lasting, less costly, and better for your health. Mill agreed with this, but thought it left out the most important source of the greater value of the "higher" pleasures, namely their intrinsic nature. This point seemed to Mill both clear and clearly compatible with Utilitarianism:

> It is quite compatible with the principle of utility to recognize the fact that some kinds of pleasure are more desirable and more valuable than others. It

would be absurd that, while in estimating all other things quality is considered as well as quantity, the estimation of pleasure should be supposed to depend on quantity alone. (See below, p. 100.)

What Mill declares absurd is just what Bentham takes to be obvious, namely that the value of a pleasure is a function of its intensity and duration. In a famous passage, Bentham explicitly denies that the "higher" pleasures are the more valuable:

> Prejudice apart, the game of push-pin is of equal value with the arts and sciences of music and poetry. If the game of push-pin furnish more pleasure, it is more valuable than either. Everybody can play at push-pin: poetry and music are relished only by a few. (See below, p. 94.)

To evaluate this dispute we need to know how Mill determines the *quality* of a pleasure. He does it by appeal to the preferences of "competent judges," i.e., people "who are equally acquainted with and equally capable of appreciating and enjoying" the pleasures under consideration. If such judges, or a majority among them, prefer the pleasures of poetry to those of push-pin, then the pleasures of poetry are more valuable than the pleasures of push-pin, irrespective of their relative intensities and durations.

It is hard to see how this procedure is actually supposed to work, and harder still to see how it can be made to yield Mill's desired results without circularity. There is, to begin with, a problem in interpreting "equally acquainted with." If it means "has experienced an equal number of both pleasures," it seems overly restrictive. A few sentences before the one using "equally acquainted," Mill employs instead "competently acquainted," and in the sentence before that he requires only that the judges "have experience of both" the pleasures. But if we require only that judges have experience of both pleasures, it will almost certainly turn out that the pleasures of watching professional football are "higher" than those of watching grand opera or reading poetry. To match Mill's ranking of pleasures we will have to lean heavily on notions like "competent acquaintance" and "equal capacity for appreciation," and it is hard to see how these notions can be explained without appeal to the notion of "higher pleasure" itself. If the competence of a judge can only be decided by seeing if she prefers "higher" pleasures to "lower" ones, we can't appeal to the notion of a "competent judge" in explicating "higher" and "lower" pleasures.

But even if Mill's method of evaluating pleasures can't be made to rank them as he thought they should be ranked, it suggests an interesting way to tackle the measurement problem, and one in fact adopted by many contemporary decision theorists. This approach, first articulated by Frank Plumpton Ramsey, begins with a person's ordinal preference ranking over a large array of possible outcomes. (An *ordinal* preference ranking requires that a person decide whether two outcomes are equally desirable, or that one is more desirable than the other, but not *how much* more desirable one is than the other.) If this ranking possesses a number of properties that it seems reasonable to think would characterize a rational agent's preferences (transitivity and additivity, for example), we can then create a "utility function" that assigns numbers to the outcomes.[17] These numbers represent, on this view, the subjective value of each of the outcomes for the person in question.

When applied to pleasures and pains, Ramsey's approach obviates the need to assign values to intensity and duration and then decide what function to use to combine them. We need only ask, roughly, which batches of pains and pleasures are preferred to which. And this seems reasonable, since, as Mill points out:

> Neither pains nor pleasures are homogeneous, and pain is always heterogeneous with pleasure. What is there to decide whether a particular pleasure is worth purchasing at the cost of a particular pain, except the feelings and judgment of the experienced? (See below, p. 103.)

Of course such preferences may vary from person to person. Smith may prefer a brief period of intense pain to a long siege of mild discomfort, while Jones may prefer the long siege, even though they agree about the intensity and duration of both experiences. And Brown may strongly prefer opera to football, while Robinson enjoys the Superbowl much more than she does *La Bohème*.

Unfortunately Ramsey's approach, even if it works, provides only what economists call an "*intra*personal" utility scale. To measure my losses against your gains, we need a way to make *inter*personal comparisons. A gain of 10 on my *intra*personal scale can't be guaranteed to outweigh a gain of 5 on yours unless we're certain that we're using "hedonic thermometers" with the same calibration. Of course to be *absolutely certain* that we're using the same scale would require solving the so-called "problem of other minds" and somehow gaining the sort of access to one another's mental states that we have to our own. But given our biological similarity and the hunch that what you say is pretty awful is just about as bad for you as what I call pretty awful is for me, we can perhaps justify the assumption that once we've decided to assign -50 to what's pretty awful and +50 to what's pretty good, we'll be more or less in agreement. And of course a Utilitarian need not claim that interpersonal comparisons can always, or even generally, be made with a high degree of precision. All that is required is that interpersonal comparisons make sense and that in some situations we can have good reason to think that some are true and others false.

A Utilitarian can, and should, also point out that *any* ethical system that accords weight to the hedonic consequences of actions will have to deal with the same measurement problems. And, the Utilitarian might gloat, "Once I've made my measurements *my* problems are over, while *yours* have just begun." But, alas, while his opponent's troubles may have just begun, the Utilitarian's are not over. Bentham's argument for the principle of utility relies on the claim that it "is capable of being consistently pursued; and it is but tautology to say, that the more consistently it is pursued, the better it must always be for mankind" (see above, p. viii). A century and a half later, Richard Brandt made the same claim at greater length:

> Let us ask ourselves: What would a set of moral prescriptions be like, such that general conformity with it...would have the best consequences? The answer is that the set would include just one rule, the prescription of the act-utilitarian: "Perform an act, among those open to you, which will have at least as good consequences as any other." There cannot be a moral rule, conformity with which could have better consequences than this one. If it really is true that doing a certain thing will have the very best consequences in the long run, everything considered, of all the things I can do, then there is nothing better I can do than this. If everyone always did the very best thing it was possible for him to do, the total intrinsic value would be at a maximum.[18]

These remarks may well sound like ringing changes on a tautology, but in fact the claim they make is false.[19] It is false because each action in a *pattern* of actions can be such that any alternative to *it* would have been worse, even though some alternative *pattern* of action would have produced more net happiness than the actual pattern.

Consider, for example, the following situation. An election is being held, and Bentham is running against Kant; if Bentham wins, there will be large Utilitarian gains. He is therefore supported by all of the 40,000,000 registered voters who are Utilitarians (and, let's suppose, only by them). Kant is backed by 39,999,990 registered voters, and all registered voters back either Bentham or Kant. Everyone knows all this, and everyone also knows that virtually all of Kant's backers will vote—they're fanatics and love voting. Bentham's backers find voting a pain in the neck. And each Bentham supporter knows that a fair percentage of the group isn't going to vote. So each knows that Kant will win whether or not he or she votes. So each stays home, Kant is elected, and things are much worse than they would have been had *all* of Bentham's supporters voted.

If we assume that the actions in this scenario are causally independent, then it will be true, of each of the Bentham supporters, that had she voted, things would have been worse (and not just for her, but for the society taken as a whole, since her loss would have produced no compensating gain).[20] So each of the actions is in conformity with what Brandt calls "the prescription of the act-utilitarian," and yet less net intrinsic good is produced than had everyone followed some alternative rule, e.g., "Vote whenever you have the opportunity, no matter what the probable outcome."

Perhaps, then, Utilitarians should look, in formulating their principle, not at individual actions, but patterns of action. One way to do this would be to formulate the principle of utility as "Do whatever you would be doing in a utilitarian optimal pattern of action." This formulation is similar to what is sometimes called "Generalized Utilitarianism." This position attempts to combine a Utilitarian characterization of the good with the requirement of universalizability set out in the first formulation of Kant's Categorical Imperative.[21] The main problem with this way of formulating the principle is that acting in accord with it may lead to disaster unless *everyone* follows it. Suppose, in our voting case, that the reason Bentham's supporters find voting bothersome is not just the wait in line at the polling place, but the danger they will face if not enough Bentham supporters vote. Suppose that voting is by nonsecret ballot, and that if Kant wins he intends to take harsh retributive measures against all those who voted for Bentham. In this situation, any single act of voting by a Bentham supporter would have produced a very large loss of utility. So adoption of the rule "Do your part in the optimal pattern for the situation" by any individual, or by any group of fewer than, say, 39,000,000 Bentham supporters, would be very bad; and the larger the group (short of 39,000,000), the worse it would be.

These results are disconcerting. It seems that a reasonable formulation of the principle of utility should meet the following two criteria:

1. It should guarantee that *anyone* who successfully follows it is performing an action that produces at least as much net utility as any alternative open to him, *and*

2. It should guarantee that if *everyone* successfully follows it, at least as much net utility will result as if everyone followed any alternative principle open to him or her.

Brandt's act-utilitarian prescription satisfies 1 but not 2. "Do your part in an optimal pattern" satisfies 2, but not 1. It is hard to see that any formulation could satisfy both 1 and 2.

I suspect that Bentham failed to see this problem because of his preoccupation with laws and legislation. A legislator can plausibly think of herself as imposing a *pattern* of action on a society, since the laws apply to everyone. Mill, more concerned than Bentham with individual moral decision making, was also more worried about the relation between the injunction to maximize total net happiness and common-sense moral principles like "It's wrong to break promises." And there is some evidence that his views on this relation changed over time. In *A System of Logic* he clearly holds that common-sense principles are only "rules of thumb":

> By a wise practitioner, therefore, rules of conduct will only be considered as provisional. Being made for the most numerous cases, or for those of most ordinary occurrence, they point out the manner in which it will be least perilous to act, where time or means do not exist for analysing the actual circumstances of the case, or where we cannot trust our judgement in estimating them. But they do not at all supersede the propriety of going through (when circumstances permit) the scientific process requisite for framing a rule from the data of the particular case before us. (See below, p. 250.)

Twenty years later, in *Utilitarianism,* Mill sometimes writes as if common-sense moral rules, which he now calls "secondary principles," have a greater weight than mere rules of thumb:

> We must remember that only in…cases of conflict between secondary principles is it requisite that first principles should be appealed to. (See below, p. 115.)

Passages like this have led some commentators to classify Mill as a "Rule Utilitarian," i.e., as someone who holds that utility provides the ultimate ground for the adoption of rules and practices, but that an individual action that violates a rule or practice cannot be justified by simply showing that it produces more net utility than any alternative. A similar position is sometimes attributed to another of Bentham's followers, John Austin, the first occupant of the Chair of Jurisprudence at the Benthamite-founded University of London. According to Austin, "Our rules would be fashioned on utility; our conduct on our rules."[22] If Austin is actually making a distinction between the justification of a rule and the justification of an action falling under a rule, and restricting the scope of Utilitarianism to the former, then he owes us an account of what to do when an action falls under an unjustified rule.[23] And the same is true of Mill, if in fact he holds a position like Austin's. It is sometimes suggested, by modern "Rule-Utilitarians," that this difficulty can be avoided by asking not about *actual* rules and practices, but about the rules and practices that would be ideal for the society.[24] Unfortunately an act which is in accord with a system of ideal but unactualized rules or practices may be much worse than one which accords with the actual but nonideal rules and practices.

It should be stressed that the difficulties in formulating a principle of utilty that we have discussed up to this point do *not* result from lack of information. Even assuming complete relevant information it is unclear what rule a Utilitarian should employ for choosing among the alternative actions open to her. But in real life lack of relevant information is ubiquitous, and the Utilitarian needs to say something about what we should do when we have only very sketchy information about the consequences of our actions. This is particularly important for Mill, who realizes quite clearly that our actions have significant effects on what sort of people we become. His primary criticisms of Bentham, in fact, center on Bentham's neglect of the causal effects actions have on character:

> All acts suppose certain dispositions, and habits of mind and heart, which may be in themselves states of enjoyment or of wretchedness, and which may be fruitful in *other* consequences besides those particular acts. No person can be a thief or a liar without being much else, and if our moral judgments and feelings with respect to a person convicted of either vice were grounded solely on the pernicious tendency of thieving and of lying, they would be partial and incomplete; many considerations would be omitted, which are at least equally "germane to the matter". . . . (See below, p. 258.)

But once we realize that becoming a person who always acts in a way that maximizes net utility, or expected net utility, is not necessarily what Utilitarianism prescribes, we may be quite at a loss as to what it *does* prescribe. A similar problem confronts teleological theories of prudential (i.e., self-interested) reason. Once the prudential teleologist realizes that following the principle "Always chose the action that will maximize self-interest" will not guarantee a prudentially optimal life, it is not clear what principle of choice she *should* adopt.[25]

Given the obscurity of its implications for action, one might question how Mill could be so certain of the truth of Utilitarianism. Part of the answer is that he assumed it was obvious that practical reason is "means-end" rationality. Thus there must be a *summum bonum,* and actions must somehow aim at maximizing it. But why was Mill so certain that the *summum bonum* is total net happiness? Mill gives his answer to this question in Chapter IV of *Utilitarianism,* where he considers "Of What Sort of Proof the Principle of Utility Is Susceptible." This section of *Utilitarianism* has provoked more commentary, and more controversy, than any other part of the book. Nonetheless, the broad outlines of Mill's argument are reasonably clear. The thesis that Mill wants to establish in Chapter IV is the claim that only happiness is intrinsically good (i.e., good in itself, and not just as a means to some other good). It is somewhat misleading, perhaps, to call this "the Principle of Utility," but it is clear in the context what Mill has in mind. And Mill is quite clear, here and earlier, that first principles do not admit of strict proof, since their role is to function as bedrock premises. Nonetheless they may be supported by "considerations capable of determining the intellect." (See below, p. 98.) The considerations Mill offers begin with the assumptions that there is, in fact, a *summum bonum*, and that it is something that *can* be desired as an end (i.e., desired for itself or intrinsically). Mill offers no explicit argument for the claim that being capable of being desired is a necessary condition for being desirable, but he does note that "the sole evidence it is possible to produce that a thing is desirable is that people do actually desire it." (See below, p. 122.) And indeed it would be odd if something was intrinsically desirable but impossible to desire. If we give Mill the premise that being capable of being desired is a necessary condition for being desirable, then to show that happiness is the *summum bonum* he need only convince us that it is impossible to desire anything but happiness as an end. And indeed the bulk of Chapter IV is an attempt to establish just this. Mill begins by noting that we do in fact desire happiness, and this of course shows that we *can* desire happiness. He then considers a number of instances in which we might be tempted to hold that things other than happiness (e.g., money) are desired as ends, and argues that in each instance it is plausible to claim that what appear to be independent ends are actually "parts" of the agent's happiness. This is the best that Mill can do. Given his belief that the only way to prove a modal claim of the form "*X* can be desired" is by producing a case in which *X* actually is desired, it will be impossible for him to *demonstrate* that only happiness can be desired as an end. The best he can do is to show that there is no reason to think that we can in fact desire anything else as an end. But even if, in fact, everyone's sole end is happiness, this will not *prove* that nothing else *could be* desired as an end. It would, however, be very strong *evidence* that happiness is the sole intrinsic good. This, I think, is why Mill withholds the claim of "proof" but maintains that he has nonetheless presented considerations capable of determining the intellect.

On this reading of Mill's argument, it contains no flawed analogies or logical lapses; but it still faces at least two serious objections. The first concerns Mill's method of dealing with apparent counterexamples to his claim that happiness is the sole end. It is quite natural to say that some people want power or posthumous fame or revenge or preservation of endangered species, and that they want these *as ends*. Indeed it seems natural to say that some of these people desire these ends more than they desire happiness. Perhaps there is some way to defuse these apparent counter-examples, but simply saying that in all such cases the agents have made power or revenge or posthumous fame "part of their happiness" is to make the claim that happiness is the sole end "true by definition," and hence trivial.[26]

The second problem facing Mill's argument is that the conclusion he wants is that the *summum bonum* is the *general* good, but his examples seem to show that what each agent desires is *her own* happiness. However implausible it may be to say that each agent desires nothing but his own happiness, it is surely *more* implausible to claim that each agent wants only the *general* happiness. Moreover, Mill's method of handling apparent counterexamples will only work for single-agent cases: the miser may make money a part of *his* happiness, but he does not thereby make it a part of *mine*. Mill seems to have been aware that there was a gap between what he argues for in Chapter IV and what he wants as a conclusion, but his attempt to bridge it is both unclear and unconvincing. He writes, in paragraph 3 of Chapter IV, that:

> No reason can be given why the general happiness is desirable, except that each person...desires his own happiness....each person's happiness is a good to that person, and the general happiness, therefore, a good to the aggregate of all persons. (See below, p. 122.)

Mill, in *Utilitarianism,* provides no explanation of *why* the fact that each person desires his own happiness makes the general happiness desirable, nor does he explain what it means to say that something is a good to an "aggregate of people." When queried about this apparent lacuna in his reasoning, Mill replied that:

> ...when I said that the general happiness is a good to the aggregate of all persons I did not mean that every human being's happiness is a good to every other human being, though I think in a good state of society and education it would be so. I merely meant in this particular sentence to argue that since A's happiness is a good, B's a good, C's a good, etc., the sum of all these goods must be a good. (See below, p. 270.)

Unfortunately the two sentences of Mill's explanation conflict. The first entails that what is a good for A may *not* be a good for B, while the second implies that if something is a good for A it is a good *simpliciter,* and hence (presumably) a good for B. But in fact no explanation of what it is to be a good *simpliciter,* as opposed to being a good for a particular agent, has been given.

These two objections to Mill's argument are quite formidable, and replies that meet one tend to exacerbate the other. One way to meet the first problem, for example, is to admit that agents have varying ends, and then to define happiness as (roughly) "getting what one wants." The *summum bonum* is then defined as total net satisfaction of desires, with everyone's desires counting equally and with a value proportionate to their intensity. This sort of position is sometimes called "preference Utilitarianism," and many contemporary philosophers and economists endorse one of its many versions. Unfortunately, while it does full justice to the diversity of what agents desire as ends, it makes it quite difficult to see why any agent would want to maximize total preference satisfaction. Suppose, for example, that agent A has as one of his most fervent ends the elimination of all Jews from Palestine, while Agent B wants nothing more than a secure Jewish state in the Middle East; why should either be interested in having the other get what he wants?[27]

This last problem surfaces in more concrete form in Mill's *On Liberty*. This work, probably Mill's most influential, presents a strong and impassioned case for many of the most basic civil liberties (e.g., freedom of thought, freedom of speech, and freedom of the press). It also argues for what at least *sounds* like a very high degree of individual freedom of action. Mill asserts that everyone should be free to do whatever she wants, as long as doing so does not harm anyone else. Neither the state nor private individuals should be allowed to restrict an agent's liberty unless the exercise of that liberty harms (or threatens to harm) others.

Mill limits this guarantee to rational agents; it is not intended to apply to small children or to adults who remain in their "nonage."[28] It is also important to note that Mill does *not* think it is permissible to limit your freedom *whenever* the exercise of that freedom harms others. Political speech, for example, often harms incumbents or leads to policies which harm one or another social class or group; but Mill thinks such speech should nonetheless be protected. Mill's principle claims that harm to others is a *necessary* condition for legitimate limitation of freedom, not that it is a *sufficient* condition for such limitation. If we ask when the exercise of a liberty that harms others should be impinged, Mill would surely answer "when the total net utility of the impingement, over the length of its employment, is greater than the total net utility of the unrestricted exercise of the liberty." Mill is quite certain that the claims made in *On Liberty* are consistent with the basic tenets of *Utilitarianism*, and his defense of civil liberties such as freedom of speech is based solely on the *utility* of the exercise of these liberties.

Nonetheless many readers feel there is a tension between the claims, or at least the tenor, of the two books. And indeed it does sometimes seem that Mill's defense of basic liberties, for example freedom of speech, is rooted in the value he himself places on these liberties, rather than on a clear perception that their exercise will in fact maximize total net utility. Mill's official opinion, of course, is that value judgments based solely on individual preference are simply expressions of sympathy or antipathy, and have to be based on "reason" if they are to be taken seriously.[29] Because of this Mill feels no hesitancy in condemning a (hypothetical) prohibition against eating pork in a predominately Muslim country, or the (actual) prohibition of Mormon polygamy in America. Yet in Chapter IV Mill allows the legitimate prohibition of certain "offences against decency." Mill is not explicit about what activities he has in mind, but presumably public nudity would be among them; but how is he to distinguish a ban on public nudity from a requirement that women wear veils or that men wear beards or that no one eat pork? More seriously, how is Mill going to justify his strong preference for individual differences and "eccentricity" as opposed to the more general preference for conformity? If in fact a growing number of people make conformity "a part of their happiness," how is Utilitarianism going to prevent the "tyranny of the majority" that Mill wants to avoid?

There will be an answer to this problem if in fact rational agents can come to an agreement on what is intrinsically desirable. If, for example, everyone were to agree that only pleasant sensations are intrinsically desirable, and that their value depends only on their being experienced (and *not* on who experiences them), such Benthamite pleasures could serve as a common coin for computing the sum of the happiness of a group of individuals, and each individual could reasonably be supposed to want to maximize that sum. But if disagreement about what is intrinsically desirable emerges, summation becomes problematic. If *you* value diversity and *I* value conformity, saying that we *both* want happiness runs a danger of becoming an empty claim, and of providing no clear reason why either of us should want to maximize *total* happiness. What the Utilitarian needs, then, is an account of the good such that all rational agents will agree that its maximization is indeed the *summum bonum*. Bentham and Mill were deeply convinced that such an account *must* exist, on pain of practical reason degenerating to the principle of sympathy and antipathy, which—as Bentham made clear—is no principle at all.[30] Their attempts to illuminate this basic Utilitarian vision, and to trace its practical implications, continue to attract followers in philosophy, economics, and public choice theory, and to inspire many to elaborate and defend their theory. The work of later Utilitarians, such as Edgeworth and Sidgwick in the 19th century, and Brandt and Hare in the 20th, provides an impressive tribute to the fecundity of the writings of Bentham and Mill. I hope that these selections from their writings will show that a deeper study of the early Utilitarians is well worth the effort.

NOTES

[1]Runes (1959), p. 250.

[2]Aristotle (1962), p. 62.

[3]Ibid., p. 6.

[4]Idem.

[5]Stillinger (1969), p. 81.

[6]Ibid., p. 85.

[7]It is worth noting that even in cases where both variables are maximized, the principle may prefer a distribution that has nothing to be said for it from *either* a Utilitarian or an egalitarian point of view. Consider, for example:

D5	D6
850 people at level 780	800 people at level 750
150 people at level 0	200 people at level 700

Here the greatest level of happiness occurs in *D5 and* more people enjoy the greatest good in *D5* than in *D6*; but both classical Utilitarians and standard egalitarians will prefer *D6* to *D5*.

[8]Edgeworth (1877), p. 39.

[9] It goes back at least to G. E. Moore's *Principia Ethica,* which takes both beauty and aesthetic appreciation, among other things, as intrinsic goods.

[10]Thomson (1993), p. 145. For an example of this sort of ecumenism, see Richard Brandt's account of what he calls "extended rule-utilitarianism" (Brandt [1950], pp. 404–405).

[11] For a useful discussion of some of these measures, see Sen (1973).

[12] For a criticism of this line of argument, see Temkin (1993), pp. 248–282.

[13] Amis (1953), p. 51.

[14] Do the verses really mean to imply, for example, that even "if *private* be" my end, I must take into account the pains of others, though I may ignore their pleasures? If so, why? And does the prose of Chapter IV really mean that I should discount once for "uncertainty" and *again* for "propinquity"? If so, why?

[15] Parekh (1973), p. 109.

[16] I don't myself think addition is a likely function for Bentham's purposes, but there are also real doubts about the appropriateness of multiplication. It isn't obvious that a pain that has intensity 100 and a duration of 1 minute is no better or worse than a pain of intensity 1 that lasts 100 minutes.

[17] For details on how this can be done, see Ramsey (1950) or Jeffrey (1983).

[18] Brandt (1963), p. 121.

[19] This was, to the best of my knowledge, first shown in Gibbard (1965).

[20] Note that each act of voting by Smith's supporters is also in accord with the act-utilitarian principle. And note also that the voting case bears a strong structural

similarity to Prisoners' Dilemma cases. In general the basic difficulties afflicting teleological theories of prudential rationality mirror those facing teleological theories of moral rationality. [For a clear introduction to Prisoners' Dilemma cases, see the Introduction to Axelrod (1984).]

[21] This sort of position is, in Mill's opinion, the one Kant himself actually held. (See below, p. 97.)

[22] Austin (1863), vol. I, p. 116.

[23] For more on the distinction Austin *might* be making, as well as the question of whether he or Mill made it, see Rawls (1955).

[24] See, for example, Brandt (1963).

[25] The fact that teleological theories carry no obvious implications for decision making, even given full relevant information, has its upside. If it isn't clear *what* Utilitarianism tells us to do, then it can't be the case that it clearly tells us to do the (intuitively) wrong things.

[26] For a good argument that people in fact have ends that transcend any experiential states of themselves or others, see Nozick's discussion of the "experience machine" (Nozick [1974], pp. 42–45.).

[27] There have been ingenious attempts to meet this and similar problems by restricting the sorts of preferences that "count," but none has gained general acceptance. The theory also faces serious problems stemming from the fact that preferences change over time. For an interesting discussion of the superiority of the "desire satisfaction" version of Utilitarianism, and a perplexing rejection of it in favor of a more traditional form, see Brandt (1979), pp. 246–266.

[28] It is a bit disconcerting to learn that Mill thinks whole societies may be in their "nonage." (See below, p. 158.) Does Mill think that "primitive" societies lack rationality, or only the information needed to make rationality useful?

[29] For a clear statement of this claim, see the first half of Chapter I of *On Liberty*.

[30] For a cogent counter to Bentham's claim, see Rawls (1971).

A Note on the Texts

The text of Bentham's *Principles of Morals and Legislation* is that of the 1823 edition, the last edition revised by Bentham. The excerpt on the phrase "Greatest happiness of the greatest number" is from a MS in the University College London collection, first printed in Bhikhu Parekh's *Bentham's Political Thought*, pp. 309–310. The selection on push-pin and poetry is from Bentham's *The Rationale of Reward*, and is available on the Bentham Project's website (http://www.ucl.ac.uk/Bentham-Project).

The text of Mill's *On Liberty* is that of the 4th edition (1869); the text of *Utilitarianism* is that of the 2nd edition (1864), the last that Mill revised. The excerpt from *A System of Logic* follows the text of the last edition printed in Mill's lifetime. The letter to Henry Jones appears in *The Later Letters of John Stuart Mill: 1849–1873* (U. of Toronto Press), p. 1414.

Selections from Bentham's
Principles of Morals and Legislation

PREFACE
(1789)

The following sheets were, as the note on the opposite page expresses, printed so long ago as the year 1780. The design, in pursuance of which they were written, was not so extensive as that announced by the present title. They had at that time no other destination than that of serving as an introduction to a plan of a penal code *in terminis,* designed to follow them, in the same volume.

The body of the work had received its completion according to the then present extent of the author's views, when, in the investigation of some flaws he had discovered, he found himself unexpectedly entangled in an unsuspected corner of the metaphysical maze. A suspension, at first not apprehended to be more than a temporary one, necessarily ensued: suspension brought on coolness, and coolness, aided by other concurrent causes, ripened into disgust.

Imperfections pervading the whole mass had already been pointed out by the sincerity of severe and discerning friends; and conscience had certified the justness of their censure. The inordinate length of some of the chapters, the apparent inutility of others, and the dry and metaphysical turn of the whole, suggested an apprehension, that, if published in its present form, the work would contend under great disadvantages for any chance, it might on other accounts possess, of being read, and consequently of being of use.

But, though in this manner the idea of completing the present work slid insensibly aside, that was not by any means the case with the considerations which had led him to engage in it. Every opening, which promised to afford the lights he stood in need of, was still pursued; as occasion arose, the several departments connected with that in which he had at first engaged, were successively explored; insomuch that, in one branch or other of the pursuit, his researches have nearly embraced the whole field of legislation.

Several causes have conspired at present to bring to light, under this new title, a work which under its original one had been imperceptibly, but as it had seemed irrevocably, doomed to oblivion. In the course of eight years, materials for various works, corresponding to the different branches of the subject of legislation, had been produced, and some nearly reduced to shape: and, in every one of those works, the principles exhibited in the present publication had been found so necessary, that, either to transcribe them piece-meal, or to exhibit them somewhere where they could be referred to in the lump, was found unavoidable. The former course would have occasioned repetitions too bulky to be employed without necessity in the execution of a plan unavoidably so voluminous: the latter was therefore indisputably the preferable one.

To publish the materials in the form in which they were already printed, or to work them up into a new one, was therefore the only alternative: the latter had all along been his wish, and, had time and the requisite degree of alacrity been at command, it would as certainly have been realised. Cogent considerations, however, concur, with the irksomeness of the task, in placing the accomplishment of it at present at an unfathomable distance.

Another consideration is, that the suppression of the present work, had it been ever so decidedly wished, is no longer altogether in his power. In the course of so long an interval, various incidents have introduced copies into various hands, from some of which they have been transferred, by deaths and other accidents, into others that are unknown to him. Detached, but considerable extracts, have even been published, without any dishonourable views, (for the name of the author was very honestly subjoined to them,) but without his privity, and in publications undertaken without his knowledge.

It may perhaps be necessary to add, to complete his excuse for offering to the public a work pervaded by blemishes, which have not escaped even the author's partial eye, that the censure, so justly bestowed upon the form, did not extend itself to the matter.

In sending it thus abroad into the world with all its imperfections upon its head, he thinks it may be of assistance to the few readers he can expect, to receive a short intimation of the chief particulars, in respect of which it fails of corresponding with his maturer views. It will thence be observed how in some respects it fails of quadrating with the design announced by its original title, as in others it does with that announced by the one it bears at present.

An introduction to a work which takes for its subject the totality of any science, ought to contain all such matters, and such matters only, as belong in common to every particular branch of that science, or at least to more branches of it than one. Compared with its present title, the present work fails in both ways of being conformable to that rule.

As an introduction to the principles of *morals,* in addition to the analysis it contains of the extensive ideas signified by the terms *pleasure, pain, motive,* and *disposition,* it ought to have given a similar analysis of the not less extensive, though much less determinate, ideas annexed to the terms *emotion, passion, appetite, virtue, vice,* and some others, including the names of the particular *virtues* and *vices.* But as the true, and, if he conceives right, the only true ground-work for the development of the latter set of terms, has been laid by the explanation of the former, the completion of such a dictionary, so to style it would, in comparison of the commencement, be little more than a mechanical operation.

Again, as an introduction to the principles of *legislation in general,* it ought rather to have included matters belonging exclusively to the *civil* branch, than matters more particularly applicable to the *penal:* the latter being but a means of compassing the ends proposed by the former. In preference therefore, or at least in priority, to the several chapters which will be found relative to *punishment,* it ought to have exhibited a set of propositions which have since presented themselves to him as affording a standard for the operations performed by government, in the creation and distribution of proprietary and other civil rights. He means certain axioms of what may be termed *mental pathology,* expressive of the connection betwixt the feelings of the parties concerned, and the several classes of incidents, which either call for, or are produced by, operations of the nature above mentioned.[1]

The consideration of the division of offences, and every thing else that belongs to offences, ought, besides, to have preceded the consideration of punishment: for the idea of *punishment* presupposes the idea of *offence:* punishment, as such, not being inflicted but in consideration of offence.

Lastly, the analytical discussions relative to the classification of offences would, according to his present views, be transferred to a separate treatise, in which the system of legislation is considered solely in respect of its form: in other words, in respect of its *method* and *terminology.*

In these respects the performance fails of coming up to the author's own ideas of what should have been exhibited in a work, bearing the title he has now given it, viz. that of an *Introduction to the Principles of Morals and Legislation.* He knows however of no other that would be less unsuitable: nor in particular would so adequate an intimation of its actual contents have been given, by a title corresponding to the more limited design, with which it was written: viz. that of serving as an *introduction to a penal code.*

Yet more. Dry and tedious as a great part of the discussions it contains must unavoidably be found by the bulk of readers, he knows not how to regret the having written them, nor even the having made them public. Under every head, the practical uses, to which the discussions contained under that head appeared applicable, are indicated: nor is there, he believes, a single proposition that he has not found occasion to build upon in the penning of some article or other of those provisions of detail, of which a body of law, authoritative or unauthoritative, must be composed. He will venture to specify particularly, in this view, the several chapters shortly characterized by the words *Sensibility, Actions, Intentionality, Consciousness, Motives, Dispositions, Consequences.* Even in the enormous chapter on the division of offences, which, notwithstanding the forced compression the plan has undergone in several of its parts, in manner there mentioned, occupies no fewer than one hundred and four closely printed quarto pages,[2] the ten concluding ones are employed in a statement of the practical advantages that may be reaped from the plan of classification which it exhibits. Those in whose sight the Defence of Usury has been fortunate enough to find favour, may reckon as one instance of those advantages the discovery of the principles developed in that little treatise. In the preface to an anonymous tract published so long ago as in 1776,[3] he had hinted at the utility of a natural classification of offences, in the character of a test for distinguishing genuine from spurious ones. The case of usury is one among a number of instances of the truth of that observation. A note at the end of Sect. xxxv. Chap. xvi. of the present publication, may serve to show how the opinions, developed in that tract, owed their origin to the difficulty experienced in the attempt to find a place in his system for that imaginary offence. To some readers, as a means of helping them to support the fatigue of wading through an analysis of such enormous length, he would almost recommend the beginning with those concluding pages.

One good at least may result from the present publication; viz. that the more he has trespassed on the patience of the reader on this occasion, the less need he will have so to do on future ones: so that this may do to those, the office which is done, by books of pure mathematics, to books of mixed mathematics and natural philosophy. The narrower the circle of readers is, within which the present work may be condemned to confine itself, the less limited may be the number of those to whom the fruits of his succeeding labours may be found accessible. He may therefore in this respect find himself in the condition of those philosophers of antiquity, who are represented as having held two bodies of doctrine, a popular and an occult one: but, with this difference, that in his instance the occult and the popular will, he hopes, be found as consistent as in those they were contradictory; and that in his production whatever there is of occultness has been the pure result of sad necessity, and in no respect of choice.

Having, in the course of this advertisement, had such frequent occasion to allude to different arrangements, as having been suggested by more extensive and maturer views, it may perhaps contribute to the satisfaction of the reader, to receive a short intimation of their nature: the rather, as, without such explanation, references, made here and there to unpublished works, might be productive of perplexity and mistake. The following then are the titles of the works by the publication of which his present designs would be completed. They are exhibited in the order which seemed to him best fitted for apprehension, and in which they would stand disposed, were the whole assemblage ready to come out at once: but the order, in which they will eventually appear, may probably enough be influenced in some degree by collateral and temporary considerations.

Part the 1st. Principles of legislation in matters of *civil,* more distinctively termed *private distributive,* or for shortness, *distributive, law.*

Part the 2nd. Principles of legislation in matters of *penal law.*

Part the 3rd. Principles of legislation in matters of *procedure:* uniting in one view the *criminal* and *civil* branches, between which no line can be drawn, but a very indistinct one, and that continually liable to variation.

Part the 4th. Principles of legislation in matters of *reward.*

Part the 5th. Principles of legislation in matters of *public distributive,* more concisely as well as familiarly termed *constitutional,* law.

Part the 6th. Principles of legislation in matters of *political tactics:* or of the art of maintaining *order* in the proceedings of political assemblies, so as to direct them to the end of their institution: viz. by a system of rules, which are to the constitutional branch, in some respects, what the law of procedure is to the civil and the penal.

Part the 7th. Principles of legislation in matters betwixt, nation and nation, or, to use a new though not inexpressive appellation, in matters of *international* law.

Part the 8th. Principles of legislation in matters of *finance.*

Part the 9th. Principles of legislation in matters of *political economy.*

Part the 10th. Plan of a body of law, complete in all its branches, considered in respect of its *form;* in other words, in respect of its method and terminology; including a view of the origination and connexion of the ideas expressed by the short list of terms, the exposition of which contains all that can be said with propriety to belong to the head of *universal jurisprudence.*[4]

The use of the principles laid down under the above several heads is to prepare the way for the body of law itself exhibited *in terminis;* and which to be complete, with reference to any political state, must consequently be calculated for the meridian, and adapted to the circumstances, of some one such state in particular.

Had he an unlimited power of drawing upon *time,* and every other condition necessary, it would be his wish to postpone the publication of each part to the completion of the whole. In particular, the use of the ten parts, which exhibit what appear to him the dictates of utility in every line, being no other than to furnish reasons for the several corresponding provisions contained in the body of law itself, the exact truth of the former can never be precisely ascertained, till the provisions, to which they are destined to apply, are themselves ascertained, and that *in terminis*. But as the infirmity of human nature renders all plans precarious in the execution, in proportion as they are extensive in the design, and as he has already made considerable advances in several branches of the theory, without having made correspondent advances in the practical applications, he deems it more than probable, that the eventual order of publication will not correspond exactly with that which, had it been equally practicable, would have appeared most eligible. Of this irregularity the unavoidable result will be, a multitude of imperfections, which, if the execution of the body of law *in terminis* had kept pace with the development of the principles, so that each part had been adjusted and corrected by the other, might have been avoided. His conduct however will be the less swayed by this inconvenience, from his suspecting it to be of the number of those in which the personal vanity of the author is much more concerned, than the instruction of the public: since whatever amendments may be suggested in the detail of the principles, by the literal fixation of the provisions to which they are relative, may easily be made in a corrected edition of the former, succeeding upon the publication of the latter.

In the course of the ensuing pages, references will be found, as already intimated, some to the plan of a penal code to which this work was meant as an introduction, some to other branches of the above-mentioned general plan, under titles somewhat different from those, by which they have been mentioned here. The giving this warning is all which it is in the author's power to do, to save the reader from the perplexity of looking out for what has not as yet any existence. The recollection of the change of plan will in like manner account for several similar incongruities not worth particularising.

Allusion was made, at the outset of this advertisement, to some unspecified difficulties, as the causes of the original suspension, and unfinished complexion, of the present work. Ashamed of his defeat, and unable to dissemble it, he knows not how to refuse himself the benefit of such an apology as a slight sketch of the nature of those difficulties may afford.

The discovery of them was produced by the attempt to solve the questions that will be found at the conclusion of the volume: *Wherein consisted the identity and completeness of a law? What the distinction, and where the separation, between a penal and a civil law? What the distinction, and where the separation, between the penal and other branches of the law?*

To give a complete and correct answer to these questions, it is but too evident that the relations and dependencies of every part of the legislative system, with respect to every other, must have been comprehended and ascertained. But it is only upon a view of these parts themselves, that such an operation could have been performed. To the accuracy of such a survey one necessary condition would therefore be, the complete existence of the fabric to be surveyed. Of the performance of this condition no example is as yet to be met with any where. *Common* law, as it styles itself in England, *judiciary* law, as it might more aptly be styled every where, that fictitious composition which has no known person for its author, no known assemblage of words for its substance, forms every where the main body of the legal fabric: like that fancied ether, which, in default of sensible matter, fills up the measure of the universe. Shreds and scraps of real law, stuck on upon that imaginary ground, compose the furniture of every national code. What follows?——that he who, for the purpose just mentioned or for any other, wants an example of a complete body of law to refer to, must begin with making one.

There is, or rather there ought to be, a *logic* of the *will,* as well as of the *understanding:* the operations of the former faculty, are neither less susceptible, nor less worthy, than those of the latter, of being delineated by rules. Of these two branches of that recondite art, Aristotle saw only the latter: succeeding logicians, treading in the steps of their great founder, have concurred in seeing with no other eyes. Yet so far as a difference can be assigned between branches so intimately connected, whatever difference there is, in point of importance, is in favour of the logic of the will. Since it is only by their capacity of directing the operations of this faculty, that the operations of the understanding are of any consequence.

Of this logic of the will, the science of *law,* considered in respect of its *form,* is the most considerable branch,——the most important application. It is, to the art of legislation, what the science of anatomy is to the art of medicine: with this difference, that the subject of it is what the artist has to work *with,* instead of being what he has to operate *upon.* Nor is the body politic less in danger from a want of acquaintance with the one science, than the body natural from ignorance in the other. One example, amongst a thousand that might be adduced in proof of this assertion, may be seen in the note which terminates this volume.

Such then were the difficulties: such the preliminaries:——an unexampled work to achieve, and then a new science to create: a new branch to add to one of the most abstruse of sciences.

Yet more: a body of proposed law, how complete soever, would be comparatively useless and uninstructive, unless explained and justified, and that in every tittle, by a continued accompaniment, a perpetual commentary of *reasons:*[5] which reasons, that the comparative value of such as point in opposite directions may be estimated, and the conjunct force, of such as point in the same direction, may be felt, must be marshalled, and put under subordination to such extensive and leading ones as are termed *principles*. There must be therefore, not one system only, but two parallel and connected systems, running on together, the one of legislative provisions, the other of political reasons, each affording to the other correction and support.

Are enterprises like these achievable? He knows not. This only he knows, that they have been undertaken, proceeded in, and that some progress has been made in all of them. He will venture to add, if at all achievable, never at least by one, to whom the fatigue of attending to discussions, as arid as those which occupy the ensuing pages, would either appear useless, or feel intolerable. He will repeat it boldly (for it has been said before him), truths that form the basis of political and moral science are not to be discovered but by investigations as severe as mathematical ones, and beyond all comparison more intricate and extensive. The familiarity of the terms is a presumption, but it is a most fallacious one, of the facility of the matter. Truths in general have been called stubborn things: the truths just mentioned are so in their own way. They are not to be forced into detached and general propositions, unincumbered with explanations and exceptions. They will not compress themselves into epigrams. They recoil from the tongue and the pen of the declaimer. They flourish not in the same soil with sentiment. They grow among thorns; and are not to be plucked, like daisies, by infants as they run. Labour, the inevitable lot of humanity, is in no track more inevitable than here. In vain would an Alexander bespeak a peculiar road for royal vanity, or a Ptolemy, a smoother one, for royal indolence. There is no *King's Road*, no *Stadtholder's Gate*, to legislative, any more than to mathematic science.

CHAPTER I
Of the Principle of Utility

I. *Mankind governed by pain and pleasure.* Nature has placed mankind under the governance of two sovereign masters, *pain* and *pleasure*. It is for them alone to point out what we ought to do, as well as to determine what we shall do. On the one hand the standard of right and wrong, on the other the chain of causes and effects, are fastened to their throne. They govern us in all we do, in all we say, in all we think: every effort we can make to throw off our subjection, will serve but to demonstrate and confirm it. In words a man may pretend to abjure their empire: but in reality he will remain subject to it all the while. The *principle of utility*[1] recognises this subjection, and assumes it for the foundation of that system, the object of which is to rear the fabric of felicity by the hands of reason and of law. Systems which attempt to question it, deal in sounds instead of sense, in caprice instead of reason, in darkness instead of light.

But enough of metaphor and declamation: it is not by such means that moral science is to be improved.

II. *Principle of utility, what.* The principle of utility is the foundation of the present work: it will be proper therefore at the outset to give an explicit and determinate account of what is meant by it. By the principle[2] of utility is meant that principle which approves or disapproves of every action whatsoever, according to the tendency which it appears to have to augment or diminish the happiness of the party whose interest is in question: or, what is the same thing in other words, to promote or to oppose that happiness. I say of every action whatsoever; and therefore not only of every action of a private individual, but of every measure of government.

III. *Utility, what.* By utility is meant that property in any object, whereby it tends to produce benefit, advantage, pleasure, good, or happiness, (all this in the present case comes to the same thing) or (what comes again to the same thing) to prevent the happening of mischief, pain, evil, or unhappiness to the party whose interest is considered: if that party be the community in general, then the happiness of the community: if a particular individual, then the happiness of that individual.

IV. *Interest of the community, what.* The interest of the community is one of the most general expressions that can occur in the phraseology of morals: no wonder that the meaning of it is often lost. When it has a meaning, it is this. The community is a fictitious *body,* composed of the individual persons who are considered as constituting as it were its *members.* The interest of the community then is, what?—the sum of the interests of the several members who compose it.

V. It is in vain to talk of the interest of the community, without understanding what is the interest of the individual.[3] A thing is said to promote the interest, or to be *for* the interest, of an individual, when it tends to add to the sum total of his pleasures: or, what comes to the same thing, to diminish the sum total of his pains.

VI. *An action conformable to the principle of utility, what.* An action then may be said to be conformable to the principle of utility, or, for shortness sake, to utility, (meaning with respect to the community at large) when the tendency it has to augment the happiness of the community is greater than any it has to diminish it.

VII. *A measure of government conformable to the principle of utility, what.* A measure of government (which is but a particular kind of action, performed by a particular person or persons) may be said to be conformable to or dictated by the principle of utility, when in like manner the tendency which it has to augment the happiness of the community is greater than any which it has to diminish it.

VIII. *Laws or dictates of utility, what.* When an action, or in particular a measure of government, is supposed by a man to be conformable to the principle of utility, it may be convenient, for the purposes of discourse, to imagine a kind of law or dictate, called a law or dictate of utility: and to speak of the action in question, as being conformable to such law or dictate.

IX. *A partizan of the principle of utility, who.* A man may be said to be a partizan of the principle of utility, when the approbation or disapprobation he annexes to any action, or to any measure, is determined by and proportioned to the tendency which he conceives it to have to augment or to diminish the happiness of the community: or in other words, to its conformity or unconformity to the laws or dictates of utility.

X. *Ought, ought not, right and wrong, &c. how to be understood.* Of an action that is conformable to the principle of utility one may always say either that it is one that ought to be done, or at least that it is not one that ought not to be done. One may say also, that it is right it should be done; at least that it is not wrong it should be done: that it is a right action; at least that it is not a wrong action. When thus interpreted, the words *ought,* and *right* and *wrong,* and others of that stamp, have a meaning: when otherwise, they have none.

XI. *To prove the rectitude of this principle is at once unnecessary and impossible.* Has the rectitude of this principle been ever formally contested? It should seem that it had, by those who have not known what they have been meaning. Is it susceptible of any direct proof? It should seem not: for that which is used to prove every thing else, cannot itself be proved: a chain of proofs must have their commencement somewhere. To give such proof is as impossible as it is needless.

XII. *It has seldom, however, as yet been consistently pursued.* Not that there is or ever has been that human creature breathing, however stupid or perverse, who has not on many, perhaps on most occasions of his life, deferred to it. By the natural constitution of the human frame, on most occasions of their lives men in general embrace this principle, without thinking of it: if not for the ordering of their own actions, yet for the trying of their own actions, as well as of those of other men. There have been, at the same time, not many, perhaps, even of the most intelligent, who have been disposed to embrace it purely and without reserve. There are even few who have not taken some occasion or other to quarrel with it, either on account of their not understanding always how to apply it, or on account of some prejudice or other which they were afraid to examine into, or could not bear to part with. For such is the stuff that man is made of: in principle and in practice, in a right track and in a wrong one, the rarest of all human qualities is consistency.

XIII. *It can never be consistently combated.* When a man attempts to combat the principle of utility, it is with reasons drawn, without his being aware of it, from that very principle itself.[4] His arguments, if they prove any thing, prove not that the principle is *wrong*, but that, according to the applications he supposes to be made of it, it is *misapplied*. Is it possible for a man to move the earth? Yes; but he must first find out another earth to stand upon.

XIV. *Course to be taken for surmounting prejudices that may have been entertained against it.* To disprove the propriety of it by arguments is impossible; but, from the causes that have been mentioned, or from some confused or partial view of it, a man may happen to be disposed not to relish it. Where this is the case, if he thinks the settling of his opinions on such a subject worth the trouble, let him take the following steps, and at length, perhaps, he may come to reconcile himself to it.

1. Let him settle with himself, whether he would wish to discard this principle altogether; if so, let him consider what it is that all his reasonings (in matters of politics especially) can amount to?

2. If he would, let him settle with himself, whether he would judge an act without any principle, or whether there is any other he would judge and act by?

3. If there be, let him examine and satisfy himself whether the principle he thinks he has found is really any separate intelligible principle; or whether it be not a mere principle in words, a kind of phrase, which at bottom expresses neither more nor less than the mere averment of his own unfounded sentiments; that is, what in another person he might be apt to call caprice?

4. If he is inclined to think that his own approbation or disapprobation, annexed to the idea of an act, without any regard to its consequences, is a sufficient foundation for him to judge and act upon, let him ask himself whether his sentiment is to be a standard of right and wrong, with respect to every other man, or whether every man's sentiment has the same privilege of being a standard to itself?

5. In the first case, let him ask himself whether his principle is not despotical, and hostile to all the rest of human race?

6. In the second case, whether it is not anarchical, and whether at this rate there are not as many different standards of right and wrong as there are men? and whether even to the same man, the same thing, which is right to-day, may not (without the least change in its nature) be wrong to-morrow? and whether the same thing is not right and wrong in the

same place at the same time? and in either case, whether an argument is not at an end? and whether, when two men have said, 'I like this,' and 'I don't like it,' they can (upon such a principle) have any thing more to say?

7. If he should have said to himself, No: for that the sentiment which he proposes as a standard must be grounded on reflection, let him say on what particulars the reflection is to turn? if on particulars having relation to the utility of the act, then let him say whether this is not deserting his own principle, and borrowing assistance from that very one in opposition to which he sets it up: or if not on those particulars, on what other particulars?

8. If he should be for compounding the matter, and adopting his own principle in part, and the principle of utility in part, let him say how far he will adopt it?

9. When he has settled with himself where he will stop, then let him ask himself how he justifies to himself the adopting it so far? and why he will not adopt it any farther?

10. Admitting any other principle than the principle of utility to be a right principle, a principle that it is right for a man to pursue; admitting (what is not true) that the word *right* can have a meaning without reference to utility, let him say whether there is any such thing as a *motive* that a man can have to pursue the dictates of it: if there is, let him say what that motive is, and how it is to be distinguished from those which enforce the dictates of utility: if not, then lastly let him say what it is this other principle can be good for?

CHAPTER II
Of Principles Adverse to That of Utility

I. *All other principles than that of utility must be wrong.* If the principle of utility be a right principle to be governed by, and that in all cases, it follows from what has been just observed, that whatever principle differs from it in any case must necessarily be a wrong one. To prove any other principle, therefore, to be a wrong one, there needs no more than just to show it to be what it is, a principle of which the dictates are in some point or other different from those of the principle of utility: to state it is to confute it.

II. *Ways in which a principle may be wrong.* A principle may be different from that of utility in two ways: 1. By being constantly opposed to it: this is the case with a principle which may be termed the principle of *asceticism.*[5] 2. By being sometimes opposed to it, and sometimes not, as it may happen: this is the case with another, which may be termed the principle of *sympathy* and *antipathy.*

III. *Principle of asceticism, what.* By the principle of asceticism I mean that principle, which, like the principle of utility, approves or disapproves of any action, according to the tendency which it appears to have to augment or diminish the happiness of the party whose interest is in question; but in an inverse manner: approving of actions in as far as they tend to diminish his happiness; disapproving of them in as far as they tend to augment it.

IV. *A partizan of the principle of asceticism, who.* It is evident that any one who reprobates any the least particle of pleasure, as such, from whatever source derived, is *pro tanto* a partizan of the principle of asceticism. It is only upon that principle, and not from the principle of utility, that the most abominable pleasure which the vilest of malefactors ever reaped from his crime would be to be reprobated, if it stood alone. The case is, that it never does stand alone; but is necessarily followed by such a quantity of pain (or, what comes to the same thing, such a chance for a certain quantity of pain) that the pleasure in comparison of it, is as nothing: and this is the true and sole, but perfectly sufficient, reason for making it a ground for punishment.

V. *This principle has had in some a philosophical, in others a religious origin.* There are two classes of men of very different complexions, by whom the principle of asceticism appears to have been embraced; the one a set of moralists, the other a set of religionists. Different accordingly have been the motives which appear to have recommended it to the notice of these different parties. Hope, that is the prospect of pleasure, seems to have animated the former: hope, the aliment of philosophic pride: the hope of honour and reputation at the hands of men. Fear, that is the prospect of pain, the latter: fear, the offspring of superstitious fancy: the fear of future punishment at the hands of a splenetic and revengeful Deity. I say in this case fear: for of the invisible future, fear is more powerful than hope. These circumstances characterize the two different parties among the partizans of the principle of asceticism; the parties and their motives different, the principle the same.

VI. *It has been carried farther by the religious party than by the philosophical.* The religious party, however, appear to have carried it farther than the philosophical: they have acted more consistently and less wisely. The philosophical party have scarcely gone farther than to reprobate pleasure: the religious party have frequently gone so far as to make it a matter of merit and of duty to court pain. The philosophical party have hardly gone farther than the making pain a matter of indifference. It is no evil, they have said: they have not said, it is a good. They have not so much as reprobated all pleasure in the lump. They have discarded only what they have called the gross; that is, such as are organical, or of which the origin is easily traced up to such as are organical: they have even cherished and magnified the refined. Yet this, however, not under the name of pleasure: to cleanse itself from the sordes of its impure original, it was necessary it should change its name: the honourable, the glorious, the reputable, the becoming, the *honestum*, the *decorum*, it was to be called: in short, any thing but pleasure.

VII. *The philosophical branch of it has had most influence among persons of education, the religious among the vulgar.* From these two sources have flowed the doctrines from which the sentiments of the bulk of mankind have all along received a tincture of this principle; some from the philosophical, some from the religious, some from both. Men of education more frequently from the philosophical, as more suited to the elevation of their sentiments: the vulgar more frequently from the superstitious, as more suited to the narrowness of their intellect, undilated by knowledge: and to the abjectness of their condition, continually open to the attacks of fear. The tinctures, however, derived from the two sources, would naturally intermingle, insomuch that a man would not always know by which of them he was most influenced: and they would often serve to corroborate and enliven one another. It was this conformity that made a kind of alliance between parties of a complexion otherwise so dissimilar: and disposed them to unite upon various occasions against the common enemy, the partizan of the principle of utility, whom they joined in branding with the odious name of Epicurean.

VIII. *The principle of asceticism has never been steadily applied by either party to the Business of Government.* The principle of asceticism, however, with whatever warmth it may have been embraced by its partizans as a rule of private conduct, seems not to have been carried to any considerable length, when applied to the business of government. In a few instances it has been carried a little way by the philosophical party: witness the Spartan regimen. Though then, perhaps, it may be considered as having been a measure of security: and an application, though a precipitate and perverse application, of the principle of utility. Scarcely in any instances, to any considerable length, by the religious: for the various monastic orders, and the societies of the Quakers, Dumplers, Moravians, and other religionists, have been free societies, whose regimen no man has been astricted to without the intervention of his own consent. Whatever merit a man may have thought there would be in making himself miserable, no such notion seems ever to have occurred to any of them, that it may be a merit, much less a duty, to make others miserable: although it should seem, that if a certain quantity of misery were a thing so desirable, it would not matter much whether it were brought by each man upon himself, or by one man upon another. It is true, that from the same source from whence, among the religionists, the attachment to the principle of asceticism took its rise, flowed other doctrines and practices, from which misery in abundance was produced in one man by the instrumentality of another: witness the holy wars, and the persecutions for religion. But the passion for producing misery in these cases proceeded upon some special ground: the exercise of it was confined to persons of particular descriptions: they were tormented, not as men, but as heretics and infidels. To have inflicted the same miseries on their fellow-believers and fellow-sectaries, would have been as blameable in the eyes even of these religionists, as in those of a partizan of the principle of utility. For a man to give himself a certain number of stripes was indeed meritorious: but to give the same number of stripes to another man, not consenting, would have been a sin. We read of saints, who for the good of their souls, and the mortification of their bodies, have voluntarily yielded themselves a prey to vermin: but though many persons of this class have wielded the reins of empire, we read of none who have set themselves to work, and made laws on purpose, with a view of stocking the body politic with the breed of highwaymen, housebreakers, or incendiaries. If at any time they have suffered the nation to be preyed upon by swarms of idle pensioners, or useless placemen, it has rather been from negligence and imbecility, than from any settled plan for oppressing and plundering of the people. If at any time they have sapped the sources of national wealth, by cramping commerce, and driving the inhabitants into emigration, it has been with other views, and in pursuit of other ends. If they have declaimed against the pursuit of pleasure, and the use of wealth, they have commonly stopped at declamation: they have not, like Lycurgus, made express ordinances for the purpose of banishing the precious metals. If they have established idleness by a law, it has been not because idleness, the mother of vice and misery, is itself a virtue, but because idleness (say they) is the road to holiness. If under the notion of fasting, they have joined in the plan of confining their subjects to a diet, thought by some to be of the most nourishing and prolific nature, it has been not for the sake of making them tributaries to the nations by whom that diet was to be supplied, but for the sake of manifesting their own power, and exercising the obedience of the people. If they have established, or suffered to be established, punishments for the breach of celibacy, they have done no more than comply with the petitions of those deluded rigorists, who, dupes to the ambitious and deep-laid policy of their rulers, first laid themselves under that idle obligation by a vow.

IX. *The principle of asceticism, in its origin, was but that of utility misapplied.* The principle of asceticism seems originally to have been the reverie of certain hasty speculators, who having perceived, or fancied, that certain pleasures, when reaped in certain circumstances, have, at the long run, been attended with pains more than equivalent to them, took occasion to quarrel with every thing that offered itself under the name of pleasure.

Having then got thus far, and having forgot the point which they set out from, they pushed on, and went so much further as to think it meritorious to fall in love with pain. Even this, we see, is at bottom but the principle of utility misapplied.

X. *It can never be consistently pursued.* The principle of utility is capable of being consistently pursued; and it is but tautology to say, that the more consistently it is pursued, the better it must ever be for humankind. The principle of asceticism never was, nor ever can be, consistently pursued by any living creature. Let but one tenth part of the inhabitants of this earth pursue it consistently, and in a day's time they will have turned it into a hell.

XI. *The principle of sympathy and antipathy, what.* Among principles adverse[6] to that of utility, that which at this day seems to have most influence in matters of government, is what may be called the principle of sympathy and antipathy. By the principle of sympathy and antipathy, I mean that principle which approves or disapproves of certain actions, not on account of their tending to augment the happiness, nor yet on account of their tending to diminish the happiness of the party whose interest is in question, but merely because a man finds himself disposed to approve or disapprove of them: holding up that approbation or disapprobation as a sufficient reason for itself, and disclaiming the necessity of looking out for any extrinsic ground. Thus far in the general department of morals: and in the particular department of politics, measuring out the quantum (as well as determining the ground) of punishment, by the degree of the disapprobation.

XII. *This is rather the negation of all principle, than any thing positive.* It is manifest, that this is rather a principle in name than in reality: it is not a positive principle of itself, so much as a term employed to signify the negation of all principle. What one expects to find in a principle is something that points out some external consideration, as a means of warranting and guiding the internal sentiments of approbation and disapprobation: this expectation is but ill fulfilled by a proposition, which does neither more nor less than hold up each of those sentiments as a ground and standard for itself.

XIII. *Sentiments of a partizan of the principle of antipathy.* In looking over the catalogue of human actions (says a partizan of this principle) in order to determine which of them are to be marked with the seal of disapprobation, you need but to take counsel of your own feelings: whatever you find in yourself a propensity to condemn, is wrong for that very reason. For the same reason it is also meet for punishment: in what proportion it is adverse to utility, or whether it be adverse to utility at all, is a matter that makes no difference. In that same *proportion* also is it meet for punishment: if you hate much, punish much: if you hate little, punish little: punish as you hate. If you hate not at all, punish not at all: the fine feelings of the soul are not to be overborne and tyrannized by the harsh and rugged dictates of political utility.

XIV. *The systems that have been formed concerning the standard of right and wrong, are all reducible to this principle.* The various systems that have been formed concerning the standard of right and wrong, may all be reduced to the principle of sympathy and antipathy. One account may serve for all of them. They consist all of them in so many contrivances for avoiding the obligation of appealing to any external standard, and for prevailing upon the reader to accept of the author's sentiment or opinion as a reason for itself. The phrases different, but the principle the same.[7]

XV. *This principle still frequently coincide with that of utility.* It is manifest, that the dictates of this principle will frequently coincide with those of utility, though perhaps without intending any such thing. Probably more frequently than not: and hence it is that the business of penal justice is carried on upon that tolerable sort of footing upon which we see it carried on in common at this day. For what more natural or more general ground of hatred to a practice can there be, than the mischievousness of such practice? What all men are exposed to suffer by, all men will be disposed to hate. It is far yet, however, from being a constant ground: for when a man suffers, it is not always that he knows what it is he suffers by. A man may suffer grievously, for instance, by a new tax, without being able to trace up the cause of his sufferings to the injustice of some neighbour, who has eluded the payment of an old one.

XVI. *This principle is most apt to err on the side of severity.* The principle of sympathy and antipathy is most apt to err on the side of severity. It is for applying punishment in many cases which deserve none: in many cases which deserve some, it is for applying more than they deserve. There is no incident imaginable, be it ever so trivial, and so remote from mischief, from which this principle may not extract a ground of punishment. Any difference in taste: any difference in opinion: upon one subject as well as upon another. No disagreement so trifling which perseverance and altercation will not render serious. Each becomes in the other's eyes an enemy, and, if laws permit, a criminal.[8] This is one of the circumstances by which the human race is distinguished (not much indeed to its advantage) from the brute creation.

XVII. *But errs, in some instances, on the side of lenity.* It is not, however, by any means unexampled for this principle to err on the side of lenity. A near and perceptible mischief moves antipathy. A remote and imperceptible mischief, though not less real, has no effect. Instances in proof of this will occur in numbers in the course of the work.[9] It would be breaking in upon the order of it to give them here.

XVIII. *The theological principle, what—not a separate principle.* It may be wondered, perhaps, that in all this while no mention has been made of the *theological* principle; meaning that principle which professes to recur for the standard of right and wrong to the will of God. But the case is, this is not in fact a distinct principle. It is never any thing more or less than one or other of the three before-mentioned principles presenting itself under another shape. The *will* of God here meant cannot be his revealed will, as contained in the sacred writings: for that is a system which nobody ever thinks of recurring to at this time of day, for the details of political administration: and even before it can be applied to the details of private conduct, it is universally allowed, by the most eminent divines of all persuasions, to stand in need of pretty ample interpretations; else to what use are the works of those divines? And for the guidance of these interpretations, it is also allowed, that some other standard must be assumed. The will then which is meant on this occasion, is that which may be called the *presumptive* will: that is to say, that which is presumed to be his will on account of the conformity of its dictates to those of some other principle. What then may be this other principle? it must be one or other of the three mentioned above: for there cannot, as we have seen, be any more. It is plain, therefore, that, setting revelation out of the question, no light can ever be thrown upon the standard of right and wrong, by any thing that can be said upon the question, what is God's will. We may be perfectly sure, indeed, that whatever is right is conformable to the will of God: but so far is that from answering the purpose of showing us what is right, that it is necessary to know first whether a thing is right, in order to know from thence whether it be conformable to the will of God.[10]

XIX. *Antipathy, let the actions it dictates be ever so right, is never of itself a right ground of action.* There are two things which are very apt to be confounded, but which it imports us carefully to distinguish:—the motive or cause, which, by operating on the mind of an individual, is productive of any act: and the ground or reason which warrants a legislator, or other bystander, in regarding that act with an eye of approbation. When the act happens, in the particular instance in question, to be productive of effects which we approve of, much more if we happen to observe that the same motive may frequently be productive, in other instances, of the like effects, we are apt to transfer our approbation to the motive itself, and to assume, as the just ground for the approbation we bestow on the act, the circumstance of its originating from that motive. It is in this way that the sentiment of antipathy has often been considered as a just ground of action. Antipathy, for instance, in such or such a case, is the cause of an action which is attended with good effects: but this does not make it a right ground of action in that case, any more than in any other. Still farther. Not only the effects are good, but the agent sees beforehand that they will be so. This may make the action indeed a perfectly right action: but it does not make antipathy a right ground of action. For the same sentiment of antipathy, if implicitly deferred to, may be, and very frequently is, productive of the very worst effects. Antipathy, therefore, can never be a right ground of action. No more, therefore, can resentment, which, as will be seen more particularly hereafter, is but a modification of antipathy. The only right ground of action, that can possibly subsist, is, after all, the consideration of utility, which, if it is a right principle of action, and of approbation, in any one case, is so in every other. Other principles in abundance, that is, other motives, may be the reasons why such and such an act *has* been done: that is, the reasons or causes of its being done: but it is this alone that can be the reason why it might or ought to have been done. Antipathy or resentment requires always to be regulated, to prevent its doing mischief: to be regulated by what? always by the principle of utility. The principle of utility neither requires nor admits of any other regulator than itself.

Chapter IV
Value of a Lot of Pleasure or Pain, How to Be Measured

I. *Use of this chapter.* Pleasures then, and the avoidance of pains, are the *ends* which the legislator has in view: it behoves him therefore to understand their *value*. Pleasures and pains are the *instruments* he has to work with: it behoves him therefore to understand their force, which is again, in other words, their value.

II. *Circumstances to be taken into the account in estimating the value of a pleasure or pain considered with reference to a single person, and by itself.* To a person considered *by himself,* the value of a pleasure or pain considered *by itself,* will be greater or less, according to the four following circumstances:[15]

1. Its *intensity*.
2. Its *duration*.
3. Its *certainty* or *uncertainty*.
4. Its *propinquity* or *remoteness*.

III. —*considered as connected with other pleasures or pains.* These are the circumstances which are to be considered in estimating a pleasure or a pain considered each of them by itself. But when the value of any pleasure or pain is considered for the purpose of estimating the tendency of any *act* by which it is produced, there are two other circumstances to be taken into the account, these are,

5. Its *fecundity,* or the chance it has of being followed by sensations of the *same* kind: that is, pleasures, if it be a pleasure: pains, if it be a pain.

6. Its *purity,* or the chance it has of *not* being followed by sensations of the *opposite* kind: that is, pains, if it be a pleasure: pleasures, if it be a pain.

These two last, however, are in strictness scarcely to be deemed properties of the pleasure or the pain itself; they are not, therefore, in strictness to be taken into the account of the value of that pleasure or that pain. They are in strictness to be deemed properties only of the act, or other event, by which such pleasure or pain has been produced; and accordingly are only to be taken into the account of the tendency of such act or such event.

IV. *—considered with reference to a number of persons.* To a *number* of persons, with reference to each of whom the value of a pleasure or a pain is considered, it will be greater or less, according to seven circumstances: to wit, the six preceding ones; *viz.*

1. Its *intensity.*

2. Its *duration.*

3. Its *certainty* or *uncertainty.*

4. Its *propinquity* or *remoteness.*

5. Its *fecundity.*

6. Its *purity.*

And one other; to wit:

7. Its *extent;* that is, the number of persons to whom it *extends;* or (in other words) who are affected by it.

V. *Process for estimating the tendency of any act or event.* To take an exact account then of the general tendency of any act, by which the interests of a community are affected, proceed as follows. Begin with any one person of those whose interests seem most immediately to be affected by it: and take an account,

1. Of the value of each distinguishable *pleasure* which appears to be produced by it in the *first* instance.

2. Of the value of each *pain* which appears to be produced by it in the *first* instance.

3. Of the value of each pleasure which appears to be produced by it *after* the first. This constitutes the *fecundity* of the first *pleasure* and the *impurity* of the first *pain.*

4. Of the value of each *pain* which appears to be produced by it after

the first. This constitutes the *fecundity* of the first *pain,* and the *impurity* of the first pleasure.

5. Sum up all the values of all the *pleasures* on the one side, and those of all the pains on the other. The balance, if it be on the side of pleasure, will give the *good* tendency of the act upon the whole, with respect to the interests of that *individual* person; if on the side of pain, the *bad* tendency of it upon the whole.

6. Take an account of the *number* of persons whose interests appear to be concerned; and repeat the above process with respect to each. *Sum up* the numbers expressive of the degrees of *good* tendency, which the act has, with respect to each individual, in regard to whom the tendency of it is *good* upon the whole: do this again with respect to each individual, in regard to whom the tendency of it is *good* upon the whole: do this again with respect to each individual, in regard to whom the tendency of it is *bad* upon the whole. Take the *balance;* which, if on the side of *pleasure,* will give the general *good tendency* of the act, with respect to the total number or community of individuals concerned; if on the side of pain, the general *evil tendency,* with respect to the same community.

VI. *Use of the foregoing process.* It is not to be expected that this process should be strictly pursued previously to every moral judgment, or to every legislative or judicial operation. It may, however, be always kept in view: and as near as the process actually pursued on these occasions approaches to it, so near will such process approach to the character of an exact one.

VII. *The same process applicable to good and evil, profit and mischief, and all other modifications of pleasure and pain.* The same process is alike applicable to pleasure and pain, in whatever shape they appear: and by whatever denomination they are distinguished: to pleasure, whether it be called *good* (which is properly the cause or instrument of pleasure) or *profit* (which is distant pleasure, or the cause or instrument of distant pleasure,) or *convenience,* or *advantage, benefit, emolument, happiness,* and so forth: to pain, whether it be called *evil,* (which corresponds to *good*) or *mischief,* or *inconvenience,* or *disadvantage,* or *loss,* or *unhappiness,* and so forth.

VIII. *Conformity of men's practice to this theory.* Nor is this a novel and unwarranted, any more than it is a useless theory. In all this there is nothing but what the practice of mankind, wheresoever they have a clear view of their own interest, is perfectly conformable to. An article of property an estate in land, for instance, is valuable, on what account? On account of the pleasures of all kinds which it enables a man to produce, and what comes to the same thing the pains of all kinds which it enables him to avert. But the value of such an article of property is universally understood to rise or fall according to the length or shortness of the time which a man has in it: the certainty or uncertainty of its coming into possession: and the nearness or remoteness of the time at which, if at all, it is to come into possession. As to the *intensity* of the pleasures which a man may derive from it, this is never thought of, because it depends upon the use which each particular person may come to make of it; which cannot be estimated till the particular pleasures he may come to derive from it, or the particular pains he may come to exclude by means of it, are brought to view. For the same reason, neither does he think of the *fecundity* or *purity* of those pleasures.

Thus much for pleasure and pain, happiness and unhappiness, in *general*. We come now to consider the several particular kinds of pain and pleasure.

Chapter VIII
Of Intentionality

I. *Recapitulation.* So much with regard to the first two of the articles upon which the evil tendency of an action may depend: *viz.* the act itself, and the general assemblage of the circumstances with which it may have been accompanied. We come now to consider the ways in which the particular circumstance of *intention* may be concerned in it.

II. *The intention may regard,* 1. *The act or,* 2. *The consequences.* First, then, the intention or will may regard either of two objects: 1. The act itself: or, 2. Its consequences. Of these objects, that which the intention regards may be styled *intentional.* If it regards the act, then the act may be said to be intentional:[71] if the consequences, so also then may the consequences. If it regards both the act and consequences, the whole *action* may be said to be intentional. Whichever of those articles is not the object of the intention, may of course be said to be *unintentional.*

III. *It may regard the act without any of the consequences.* The act may very easily be intentional without the consequences; and often is so. Thus, you intend to touch a man, without intending to hurt him: and yet, as the consequences turn out, you may chance to hurt him.

IV. *—or the consequences without regarding the act in all its stages.* The consequences of an act may also be intentional, without the act's being intentional throughout; that is, without its being intentional in every stage of it: but this is not so frequent a case as the former. You intend to hurt a man, suppose, by running against him, and pushing him down: and you run towards him accordingly: but a second man coming in on a sudden between you and the first man, before you can stop yourself, you run against the second man, and by him push down the first.

V. —*but not without regarding the first stage.* But the consequences of an act cannot be intentional, without the act's being itself intentional in at least the first stage. If the act be not intentional in the first stage, it is no act of yours: there is accordingly no intention on your part to produce the consequences: that is to say, the individual consequences. All there can have been on your part is a distant intention to produce other consequences, of the same nature, by some act of yours, at a future time: or else, without any intention, a bare *wish* to see such event take place. The second man, suppose, runs of his own accord against the first, and pushes him down. You had intentions of doing a thing of the same nature: *viz.* To run against him, and push him down yourself; but you had done nothing in pursuance of those intentions: the individual consequences therefore of the act, which the second man performed in pushing down the first, cannot be said to have been on your part intentional.[72]

VI. Second. A *consequence, when intentional, may be directly so, or obliquely. A* consequence, when it is intentional, may either be *directly* so, or only *obliquely.* It may be said to be directly or lineally intentional, when the prospect of producing it constituted one of the links in the chain of causes by which the person was determined to do the act. It may be said to be obliquely or collaterally intentional, when, although the consequence was in contemplation, and appeared likely to ensue in case of the act's being performed, yet the prospect of producing such consequence did not constitute a link in the aforesaid chain.

VII. Third. *When directly, ultimately so, or mediately.* An incident, which is directly intentional, may either be *ultimately* so, or only *mediately.* It may be said to be ultimately intentional, when it stands last of all exterior events in the aforesaid chain of motives; insomuch that the prospect of the production of such incident, could there be a certainty of its taking place, would be sufficient to determine the will, without the prospect of its producing any other. It may be said to be mediately intentional, and no more, when there is some other incident, the prospect of producing which forms a subsequent link in the same chain: insomuch that the prospect of producing the former would not have operated as a motive, but for the tendency which it seemed to have towards the production of the latter.

VIII. Fourth. *When directly intentional, it may be exclusively so, or inexclusively.* When an incident is directly intentional, it may either be *exclusively* so, or *inexclusively.* It may be said to be exclusively intentional, when no other but that very individual incident would have answered the purpose, insomuch that no other incident had any share in determining the will to the act in question. It may be said to have been inexclusively[73] intentional, when there was some other incident, the prospect of which was acting upon the will at the same time.

IX. Fifth. *When inexclusively, it may be conjunctively, disjunctively, or indiscriminately so.* When an incident is inexclusively intentional, it may be either *con*junctively so, *dis*junctively, or *indiscriminately.* It may be said to be conjunctively intentional with regard to such other incident, when the intention is to produce both: disjunctively, when the intention is to produce either the one or the other indifferently, but not both: indiscriminately, when the intention is indifferently to produce either the one or the other, or both, as it may happen.

X. Sixth. *When disjunctively, it may be with or without preference.* When two incidents are disjunctively intentional, they may be so with or without *preference.* They may be said to be so with preference, when the intention is, that one of them in particular should happen rather than the other: without preference, when the intention is equally fulfilled, whichever of them happens.[74]

XI. *Example.* One example will make all this clear. William II. king of England, being out a stag-hunting, received from Sir Walter Tyrrel a wound, of which he died.[75] Let us take this case, and diversify it with a variety of suppositions, correspondent to the distinctions just laid down.

1. First then, Tyrrel did not so much as entertain a thought of the king's death; or, if he did, looked upon it as an event of which there was no danger. In either of these cases the incident of his killing the king was altogether unintentional.

2. He saw a stag running that way, and he saw the king riding that way at the same time: what he aimed at was to kill the stag: he did not wish to kill the king: at the same time he saw, that if he shot, it was as likely he should kill the king as the stag: yet for all that he shot, and killed the king accordingly. In this case the incident of his killing the king was intentional, but obliquely so.

3. He killed the king on account of the hatred he bore him, and for no other reason than the pleasure of destroying him. In this case the incident of the king's death was not only directly but ultimately intentional.

4. He killed the king, intending fully so to do; not for any hatred he bore him, but for the sake of plundering him when dead. In this case the incident of the king's death was directly intentional, but not ultimately: it was mediately intentional.

5. He intended neither more nor less than to kill the king. He had no other aim nor wish. In this case it was exclusively as well as directly intentional: exclusively, to wit, with regard to every other material incident.

6. Sir Walter shot the king in the right leg, as he was plucking a thorn out of it with his left hand. His intention was, by shooting the arrow into his leg through his hand, to cripple him in both those limbs at the same time. In this case the incident of the king's being shot in the leg was intentional: and that conjunctively with another which did not happen; *viz.* his being shot in the hand.

7. The intention of Tyrrel was to shoot the king either in the hand or in the leg, but not in both; and rather in the hand than in the leg. In this case the intention of shooting in the hand was disjunctively con-current, with regard to the other incident, and that with preference.

8. His intention was to shoot the king either in the leg or the hand, whichever might happen: but not in both. In this case the intention was inexclusive, but disjunctively so: yet that, however, without preference.

9. His intention was to shoot the king either in the leg or the hand, or in both, as it might happen. In this case the intention was indiscrim-inately concurrent, with respect to the two incidents.

XII. *Intentionality of the act with respect to its different* stages, *how far material.* It is to be observed, that an act may be unintentional in any stage or stages of it, though intentional in the preceding: and, on the other hand, it may be intentional in any stage or stages of it, and yet uninten-tional in the succeeding.[76] But whether it be intentional or no in any pre-ceding stage, is immaterial, with respect to the consequences, so it be unintentional in the last. The only point, with respect to which it is mate-rial, is the proof. The more stages the act is unintentional in, the more ap-parent it will commonly be, that it was unintentional with respect to the last. If a man, intending to strike you on the cheek, strikes you in the eye, and puts it out, it will probably be difficult for him to prove that it was not his intention to strike you in the eye. It will probably be easier, if his in-tention was really not to strike you, or even not to strike at all.

XIII. *Goodness and badness of intention dismissed.* It is frequent to hear men speak of a good intention, of a bad intention; of the goodness and badness of a man's intention: a circumstance on which great stress is gen-erally laid. It is indeed of no small importance, when properly under-stood: but the import of it is to the last degree ambiguous and obscure.

Strictly speaking, nothing can be said to be good or bad, but either in itself; which is the case only with pain or pleasure: or on account of its effects; which is the case only with things that are the causes or preventives of pain and pleasure. But in a figurative and less proper way of speech, a thing may also be styled good or bad, in consideration of its cause. Now the effects of an intention to do such or such an act, are the same objects which we have been speaking of under the appellation of its *consequences:* and the causes of intention are called *motives.* A man's intention then on any occasion may be styled good or bad, with reference either to the consequences of the act, or with reference to his motives. If it be deemed good or bad in any sense, it must be either because it is deemed to be productive of good or of bad consequences, or because it is deemed to originate from a good or from a bad motive. But the goodness or badness of the consequences depend upon the circumstances. Now the circumstances are no objects of the intention. A man intends the act: and by his intention produces the act: but as to the circumstances, he does not intend *them:* he does not, inasmuch as they are circumstances of it, produce them. If by accident there be a few which he has been instrumental in producing, it has been by former intentions, directed to former acts, productive of those circumstances as the consequences: at the time in question he takes them as he finds them. Acts, with their consequences, are objects of the will as well as of the understanding: circumstances, as such, are objects of the understanding only. All he can do with these, as such, is to know or not to know them: in other words, to be conscious of them, or not conscious. To the title of Consciousness belongs what is to be said of the goodness or badness of a man's intention, as resulting from the consequences of the act: and to the head of Motives, what is to be said of his intention, as resulting from the motive.

CHAPTER XIII
Cases Unmeet for Punishment

§ 1. *General view of cases unmeet for punishment.*

I. *The end of law is, to augment happiness.* The general object which all laws have, or ought to have, in common, is to augment the total happiness of the community; and therefore, in the first place, to exclude, as far as may be, every thing that tends to subtract from that happiness: in other words, to exclude mischief.

II. *But punishment is an evil.* But all punishment is mischief: all punishment in itself is evil. Upon the principle of utility, if it ought at all to be admitted, it ought only to be admitted in as far as it promises to exclude some greater evil.[155]

III. *Therefore ought not to be admitted;* It is plain, therefore, that in the following cases punishment ought not to be inflicted.

1. *Where groundless.* Where it is *groundless:* where there is no mischief for it to prevent; the act not being mischievous upon the whole.

2. *Inefficacious.* Where it must be *inefficacious:* where it cannot act so as to prevent the *mischief.*

3. *Unprofitable.* Where it is *unprofitable,* or too *expensive:* where the mischief it would produce would be greater than what it prevented.

4. *Or needless.* Where it is *needless:* where the mischief may be prevented, or cease of itself, without it: that is, at a cheaper rate.

§ 2. *Cases in which punishment is groundless.*

These are,

IV. 1. *Where there has never been any mischief: as in the case of consent.* Where there has never been any mischief: where no mischief has been produced to any body by the act in question. Of this number are those in which the act was such as might, on some occasions, be mischievous or disagreeable, but the person whose interest it concerns gave his *consent* to the performance of it.[156] This consent, provided it be free, and fairly obtained,[156] is the best proof that can be produced, that, to the person who gives it, no mischief, at least no immediate mischief, upon the whole, is done. For no man can be so good a judge as the man himself, what it is gives him pleasure or displeasure.

V. 2. *Where the mischief was outweighed: as in precaution against calamity, and the exercise of powers.* Where the mischief was *outweighed:* although a mischief was produced by that act, yet the same act was necessary to the production of a benefit which was of greater value[157] than the mischief. This may be the case with any thing that is done in the way of precaution against instant calamity, as also with any thing that is done in the exercise of the several sorts of powers necessary to be established in every community, to wit, domestic, judicial, military, and supreme.[158]

VI. 3. *—or will, for a certainty be cured by compensation.* Where there is a certainty of an adequate compensation: and that in all cases where the offence can be committed. This supposes two things: 1. That the offence is such as admits of an adequate compensation: 2. That such a compensation is sure to be forthcoming. Of these suppositions, the latter will be found to be a merely ideal one: a supposition that cannot, in the universality here given to it, be verified by fact. It cannot, therefore, in practice, be numbered amongst the grounds of absolute impunity. It may, however, be admitted as a ground for an abatement of that punishment, which other considerations, standing by themselves, would seem to dictate.[159]

§ 3. Cases in which punishment must be inefficacious.

These are,

VII. 1. *Where the penal provision comes too late: as in, 1. An ex-post-facto law, 2. An ultra-legal sentence.* Where the penal provision is *not established* until after the act is done. Such are the cases, 1. Of an *ex-post-facto* law; where the legislator himself appoints not a punishment till after the act is done. 2. Of a sentence beyond the law; where the judge, of his own authority, appoints a punishment which the legislator had not appointed.

VIII. 2. *Or is not made known: as in a law not sufficiently promulgated.* Where the penal provision, though established, is *not conveyed* to the notice of the person on whom it seems intended that it should operate. Such is the case where the law has omitted to employ any of the expedients which are necessary, to make sure that every person whatsoever, who is within the reach of the law, be apprized of all the cases whatsoever, in which (being in the station of life he is in) he can be subjected to the penalties of the law.[160]

IX. 3. *Where the will cannot be deterred from* any *act: as in,* Where the penal provision, though it were conveyed to a man's notice, *could produce no effect* on him, with respect to the preventing him from engaging in any act of the *sort* in question. Such is the case, 1. In extreme *infancy;* where a man has not yet attained that state or disposition of mind in which the prospect of evils so distant as those which are held forth by the law, has the effect of influencing his conduct. 2. In *insanity;* where the person, if he has attained to that disposition, has since been deprived of it through the influence of some permanent though unseen cause. 3. In *intoxication;* where he has been deprived of it by the transient influence of a visible cause: such as the use of wine, or opium, or other drugs, that act in this manner on the nervous system: which condition is indeed neither more nor less than a temporary insanity produced by an assignable cause.[161]

X. 4. *Or not from the individual act in question, as in,* Where the penal provision (although, being conveyed to the party's notice, it might very well prevent his engaging in acts of the sort in question, provided he knew that it related to those acts) could not have this effect, with regard to the *individual* act he is about to engage in: to wit, because he knows not that it is of the number of those to which the penal provision relates. This may happen, 1. In the case of *unintentionality;* where he intends not to engage, and thereby knows not that he is about to engage, in the *act* in which eventually he is about to engage.[162] 2. In the case of *unconsciousness;* where, although he may know that he is about to engage in the *act* itself, yet, from not knowing all the material *circumstances* attending it, he knows not of the *tendency* it has to produce that mischief, in contemplation of which it has been made penal in most instances. 3. In the case of *missupposal;* where, although he may know of the tendency the act has to produce that degree of mischief, he supposes it, though mistakenly, to be attended with some circumstance, or set of circumstances, which, if it had been attended with, it would either not have been productive of that mischief, or have been productive of such a greater degree of good, as has determined the legislator in such a case not to make it penal.[163]

XI. 5. *Or is acted on by an opposite superior force: as by,* Where, though the penal clause might exercise a full and prevailing influence, were it to act alone, yet by the *predominant* influence of some opposite cause upon the will, it must necessarily be ineffectual; because the evil which he sets himself about to undergo, in the case of his *not* engaging in the act, is so great, that the evil denounced by the penal clause, in case of his engaging in it, cannot appear greater. This may happen, 1. In the case of *physical danger;* where the evil is such as appears likely to be brought about by the unassisted powers of *nature.* 2. In the case of a *threatened mischief;* where it is such as appears likely to be brought about through the intentional and conscious agency of *man.*[164]

XII. 6. —*or the bodily organs cannot follow its determination: as under* Where (though the penal clause may exert a full and prevailing influence over the *will* of the party) yet his *physical faculties* (owing to the predominant influence of some physical cause) are not in a condition to follow the determination of the will: insomuch that the act is absolutely *involuntary.* Such is the case of physical *compulsion* or *restraint,* by whatever means brought about; where the man's hand, for instance, is pushed against some object which his will disposes him *not* to touch; or tied down from touching some object which his will disposes him to touch.

§ 4. Cases where punishment is unprofitable.

These are,

XIII. 1. *Where, in the* sort *of case in question, the punishment would produce more evil than the offence would.* Where, on the one hand, the nature of the offence, on the other hand, that of the punishment, are, *in the ordinary state of things,* such, that when compared together, the evil of the latter will turn out to be greater than that of the former.

XIV. *Evil producible by a punishment—its four branches—viz.* Now the evil of the punishment divides itself into four branches, by which so many different sets of persons are affected. 1. The evil of *coercion* or *restraint:* or the pain which it gives a man not to be able to do the act, whatever it be, which by the apprehension of the punishment he is deterred from doing.

This is felt by those by whom the law is *observed.* 2. The evil of *apprehension:* or the pain which a man, who has exposed himself to punishment, feels at the thoughts of undergoing it. This is felt by those by whom the law has been *broken,* and who feel themselves in *danger* of its being executed upon them. 3. The evil of *sufferance:*[165] or the pain which a man feels, in virtue of the punishment itself, from the time when he begins to undergo it. This is felt by those by whom the law is broken, and upon whom it comes actually to be executed. 4. The pain of sympathy, and the other *derivative* evils resulting to the persons who are in *connection* with the several classes of original sufferers just mentioned.[166] Now of these four lots of evil, the first will be greater or less, according to the nature of the act from which the party is restrained: the second and third according to the nature of the punishment which stands annexed to that offence.

XV. *(The evil of the offence being different, according to the nature of the offence, cannot be represented here.)* On the other hand, as to the evil of the offence, this will also, of course, be greater or less, according to the nature of each offence. The proportion between the one evil and the other will therefore be different in the case of each particular offence. The cases, therefore, where punishment is unprofitable on this ground, can by no other means be discovered, than by an examination of each particular offence; which is what will be the business of the body of the work.

XVI. 2. —*or in the* individual *case in question: by reason of* Where, although in the *ordinary state* of things, the evil resulting from the punishment is not greater than the benefit which is likely to result from the force with which it operates, during the same space of time, towards the excluding the evil of the offences, yet it may have been rendered so by the influence of some *occasional circumstances.* In the number of these circumstances may be, 1. *The multitude of delinquents.* The multitude of delinquents at a particular juncture; being such as would increase, beyond the ordinary measure, the *quantum* of the second and third lots, and thereby also of a part of the fourth lot, in the evil of the punishment. 2. *The value of a delinquent's service.* The extraordinary value of the services of some one delinquent; in the case where the effect of the punishment would be to deprive the community of the benefit of those services. 3. *The displeasure of the people.* The displeasure of the *people;* that is, of an indefinite number of the members of the *same* community, in cases where (owing to the influence of some occasional incident) they happen to conceive, that the offence or the offender ought not to be punished at all, or at least ought not to be punished in the way in question. 4. *The displeasure of foreign powers.* The displeasure of *foreign powers;* that is, of the governing body, or a considerable number of the members of some *foreign* community or communities, with which the community in question is connected.

§ 5. Cases where punishment is needless.

These are,

XVII. 1. *Where the mischief is to be prevented at a cheaper rate; as,* Where the purpose of putting an end to the practice may be attained as effectually at a cheaper rate: by instruction, for instance, as well as by terror: by informing the understanding; as well as by exercising an immediate influence on the will. *By instruction.* This seems to be the case with respect to all those offences which consist in the disseminating pernicious principles in matters of *duty;* of whatever kind the duty be; whether political, or moral, or religious. And this, whether such principles be disseminated *under,* or even *without,* a sincere persuasion of their being beneficial. I say, even *without:* for though in such a case it is not instruction that can prevent the writer from endeavouring to inculcate his principles, yet it may the readers from adopting them: without which, his endeavouring to inculcate them will do no harm. In such a case, the sovereign will commonly have little need to take an active part: if it be the interest of *one* individual to inculcate principles that are pernicious, it will as surely be the interest of *other* individuals to expose them. But if the sovereign must needs take a part in the controversy, the pen is the proper weapon to combat error with, not the sword.

CHAPTER XIV
Of the Proportion Between Punishments and Offences

I. *Recapitulation.* We have seen that the general object of all laws is to prevent mischief; that is to say, when it is worth while; but that, where there are no other means of doing this than punishment, there are four cases in which it is *not* worth while.

II. *Four objects of punishment.* When it *is* worth while, there are four subordinate designs or objects, which, in the course of his endeavours to compass, as far as may be, that one general object, a legislator, whose views are governed by the principle of utility, comes naturally to propose to himself.

III. 1. *1st Object—to prevent all offences.* His first, most extensive, and most eligible object, is to prevent, in as far as it is possible, and worth while, all sorts of offences whatsoever:[167] in other words, so to manage, that no offence whatsoever may be committed.

IV. 2. *2d Object—to prevent the worst.* But if a man must needs commit an offence of some kind or other, the next object is to induce him to commit an offence *less* mischievous, *rather* than one *more* mischievous: in other words, to choose always the *least* mischievous, of two offences that will either of them suit his purpose.

V. 3. *3d Object—to keep down the mischief.* When a man has resolved upon a particular offence, the next object is to dispose him to do *no more* mischief than is *necessary* to his purpose: in other words, to do as little mischief, as is consistent with the benefit he has in view.

V. 4. *4th Object—to act at the least expense.* The last object is, whatever the mischief be, which it is proposed to prevent, to prevent it at as *cheap* a rate as possible.

VII. *Rules of proportion between punishments and offences.* Subservient to these four objects, or purposes, must be the rules or canons by which the proportion of punishments[168] to offences is to be governed.

VIII. Rule 1. *Outweigh the profit of the offence.* The first object, it has been seen, is to prevent, in as far as it is worth while, all sorts of offences; therefore,

The value of the punishment must not be less in any case than what is sufficient to outweigh that of the profit[169] *of the offence.*[170]

If it be, the offence (unless some other considerations, independent of the punishment, should intervene and operate efficaciously in the character of tutelary motives)[171] will be sure to be committed notwithstanding:[172] the whole lot of punishment will be thrown away: it will be altogether *inefficacious.*[173]

IX. *The propriety of taking the strength of the temptation for a ground of abatement, no objection to this rule.* The above rule has been often objected to, on account of its seeming harshness: but this can only have happened for want of its being properly understood. The strength of the temptation, *cæteris paribus*, is as the profit of the offence: the quantum of the punishment must rise with the profit of the offence: *cæteris paribus*, it must therefore rise with the strength of the temptation. This there is no disputing. True it is, that the stronger the temptation, the less conclusive is the indication which the act of delinquency affords of the depravity of the offender's disposition.[174] So far then as the absence of any aggravation, arising from extraordinary depravity of disposition, may operate, or at the utmost, so far as the presence of a ground of extenuation, resulting from the innocence or beneficence of the offender's disposition, can operate, the strength of the temptation may operate in abatement of the demand for punishment. But it can never operate so far as to indicate the propriety of making the punishment ineffectual, which it is sure to be when brought below the level of the apparent profit of the offence.

The partial benevolence which should prevail for the reduction of it below this level, would counteract as well those purposes which such a motive would actually have in view, as those more extensive purposes which benevolence ought to have in view: it would be cruelty not only to the public, but to the very persons in whose behalf it pleads: in its effects, I mean, however opposite in its intention. Cruelty to the public, that is cruelty to the innocent, by suffering them, for want of an adequate protection, to lie exposed to the mischief of the offence: cruelty even to the offender himself, by punishing him to no purpose, and without the chance of compassing that beneficial end, by which alone the introduction of the evil of punishment is to be justified.

X. Rule 2. *Venture more against a great offence than a small one.* But whether a given offence shall be prevented in a given degree by a given quantity of punishment, is never any thing better than a chance; for the purchasing of which, whatever punishment is employed, is so much expended in advance. However, for the sake of giving it the better chance of outweighing the profit of the offence,

The greater the mischief of the offence, the greater is the expense, which it may be worth while to be at, in the way of punishment.[175]

XI. Rule 3. *Cause the least of two offences to be preferred.* The next object is, to induce a man to choose always the least mischievous of two offences; therefore

Where two offences come in competition, the punishment for the greater offence must be sufficient to induce a man to prefer the less.[176]

XII. Rule 4. *Punish for each particle of the mischief.* When a man has resolved upon a particular offence, the next object is, to induce him to do no more mischief than what is necessary for his purpose: therefore

The punishment should be adjusted in such manner to each particular offence, that for every part of the mischief there may be a motive to restrain the offender from giving birth to it.[177]

XIII. Rule 5. *Punish in no degree without special reason.* The last object is, whatever mischief is guarded against, to guard against it at as cheap a rate as possible: therefore

The punishment ought in no case to be more than what is necessary to bring it into conformity with the rules here given.

XIV. Rule 6. *Attend to circumstances influencing sensibility.* It is further to be observed, that owing to the different manners and degrees in which persons under different circumstances are affected by the same exciting cause, a punishment which is the same in name will not always either really produce, or even so much as appear to others to produce, in two different persons the same degree of pain: therefore

That the quantity actually inflicted on each individual offender may correspond to the quantity intended for similar offenders in general, the several circumstances influencing sensibility ought always to be taken into. account.[178]

XV. *Comparative view of the above rules.* Of the above rules of proportion, the four first we may perceive, serve to mark out the limits on the side of diminution; the limits *below* which a punishment ought not to be *diminished:* the fifth, the limits on the side of increase; the limits *above* which it ought not to be *increased.* The five first are calculated to serve as guides to the legislator: the sixth is calculated, in some measure, indeed, for the same purpose, but principally for guiding the judge in his endeavours to conform, on both sides, to the intentions of the legislator.

XVI. *Into the account of the* value *of a punishment must be taken its deficiency in point of certainty and proximity.* Let us look back a little. The first rule, in order to render it more conveniently applicable to practice, may need perhaps to be a little more particularly unfolded. It is to be observed, then, that for the sake of accuracy, it was necessary, instead of the word *quantity* to make use of the less perspicuous term *value.* For the word *quantity* will not properly include the circumstances either of certainty or proximity: circumstances which, in estimating the value of a lot of pain or pleasure, must always be taken into the account.[179] Now, on the one hand, a lot of punishment is a lot of pain; on the other hand, the profit of an offence is a lot of pleasure, or what is equivalent to it. But the profit of the offence *is* commonly more *certain* than the punishment, or, what comes to the same thing, *appears* so at least to the offender. It is at any rate commonly more *immediate.* It follows, therefore, that, in order to maintain its superiority over the profit of the offence, the punishment must have its value made up in some other way, in proportion to that whereby it falls short in the two points of *certainty* and *proximity.* Now there is no other way in which it can receive any addition to its *value,* but by receiving an addition in point of *magnitude.* Wherever then the value of the punishment falls short, either in point of *certainty,* or of *proximity,* of that of the profit of the offence, it must receive a proportionable addition in point of *magnitude.*[180]

XVII. *Also, into the account of the mischief, and profit of the offence, the mischief and profit of other offences of the same* habit. Yet farther. To make sure of giving the value of the punishment the superiority over that of the offence, it may be necessary, in some cases, to take into the account the profit not only of the *individual* offence to which the punishment is to be annexed, but also of such *other* offences of the *same sort* as the offender is likely to have already committed without detection. This random mode of calculation, severe as it is, it will be impossible to avoid having recourse to, in certain cases: in such, to wit, in which the profit is pecuniary, the chance of detection very small, and the obnoxious act of such a nature as indicates a habit: for example, in the case of frauds against the coin. If it be *not* recurred to, the practice of committing the offence will be sure to be, upon the balance of the account, a gainful practice. That being the case, the legislator will be absolutely sure of *not* being able to suppress it, and the whole punishment that is bestowed upon it will be thrown away. In a word (to keep to the same expressions we set out with) that whole quantity of punishment will be *inefficacious*.

XVIII. Rule 7. *Want of certainty must be made up in magnitude.* These things being considered, the three following rules may be laid down by way of supplement and explanation to Rule 1.

To enable the value of the punishment to outweigh that of the profit of the offence, it must be increased, in point of magnitude, in proportion as it falls short in point of certainty.

XIX Rule 8. *(So also want of proximity.) Punishment must be further increased in point of magnitude, in proportion as it falls short in point of proximity.*

XX Rule 9. *(For acts indicative of a habit punish as for the habit.) Where the act is conclusively indicative of a habit, such an increase must be given to the punishment as may enable it to outweigh the profit not only of the individual offence, but of such other like offences as are likely to have been committed with impunity by the same offender.*

XXI. *The remaining rules are of less importance.* There may be a few other circumstances or considerations which may influence, in some small degree, the demand for punishment: but as the propriety of these is either not so demonstrable, or not so constant, or the application of them not so determinate, as that of the foregoing, it may be doubted whether they be worth putting on a level with the others.

XXII. Rule 10. *(For the sake of quality, increase in quantity.) When a punishment, which in point of quality is particularly well calculated to answer its intention, cannot exist in less than a certain quantity, it may sometimes be of use, for the sake of employing it, to stretch a little beyond that quantity which, on other accounts, would be strictly necessary.*

XXIII. Rule 11. *(Particularly for a moral lesson.) In particular, this may sometimes be the case, where the punishment proposed is of such a nature as to be particularly well calculated to answer the purpose of a moral lesson.*[181]

XXIV. Rule 12. *Attend to circumstances which may render punishment unprofitable.* The tendency of the above considerations is to dictate an augmentation in the punishment: the following rule operates in the way of diminution. There are certain cases (it has been seen)[182] in which, by the influence of accidental circumstances, punishment may be rendered unprofitable in the whole: in the same cases it may chance to be rendered unprofitable as to a part only. Accordingly,

In adjusting the quantum of punishment, the circumstances, by which all punishment may be rendered unprofitable, ought to be attended to.

XXV. Rule 13. *For simplicity's sake, small disproportions may be neglected.* It is to be observed that the more various and minute any set of provisions are, the greater the chance is that any given article in them will not be borne in mind: without which, no benefit can ensue from it. Distinctions, which are more complex than what the conceptions of those whose conduct it is designed to influence can take in, will even be worse than useless. The whole system will present a confused appearance: and thus the effect, not only of the proportions established by the articles in question, but of whatever is connected with them, will be destroyed.[183] To draw a precise line of direction in such case seems impossible. However, by way of memento, it may be of some use to subjoin the following rule.

Among provisions designed to perfect the proportion between punishments and offences, if any occur, which, by their own particular good effects, would not make up for the harm they would do by adding to the intricacy of the Code, they should be omitted.[184]

XXVI. *Auxiliary force of the physical, moral, and religious sanction, not here allowed for—why.* It may be remembered, that the political sanction, being that to which the sort of punishment belongs, which in this chapter is all along in view, is but one of four sanctions, which may all of them contribute their share towards producing the same effects. It may be expected, therefore, that in adjusting the quantity of political punishment, allowance should be made for the assistance it may meet with from those other controlling powers. True it is, that from each of these several sources a very powerful assistance may sometimes be derived. But the case is, that (setting aside the moral sanction, in the case where the force of it is expressly adopted into and modified by the political)[185] the force of those other powers is never determinate enough to be depended upon. It can never be reduced, like political punishment, into exact lots, nor meted out in number, quantity, and value. The legislator is therefore obliged to provide the full complement of punishment, as if he were sure of not receiving any assistance whatever from any of those quarters. If he does, so much the better: but lest he should not, it is necessary he should, at all events, make that provision which depends upon himself.

XXVII. *Recapitulation.* It may be of use, in this place, to recapitulate the several circumstances, which, in establishing the proportion betwixt punishments and offences, are to be attended to. These seem to be as follows:

I. *On the part of the offence:*
1. The profit of the offence;
2. The mischief of the offence;
3. The profit and mischief of other greater or lesser offences, of different sorts, which the offender may have to choose out of;
4. The profit and mischief of other offences, of the same sort, which the same offender may probably have been guilty of already.

II. *On the part of the punishment:*
   5. The magnitude of the punishment: composed of its intensity and duration;
   6. The deficiency of the punishment in point of certainty;
   7. The deficiency of the punishment in point of proximity;
   8. The quality of the punishment;
   9. The accidental advantage in point of quality of a punishment, not strictly needed in point of quantity,
   10. The use of a punishment of a particular quality, in the character of a moral lesson.

III. *On the part of the offender:*
   11. The responsibility of the class of persons in a way to offend;
   12. The sensibility of each particular offender;
   13. The particular merits or useful qualities of any particular offender, in case of a punishment which might deprive the community of the benefit of them;
   14. The multitude of offenders on any particular occasion.

IV. *On the part of the public,* at any particular conjuncture:
   15. The inclinations of the people, for or against any quantity or mode of punishment;
   16. The inclinations of foreign powers.

V. *On the part of the law:* that is, of the public for a continuance:
   17. The necessity of making small sacrifices, in point of proportionality, for the sake of simplicity.

XXVIII. *The nicety here observed vindicated from the charge of inutility.* There are some, perhaps, who, at first sight, may look upon the nicety employed in the adjustment of such rules, as so much labour lost: for gross ignorance, they will say, never troubles itself about laws, and passion does not calculate. But the evil of ignorance admits of cure:[186] and as to the proposition that passion does not calculate, this, like most of these very general and oracular propositions, is not true. When matters of such importance as pain and pleasure are at stake, and these in the highest degree (the only matters, in short, that can be of importance) who is there that does not calculate? Men calculate, some with less exactness, indeed, some with more: but all men calculate. I would not say, that even a madman does not calculate.[187] Passion calculates, more or less, in every man: in different men, according to the warmth or coolness of their dispositions: according to the firmness or irritability of their minds: according to the nature of the motives by which they are acted upon. Happily, of all passions, that is the most given to calculation, from the excesses of which, by reason of its strength, constancy, and universality, society has most to apprehend:[188] I mean that which corresponds to the motive of pecuniary interest: so that these niceties, if such they are to be called, have the best chance of being efficacious, where efficacy is of the most importance.

CHAPTER XV
Of the Properties to Be Given to a Lot of Punishment

I. *Properties are to be governed by proportion.* It has been shown what the rules are, which ought to be observed in adjusting the proportion between the punishment and the offence. The properties to be given to a lot of punishment, in every instance, will of course be such as it stands in need of, in order to be capable of being applied, in conformity to those rules: the *quality* will be regulated by the *quantity*.

II. *Property 1. Variability.* The first of those rules, we may remember, was, that the quantity of punishment must not be less, in any case, than what is sufficient to outweigh the profit of the offence: since, as often as it is less, the whole lot (unless by accident the deficiency should be supplied from some of the other sanctions) is thrown away: it is *inefficacious*. The fifth was, that the punishment ought in no case to be more than what is required by the several other rules: since, if it be, all that is above that quantity is *needless*. The fourth was, that the punishment should be adjusted in such manner to each individual offence, that every part of the mischief of that offence may have a penalty (that is, a tutelary motive) to encounter it: otherwise, with respect to so much of the offence as has not a penalty to correspond to it, it is as if there were no punishment in the case. Now to none of those rules can a lot of punishment be conformable, unless, for every variation in point of quantity, in the mischief of the species of offence to which it is annexed, such lot of punishment admits of a correspondent variation. To prove this, let the profit of the offence admit of a multitude of degrees. Suppose it, then, at any one of these degrees: if the punishment be less than what is suitable to that degree, it will be *inefficacious;* it will be so much thrown away: if it be more, as far as the difference extends, it will be *needless;* it will therefore be thrown away also in that case.

The first property, therefore, that ought to be given to a lot of punishment, is that of being variable in point of quantity, in conformity to every variation which can take place in either the profit or mischief of the offence. This property might, perhaps, be termed, in a single word, *variability*.

III. *Property 2. Equability.* A second property, intimately connected with the former, may be styled *equability*. It will avail but little, that a mode of punishment (proper in all other respects) has been established by the legislator; and that capable of being screwed up or let down to any degree that can be required; if, after all, whatever degree of it be pitched upon, that same degree shall be liable, according to circumstances, to produce a very heavy degree of pain, or a very slight one, or even none at all. In this case, as in the former, if circumstances happen one way, there will be a great deal of pain produced which will be *needless:* if the other way, there will be no pain at all applied, or none that will be *efficacious.* A punishment, when liable to this irregularity, may be styled an unequable one: when free from it, an equable one. The quantity of pain produced by the punishment will, it is true, depend in a considerable degree upon circumstances distinct from the nature of the punishment itself: upon the condition which the offender is in, with respect to the circumstances by which a man's sensibility is liable to be influenced. But the influence of these very circumstances will in many cases be reciprocally influenced by the nature of the punishment: in other words, the pain which is produced by any mode of punishment, will be the joint effect of the punishment which is applied to him, and the circumstances in which he is exposed to it. Now there are some punishments, of which the effect may be liable to undergo a greater alteration by the influence of such foreign circumstances, than the effect of other punishments is liable to undergo. So far, then, as this is the case, equability or unequability may be regarded as properties belonging to the punishment itself.

IV. *Punishments which are apt to be deficient in this respect.* An example of a mode of punishment which is apt to be unequable, is that of *banishment,* when the *locus a quo* (or place the party is banished from) is some determinate place appointed by the law, which perhaps the offender cares not whether he ever see or no. This is also the case with *pecuniary,* or *quasi-pecuniary* punishment, when it respects some particular species of property, which the offender may have been possessed of, or not, as it may happen. All these punishments may be split down into parcels, and measured out with the utmost nicety: being divisible by time, at least, if by nothing else. They are not, therefore, any of them defective in point of variability: and yet, in many cases, this defect in point of equability may make them as unfit for use as if they were.[189]

V. *Property 3. Commensurability to other punishments.* The third rule of proportion was, that where two offences come in competition, the punishment for the greater offence must be sufficient to induce a man to prefer the less. Now, to be sufficient for this purpose, it must be evidently and uniformly greater: greater, not in the eyes of some men only, but of all men who are liable to be in a situation to take their choice between the two offences; that is, in effect, of all mankind. In other words, the two punishments must be perfectly *commensurable.* Hence arises a third property, which may be termed *commensurability:* to wit, with reference to other punishments.[190]

VI. *How two lots of punishment may be rendered perfectly commensurable.* But punishments of different kinds are in very few instances uniformly greater one than another; especially when the lowest degrees of that which is ordinarily the greater, are compared with the highest degrees of that which is ordinarily the less: in other words, punishments of different kinds are in few instances uniformly commensurable. The only certain and universal means of making two lots of punishment perfectly commensurable, is by making the lesser an ingredient in the composition of the greater. This may be done in either of two ways. 1. By adding to the lesser punishment another quantity of punishment of the same kind. 2. By adding to it another quantity of a different kind. The latter mode is not less certain than the former: for though one cannot always be absolutely sure, that to the same person a given punishment will appear greater than another given punishment; yet one may be always absolutely sure, that any given punishment, so as it does but come into contemplation, will appear greater than none at all.

VII. *Property 4. Characteristicalness.* Again: Punishment cannot act any farther than in as far as the idea of it, and of its connection with the offence, is present in the mind. The idea of it, if not present, cannot act at all; and then the punishment itself must be *inefficacious.* Now, to be present, it must be remembered, and to be remembered it must have been learnt. But of all punishments that can be imagined, there are none of which the connection with the offence is either so easily learnt, or so efficaciously remembered, as those of which the idea is already in part associated with some part of the idea of the offence: which is the case when the one and the other have some circumstance that belongs to them in common. When this is the case with a punishment and an offence, the punishment is said to bear an *analogy* to, or to be *characteristic* of, the offence.[191] *Characteristicalness* is, therefore, a fourth property, which on this account ought to be given, whenever it can conveniently be given, to a lot of punishment.

VIII. *The mode of punishment the most eminently characteristic, is that of retaliation.* It is obvious, that the effect of this contrivance will be the greater, as the analogy is the closer. The analogy will be the closer, the more *material*[192] that circumstance is, which is in common. Now the most material circumstance that can belong to an offence and a punishment in common, is the hurt or damage which they produce. The closest analogy, therefore, that can subsist between an offence and the punishment annexed to it, is that which subsists between them when the hurt or damage they produce is of the same nature: in other words, that which is constituted by the circumstance of identity in point of damage.[193] Accordingly, the mode of punishment, which of all others bears the closest analogy to the offence, is that which in the proper and exact sense of the word is termed *retaliation*. Retaliation, therefore, in the few cases in which it is practicable, and not too expensive, will have one great advantage over every other mode of punishment.

IX. *Property 5. Exemplarity.* Again: It is the idea only of the punishment (or, in other words, the *apparent* punishment) that really acts upon the mind; the punishment itself (the *real* punishment) acts not any farther than as giving rise to that idea. It is the apparent punishment, therefore, that does all the service, I mean in the way of example, which is the principal object.[194] It is the real punishment that does all the mischief.[195] Now the ordinary and obvious way of increasing the magnitude of the apparent punishment, is by increasing the magnitude of the real. The apparent magnitude, however, may to a certain degree be increased by other less expensive means: whenever, therefore, at the same time that these less expensive means would have answered that purpose, an additional real punishment is employed, this additional real punishment is *needless*. As to these less expensive means, they consist, 1. In the choice of a particular mode of punishment, a punishment of a particular quality, independent of the quantity.[196] 2. In a particular set of *solemnities* distinct from the punishment itself, and accompanying the execution of it.[197]

X. *The most effectual way of rendering a punishment exemplary is by means of analogy.* A mode of punishment, according as the appearance of it bears a greater proportion to the reality, may be said to be the more *exemplary*. Now as to what concerns the choice of the punishment itself, there is not any means by which a given quantity of punishment can be rendered more exemplary, than by choosing it of such a sort as shall bear an *analogy* to the offence. Hence another reason for rendering the punishment analogous to, or in other words characteristic of, the offence.

XI. *Property 6. Frugality.* Punishment, it is still to be remembered, is in itself an expense: it is in itself an evil.[198] Accordingly the fifth rule of proportion is, not to produce more of it than what is demanded by the other rules. But this is the case as often as any particle of pain is produced, which contributes nothing to the effect proposed. Now if any mode of punishment is more apt than another to produce any such superfluous and needless pain, it may be styled *unfrugal;* if less, it may be styled *frugal*. *Frugality*, therefore, is a sixth property to be wished for in a mode of punishment.

XII. *Frugality belongs in perfection to pecuniary punishment.* The perfection of frugality, in a mode of punishment, is where not only no superfluous pain is produced on the part of the person punished, but even that same operation, by which he is subjected to pain, is made to answer the purpose of producing pleasure on the part of some other person. Understand a profit or stock of pleasure of the self-regarding kind: for a pleasure of the dissocial kind is produced almost of course, on the part of all persons in whose breasts the offence has excited the sentiment of ill-will. Now this is the case with pecuniary punishment, as also with such punishments of the *quasi-pecuniary* kind as consist in the subtraction of such a species of possession as is transferable from one party to another. The pleasure, indeed, produced by such an operation, is not in general equal to the pain:[199] it may, however, be so in particular circumstances, as where he, from whom the thing is taken, is very rich, and he, to whom it is given, very poor: and, be it what it will, it is always so much more than can be produced by any other mode of punishment.

XIII. *Exemplarity and frugality, in what they differ and agree.* The properties of exemplarity and frugality seem to pursue the same immediate end, though by different courses. Both are occupied in diminishing the ratio of the real suffering to the apparent: but exemplarity tends to increase the apparent; frugality to reduce the real.

XIV. *Other properties of inferior importance.* Thus much concerning the properties to be given to punishments in general, to whatsoever offences they are to be applied. Those which follow are of less importance, either as referring only to certain offences in particular, or depending upon the influence of transitory and local circumstances.

In the first place, the four distinct ends into which the main and general end of punishment is divisible,[200] may give rise to so many distinct properties, according as any particular mode of punishment appears to be more particularly adapted to the compassing of one or of another of those ends. To that of *example,* as being the principal one, a particular property has already been adapted. There remains the three inferior ones of *reformation, disablement,* and *compensation.*

XV. *Property 7. Subserviency to reformation.* A seventh property, therefore, to be wished for in a mode of punishment, is that of *subserviency to reformation,* or *reforming tendency.* Now any punishment is subservient to reformation in proportion to its *quantity:* since the greater the punishment a man has experienced, the stronger is the tendency it has to create in him an aversion towards the offence which was the cause of it: and that with respect to all offences alike. But there are certain punishments which, with regard to certain offences, have a particular tendency to produce that effect by reason of their *quality:* and where this is the case, the punishments in question, as applied to the offences in question, will *pro tanto* have the advantage over all others. This influence will depend upon the nature of the motive which is the cause of the offence: the punishment most subservient to reformation will be the sort of punishment that is best calculated to invalidate the force of that motive.

XVI. —*applied to offences originating in ill-will.* Thus, in offences originating from the motive of ill-will,[201] that punishment has the strongest reforming tendency, which is best calculated to weaken the force of the irascible affections. And more particularly, in that sort of offence which consists in an obstinate refusal, on the part of the offender, to do something which is lawfully required of him,[202] and in which the obstinacy is in great measure kept up by his resentment against those who have an interest in forcing him to compliance, the most efficacious punishment seems to be that of confinement to spare diet.

XVII. —*to offences originating in indolence joined to pecuniary interest.* Thus, also, in offences which owe their birth to the joint influence of indolence and pecuniary interest, that punishment seems to possess the strongest reforming tendency, which is best calculated to weaken the force of the former of those dispositions. And more particularly, in the cases of theft, embezzlement, and every species of defraudment, the mode of punishment best adapted to this purpose seems, in most cases, to be that of penal labour.

XVIII. *Property 8. Efficacy with respect to disablement.* An eighth property to be given to a lot of punishment in certain cases, is that of *efficacy with respect to disablement,* or, as it might be styled more briefly, *disabling efficacy.* This is a property which may be given in perfection to a lot of punishment; and that with much greater certainty than the property of subserviency to reformation. The inconvenience is, that this property is apt, in general, to run counter to that of frugality: there being, in most cases, no certain way of disabling a man from doing mischief, without, at the same time, disabling him, in a great measure, from doing good, either to himself or others. The mischief therefore of the offence must be so great as to demand a very considerable lot of punishment, for the purpose of example, before it can warrant the application of a punishment equal to that which is necessary for the purpose of disablement.

XIX. —*is most conspicuous in capital punishment.* The punishment, of which the efficacy in this way is the greatest, is evidently that of death. In this case the efficacy of it is certain. This accordingly is the punishment peculiarly adapted to those cases in which the name of the offender, so long as he lives, may be sufficient to keep a whole nation in a flame. This will now and then be the case with competitors for the sovereignty, and leaders of the factions in civil wars: though, when applied to offences of so questionable a nature, in which the question concerning criminality turns more upon success than any thing else; an infliction of this sort may seem more to savour of hostility than punishment. At the same time this punishment, it is evident, is in an eminent degree *unfrugal;* which forms one among the many objections there are against the use of it, in any but very extraordinary cases.[203]

XX. *Other punishments in which it is to be found.* In ordinary cases the purpose may be sufficiently answered by one or other of the various kinds of confinement and banishment: of which, imprisonment is the most strict and efficacious. For when an offence is so circumstanced that it cannot be committed but in a certain place, as is the case, for the most part, with offences against the person, all the law has to do, in order to disable the offender from committing it, is to prevent his being in that place. In any of the offences which consist in the breach or the abuse of any kind of trust, the purpose may be compassed at a still cheaper rate, merely by forfeiture of the trust: and in general, in any of those offences which can only be committed under favour of some relation in which the offender stands with reference to any person, or sets of persons, merely by forfeiture of that relation: that is, of the right of continuing to reap the advantages belonging to it. This is the case, for instance, with any of those offences which consist in an abuse of the privileges of marriage, or of the liberty of carrying on any lucrative or other occupation.

XXI. *Property 9. Subserviency to compensation.* The *ninth* property is that of *subserviency to compensation.* This property of punishment, if it be *vindictive* compensation that is in view, will, with little variation, be in proportion to the quantity: if *lucrative,* it is the peculiar and characteristic property of pecuniary punishment.

XXII. *Property 10. Popularity.* In the rear of all these properties may be introduced that of *popularity;* a very fleeting and indeterminate kind of property, which may belong to a lot of punishment one moment, and be lost by it the next. By popularity is meant the property of being acceptable, or rather not unacceptable, to the bulk of the people, among whom it is proposed to be established. In strictness of speech, it should rather be called *absence of unpopularity:* for it cannot be expected, in regard to such a matter as punishment, that any species or lot of it should be positively acceptable and grateful to the people: it is sufficient, for the most part, if they have no decided aversion to the thoughts of it. Now the property of characteristicalness, above noticed, seems to go as far towards conciliating the approbation of the people to a mode of punishment, as any; insomuch that popularity may be regarded as a kind of secondary quality, depending upon that of characteristicalness.[204] The use of inserting this property in the catalogue, is chiefly to make it serve by way of memento to the legislator not to introduce, without a cogent necessity, any mode or lot of punishment, towards which he happens to perceive any violent aversion entertained by the body of the people.

XXIII. *Mischiefs resulting from the unpopularity of a punishment—discontent among the people, and weakness in the law.* The effects of unpopularity in a mode of punishment are analogous to those of unfrugality. The unnecessary pain which denominates a punishment unfrugal, is most apt to be that which is produced on the part of the offender. A portion of superfluous pain is in like manner produced when the punishment is unpopular: but in this case it is produced on the part of persons altogether innocent, the people at large. This is already one mischief; and another is, the weakness which it is apt to introduce into the law. When the people are satisfied with the law, they voluntarily lend their assistance in the execution: when they are dissatisfied, they will naturally withhold that assistance, it is well if they do not take a positive part in raising impediments. This contributes greatly to the uncertainty of the punishment; by which, in the first instance, the frequency of the offence receives an increase. In process of time that deficiency, as usual, is apt to draw on an increase in magnitude: an addition of a certain quantity which otherwise would be *needless.*[205]

XXIV. *This property supposes a prejudice which the legislator ought to cure.* This property, it is to be observed, necessarily supposes, on the part of the people, some prejudice or other, which it is the business of the legislator to endeavour to correct. For if the aversion to the punishment in question were grounded on the principle of utility, the punishment would be such as, on other accounts, ought not to be employed: in which case its popularity or unpopularity would never be worth drawing into question. It is properly therefore a property not so much of the punishment as of the people: a disposition to entertain an unreasonable dislike against an object which merits their approbation. It is the sign also of another property, to wit, indolence or weakness, on the part of the legislator: in suffering the people, for the want of some instruction, which ought to be and might be given them, to quarrel with their own interest. Be this as it may, so long as any such dissatisfaction subsists, it behoves the legislator to have an eye to it, as much as if it were ever so well grounded. Every nation is liable to have its prejudices and its caprices, which it is the business of the legislator to look out for, to study, and to cure.[206]

XXV. *Property 11. Remissibility.* The eleventh and last of all the properties that seem to be requisite in a lot of punishment, is that of *remissibility.*[207] The general presumption is, that when punishment is applied, punishment is needful: that it ought to be applied, and therefore cannot want to be *remitted.* But in very particular, and those always very deplorable cases, it may by accident happen otherwise. It may happen that punishment shall have been inflicted, where, according to the intention of the law itself, it ought not to have been inflicted: that is, where the sufferer is innocent of the offence. At the time of the sentence passed he appeared guilty: but since then, accident has brought his innocence to light. This being the case, so much of the destined punishment as he has suffered already, there is no help for. The business is then to free him from as much as is yet to come. But *is* there any yet to come? There is very little chance of there being any, unless it be so much as consists of *chronical* punishment: such as imprisonment, banishment, penal labour, and the like. So much as consists of *acute* punishment, to wit where the penal process itself is over presently, however permanent the punishment may be in its effects, may be considered as *ir*remissible. This is the case, for example, with whipping, branding, mutilation, and capital punishment. The most perfectly irremissible of any is capital punishment. For though other punishments cannot, when they are over, be remitted, they may be compensated for; and although the unfortunate victim cannot be put into the same condition, yet possibly means may be found of putting him into as good a condition, as he would have been in if he had never suffered. This may in general be done very effectually where the punishment has been no other than pecuniary.

There is another case in which the property of remissibility may appear to be of use: this is, where, although the offender has been justly punished, yet on account of some good behaviour of his, displayed at a time subsequent to that of the commencement of the punishment, it may seem expedient to remit a part of it. But this it can scarcely be, if the proportion of the punishment is, in other respects, what it ought to be. The purpose of example is the more important object, in comparison of that of reformation.[208] It is not very likely, that less punishment should be required for the former purpose than for the latter. For it must be rather an extraordinary case, if a punishment, which is sufficient to deter a man who has only thought of it for a few moments, should not be sufficient to deter a man who has been feeling it all the time. Whatever, then, is required for the purpose of example, must abide at all events: it is not any reformation on the part of the offender, that can warrant the remitting of any part of it: if it could, a man would have nothing to do but to reform immediately, and so free himself from the greatest part of that punishment which was deemed necessary. In order, then, to warrant the remitting of any part of a punishment upon this ground, it must first be supposed that the punishment at first appointed was more than was necessary for the purpose of example, and consequently that a part of it was *needless* upon the whole. This, indeed, is apt enough to be the case, under the imperfect systems that are as yet on foot: and therefore, during the continuance of those systems, the property of remissibility may, on this second ground likewise, as well as on the former, be deemed a useful one. But this would not be the case in any new-constructed system, in which the rules of proportion above laid down should be observed. In such a system, therefore, the utility of this property would rest solely on the former ground.

XXVI. *To obtain all these properties, punishments must be mixed.* Upon taking a survey of the various possible modes of punishment, it will appear evidently, that there is not any one of them that possesses all the above properties in perfection. To do the best that can be done in the way of punishment, it will therefore be necessary, upon most occasions, to compound them, and make them into complex lots, each consisting of a number of different modes of punishment put together: the nature and proportions of the constituent parts of each lot being different, according to the nature of the offence which it is designed to combat.

XXVII. *The foregoing properties recapitulated.* It may not be amiss to bring together, and exhibit in one view, the eleven properties above established. They are as follows:

Two of them are concerned in establishing a proper proportion between a single offence and its punishment; viz.

1. Variability.
2. Equability.

One, in establishing a proportion, between more offences than one, and more punishments than one; viz.

3. Commensurability.

A fourth contributes to place the punishment in that situation in which alone it can be efficacious; and at the same time to be bestowing on it the two farther properties of exemplarity and popularity; viz.

4. Characteristicalness.

Two others are concerned in excluding all useless punishment; the one indirectly, by heightening the efficacy of what is useful; the other in a direct way; viz.

5. Exemplarity.
6. Frugality.

Three others contribute severally to the three inferior ends of punishment; viz.

7. Subserviency to reformation.

8. Efficacy in disabling.

9. Subserviency to compensation.

Another property tends to exclude a collateral mischief, which a particular mode of punishment is liable accidentally to produce, viz.

10. Popularity.

The remaining property tends to palliate a mischief, which all punishment, as such, is liable accidentally to produce; viz.

11. Remissibility.

The properties of commensurability, characteristicalness, exemplarity, subserviency to reformation, and efficacy in disabling, are more particularly calculated to augment the *profit* which is to be made by punishment: frugality, subserviency to compensation, popularity, and remissibility, to diminish the *expense:* variability and equability are alike subservient to both those purposes.

XXVIII. *Connection of this with the ensuing chapter.* We now come to take a general survey of the system of *offences:* that is, of such *acts* to which, on account of the mischievous *consequences* they have a *natural* tendency to produce, and in the view of putting a stop to those consequences, it may be proper to annex a certain *artificial* consequence, consisting of punishment, to be inflicted on the authors of such acts, according to the principles just established.

CHAPTER XVII
Of the Limits of the Penal Branch of Jurisprudence

§ 1. Limits between Private Ethics and the Art of Legislation.

I. *Use of this chapter.* So much for the division of offences in general. Now an offence is an act prohibited, or (what comes to the same thing) an act of which the contrary is commanded, by the law: and what is it that the law can be employed in doing, besides prohibiting and commanding? It should seem then, according to this view of the matter, that were we to have settled what may be proper to be done with relation to offences, we should thereby have settled every thing that may be proper to be done in the way of law. Yet that branch which concerns the method of dealing with offences, and which is termed sometimes the *criminal,* sometimes the *penal,* branch, is universally understood to be but one out of two branches which compose the whole subject of the art of legislation; that which is termed the *civil* being the other.[329] Between these two branches then, it is evident enough, there cannot but be a very intimate connection; so intimate is it indeed, that the limits between them are by no means easy to mark out. The case is the same in some degree between the whole business of legislation (civil and penal branches taken together) and that of private ethics. Of these several limits however it will be in a manner necessary to exhibit some idea: lest, on the one hand, we should seem to leave any part of the subject that *does* belong to us untouched, or, on the other hand, to deviate on any side into a track which does not belong to us.

In the course of this enquiry, that part of it I mean which concerns the limits between the civil and the penal branch of law, it will be necessary to settle a number of points, of which the connection with the main question might not at first sight be suspected. To ascertain what sort of a thing *a* law is; what the *parts* are that are to be found in it; what it must contain in order to be *complete;* what the connection is between that part of a body of laws which belongs to the subject of *procedure* and the rest of the law at large:—all these, it will be seen, are so many problems, which must be solved before any satisfactory answer can be given to the main question above mentioned.

Nor is this their only use: for it is evident enough, that the notion of a complete law must first be fixed, before the legislator can in any case know what it is he has to do, or when his work is done.

II. *Ethics in general, what.* Ethics at large may be defined, the art of directing men's actions to the production of the greatest possible quantity of happiness, on the part of those whose interest is in view.

III. *Private ethics.* What then are the actions which it can be in a man's power to direct? They must be either his own actions, or those of other agents. Ethics, in as far as it is the art of directing a man's own actions, may be styled the *art of self-government,* or *private ethics.*

IV. *The art of government: that is, of legislation and administration.* What other agents then are there, which, at the same time that they are under the influence of man's direction, are susceptible of happiness? They are of two sorts: 1. Other human beings who are styled persons. 2. Other animals, which, on account of their interests having been neglected by the insensibility of the ancient jurists, stand degraded into the class of *things.*[330] As to other human beings, the art of directing their actions to the above end is what we mean, or at least the only thing which, upon the principle of utility, we *ought* to mean, by the art of government: which, in as far as the measures it displays itself in are of a permanent nature, is generally distinguished by the name of *legislation:* as it is by that of *administration,* when they are of a temporary nature, determined by the occurrences of the day.

V. *Art of education.* Now human creatures, considered with respect to
the maturity of their faculties, are either in an *adult,* or in a *non-adult* state.
The art of government, in as far as it concerns the direction of the actions
of persons in a non-adult state, may be termed the art of *education.* In as
far as this business is entrusted with those who, in virtue of some private
relationship, are in the main the best disposed to take upon them, and the
best able to discharge, this office, it may be termed the art of *private education;* in as far as it is exercised by those whose province it is to superin-
tend the conduct of the whole community, it may be termed the art of
public education.

VI. *Ethics exhibits the rules of, 1. Prudence. 2. Probity. 3. Beneficence.* As
to ethics in general, a man's happiness will depend, in the first place, upon
such parts of his behaviour as none but himself are interested in; in the
next place, upon such parts of it as may affect the happiness of those about
him. In as far as his happiness depends upon the first-mentioned part of
his behaviour, it is said to depend upon his *duty to himself.* Ethics then, in
as far as it is the art of directing a man's actions in this respect, may be
termed the art of discharging one's duty to one's self: and the quality
which a man manifests by the discharge of this branch of duty (if duty it
is to be called) is that of *prudence.* In as far as his happiness, and that of any
other person or persons whose interests are considered, depends upon
such parts of his behaviour as may affect the interests of those about him,
it may be said to depend upon his *duty to others;* or, to use a phrase now
somewhat antiquated, his *duty to his neighbour.* Ethics then, in as far as it is
the art of directing a man's actions in this respect, may be termed the art
of discharging one's duty to one's neighbour. Now the happiness of one's
neighbour may be consulted in two ways: 1. In a negative way, by forbear-
ing to diminish it. 2. In a positive way, by studying to increase it. A man's
duty to his neighbour is accordingly partly negative and partly positive: to
discharge the negative branch of it, is *probity:* to discharge the positive
branch, *beneficence.*

VII. *Probity and beneficence, how they connect with prudence.* It may here
be asked, How it is that upon the principle of private ethics, legislation
and religion out of the question, a man's happiness depends upon such
parts of his conduct as affect, immediately at least, the happiness of no
one but himself: this is as much as to ask, What motives (independent of
such as legislation and religion may chance to furnish) can one man have
to consult the happiness of another? by what motives, or, which comes to
the same thing, by what obligations, can he be bound to obey the dictates
of *probity* and *beneficence?* In answer to this, it cannot but be admitted, that
the only interests which a man at all times and upon all occasions is sure to
find *adequate* motives for consulting, are his own. Notwithstanding this,

there are no occasions in which a man has not some motives for consulting the happiness of other men. In the first place, he has, on all occasions, the purely social motive of sympathy or benevolence: in the next place, he has, on most occasions, the semisocial motives of love of amity and love of reputation. The motive of sympathy will act upon him with more or less effect, according to the *bias* of his sensibility:[331] the two other motives, according to a variety of circumstances, principally according to the strength of his intellectual powers, the firmness and steadiness of his mind, the quantum of his moral sensibility, and the characters of the people he has to deal with.

VIII. *Every act which is a proper object of ethics is not of legislation.* Now private ethics has happiness for its end: and legislation can have no other. Private ethics concerns every member, that is, the happiness and the actions of every member, of any community that can be proposed, and legislation can concern no more. Thus far, then, private ethics and the art of legislation go hand in hand. The end they have, or ought to have, in view, is of the same nature. The persons whose happiness they ought to have in view, as also the persons whose conduct they ought to be occupied in directing, are precisely the same. The very acts they ought to be conversant about, are even in a *great measure* the same. Where then lies the difference? In that the acts which they ought to be conversant about, though in a great measure, are not *perfectly and throughout* the same. There is no case in which a private man ought not to direct his own conduct to the production of his own happiness, and of that of his fellow creatures: but there are cases in which the legislator ought not (in a direct way at least, and by means of punishment applied immediately to particular *individual* acts) to attempt to direct the conduct of the several other members of the community. Every act which promises to be beneficial upon the whole to the community (himself included) each individual ought to perform of himself: but it is not every such act that the legislator ought to compel him to perform. Every act which promises to be pernicious upon the whole to the community (himself included) each individual ought to abstain from of himself: but it is not every such act that the legislator ought to compel him to abstain from.

IX. *The limits between the provinces of private ethics and legislation, marked out by the cases unmeet for punishment.* Where then is the line to be drawn?—We shall not have far to seek for it. The business is to give an idea of the cases in which ethics ought, and in which legislation ought not (in a direct manner at least) to interfere. If legislation interferes in a direct manner, it must be by punishment.[332] Now the cases in which punishment, meaning the punishment of the political sanction, ought not to be inflicted, have been already stated.[333] If then there be any of these cases in which, although legislation ought not, private ethics does or ought to interfere, these cases will serve to point out the limits between the two arts or branches of science. These cases, it may be remembered, are of four sorts: 1. Where punishment would be groundless. 2. Where it would be inefficacious. 3. Where it would be unprofitable. 4. Where it would be needless. Let us look over all these cases, and see whether in any of them there is room for the interference of private ethics, at the same time that there is none for the direct interference of legislation.

X. 1. *Neither ought to apply where punishment is* groundless. First then, as to the cases where punishment would be *groundless*. In these cases it is evident, that the restrictive interference of ethics would be groundless too. It is because, upon the whole, there is no evil in the act, that legislation ought not to endeavour to prevent it. No more, for the same reason, ought private ethics.

XI. 2. *How far private ethics can apply in the cases where punishment would be* inefficacious. As to the cases in which punishment would be *inefficacious*. These, we may observe, may be divided into two sets or classes. The first do not depend at all upon the nature of the act: they turn only upon a defect in the timing of the punishment. The punishment in question is no more than what, for any thing that appears, ought to have been applied to the act in question. It ought, however, to have been applied at a different time, viz. not till after it had been properly denounced. These are the cases of an *ex-post-facto* law; of a judicial sentence beyond the law; and of a law not sufficiently promulgated. The acts here in question then might, for anything that appears, come properly under the department even of coercive legislation: of course do they under that of private ethics. As to the other set of cases, in which punishment would be inefficacious; neither do these depend upon the nature of the act, that is, of the *sort* of act: they turn only upon some extraneous cir*cumstances,* with which an act of *any* sort may chance to be accompanied. These, however, are of such a nature as not only to exclude the application of legal punishment, but in general to leave little room for the influence of private ethics. These are the cases where the will could not be deterred from any act, even by the extraordinary force of artificial punishment: as in the cases of extreme infancy, insanity, and perfect intoxication: of course, therefore, it could not by such slender and precarious force as could be applied by private ethics. The case is in this respect the same, under the circumstances of unintentionality with respect to the event of the action, unconsciousness with regard to the circumstances, and missupposal with regard to the existence of circumstances which have not existed; as also where the force, even of extraordinary punishment, is rendered inoperative by the superior force of a physical danger or threatened mischief. It is evident, that in these cases, if the thunders of the law prove impotent, the whispers of simple morality can have but little influence.

XII. 3. *How far, where it would be* unprofitable. As to the cases where punishment would be *unprofitable*. These are the cases which constitute the great field for the exclusive interference of private ethics. When a punishment is unprofitable, or in other words too expensive, it is because the evil of the punishment exceeds that of the offence. Now the evil of the punishment, we may remember,[334] is distinguishable into four branches: 1. The evil of coercion, including constraint or restraint, according as the act commanded is of the positive kind or the negative. 2. The evil of apprehension. 3. The evil of sufferance. 4. The derivative evils resulting to persons in *connection* with those by whom the three above-mentioned original evils are sustained. Now with respect to those original evils, the persons who lie exposed to them may be two very different sets of persons. In the first place, persons who may have actually committed, or been prompted to commit, the acts really meant to be prohibited. In the next place, persons who may have performed, or been prompted to perform, such other acts as they fear may be in danger of being involved in the punishment designed only for the former. But of these two sets of acts, it is the former only that are pernicious: it is, therefore, the former only that it can be the business of private ethics to endeavour to prevent. The latter being by the supposition not mischievous, to prevent them is what it can no more be the business of ethics to endeavour at, than of legislation. It remains to show how it may happen, that there should be acts really pernicious, which, although they may very properly come under the censure of private ethics, may yet be no fit objects for the legislator to control.

XIII. *Which it may be, 1. Although confined to the guilty.* Punishment then, as applied to delinquency, may be unprofitable in both or either of two ways: 1. By the expense it would amount to, even supposing the application of it to be confined altogether to delinquency: 2. By the danger there may be of its involving the innocent in the fate designed only for the guilty. First then, with regard to the cases in which the expense of the punishment, as applied to the guilty, would outweigh the profit to be made by it. These cases, it is evident, depend upon a certain proportion between the evil of the punishment and the evil of the offence. Now were the offence of such a nature, that a punishment which, in point of *magnitude*, should but just exceed the profit of it, would be sufficient to prevent it, it might be rather difficult perhaps to find an instance in which such punishment would clearly appear to be unprofitable. But the fact is, there are many cases in which a punishment, in order to have any chance of being efficacious, must, in point of magnitude, be raised a great deal above that level. Thus it is, wherever the danger of detection is, or, what comes to the same thing, is likely to appear to be, so small, as to make the punishment appear in a high degree uncertain. In this case it is necessary, as has been shown,[335] if punishment be at all applied, to raise it in point of magnitude as much as it falls short in point of certainty. It is evident, however, that all this can be but guess-work: and that the effect of such a proportion will be rendered precarious, by a variety of circumstances: by the want of sufficient promulgation on the part of the law:[336] by the particular circumstances of the temptation:[337] and by the circumstances influencing the sensibility of the several individuals who are exposed to it.[338] Let the *seducing* motives be strong, the offence then will at any rate be frequently committed. Now and then indeed, owing to a coincidence of circumstances more or less extraordinary, it will be detected, and by that means punished. But for the purpose of example, which is the principal one, an act of punishment, considered in itself, is of no use: what use it can be of, depends altogether upon the expectation it raises of similar punishment, in future cases of similar delinquency. But this future punishment, it is evident, must always depend upon detection. If then the want of detection is such as must in general (especially to eyes fascinated by the force of the seducing motives) appear too improbable to be reckoned upon, the punishment, though it should be inflicted, may come to be of no use. Here then will be two opposite evils running on at the same time, yet neither of them reducing the quantum of the other: the evil of the disease and the evil of the painful and inefficacious remedy. It seems to be partly owing to some such considerations, that fornication, for example, or the illicit commerce between the sexes, has commonly either gone altogether unpunished, or been punished in a degree inferior to that in which, on other accounts, legislators might have been disposed to punish it.

XIV. *2. By enveloping the innocent.* Secondly, with regard to the cases in which political punishment, as applied to delinquency, may be unprofitable, in virtue of the danger there may be of its involving the innocent in the fate designed only for the guilty. Whence should this danger then arise? From the difficulty there may be of fixing the idea of the guilty action: that is, of subjecting it to such a definition as shall be clear and precise enough to guard effectually against misapplication. This difficulty may arise from either of two sources: the one permanent, to wit, the nature of the *actions* themselves: the other occasional, I mean the qualities of the *men* who may have to deal with those actions in the way of government. In as far as it arises from the latter of these sources, it may depend partly upon the use which the *legislator* may be *able* to make of language; partly upon the use which, according to the apprehension of the legislator, the *judge* may be *disposed* to make of it. As far as legislation is concerned, it will depend upon the degree of perfection to which the arts of language may have been carried, in the first place, in the nation in general; in the next place, by the *legislator* in particular. It is to a sense of this difficulty, as it should seem, that we may attribute the caution with which most legislators have abstained from subjecting to censure, on the part of the law, such actions as come under the notion of rudeness, for example, or treachery, or ingratitude. The attempt to bring acts of so vague and questionable a nature under the control of law, will argue either a very immature age, in which the difficulties which give birth to that danger are not descried; or a very enlightened age, in which they are overcome.[339]

XV. *Legislation how far necessary for the enforcement of the dictates of* prudence. For the sake of obtaining the clearer idea of the limits between the art of legislation and private ethics, it may now be time to call to mind the distinctions above established with regard to ethics in general. The degree in which private ethics stands in need of the assistance of legislation, is different in the three branches of duty above distinguished. Of the rules of moral duty, those which seem to stand least in need of the assistance of legislation are the rules of *prudence*. It can only be through some defect on the part of the understanding, if a man be ever deficient in point of duty to himself. If he does wrong, there is nothing else that it can be owing to but either some *inadvertence*[340] or some *mis-supposal*[340] with regard to the circumstances on which his happiness depends. It is a standing topic of complaint, that a man knows too little of himself. Be it so: but is it so certain that the legislator must know more?[341] It is plain, that of individuals the legislator can know nothing: concerning those points of conduct which depend upon the particular circumstances of each individual, it is plain, therefore, that he can determine nothing to advantage. It is only with respect to those broad lines of conduct in which all persons, or very large and permanent descriptions of persons, may be in a way to engage, that he can have any pretence for interfering; and even here the propriety of his interference will, in most instances, lie very open to dispute. At any rate, he must never expect to produce a perfect compliance by the mere force of the sanction of which he is himself the author. All he can hope to do, is to increase the efficacy of private ethics, by giving strength and direction to the influence of the moral sanction. With what chance of success, for example, would a legislator go about to extirpate drunkenness and fornication by dint of legal punishment? Not all the tortures which ingenuity could invent would compass it: and, before he had made any progress worth regarding, such a mass of evil would be produced by the punishment, as would exceed, a thousandfold, the utmost possible mischief of the offence. The great difficulty would be in the procuring evidence; an object which could not be attempted, with any probability of success, without spreading dismay through every family,[342] tearing the bonds of sympathy asunder,[343] and rooting out the influence of all the social motives. All that he can do then, against offences of this nature, with any prospect of advantage, in the way of direct legislation, is to subject them, in cases of notoriety, to a slight censure, so as thereby to cover them with a slight shade of artificial disrepute.

XVI. —*Apt to go too far in this respect.* It may be observed, that with regard to this branch of duty, legislators have, in general, been disposed to carry their interference full as far as is expedient. The great difficulty here is, to persuade them to confine themselves within bounds. A thousand little passions and prejudices have led them to narrow the liberty of the subject in this line, in cases in which the punishment is either attended with no profit at all, or with none that will make up for the expense.

XVII. —*Particularly in matters of religion.* The mischief of this sort of interference is more particularly conspicuous in the article of religion. The reasoning, in this case, is of the following stamp. There are certain errors, in matters of belief, to which all mankind are prone: and for these errors in judgment, it is the determination of a Being of infinite benevolence, to punish them with an infinity of torments. But from these errors the legislator himself is necessarily free: for the men, who happen to be at hand for him to consult with, being men perfectly enlightened, unfettered, and unbiassed, have such advantages over all the rest of the world, that when they sit down to enquire out the truth relative to points so plain and so familiar as those in question, they cannot fail to find it. This being the case, when the sovereign sees his people ready to plunge headlong into an abyss of fire, shall he not stretch out a hand to save them? Such, for example, seems to have been the train of reasoning, and such the motives, which led Lewis the XIVth into those coercive measures which he took for the conversion of heretics and the confirmation of true believers. The ground-work, pure sympathy and loving-kindness: the superstructure, all the miseries which the most determined malevolence could have devised.[344] But of this more fully in another place.[345]

XVIII. —*How far necessary for the enforcement of the dictates of probity.* The rules of *probity* are those, which in point of expediency stand most in need of assistance on the part of the legislator, and in which, in point of fact, his interference has been most extensive. There are few cases in which it *would* be expedient to punish a man for hurting *himself:* but there are few cases, if any, in which it would *not* be expedient to punish a man for injuring his neighbour. With regard to that branch of probity which is opposed to offences against property, private ethics depends in a manner for its very existence upon legislation. Legislation must first determine what things are to be regarded as each man's property, before the general rules of ethics, on this head, can have any particular application. The case is the same with regard to offences against the state. Without legislation there would be no such thing as a *state:* no particular persons invested with powers to be exercised for the benefit of the rest. It is plain, therefore, that in this branch the interference of the legislator cannot any where be dispensed with. We must first know what are the dictates of legislation, before we can know what are the dictates of private ethics.[346]

XIX. —*of the dictates of beneficence.* As to the rules of beneficence, these, as far as concerns matters of detail, must necessarily be abandoned in great measure to the jurisdiction of private ethics. In many cases the beneficial quality of the act depends essentially upon the disposition of the agent; that is, upon the motives by which he appears to have been prompted to perform it: upon their belonging to the head of sympathy, love of amity, or love of reputation; and not to any head of self-regarding motives, brought into play by the force of political constraint: in a word, upon their being such as denominate his conduct *free* and *voluntary,* according to one of the many senses given to those ambiguous expressions.[347] The limits of the law on this head seem, however, to be capable of being extended a good deal farther than they seem ever to have been extended hitherto. In particular, in cases where the person is in danger, why should it not be made the duty of every man to save another from mischief, when it can be done without prejudicing himself, as well as to abstain from bringing it on him? This accordingly is the idea pursued in the body of the work.[348]

XX. *Difference between private ethics and the art of legislation recapitulated.* To conclude this section, let us recapitulate and bring to a point the difference between private ethics, considered as an art or science, on the one hand, and that branch of jurisprudence which contains the art or science of legislation, on the other. Private ethics teaches how each man may dispose himself to pursue the course most conducive to his own happiness, by means of such motives as offer of themselves: the art of legislation (which may be considered as one branch of the science of jurisprudence) teaches how a multitude of men, composing a community, may be disposed to pursue that course which upon the whole is the most conducive to the happiness of the whole community, by means of motives to be applied by the legislator.

We come now to exhibit the limits between penal and civil jurisprudence. For this purpose it may be of use to give a distinct though summary view of the principal branches into which jurisprudence, considered in its utmost extent, is wont to be divided.

§ 2. *Jurisprudence, its branches.*

XXI. *Jurisprudence, expository—censorial.* Jurisprudence is a fictitious entity: nor can any meaning be found for the word, but by placing it in company with some word that shall be significative of a real entity. To know what is meant by jurisprudence, we must know, for example, what is meant by a book of jurisprudence. A book of jurisprudence can have but one or the other of two objects: 1. To ascertain what the law[349] is: 2. To ascertain what it ought to be. In the former case it may be styled a book of *expository* jurisprudence; in the latter, a book of *censorial* jurisprudence: or, in other words, a book on the *art of legislation.*

XXII. *Expository jurisprudence, authoritative—unauthoritative.* A book of expository jurisprudence, is either *authoritative* or *unauthoritative.* It is styled authoritative, when it is composed by him who, by representing the state of the law to be so and so, causeth it so to be; that is, of the legislator himself: unauthoritative, when it is the work of any other person at large.

XXIII. *Sources of the distinctions yet remaining.* Now *law,* or *the law,* taken indefinitely, is an abstract and collective term; which, when it means any thing, can mean neither more nor less than the sum total of a number of individual laws taken together.[350] It follows, that of whatever other modifications the subject of a book of jurisprudence is susceptible, they must all of them be taken from some circumstance or other of which such individual laws, or the assemblages into which they may be sorted, are susceptible. The circumstances that have given rise to the principal branches of jurisprudence we are wont to hear of, seem to be as follows: 1. The *extent* of the laws in question in point of dominion. 2. The *political quality* of the persons whose conduct they undertake to regulate. 3. The *time* of their being in force. 4. The manner in which they are *expressed.* 5. The concern which they have with the article of *punishment.*

XXIV. *Jurisprudence, local—universal.* In the first place, in point of extent, what is delivered concerning the laws in question, may have reference either to the laws of such or such a nation or nations in particular, or to the laws of all nations whatsoever: in the first case, the book may be said to relate to *local,* in the other, to *universal, jurisprudence.*

Now of the infinite variety of nations there are upon the earth, there are no two which agree exactly in their laws: certainly not in the whole: perhaps not even in any single article: and let them agree to-day, they would disagree to-morrow. This is evident enough with regard to the *substance* of the laws: and it would be still more extraordinary if they agreed in point of *form;* that is, if they were conceived in precisely the same strings of words. What is more, as the languages of nations are commonly different, as well as their laws, it is seldom that, strictly speaking, they have so much as a single *word* in common. However, among the words that are appropriated to the subject of law, there are some that in all languages are pretty exactly correspondent to one another: which comes to the same thing nearly as if they were the same. Of this stamp, for example, are those which correspond to the words *power, right, obligation, liberty,* and many others.

It follows, that if there are any books which can, properly speaking, be styled books of universal jurisprudence, they must be looked for within very narrow limits. Among such as are expository, there can be none that are authoritative: nor even, as far as the *substance* of the laws is concerned, any that are unauthoritative. To be susceptible of an universal application, all that a book of the expository kind can have to treat of, is the import of words: to be, strictly speaking, universal, it must confine itself to terminology. Accordingly the definitions which there has been occasion here and there to intersperse in the course of the present work, and particularly the definition hereafter given of the word *law,* may be considered as matter belonging to the head of universal jurisprudence. Thus far in strictness of speech: though in point of usage, where a man, in laying down what he apprehends to be the law, extends his views to a few of the nations with which his own is most connected, it is common enough to consider what he writes as relating to universal jurisprudence.

It is in the censorial line that there is the greatest room for disquisitions that apply to the circumstances of all nations alike: and in this line what regards the substance of the laws in question is as susceptible of an universal application, as what regards the words. That the laws of all nations, or even of any two nations, should coincide in all points, would be as ineligible as it is impossible: some leading points, however, there seem to be, in respect of which the laws of all civilised nations might, without inconvenience, be the same. To mark out some of these points will, as far as it goes, be the business of the body of this work.

XXV. —*internal and international.* In the second place, with regard to the *political quality* of the persons whose conduct is the object of the law. These may, on any given occasion, be considered either as members of the same state, or as members of different states: in the first case, the law may be referred to the head of *internal,* in the second case, to that of *international*[351] jurisprudence.

Now as to any transactions which may take place between individuals who are subjects of different states, these are regulated by the internal laws, and decided upon by the internal tribunals, of the one or the other of those states: the case is the same where the sovereign of the one has any immediate transactions with a private member of the other: the sovereign reducing himself, *pro re natâ,* to the condition of a private person, as often as he submits his cause to either tribunal; whether by claiming a benefit, or defending himself against a burthen. There remain then the mutual transactions between sovereigns, as such, for the subject of that branch of jurisprudence which may be properly and exclusively termed *international.*[352]

With what degree of propriety rules for the conduct of persons of this description can come under the appellation of *laws*, is a question that must rest till the nature of the thing called *a law* shall have been more particularly unfolded.

It is evident enough, that international jurisprudence may, as well as internal, be censorial as well as expository, unauthoritative as well as authoritative.

XXVI. *Internal jurisprudence, national and provincial, local or particular.* Internal jurisprudence, again, may either concern all the members of a state indiscriminately, or such of them only as are connected in the way of residence, or otherwise, with a particular district. Jurisprudence is accordingly sometimes distinguished into *national* and *provincial.* But as the epithet *provincial* is hardly applicable to districts so small as many of those which have laws of their own are wont to be, such as towns, parishes, and manors; the term *local* (where universal jurisprudence is plainly out of the question) or the term *particular,* though this latter is not very characteristic, might either of them be more commodious.[353]

XXVII. *Jurisprudence, ancient—living.* Thirdly, with respect to *time.* In a work of the expository kind, the laws that are in question may either be such as are still in force at the time when the book is writing, or such as have ceased to be in force. In the latter case the subject of it might be termed *ancient;* in the former, *present* or *living* jurisprudence: that is, if the substantive *jurisprudence,* and no other, must at any rate be employed, and that with an epithet in both cases. But the truth is, that a book of the former kind is rather a book of history than a book of jurisprudence; and, if the word *jurisprudence* be expressive of the subject, it is only with some such words as *history* or *antiquities* prefixed. And as the laws which are any where in question are supposed, if nothing appears to the contrary, to be those which are in force, no such epithet as that of *present* or *living* commonly appears.

Where a book is so circumstanced, that the laws which form the subject of it, though in force at the time of its being written, are in force no longer, that book is neither a book of living jurisprudence, nor a book on the history of jurisprudence: it is no longer the former, and it never was the latter. It is evident that, owing to the changes which from time to time must take place, in a greater or less degree, in every body of laws, every book of jurisprudence, which is of an expository nature, must in the course of a few years, come to partake more or less of this condition.

The most common and most useful object of a history of jurispru-

dence, is to exhibit the circumstances that have attended the establishment of laws actually in force. But the exposition of the dead laws which
have been superseded, is inseparably interwoven with that of the living
ones which have superseded them. The great use of both these branches
of *science*, is to furnish examples for the *art* of legislation.[354]

XXVIII. *Jurisprudence, statutory—customary.* Fourthly, in point of *expression*, the laws in question may subsist either in the form of *statute* or in
that of *customary* law.

As to the difference between these two branches (which respects only
the article of form or expression) it cannot properly be made appear till
some progress has been made in the definition of a law.

XXIX. *Jurisprudence, civil—penal—criminal.* Lastly, the most intricate
distinction of all, and that which comes most frequently on the carpet, is
that which is made between the *civil* branch of jurisprudence and the
penal, which latter is wont, in certain circumstances, to receive the name
of *criminal*.

*Question concerning the distinction between the civil branch and the penal,
stated.* What is a penal code of laws? What a civil code? Of what nature are
their contents? Is it that there are two sorts of laws, the one penal the
other civil, so that the laws in a penal code are all penal laws, while the laws
in a civil code are all civil laws? Or is it, that in every law there is some
matter which is of a penal nature, and which therefore belongs to the
penal code; and at the same time other matter which is of a civil nature,
and which therefore belongs to the civil code? Or is it, that some laws belong to one code or the other exclusively, while others are divided between
the two? To answer these questions in any manner that shall be tolerably
satisfactory, it will be necessary to ascertain what *a law* is; meaning one
entire but single law: and what are the parts into which a law, as such, is
capable of being distinguished: or, in other words, to ascertain what the
properties are that are to be found in every object which can with propriety receive the appellation of *a* law. This then will be the business of the
third and fourth sections: what concerns the import of the word *criminal*,
as applied to law, will be discussed separately in the fifth.[355]

NOTES

PREFACE
(1789)

[1]*For example.*—*It is worse to lose than simply not to gain.*—*A loss falls the lighter by
being divided.*—*The suffering, of a person hurt in gratification of enmity, is greater
than the gratification produced by the same cause.*—These, and a few others which he
will have occasion to exhibit at the head of another publication, have the same

claim to the appellation of axioms, as those given by mathematicians under that name; since, referring to universal experience as their immediate basis, they are incapable of demonstration, and require only to be developed and illustrated, in order to be recognised as incontestable.

[2]The first edition was published in 1789, in quarto.

[3]A Fragment on Government, &c., reprinted 1822.

[4]Such as obligation, right, power, possession, title, exemption, immunity, franchise, privilege, nullity, validity, and the like.

[5]To the aggregate of them a common denomination has since been allotted—*the rationale*.

CHAPTER I

[1]Note by the Author, July 1822.

To this denomination has of late been added, or substituted, the *greatest happiness* or *greatest felicity* principle: this for shortness, instead of saying at length *that principle* which states the greatest happiness of all those whose interest is in question, as being the right and proper, and only right and proper and universally desirable, end of human action: of human action in every situation, and in particular in that of a functionary or set of functionaries exercising the powers of Government. The word *utility* does not so clearly point to the ideas of *pleasure* and *pain* as the words *happiness* and *felicity* do: nor does it lead us to the consideration of the *number,* of the interests affected; to the *number,* as being the circumstance, which contributes, in the largest proportion, to the formation of the standard here in question; the *standard of right and wrong,* by which alone the propriety of human conduct, in every situation, can with propriety be tried. This want of a sufficiently manifest connexion between the ideas of *happiness* and *pleasure* on the one hand, and the idea of *utility* on the other, I have every now and then found operating, and with but too much efficiency, as a bar to the acceptance, that might otherwise have been given, to this principle.

[2]*A principle, what.* The word principle is derived from the Latin principium: which seems to be compounded of the two words *primus,* first, or chief, and *cipium,* a termination which seems to be derived from *capio,* to take, as in *mancipium, municipium;* to which are analogous, *auceps, forceps,* and others. It is a term of very vague and very extensive signification: it is applied to any thing which is conceived to serve as a foundation or beginning to any series of operations: in some cases, of physical operations; but of mental operations in the present case.

The principle here in question may be taken for an act of the mind; a sentiment; a sentiment of approbation; a sentiment which, when applied to an action, approves of its utility, as that quality of it by which the measure of approbation or disapprobation bestowed upon it ought to be governed.

[3]Interest is one of those words, which not having any superior *genus,* cannot in the ordinary way be defined.

[4]'The principle of utility, (I have heard it said) is a dangerous principle: it is dangerous on certain occasions to consult it.' This is as much as to say, what? that it is

not consonant to utility, to consult utility: in short, that it is *not* consulting it, to consult it.

Addition by the Author, July 1822.

Not long after the publication of the Fragment on Government, anno 1776, in which, in the character of an all-comprehensive and all-commanding principle, the principle of *utility* was brought to view, one person by whom observation to the above effect was made was *Alexander Wedderburn*, at that time Attorney or Solicitor General, afterwards successively Chief Justice of the Common Pleas, and Chancellor of England, under the successive titles of Lord Loughborough and Earl of Rosslyn. It was made—not indeed in my hearing, but in the hearing of a person by whom it was almost immediately communicated to me. So far from being self-contradictory, it was a shrewd and perfectly true one. By that distinguished functionary, the state of the Government was thoroughly understood: by the obscure individual, at that time not so much as supposed to be so: his disquistions had not been as yet applied, with any thing like a comprehensive view, to the field of Constitutional Law, nor therefore to those features of the English Government, by which the greatest happiness of the ruling *one* with or without that of a favoured few, are now so plainly seen to be the only ends to which the course of it has at any time been directed. The *principle of utility* was an appellative, at that time employed—employed by me, as it bad been by others, to designate that which, in a more perspicuous and instructive manner, may, as above, be designated by the name of the *greatest happiness principle*. 'This principle (said Wedderburn) is a dangerous one.' Saying so, he said that which, to a certain extent, is strictly true: a principle, which lays down, as the only *right* and justifiable end of Government, the greatest happiness of the greatest number—how can it be denied to be a dangerous one? dangerous it unquestionably is, to every government which has for its *actual* end or object, the greatest happiness of a certain *one,* with or without the addition of some comparatively small number of others, whom it is matter of pleasure or accommodation to him to admit, each of them, to a share in the concern, on the footing of so many junior partners. *Dangerous* it therefore really was, to the interest—the sinister interest—of all those functionaries, himself included, whose interest it was, to maximize delay, vexation, and expense, in judicial and other modes of procedure, for the sake of the profit, extractible out of the expense. In a Government which had for its end in view the greatest happiness of the greatest number, Alexander Wedderburn might have been Attorney General and then Chancellor: but he would not have been Attorney General with £15,000 a year, nor Chancellor, with a peerage with a veto upon all justice, with £25,000 a year, and with 500 sinecures at his disposal, under the name of Ecclesiastical Benefices, besides *et cæteras*.

CHAPTER II

[5]*Asceticism, origin of the word. Principles of the Monks.* Ascetic is a term that has been sometimes applied to Monks. It comes from a Greek word which signifies *exercise.* The practices by which Monks sought to distinguish themselves from other men were called their Exercises. These exercises consisted in so many contrivances they had for tormenting themselves. By this they thought to ingratiate themselves

with the Deity. For the Deity, said they, is a Being of infinite benevolence: now a Being of the most ordinary benevolence is pleased to see others make themselves as happy as they can: therefore to make ourselves as unhappy as we can is the way to please the Deity. If any body asked them, what motive they could find for doing all this? Oh! said they, you are not to imagine that we are punishing ourselves for nothing: we know very well what we are about. You are to know, that for every grain of pain it costs us now, we are to have a hundred grains of pleasure by and by. The case is, that God loves to see us torment ourselves at present: indeed he has as good as told us so. But this is done only to try us, in order just to see how we should behave: which it is plain he could not know, without making the experiment. Now then, from the satisfaction it gives him to see us make ourselves as unhappy as we can make ourselves in this present life, we have a sure proof of the satisfaction it will give him to see us as happy as he can make us in a life to come.

[6]The following Note was first printed in January 1789.

It ought rather to have been styled, more extensively, the principle of *caprice*. Where it applies to the choice of actions to be marked out for injunction or prohibition, for reward or punishment, (to stand, in a word, as subjects for *obligations* to be imposed,) it may indeed with propriety be termed, as in the text, the principle of *sympathy* and *antipathy*. But this appellative does not so well apply to it, when occupied in the choice of the *events* which are to serve as sources of *title* with respect to *rights:* where the actions prohibited and allowed the obligations and rights, being already fixed, the only question is, under what circumstances a man is to be invested with the one or subjected to the other? from what incidents occasion is to be taken to invest a man, or to refuse to invest him, with the one, or to subject him to the other? In this latter case it may more appositely be characterized by the name of the *phantastic principle.* Sympathy and antipathy are affections of the *sensible* faculty. But the choice of *titles* with respect to *rights,* especially with respect to proprietary rights, upon grounds unconnected with utility, has been in many instances the work, not of the affections but of the imagination.

When, in justification of an article of English Common Law, calling uncles to succeed in certain cases in preference to fathers, Lord Coke produced a sort of ponderosity he had discovered in rights, disqualifying them from ascending in a straight line, it was not that he *loved* uncles particularly, or *hated* fathers, but because the analogy, such as it was, was what his imagination presented him with, instead of a reason, and because, to a judgment unobservant of the standard of utility, or unacquainted with the art of consulting it, where affection is out of the way, imagination is the only guide.

When I know not what ingenious grammarian invented the proposition *Delegatus non potest delegare,* to serve as a rule of law, it was not surely that he had any antipathy to delegates of the second order, or that it was any pleasure to him to think of the ruin which, for want of a manager at home, may befal the affairs of a traveller, whom an unforeseen accident has deprived of the object of his choice: it was, that the incongruity, of giving the same law to objects so contrasted as *active* and *passive* are, was not to be surmounted, and that *-atus* chimes, as well as it contrasts, with *-are.*

When that inexorable maxim, (of which the dominion is no more to be defined, than the date of its birth, or the name of its father, is to be found,) was imported from England for the government of Bengal, and the whole fabric of judicature was crushed by the thunders of *ex post facto* justice, it was not surely that the prospect of a blameless magistracy perishing in prison afforded any enjoyment to the unoffended authors of their misery; but that the music of the maxim, absorbing the whole imagination, had drowned the cries of humanity along with the dictates of common sense.† *Fiat Justitia, ruat coelum,* says another maxim, as full of extravagance as it is of harmony: Go heaven to wreck—so justice be but done:— and what is the ruin of kingdoms, in comparison of the wreck of heaven?

So again, when the Prussian chancellor, inspired with the wisdom of I know not what Roman sage, proclaimed in good Latin, for the edification of German ears, *Servitus servitutis non datur,* [Cod. Fred. tom. ii. par. 2. liv. 2. tit. x. § 6. p. 308.] it was not that he had conceived any aversion to the lifeholder who, during the continuance of his term, should wish to gratify a neighbour with a right of way or water, or to the neighbour who should wish to accept of the indulgence; but that, to a jurisprudential ear, *-tus -tutis* sound little less melodious than *-atus -are.* Whether the melody of the maxim was the real reason of the rule, is not left open to dispute: for it is ushered in by the conjunction *quia,* reason's appointed harbinger: *quia servitus servitutis non datur.*

Neither would equal melody have been produced, nor indeed could similar melody have been called for, in either of these instances, by the opposite provision: it is only when they are opposed to general rules, and not when by their conformity they are absorbed in them, that more specific ones can obtain a separate existence. *Delegatus potest delegare,* and *Servitus servitutis datur,* provisions already included under the general adoption of contracts, would have been as unnecessary to the apprehension and the memory, as, in comparison of their energetic negatives, they are insipid to the ear.

Were the inquiry diligently made, it would be found that the goddess of harmony has exercised more influence, however latent, over the dispensations of Themis, than her most diligent historiographers, or even her most passionate panegyrists, seem to have been aware of. Every one knows, how, by the ministry of Orpheus, it was she who first collected the sons of men beneath the shadow of the sceptre: yet, in the midst of continual experience, men seem yet to learn, with what successful diligence she has laboured to guide it in its course. Every one knows, that measured numbers were the language of the infancy of law: none seem to have observed, with what imperious sway they have governed her maturer age. In English jurisprudence in particular, the connexion betwixt law and music, however less perceived than in Spartan legislation, is not perhaps less real nor less close. The music of the Office, though not of the same kind, is not less musical in its kind, than the music of the Theatre; that which hardens the heart, than that which softens it:—sostenutos as long, cadences as sonorous; and those governed by rules, though not yet promulgated, not less determinate. Search indictments, pleadings, proceedings in chancery, conveyances: whatever trespasses you may find against truth or common sense, you will find none against the laws of harmony. The English Liturgy, justly as this quality has been extolled in that sacred office, possesses not a greater measure of it, than is commonly to be found in an English Act of Parliament. Dignity, simplicity, brevity, precision, intelligibility, possibility of being retained or so much as apprehended, every thing yields to Harmony. Volumes might be filled, shelves loaded, with the sacrifices that are made to this insatiate power. Expletives, her ministers in Grecian poetry are not less busy, though in different shape and bulk, in English legislation: in the former, they are monosyllables [*men, toi, ge, nun, &c.*]: in the latter, they are whole lines [And be it further enacted by the authority aforesaid, that—Provided always, and it is hereby further enacted and declared that—&c. &c.].

To return to the *principle of sympathy and antipathy:* a term preferred at first, on account of its impartiality, to the *principle of caprice.* The choice of an appellative, in the above respects too narrow, was owing to my not having, at that time, extended my views over the civil branch of law, any otherwise than as I had found it inseparably involved in the penal. But when we come to the former branch, we shall see the *phantastic* principle making at least as great a figure there, as the principle of *sympathy and antipathy* in the latter.

In the days of Lord Coke, the light of utility can scarcely be said to have as yet shone upon the face of Common Law. If a faint ray of it, under the name of the *argumentum ab inconvenienti,* is to be found in a list of about twenty topics exhibited by that great lawyer as the co-ordinate leaders of that all-perfect system, the admission, so circumstanced, is as sure a proof of neglect, as, to the statues of Brutus and Cassius, exclusion was a cause of notice. It stands, neither in the front, nor in the rear, nor in any post of honour; but huddled in towards the middle, without the smallest mark of preference. [Coke, Littleton, 11. a.] Nor is this Latin *inconvenience* by any means. the same thing with the English one. It stands distinguished from *mischief:* and because by the vulgar it is taken for something less bad, it is given by the learned as something worse. *The law prefers a mischief to an inconvenience,* says an admired maxim, and the more admired, because as nothing is expressed by it, the more is supposed to be understood.

Not that there is any avowed, much less a constant opposition, between the prescriptions of utility and the operations of the common law: such constancy we have seen to be too much even for ascetic fervor. [Supra, par. x] From time to time instinct would unavoidably betray them into the paths of reason: instinct which, however it may be cramped, can never be killed by education. The cobwebs spun out of the materials brought together by 'the competition of opposite analogies,' can never have ceased being warped by the silent attraction of the rational principle: though it should have been as the needle is by the magnet, without the privity of conscience.

†Additional Note by the Author, July 1822.

Add, and that the bad system, of Mahometan and other native law was to be put down at all events, to make way for the inapplicable and still more mischievous system of English Judge-made law, and, by the hand of his accomplice Hastings, was to be put into the pocket of Impey—Importer of this instrument of subversion, £8,000 a-year contrary to law, in addition to the £8,000 a-year lavished upon him, with the customary profusion, by the hand of law.—See the Account of this transaction in *Mill's British India.*

To this Governor a statue is erecting by a vote of East India Directors and Proprietors: on it should be inscribed—*Let it but put money into our pockets, no tyranny too flagitious to be worshipped by us.*

To this statue of the Arch-malefactor should be added, for a companion, that of the long-robed accomplice: the one lodging the bribe in the hand of the other. The hundred millions of plundered and oppressed Hindoos and Mahometans pay for the one: a Westminster Hall subscription might pay for the other.

What they have done for Ireland with her seven millions of souls, the authorised deniers and perverters of justice have done for Hindostan with her hundred millions. In this there is nothing wonderful. The wonder is—that under such institutions, men, though in ever such small number, should be found, whom the view of the injustices which, by *English Judge-made law,* they are compelled to commit, and the miseries they are thus compelled to produce, deprive of health and rest. Witness the Letter of an English Hindostan Judge, Sept. 1, 1819, which lies before me. I will not make so cruel a requital for his honesty, as to put his name in print: indeed the House of Commons' Documents already published leave little need of it.

[7]*Various phrases that have served as the characteristic marks of so many pretended systems.* It is curious enough to observe the variety of inventions men have hit upon, and the variety of phrases they have brought forward, in order to conceal from the world, and, if possible, from themselves, this very general and therefore very pardonable self-sufficiency.

1. *Moral Sense.* One man says, he has a thing made on purpose to tell him what is right and what is wrong; and that it is called a *moral sense:* and then he goes to work at his ease, and says, such a thing is right, and such a thing is wrong—why? 'because my moral sense tells me it is.'

2. *Common Sense.* Another man comes and alters the phrase: leaving out *moral,* and putting in *common,* in the room of it. He then tells you, that his common sense teaches him what is right and wrong, as surely as the other's moral sense did: meaning by common sense, a sense of some kind or other, which, he says, is possessed by all mankind: the sense of those, whose sense is not the same as the author's, being struck out of the account as not worth taking. This contrivance does better than the other; for a moral sense, being a new thing, a man may feel about him a good while without being able to find it out: but common sense is as old as the creation; and there is no man but would be ashamed to be thought not to have as much of it as his neighbours. It has another great advantage: by appearing to share power, it lessens envy: for when a man gets up upon this ground, in order to anathematize those who differ from him, it is not by a *sic volo sic jubeo,* but by a *velitis jubeatis.*

3. *Understanding.* Another man comes, and says, that as to a moral sense indeed, he cannot find that he has any such thing: that however he has an *understanding,* which will do quite as well. This understanding, he says, is the standard of right

and wrong: it tells him so and so. All good and wise men understand as he does: if other men's understandings differ in any point from his, so much the worse for them: it is a sure sign they are either defective or corrupt.

4. *Rule of Right.* Another man says, that there is an eternal and immutable Rule of Right: that that rule of right dictates so and so: and then he begins giving you his sentiments upon any thing that comes uppermost: and these sentiments (you are to take for granted) are so many branches of the eternal rule of right.

5. *Fitness of Things.* Another man, or perhaps the same man (it's no matter) says, that there are certain practices conformable, and others repugnant, to the Fitness of Things; and then he tells you, at his leisure, what practices are conformable and what repugnant: just as he happens to like a practice or dislike it.

6. *Law of Nature.* A great multitude of people are continually talking of the Law of Nature; and then they go on giving you their sentiments about what is right and what is wrong: and these sentiments, you are to understand, are so many chapters and sections of the Law of Nature.

7. *Law of Reason, Right Reason, Natural Justice, Natural Equity, Good Order.* Instead of the phrase, Law of Nature, you have sometimes, Law of Reason, Right Reason, Natural Justice, Natural Equity, Good Order. Any of them will do equally well. This latter is most used in politics. The three last are much more tolerable than the others, because they do not very explicitly claim to be any thing more than phrases: they insist but feebly upon the being looked upon as so many positive standards of themselves, and seem content to be taken, upon occasion, for phrases expressive of the conformity of the thing in question to the proper standard, whatever that may be. On most occasions, however, it will be better to say *utility: utility* is clearer, as referring more explicitly to pain and pleasure.

8. *Truth.* We have one philosopher, who says, there is no harm in any thing in the world but in telling a lie: and that if, for example, you were to murder your own father, this would only be a particular way of saying, he was not your father. Of course, when this philosopher sees any thing that he does not like, he says, it is a particular way of telling a lie. It is saying, that the act ought to be done, or may be done, when, *in truth,* it ought not to be done.

9. *Doctrine of Election.* The fairest and openest of them all is that sort of man who speaks out, and says, I am of the number of the Elect: now God himself takes care to inform the Elect what is right: and that with so good effect, and let them strive ever so, they cannot help not only knowing it but practising it. If therefore a man wants to know what is right and what is wrong, he has nothing to do but to come to me.

Repugnancy to Nature. It is upon the principle of antipathy that such and such acts are often reprobated on the score of their being *unnatural:* the practice of exposing children, established among the Greeks and Romans, was an unnatural practice. Unnatural, when it means any thing, means unfrequent: and there it means something; although nothing to the present purpose. But here it means no such thing: for the frequency of such acts is perhaps the great complaint. It therefore means nothing; nothing, I mean, which there is in the act itself. All it can serve to express is, the disposition of the person who is talking of it: the disposition he is in to be angry at the thoughts of it. Does it merit his anger? Very likely it may: but whether it does or no is a question, which, to be answered rightly, can only be answered upon the principle of utility.

Unnatural, is as good a word as moral sense, or common sense; and would be as good a foundation for a system. Such an act is unnatural; that is, repugnant to nature: for I do not like to practise it: and, consequently, do not practise it. It is therefore repugnant to what ought to be the nature of every body else.

Mischief they produce. The mischief common to all these ways of thinking and arguing (which, in truth, as we have seen, are but one and the same method, couched in different forms of words) is their serving as a cloke, and pretence, and aliment, to despotism: if not a despotism in practice, a despotism however in disposition: which is but too apt, when pretence and power offer, to show itself in practice. The consequence is, that with intentions very commonly of the purest kind, a man becomes a torment either to himself or his fellow-creatures. If he be of the melancholy cast, he sits in silent grief, bewailing their blindness and depravity: if of the irascible, he declaims with fury and virulence against all who differ from him; blowing up the coals of fanaticism, and branding with the charge of corruption and insincerity, every man who does not think, or profess to think, as he does.

If such a man happens to possess the advantages of style, his book may do a considerable deal of mischief before the nothingness of it is understood.

These principles, if such they can be called, it is more frequent to see applied to morals than to politics: but their influence extends itself to both. In politics, as well as morals, a man will be at least equally glad of a pretence for deciding any question in the manner that best pleases him, without the trouble of inquiry. If a man is an infallible judge of what is right and wrong in the actions of private individuals, why not in the measures to be observed by public men in the direction of those actions? accordingly (not to mention other chimeras) I have more than once known the pretended law of nature set up in legislative debates, in opposition to arguments derived from the principle of utility.

Whether utility is actually the sole ground of all the approbation we ever bestow, is a different consideration. 'But is it never, then, from any other considerations than those of utility, that we derive our notions of right and wrong?' I do not know: I do not care. Whether a moral sentiment can be originally conceived from any other source than a view of utility, is one question: whether upon examination and reflection it can, in point of fact, be actually persisted in and justified on any other ground, by a person reflecting within himself, is another: whether in point of right it can properly be justified on any other ground, by a person addressing himself to the community, is a third. The two first are questions of speculation: it matters not, comparatively speaking, how they are decided. The last is a question of practice: the decision of it is of as much importance as that of any can be.

'I feel in myself,' (say you) 'a disposition to approve of such or such an action in a moral view: but this is not owing to any notions I have of its being a useful one to the community. I do not pretend to know whether it be an useful one or not: it may be, for aught I know, a mischievous one.' 'But is it then,' (say I) 'a mischievous one? examine; and if you can make yourself sensible that it is so, then, if duty means any thing, that is, moral duty, it is your *duty* at least to abstain from it: and more than that, if it is what lies in your power, and can be done without too great a sacrifice, to endeavour to prevent it. It is not your cherishing the notion of it in your bosom, and giving it the name of virtue, that will excuse you.'

'I feel in myself,' (say you again) 'a disposition to detest such or such an action in a moral view; but this is not owing to any notions I have of its being a mischievous one to the community. I do not pretend to know whether it be a mischievous one or not: it may be not a mischievous one: it may be, for aught I know, an useful one.'—'May it indeed,' (say I) 'an useful one? but let me tell you then, that unless duty, and right and wrong, be just what you please to make them, if it really be not a mischievous one, and any body has a mind to do it, it is no duty of yours, but, on the contrary, it would be very wrong in you, to take upon you to prevent him: detest it within yourself as much as you please; that may be a very good reason (unless it be also a useful one) for your not doing it yourself: but if you go about, by word or deed, to do any thing to hinder him, or make him suffer for it, it is you, and not he, that have done wrong: it is not your setting yourself to blame his conduct, or branding it with the name of vice, that will make him culpable, or you blameless. Therefore, if you can make yourself content that he shall be of one mind, and you of another, about that matter, and so continue, it is well: but if nothing will serve you, but that you and he must needs be of the same mind, I'll tell you what you have to do: it is for you to get the better of your antipathy, not for him to truckle to it.'

[8]King James the First of England had conceived a violent antipathy against Arians: two of whom he burnt [Hume's Hist. vol. 6.]. This gratification he procured himself without much difficulty: the notions of the times were favourable to it. He wrote a furious book against Vorstius, for being what was called an Arminian: for Vorstius was at a distance. He also wrote a furious book, called 'A Counterblast to Tobacco,' against the use of that drug, which Sir Walter Raleigh had then lately introduced. Had the notions of the times co-operated with him, he would have burnt the Anabaptist and the smoker of tobacco in the same fire. However he had the satisfaction of putting Raleigh to death afterwards, though for another crime.

Disputes concerning the comparative excellence of French and Italian music have occasioned very serious bickerings at Paris. One of the parties would not have been sorry (says Mr. D'Alembert [Melanges Essai sur la Liberté de la Musique.]) to have brought government into the quarrel. Pretences were sought after and urged. Long before that, a dispute of like nature, and of at least equal warmth, had been kindled at London upon the comparative merits of two composers at London; where riots between the approvers and disapprovers of a new play are, at this day, not unfrequent. The ground of quarrel between the Big-endians and the Little-endians in the fable, was not more frivolous than many an one which has laid empires desolate. In Russia, it is said, there was a time when some thousands of persons lost their lives in a quarrel, in which the government had taken part, about the number of fingers to be used in making the sign of the cross. This was in days of yore: the ministers of Catherine II. are better *instructed* [Instruct. art. 474, 475, 476.] than to take any other part in such disputes, than that of preventing the parties concerned from doing one another a mischief.

[9]See ch. xvi. [Division], par. 42, 44.

[10]*The principle of theology how reducible to one or another of the other three principles.*
The principle of theology refers every thing to God's pleasure. But what is God's
pleasure? God does not, he confessedly does not now, either speak or write to us.
How then are we to know what is his pleasure? By observing what is our own pleasure, and pronouncing it to be his. Accordingly, what is called the pleasure of God,
is and must necessarily be (revelation apart) neither more nor less than the good
pleasure of the person, whoever he be, who is pronouncing what he believes, or
pretends, to be God's pleasure. How know you it to be God's pleasure that such or
such an act should be abstained from? whence come you even to suppose as much?
'Because the engaging in it would, I imagine, be prejudicial upon the whole to the
happiness of mankind;' says the partizan of the principle of utility: 'Because the
commission of it is attended with a gross and sensual, or at least with a trifling and
transient satisfaction;' says the partizan of the principle of asceticism: 'Because I
detest the thoughts of it; and I cannot, neither ought I to be called upon to tell
why;' says he who proceeds upon the principle of antipathy. In the words of one or
other of these must that person necessarily answer (revelation apart) who professes to take for his standard the will of God.

CHAPTER IV

[15]These circumstances have since been denominated *elements* or *dimensions* of
value in a pleasure or a pain.

Not long after the publication of the first edition, the following memoriter
verses were framed, in the view of lodging more effectually, in the memory, these
points, on which the whole fabric of morals and legislation may be seen to rest.

> *Intense, long, certain, speedy, fruitful, pure*—
> Such marks in *pleasures* and in *pains* endure.
> Such pleasures seek if *private* be thy end:
> If it be *public,* wide let them *extend.*
> Such *pains* avoid, whichever be thy view:
> If pains *must* come, let them *extend* to few.

CHAPTER VIII

[71]*Ambiguity of the words* voluntary *and* involuntary. On this occasion the words
voluntary and *involuntary* are commonly employed. These, however, I purposely
abstain from, on account of the extreme ambiguity of their signification. By a voluntary act is meant sometimes, any act, in the performance of which the will has
had any concern at all; in this sense it is synonymous to *intentional:* sometimes
such acts only, in the production of which the will has been determined by motives not of a painful nature; in this sense it is synonymous to unconstrained, or
uncoerced: sometimes such acts only, in the production of which the will has been
determined by motives, which, whether of the pleasurable or painful kind, occurred to a man himself, without being suggested by any body else; in this sense it
is synonymous to *spontaneous.* The sense of the word involuntary does not correspond completely to that of the word voluntary. Involuntary is used in opposition
to intentional; and to unconstrained: but not to spontaneous. It might be of use to

confine the signification of the words voluntary and involuntary to one single and very narrow case, which will be mentioned in the next note.

[72]*An act unintentional in its first stage, may be so with respect to, 1. Quantity of matter moved; 2. Direction; 3. Velocity.* To render the analysis here given of the possible states of the mind in point of intentionality absolutely complete, it must be pushed to such a farther degree of minuteness, as to some eyes will be apt to appear trifling. On this account it seemed advisable to discard what follows, from the text to a place where any one who thinks proper may pass by it. An act of the body, when of the positive kind, is a motion: now in motion there are always three articles to be considered: 1. The quantity of matter that moves: 2. The direction in which it moves: and, 3. The velocity with which it moves. Correspondent to these three articles, are so many modes of intentionality, with regard to an act, considered as being only in its first stage. To be completely unintentional, it must be unintentional with respect to every one of these three particulars. This is the case with those acts which alone are properly termed *involuntary:* acts, in the performance of which the will has no sort of share: such as the contraction of the heart and arteries.

Upon this principle, acts that are unintentional in their first stage, may be distinguished into such as are completely unintentional, and such as are incompletely unintentional: and these again may be unintentional, either in point of quantity of matter alone, in point of direction alone, in point of velocity alone, or in any two of these points together.

The example given further on may easily be extended to this part of the analysis, by any one who thinks it worth the while.

There seem to be occasions in which even these disquisitions, minute as they may appear, may not be without their use in practice. In the case of homicide, for example, and other corporal injuries, all the distinctions here specified may occur, and in the course of trial may, for some purpose or other, require to be brought to mind, and made the subject of discourse. What may contribute to render the mention of them pardonable, is the use that might possibly be made of them in natural philosophy. In the hands of an expert metaphysician, these, together with the foregoing chapter on human actions, and the section on facts in general, in title Evidence of the Book of Procedure, might, perhaps, be made to contribute something towards an exhaustive analysis of the possible varieties of mechanical inventions.

[73]Or concurrently.

[74]*Difference between an incident's being unintentional, and disjunctively intentional when the election is in favour of the other.* There is a difference between the case where an incident is altogether unintentional, and that in which, it being disjunctively intentional with reference to another, the preference is in favour of that other. In the first case, it is not the intention of the party that the incident in question should happen at all: in the latter case, the intention is rather that the other should happen: but if that cannot be, then that this in question should happen rather than that neither should, and that both, at any rate, should not happen.

All these are distinctions to be attended to in the use of the particle *or:* a particle of very ambiguous import, and of great importance in legislation. See Append. tit. [Composition].

[75]Hume's Hist.

[76]See ch. vii. [Actions], par. 14.

CHAPTER XIII

[155]*What concerns the* end, *and several other topics relative to punishment, dismissed to another work.* What follows, relative to the subject of punishment, ought regularly to be preceded by a distinct chapter on the ends of punishment. But having little to say on that particular branch of the subject, which has not been said before, it seemed better, in a work, which will at any rate be but too voluminous, to omit this title, reserving it for another, hereafter to be published intituled *The Theory of Punishment.*† To the same work I must refer the analysis of the several possible modes of punishment, a particular and minute examination of the nature of each, and of its advantages and disadvantages, and various other disquisitions, which did not seem absolutely necessary to be inserted here. A very few words, however, concerning the *ends* of punishment, can scarcely be dispensed with.

Concise view of the ends of punishment. The immediate principal end of punishment is to control action. This action is either that of the offender, or of others: that of the offender it controls by its influence, either on his will, in which case it is said to operate in the way of *reformation;* or on his physical power, in which case it is said to operate by *disablement:* that of others it can influence no otherwise than by its influence over their wills; in which case it is said to operate in the way of *example.* A kind of collateral end, which it has a natural tendency to answer, is that of affording a pleasure or satisfaction to the party injured, where there is one, and, in general, to parties whose ill-will, whether on a self-regarding account, or on the account of sympathy or antipathy, has been excited by the offence. This purpose, as far as it can be answered *gratis,* is a beneficial one. But no punishment ought to be allotted merely to this purpose, because (setting aside its effects in the way of control) no such pleasure is ever produced by punishment as can be equivalent to the pain. The punishment, however, which is allotted to the other purpose, ought, as far as it can be done without expense, to be accommodated to this. Satisfaction thus administered to a party injured, in the shape of a dissocial pleasure [See ch. x. [Motives].], may be styled a vindictive satisfaction or compensation: as a compensation, administered in the shape of a self-regarding profit, or stock of pleasure, may be styled a lucrative one. See B. I. tit. vi. [Compensation]. Example is the most important end of all, in proportion as the *number* of the persons under temptation to offend is to *one.*

†This is the work which, from the Author's papers, has since been published by Mr. Dumont in French, in company with *The Theory of Reward* added to it, for the purpose of mutual illustration. It is in contemplation to publish them both in English, from the Author's manuscripts, with the benefit of any amendments that have been made by Mr. Dumont. *[Note to Edition of 1823.]*

[156]See B. I. tit. [Justifications].

[157]See supra, ch. iv. [Value].

[158]See Book I. tit. [Justifications].

[159]*Hence the favour shown to the offences of responsible offenders: such as simple mercantile frauds.* This, for example, seems to have been one ground, at least, of the favour shown by perhaps all systems of laws, to such offenders as stand upon a footing of responsibility: shown, not directly indeed to the persons themselves; but to such offences as none but responsible persons are likely to have the opportunity of engaging in. In particular, this seems to be the reason why embezzlement, in certain cases, has not commonly been punished upon the footing of theft: nor mercantile frauds upon that of common sharping. [See tit. [Simple merc. Defraudment].]

[160]See B. II. Appendix, tit. iii. [Promulgation].

[161]*In infancy and intoxication the case can hardly be proved to come under the rule.* Notwithstanding what is here said, the cases of infancy and intoxication (as we shall see hereafter) cannot be looked upon in practice as affording sufficient grounds for absolute impunity. But this exception in point of practice is no objection to the propriety of the rule in point of theory. The ground of the exception is neither more nor less than the difficulty there is of ascertaining the matter of fact: viz. whether at the requisite point of time the party was actually in the state in question; that is, whether a given case comes really under the rule. Suppose the matter of fact capable of being perfectly ascertained, without danger or mistake, the impropriety of punishment would be as indubitable in these cases as in any other. [See B. I. tit. iv. [Exemptions], and tit. vii. [Extenuations].]

    The reason for not punishing in these three cases is commonly put upon a wrong footing. The reason that is commonly assigned for the establishing an exemption from punishment in favour of infants, insane persons, and persons under intoxication, is either false in fact, or confusedly expressed. The phrase is, that the will of these persons concurs not with the act; that they have no vicious will; or, that they have not the free use of their will. But suppose all this to be true? What is it to the purpose? Nothing: except in as far as it implies the reason given in the text.

[162]See ch. viii. [Intentionality].

[163]See ch. ix. [Consciousness].

[164]*Why the influence of the moral and religious sanctions is not mentioned in the same view.* The influences of the *moral* and *religious* sanctions, or, in other words, of the motives of *love of reputation* and *religion,* are other causes, the force of which may, upon particular occasions, come to be greater than that of any punishment which the legislator is *able,* or at least which he will *think proper,* to apply. These, therefore, it will be proper for him to have his eye upon. But the force of these influences is variable and different in different times and places: the force of the foregoing influences is constant and the same, at all times and every where. These, therefore, it can never be proper to look upon as safe grounds for establishing absolute impunity: owing (as in the above-mentioned cases of infancy and intoxication) to the impracticability of ascertaining the matter of fact.

[165]See ch. v. [Pleasures and Pains].

[166]See ch. xii. [Consequences] iv.

CHAPTER XIV

[167]By *offences* I mean, at present, acts which appear to him to have a tendency to produce mischief.

[168]*The same rule applicable to motives in general.* The same rules (it is to be observed) may be applied, with little variation, to rewards as well as punishment: in short, to motives in general, which, according as they are of the pleasurable or painful kind, are of the nature of *reward* or *punishment:* and, according as the act they are applied to produce is of the positive or negative kind, are styled impelling or restraining. See ch. x. [Motives] xliii.

[169]*Profit may be of any other kind, as well as pecuniary.* By the profit of an offence, is to be understood, not merely the pecuniary profit, but the pleasure or advantage, of whatever kind it be, which a man reaps, or expects to reap, from the gratification of the desire which prompted him to engage in the offence. [See ch. x. [Motives] § 1.]

Impropriety of the notion that the punishment ought not to increase with the temptation. It is the profit (that is, the expectation of the profit) of the offence that constitutes the *impelling* motive, or, where there are several, the sum of the impelling motives, by which a man is prompted to engage in the offence. It is the punishment, that is, the expectation of the punishment, that constitutes the *restraining* motive, which, either by itself, or in conjunction with others, is to act upon him in a *contrary* direction, so as to induce him to abstain from engaging in the offence. Accidental circumstances apart, the strength of the temptation is as the force of the seducing, that is, of the impelling motive or motives. To say then, as authors of great merit and great name have said, that the punishment ought not to increase with the strength of the temptation, is as much as to say in mechanics, that the moving force or *momentum* of the *power* need not increase in proportion to the momentum of the *burthen.*

[170]Beccaria, dei diletti, § 6. id. trad. par. Morellet, § 23.

[171]See ch. xi. [Dispositions] xxix.

[172]It is a well-known adage, though it is to be hoped not a true one, that every man has his price. It is commonly meant of a man's virtue. This saying, though in a very different sense, was strictly verified by some of the Anglo–Saxon laws: by which a fixed price was set, not upon a man's virtue indeed, but upon his life: that of the sovereign himself among the rest. For 200 shillings you might have killed a peasant: for six times as much, a nobleman: for six-and-thirty times as much you might have killed the king. [Wilkins' Leg. Anglo-Sax. p. 71, 72. See Hume, Vol. I. App. 1. p. 219.] A king in those days was worth exactly 7,200 shillings. If then the heir to the throne, for example, grew weary of waiting for it, he had a secure and legal way of gratifying his impatience: he had but to kill the king with one hand, and pay himself with the. other, and all was right. An earl Godwin, or a duke Streon, could have bought the lives of a whole dynasty. It is plain, that if ever a king in those days died in his bed, he must have had something else, besides this law, to thank for it. This being the production of a remote and barbarous age, the absurdity of it is presently recognised: but, upon examination, it would be found, that the freshest laws of the most civilised nations are continually falling into the

same error. [See in particular the *English Statute laws* throughout, *Bonaparte's* Penal Code, and the recently enacted or not enacted *Spanish* Penal Code.—*Note by the Author, July 1822.*] This, in short, is the case wheresoever the punishment is fixed while the profit of delinquency is indefinite: or, to speak more precisely, where the punishment is limited to such a mark, that the profit of delinquency may reach beyond it.

[173]See ch. xiii. [Cases unmeet], § 1.

[174]See ch. xi. [Dispositions], xlii.

[175]*Example—Incendiarism and coining.* For example, if it can ever be worth while to be at the expense of so horrible a punishment as that of burning alive, it will be more so in the view of preventing such a crime as that of murder or incendiarism, than in the view of preventing the uttering of a piece of bad money. See B. L tit. [Defraudment touching the Coin] and [Incendiarism].

[176]Espr. des Loix, L. vi. c. 16.

[177]*Example.—In blows given and money stolen.* If any one have any doubt of this, let him conceive the offence to be divided into as many separate offences as there are distinguishable parcels of mischief that result from it. Let it consist, for example, in a man's giving you ten blows, or stealing from you ten shillings. If then, for giving you ten blows, he is punished no more than for giving you five, the giving you five of these ten blows is an offence for which there is no punishment at all: which being understood, as often as a man gives you five blows, he will be sure to give you five more, since he may have the pleasure of giving you these five for nothing. In like manner, if for stealing from you ten shillings, he is punished no more than for stealing five, the stealing of the remaining five of those ten shillings is an offence for which there is no punishment at all. This rule is violated in almost every page of every body of laws I have ever seen.

The profit, it is to be observed, though frequently, is not constantly, proportioned to the mischief: for example, where a thief, along with the things he covets, steals others which are of no use to him. This may happen through wantonness, indolence, precipitation, &c. &c.

[178]See ch. vi. [Sensibility].

[179]See ch. iv. [Value].

[180]It is for this reason, for example, that simple compensation is never looked upon as sufficient punishment for theft or robbery.

[181]*A punishment applied by way of moral lesson, what.* A punishment may be said to be calculated to answer the purpose of a moral lesson, when, by reason of the ignominy it stamps upon the offence, it is calculated to inspire the public with sentiments of aversion towards those pernicious habits and dispositions with which the offence appears to be connected; and thereby to inculcate the opposite beneficial habits and dispositions.

Example.—In simple corporal injuries. It is this, for example, if any thing, that must justify the application of so severe a punishment as the infamy of a public exhibition, hereinafter proposed, for him who lifts up his hand against a woman, or against his father. See B. I. tit. [Simp. corporal injuries].

Example.—In military laws. It is partly on this principle, I suppose, that military legislators have justified to themselves the inflicting death on the soldier who lifts up his hand against his superior officer.

[182]See ch. xiii. [Cases unmeet], § 4.

[183]See B. II. tit. [Purposes], Append. tit. [Composition].

[184]*Proportionality carried very far in the present work—why.* Notwithstanding this rule, my fear is, that in the ensuing model, I may be thought to have carried my endeavours at proportionality too far. Hitherto scarce any attention has been paid to it. Montesquieu seems to have been almost the first who has had the least idea of any such thing. In such a matter, therefore, excess seemed more eligible than defect. The difficulty is to invent: that done, if any thing seems superfluous, it is easy to retrench.

[185]See B. I. tit. [Punishments].

[186]See Append. tit. [Promulgation].

[187]There are few madmen but what are observed to be afraid of the strait waistcoat.

[188]See ch. xii. [Consequences], xxxiii.

CHAPTER XV

[189]By the English law, there are several offences which are punished by a total forfeiture of moveables, not extending to immoveables. This is the case with suicide, and with certain species of theft and homicide. In some cases, this is the principal punishment: in others, even the only one. The consequence is, that if a man's fortune happens to consist in moveables, he is ruined; if in immoveables, he suffers nothing.

[190]See *View of the Hard-Labour Bill,* Lond. 1778, p. 100.

For the idea of this property, I must acknowledge myself indebted to an anonymous letter in the St. James's Chronicle, of the 27th of September, 1777; the author of which is totally unknown to me. If any one should be disposed to think lightly of the instruction, on account of the channel by which it was first communicated, let him tell me where I can find an idea more ingenious or original.

[191]See Montesq. Esp. des Loix, L. xii. ch. iv. He seems to have the property of characteristicalness in view; but that the idea he had of it was very indistinct, appears from the extravagant advantages he attributes to it.

[192]See ch. vii. [Actions], iii.

[193]Besides this, there are a variety of other ways in which the punishment may bear an analogy to the offence. This will be seen by looking over the table of punishments.

[194]See ch. xiii. [Cases unmeet], § 1, 2. note.

[195]Ib. § 4. par. iii.

[196]See B. I. tit. [Punishments].

[197]See B. II. tit. [Execution].

[198]Ch. xiii. [Cases unmeet], par. iii.

[199]Ib. note.

[200]See ch. xiii. [Cases unmeet], par. ii. note.

[201]See ch. x. [Motives].

[202]See B. I. tit. [Offences against Justice].

[203]See B. I. tit. [Punishments].

[204]*Characteristicalness renders a punishment, 1. memorable: 2. exemplary: 3. popular.*
The property of characteristicalness, therefore, is useful in a mode of punishment
in three different ways: 1. It renders a mode of punishment, before infliction,
more easy to be borne in mind: 2. It enables it, especially after infliction, to make
the stronger impression, when it is there; that is, renders it the more *exemplary:* 3.
It tends to render it more acceptable to the people, that is, it renders it the more
popular.

[205]See ch. xiii. [Cases unmeet], § v.

[206]See ch. xiii. [Cases unmeet], § iv. par. iv.

[207]See View of the Hard Labour Bill, p. 109.

[208]See ch. xiii. (Cases unmeet], ii. note.

CHAPTER XVII

[329]And the *constitutional* branch, what is become of it? Such is the question which
many a reader will be apt to put. An answer that might be given is—that the matter of it might without much violence be distributed under the two other heads.
But, as far as recollection serves, that branch, notwithstanding its importance, and
its capacity of being lodged separately from the other matter, had at that time
scarcely presented itself to my view in the character of a distinct one: the thread of
my enquiries had not as yet reached it. But in the concluding note of this same
chapter, in paragraphs xxii to the end, the omission may be seen in some measure
supplied.

[330]*Interests of the inferior animals improperly neglected in legislation.* Under the Gen-
too and Mahometan religions, the interests of the rest of the animal creation seem
to have met with some attention. Why have they not, universally, with as much as
those of human creatures, allowance made for the difference in point of sensibility? Because the laws that are have been the work of mutual fear; a sentiment
which the less rational animals have not had the same means as man has of turning
to account. Why *ought* they not? No reason can be given. If the being eaten were
all, there is very good reason why we should be suffered to eat such of them as we
like to eat: we are the better for it, and they are never the worse. They have none of
those long-protracted anticipations of future misery which we have. The death
they suffer in our hands commonly is, and always may be, a speedier, and by that
means a less painful one, than that which would await them in the inevitable
course of nature. If the being killed were all, there is very good reason why we
should be suffered to kill such as molest us: we should be the worse for their living
and they are never the worse for being dead. But is there any reason why we
should be suffered to torment them? Not any that I can see. Are there any why we
should *not* be suffered to torment them? Yes, several. See B. I. tit. [Cruelty to ani-
mals]. The day has been, I grieve to say in many places it is not yet past, in which

the greater part of the species, under the denomination of slaves, have been treated by the law exactly upon the same footing as, in England for example, the inferior races of animals are still. The day *may* come, when the rest of the animal creation may acquire those rights which never could have been withholden from them but by the hand of tyranny. The French have already discovered that the blackness of the skin is no reason why a human being should be abandoned without redress to the caprice of a tormentor [See Lewis XIVth's Code Noir.]. It may come one day to be recognized, that the number of the legs, the villosity of the skin, or the termination of the *os sacrum*, are reasons equally insufficient for abandoning a sensitive being to the same fate. What else is it that should trace the insuperable line? Is it the faculty of reason, or, perhaps, the faculty of discourse? But a full-grown horse or dog is beyond comparison a more rational, as well as a more conversable animal, than an infant of a day, or a week, or even a month, old. But suppose the case were otherwise, what would it avail? the question is not, Can they *reason?* nor, Can they *talk?* but, Can they *suffer?*

[331]Ch. vi. [Sensibility] iii.

[332]I say nothing in this place of reward: because it is only in a few extraordinary cases that it can be applied, and because even where it is applied, it may be doubted perhaps whether the application of it can, properly speaking, be termed an act of legislation. See infra, § 3.

[333]Ch. xiii. [Cases unmeet].

[334]See ch. xiii. [Cases unmeet], § iv.

[335]Ch. xiv. [Proportion] xviii. Rule 7.

[336]Ch. xiii. [Cases unmeet] § iii. Append. tit. [Promulgation].

[337]Ch. xi. [Disposition] xxxv. &c.

[338]Ch. vi. [Sensibility].

[339]In certain countries, in which the voice of the people has a more especial control over the hand of the legislator, nothing can exceed the dread which they are under of seeing any effectual provision made against the offences which come under the head of *defamation*, particularly that branch of it which may be styled the *political*. This dread seems to depend partly upon the apprehension they may think it prudent to entertain of a defect in point of ability or integrity on the part of the legislator, partly upon a similar appehension of a defect in point of integrity on the part of the judge.

[340]See ch. ix. [Consciousness].

[341]Ch. xvi. [Division] lii.

On occasions like this the legislator should never lose sight of the well-known story of the oculist and the sot. A countryman who had hurt his eyes by drinking, went to a celebrated oculist for advice. He found him at table, with a glass of wine before him. 'You must leave off drinking,' said the oculist. 'How so?' says the countryman. '*You* don't, and yet methinks your own eyes are none of the best.'— 'That's very true, friend,' replied the oculist: 'but you are to know, I love my bottle better than my eyes.'

[342]Evil of apprehension: third branch of the evil of a punishment. Ch. xiii. § iv.

[343]Derivative evils: fourth branch of the evil of a punishment. Ib.

[344]I do not mean but that other motives of a less social nature might have introduced themselves, and probably, in point of fact, did introduce themselves, in the progress of the enterprise. But in point of possibility, the motive above mentioned, when accompanied with such a thread of reasoning, is sufficient without any other, to account for all the effects above alluded to. If any others interfere, their interference, how natural soever, may be looked upon as an accidental and inessential circumstance, not necessary to the production of the effect. Sympathy, a concern for the danger they appear to be exposed to, gives birth to the wish of freeing them from it: that wish shows itself in the shape of a command: this command produces disobedience: disobedience on the one part produces disappointment on the other: the pain of disappointment produces ill-will towards those who are the authors of it. The affections will often make this progress in less time than it would take to describe it. The sentiment of wounded pride, and other modifications of the love of reputation and the love of power, add fuel to the flame. A kind of revenge exasperates the severities of coercive policy.

[345]See B. I. tit. [Self-regarding offences.]

[346]But suppose the dictates of legislation *are* not what they *ought to be:* what are then, or (what in this case comes to the same thing) what ought to be, the dictates of private ethics? Do they coincide with the dictates of legislation, or do they oppose them, or do they remain neuter? a very interesting question this, but one that belongs not to the present subject. It belongs exclusively to that of private ethics. Principles which may lead to the solution of it may be seen in A Fragment on Government, p. 150, Lond. edit. 1776—and p. 114, edit. 1823.

[347]If we may believe M. Voltaire [Quest. sur l'Encyclop. tom. 7. art. Impuissance.], there was a time when the French ladies who thought themselves neglected by their husbands, used to petition *pourétre embesoignèes:* the technical word, which, he says, was appropriated to this purpose. This sort of law-proceedings seems not very well calculated to answer the design: accordingly we hear nothing of them now-a-days. The French ladies of the present age seem to be under no such difficulties.

[348]A woman's head-dress catches fire: water is at hand: a man, instead of assisting to quench the fire, looks on, and laughs at it. A drunken man, falling with his face downwards into a puddle, is in danger of suffocation: lifting his head a little on one side would save him: another man sees this and lets him lie. A quantity of gunpowder lies scattered about a room: a man is going into it with a lighted candle: another, knowing this, lets him go in without warning. Who is there that in any of these cases would think punishment misapplied?

[349]The word *law* itself, which stands so much in need of a definition, must wait for it awhile (see § 3): for there is no doing every thing at once. In the mean time every reader will understand it according to the notion he has been accustomed to annex to it.

[350]In most of the European languages there are two different words for distin-

guishing the abstract and the concrete senses of the word *law:* which words are so wide asunder as not even to have any etymological affinity. In Latin, for example, there is *lex* for the concrete sense, *jus* for the abstract: in Italian, *legge* and *diritto*. in French, *loi* and *droit:* in Spanish *ley* and *derecho:* in German, *gesetz* and *recht*. The English is at present destitute of this advantage.

In the Anglo-Saxon, besides *lage*, and several other words, for the concrete sense, there was the word *right*, answering to the German *recht*, for the abstract as may be seen in the compound *folc-right*, and in other instances. But the word *right* having long ago lost this sense, the modern English no longer possesses this advantage.

351The word *international*, it must be acknowledged, is a new one; though, it is hoped, sufficiently analogous and intelligible. It is calculated to express, in a more significant way, the branch of law which goes commonly under the name of the *law of nations:* an appellation so uncharacteristic, that, were it not for the force of custom, it would seem rather to refer to internal jurisprudence. The chancellor D'Aguesseau has already made, I find, a similar remark: he says that what is commonly called *droit* des *gens*, ought rather to be termed *droit* entre *les gens* [Œuvres, Tom. ii. p. 337, edit. 1773, 12 no.].

352In the times of James I. of England and Philip III. of Spain, certain merchants at London happened to have a claim upon Philip, which his ambassador Gondemar did not think fit to satisfy. They applied for counsel to Selden, who advised them to sue the Spanish monarch in the court of King's Bench, and prosecute him to an outlawry. They did so: and the sheriffs of London were accordingly commanded, in the usual form, to take the body of the defendant Philip, wherever it was to be found within their bailiwick. As to the sheriffs, Philip, we may believe, was in no great fear of them: but, what answered the same purpose, he happened on his part to have demands upon some other merchants, whom, so long as the outlawry remained in force, there was no proceeding against. Gondemar paid the money [Selden's Table-Talk, tit. Law.]. This was internal jurisprudence: if the dispute had been betwixt Philip and James himself, it would have been international.

As to the word *international*, from this work, or the first of the works edited in French by Mr. Dumont, it has taken root in the language. Witness reviews and newspapers.

353The term *municipal* seemed to answer the purpose very well, till it was taken by an English author of the first eminence to signify internal law in general, in contradistinction to international law, and the imaginary law of nature. It might still be used in this sense, without scruple, in any other language.

354Of what stamp are the works of Grotius, Puffendorf, and Burlamaqui? Are they political or ethical, historical or juridical, expository or censorial?—Sometimes one thing, sometimes another: they seem hardly to have settled the matter with themselves. A defect this to which all books must almost unavoidably be liable, which take for their subject the pretended *law of nature;* an obscure phantom, which, in the imaginations of those who go in chase of it, points sometimes to *manners*, sometimes to *laws*; sometimes to what law *is*, sometimes to what it *ought* to be [See Chap. II. [Principles Adverse] xiv.]. Montesquieu sets out upon the censorial plan: but long before the conclusion, as if he had forgot his first design, he throws off the censor, and puts on the antiquarian. The Marquis Beccaria's book, the first of any account that is uniformly censorial, concludes as it sets out, with penal jurisprudence.

[355]*Occasion and purpose of this concluding note.* Here ends the original work, in the state into which it was brought in November, 1780. What follows is now added in January, 1789

The third, fourth, and fifth sections intended, as expressed in the text, to have been added to this chapter, will not here, nor now be given; because to give them in a manner tolerably complete and satisfactory, might require a considerable volume. This volume will form a work of itself, closing the series of works mentioned in the preface.

What follows here may serve to give a slight intimation of the nature of the task, which such a work will have to achieve: it will at the same time furnish, not any thing like a satisfactory answer to the questions mentioned in the text, but a slight and general indication of the course to be taken for giving them such an answer.

By a law *here is not meant a* statute. What is a law? What the parts of a law? The subject of these questions, it is to be observed, is the *logical,* the *ideal,* the *intellectual* whole, not the *physical* one: the *law,* and not the *statute.* An enquiry, directed to the latter sort of object, could neither admit of difficulty nor afford instruction. In this sense whatever is given for law by the person or persons recognised as possessing the power of making laws, is *law.* The Metamorphoses of Ovid, if thus given, would be law. So much as was embraced by one and the same act of authentication, so much as received the touch of the sceptre at one stroke, is *one* law: a whole law, and nothing more. A statute of George II. made to substitute an *or* instead of an *and* in a former statute is a complete law; a statute containing an entire body of laws, perfect in all its parts, would not be more so. By the word *law* then, as often as it occurs in the succeeding pages is meant that ideal object, of which the part, the whole, or the multiple, or an assemblage of parts, wholes, and multiples mixed together, is exhibited by a statute; not the statute which exhibits them.

Every law is either a command, or a revocation of one. Every law, when complete, is either of a *coercive* or an *uncoercive* nature.

A coercive law is a *command.*

An uncoercive, or rather a *discoercive,* law is the *revocation,* in whole or in part, of a coercive law.

A declaratory law is not, properly speaking, a law. What has been termed a *declaratory* law, so far as it stands distinguished from either a coercive or a discoercive law, is not properly speaking a law. It is not the expression of an act of the will exercised at the time: it is a mere notification of the existence of a law, either of the coercive or the discoercive kind, as already subsisting: of the existence of some document expressive of some act of the will, exercised, not at the time, but at some former period. If it does any thing more than give information of this fact, viz. of the prior existence of a law of either the coercive or the discoercive kind, it ceases *pro tanto* to be what is meant by a declaratory law, and assuming either the coercive or the discoercive quality.

Every coercive law creates an offence. Every coercive law creates an *offence,* that is converts an act of some sort, or other into an offence. It is only by so doing that it can *impose obligation*, that it can *produce coercion*.

VI. *A law creating an offence, and one appointing punishment, are distinct laws.* A law confining itself to the creation of an offence, and a law commanding a punishment to be administered in case of the commission of such an offence, are two distinct laws; not parts (as they seem to have been generally accounted hitherto) of one and the same law. The acts they command are altogether different; the persons they are addressed to are altogether different Instance, *Let no man steal;* and, *Let the judge cause whoever is convicted of stealing to be hanged.*

They might be styled; the former, a *simply imperative* law; the other a *punitory:* but the punitory, if it commands the punishment to be inflicted, and does not merely permit it, is as truly *imperative* as the other: only it is punitory besides, which the other is not.

VII. *A discoercive law can have no punitory one appertaining to it but through the intervention of coercive one.* A law of the discoercive kind, considered in itself, can have no punitory law belonging to it: to receive the assistance and support of a punitory law, it must first receive that of a simply imperative or coercive law, and it is to this latter that the punitory law will attach itself, and not to the discoercive one. Example; discoercive law. *The sheriff has power to hang all such as the judge, proceeding in due course of law, shall order him to hang.* Example of a coercive law, made in support of the above discoercive one. *Let no man hinder the sheriff from hanging such as the judge, proceeding in due course of law, shall order him to hang.* Example of a punitory law, made in support of the above coercive one. *Let the judge cause to be imprisoned whosoever attempts to hinder the sheriff from hanging one, whom the judge, proceeding in due course of law, has ordered him to hang.*

VIII. *But a punitory law involves the simply imperative one it belongs to.* But though a simply imperative law, and the punitory law attached to it, are so far distinct laws, that the former contains nothing of the latter, and the latter, in its direct tenor, contains nothing of the former, yet by *implication,* and that a necessary one, the punitory does involve and include the import of the simply imperative law to which it is appended. To say to the judge, *Cause to be hanged whoever in due form of law is convicted of stealing,* is, though not a direct, yet as intelligible a way of intimating to men in general that they must not steal, as to say to them directly, *Do not steal:* and one sees, how much more likely to be efficacious.

IX. *The simply imperative one might therefore be spared, but for its expository matter.* It should seem then, that, wherever a simply imperative law is to have a punitory one appended to it, the former might be spared altogether: in which case, saving the exception (which naturally should seem not likely to be a frequent one) of a law capable of answering its purpose without such an appendage, there should be no occasion in the whole body of the law for any other than punitory, or in other words than *penal,* laws. And this, perhaps, would be the case, were it not for the necessity of a large quantity of matter of the *expository* kind, of which we come now to speak.

X. *Nature of such expository matter.* It will happen in the instance of many, probably of most, possibly of all commands endued with the force of a public law, that, in the expression given to such a command, it shall be necessary to have recourse to terms too complex in their signification to exhibit the requisite ideas, without the assistance of a greater or less quantity of matter of an expository nature. Such terms, like the symbols used in algebraical notation, are rather substitutes and indexes to the terms capable of themselves of exhibiting the ideas in question, than the real and immediate representatives of those ideas.

Take for instance the law, *Thou shalt not steal.* Such a command, were it to rest there, could never sufficiently answer the purpose of a law. A word of so vague and unexplicit a meaning can no otherwise perform this office, than by giving a general intimation of a variety of propositions, each requiring, to convey it to the apprehension, a more particular and ample assemblage of terms. Stealing, for example (according to a definition not accurate enough for use, but sufficiently so for the present purpose), is *the taking of a thing which is another's, by one who has no* TITLE *so to do,* and is *conscious of his having none.* Even after this exposition, supposing it a correct one, can the law be regarded as completely expressed? Certainly not. For what is meant by *a man's having a* TITLE *to take a thing?* To be complete, the law must have exhibited, amongst a multitude of other things, two catalogues: the one of events to which it has given the quality of *conferring title* in such a case; the other of the events to which it has given the quality of *taking it away.* What follows? That for a man to have *stolen,* for a man to *have had no title to what he took,* either no one of the articles contained in the first of those lists must have happened in his favour, or if there has, some one of the number of those contained in the second must have happened to his prejudice.

XI. *The vastness of its comparative bulk is not peculiar to legislative commands.* Such then is the nature of a general law, that while the imperative part of it, the *punctum saliens* as it may be termed, of this artificial body, shall not take up above two or three words, its expository appendage, without which that imperative part could not rightly perform its office, may occupy a considerable volume.

But this may equally be the case with a private order given in a family. Take for instance one from a bookseller to his foreman. *Remove, from this shop to my new one, my whole stock, according to this printed catalogue.—Remove, from this shop to my new one, my whole stock,* is the imperative matter of this order, the catalogue referred to contains the expository appendage.

XII. *The same mass of expository matter may serve in common for many laws.* The same mass of expository matter may serve in common for, may appertain in common to, many commands, many masses of imperative matter. Thus, amongst other things, the catalogue of *collative* and *ablative* events, with respect to *titles* above spoken of (see No. IX. of this note), will belong in common to all or most of the laws constitutive of the various offences against property. Thus, in mathematical diagrams, one and the same base shall serve for a whole cluster of triangles.

XIII. *The imperative character essential to law, is apt to be concealed in and by expository matter.* Such expository matter, being of a complexion so different from the imperative it would be no wonder if the connection of the former with the latter should escape the observation: which, indeed, is perhaps pretty generally the case. And so long as any mass of legislative matter presents itself, which is not itself imperative or the contrary, or of which the connection with matter of one of those two descriptions is not apprehended, so long and so far the truth of the proposition, *That every law is a command or its opposite,* may remain unsuspected, or appear questionable; so long also may the incompleteness of the greater part of those masses of legislative matter, which wear the complexion of complete laws upon the face of them, also the method to be taken for rendering them really complete, remain undiscovered.

XIV. *The concealment is favoured by the multitude of indirect forms in which imperative matter is capable of being couched.* A circumstance, that will naturally contribute to increase the difficulty of the discovery, is the great variety of ways in which the imperation of a law may be conveyed—the great variety of forms which the imperative part of a law may indiscriminately assume: some more directly, some less directly expressive of the imperative quality. *Thou shalt not steal. Let no man steal. Whoso stealeth shall be punished so and so. If any man steal, he shall be punished so and so. Stealing is where a man does so and so; the punishment for stealing is so and so. To judges* so and so named, and so and so constituted, *belong the cognizance of such and such offences;* viz. *stealing*—and so on. These are but part of a multitude of forms of words, in any of which the command by which stealing is prohibited might equally be couched: and it is manifest to what a degree, in some of them, the imperative quality is clouded and concealed from ordinary apprehension.

XV. *Number and nature of the laws in a code how determined.* After this explanation, a general proposition or two, that may be laid down, may help to afford some little insight into the structure and contents of a complete body of laws.—So many different sorts of *offences* created, so many different laws of the *coercive* kind: so many *exceptions* taken out of the descriptions of those offences, so many laws of the *discoercive* kind.

To class *offences,* as hath been attempted to be done in the preceding chapter, is therefore to class *laws:* to exhibit a complete catalogue of all the offences created by law, including the whole mass of expository matter necessary for fixing and exhibiting the import of the terms contained in the several laws, by which those offences are respectively created, would be to exhibit a complete collection of the laws in force: in a word a complete body of law; a *pannomion,* if so it might be termed.

XVI. *General idea of the limits between a civil and a penal code.* From the obscurity in which the limits of a *law,* and the distinction betwixt a law of the civil or simply imperative kind and a punitory law, are naturally involved, results the obscurity of the limits betwixt a civil and a penal *code,* betwixt a civil branch of the law and the penal.

The question, *What parts of the total mass of legislative matter belong to the civil branch, and what to the penal?* supposes that divers political states, or at least that some one such state, are to be found, having as well a civil code as a penal code, each of them complete in its kind, and marked out by certain limits. But no *one* such state has ever yet existed.

To put a question to which a true answer can be given, we must substitute to the foregoing question some such a one as that which follows:

Suppose two masses of legislative matter to be drawn up at this time of day, the one under the name of a civil code, the other of a penal code, each meant to be complete in its kind—in what general way, is it natural to suppose, that the different sorts of matter, as above distinguished, would be distributed between them?

To this question the following answer seems likely to come as near as any other to the truth.

The *civil* code would not consist of a collection of civil laws, each complete in itself, as well as clear of all penal ones:

Neither would the *penal* code (since we have seen that it *could* not) consist of a collection of punitive laws, each not only complete in itself, but clear of all civil ones. But

XVII. *Contents of a civil code.* The civil code would consist chiefly of mere masses of expository matter. The imperative matter, to which those masses of expository matter respectively appertained, would be found—not in that same code—not in the civil code—nor in a pure state, free from all admixture of punitory laws; but in the penal code—in a state of combination—involved, in manner as above explained, in so many correspondent punitory laws.

XVIII. *Contents of a penal code.* The penal code then would consist principally of punitive laws, involving the imperative matter of the whole number of civil laws: along with which would probably also be found various masses of expository matter, appertaining not to the civil, but to the punitory laws. The body of penal law, enacted by the Empress-Queen Maria Theresa, agrees pretty well with this account.

XIX. *In the Code Frederic the imperative character is almost lost in the expository matter.* The mass of legislative matter published in French as well as German, under the auspices of Frederic II. of Prussia, by the name of Code Frederic, but never established with force of law [Mirabeau sur la Monarchie Prussienne, Tom. v. Liv. 8. p. 215.], appears, for example, to be almost wholly composed of masses of expository matter, the relation of which to any imperative matter appears to have been but very imperfectly apprehended.

XX. *So in the Roman law.* In that enormous mass of confusion and inconsistency, the ancient Roman, or, as it is termed by way of eminence, the *civil* law, the imperative matter, and even all traces of the imperative character, seem at last to have been smothered in the expository. *Esto* had been the language of primæval simplicity: *esto* had been the language of the twelve tables. By the time of Justinian (so thick was the darkness raised by clouds of commentators) the penal law had been crammed into an odd corner of the civil—the whole catalogue of offences, and even of crimes, lay buried under a heap of *obligations*—*will* was hid in *opinion*—and the original *esto* had transformed itself into *videtur,* in the mouths even of the most despotic sovereigns.

XXI. *In the barbarian codes it stands conspicuous.* Among the barbarous nations that grew up out of the ruins of the Roman Empire, Law, emerging from under the mountain of expository rubbish, reassumed for a while the language of command: and then she had simplicity at least, if nothing else, to recommend her.

XXII. *Constitutional code, its connexion with the two others.* Besides the civil and the penal, every complete body of law must contain a third branch, the *constitutional.*

The constitutional branch is chiefly employed in conferring, on particular classes of persons, *powers,* to be exercised for the good of the whole society, or of considerable parts of it, and prescribing *duties* to the persons invested with those powers.

The powers are principally constituted, in the first instance, by discoercive or permissive laws, operating as exceptions to certain laws of the coercive or imperative kind. Instance: *A tax-gatherer, as such, may, on such and such an occasion, take such and such things, without any other* TITLE.

The duties are created by imperative laws, addressed to the persons on whom the powers are conferred. Instance: *On such and such an occasion, such and such a tax-gatherer shall take such and such things. Such and such a judge shall, in such and such a case, cause persons so and so offending to be hanged.*

The parts which perform the function of indicating who the individuals are, who, in every case, shall be considered as belonging to those classes, have neither a permissive complexion, nor an imperative.

They are so many masses of expository matter, appertaining in common to all laws, into the texture of which, the names of those classes of persons have occasion to be inserted. Instance; imperative matter:—*Let the judge cause whoever, in due course of law, is convicted of stealing, to be hanged.* Nature of the expository matter:—Who is the person meant by the word *judge?* He who has been *invested* with that office in such a manner: and in respect of whom no *event* has happened, of the number of those, to which the effect is given, of reducing him to the condition of one *divested* of that office.

XXIII. *Thus the matter of one law may be divided among all three codes.* Thus it is, that one and the same law, one and the same command, will have its matter divided, not only between two great codes, or main branches of the whole body of the laws, the civil and the penal; but amongst three such branches, the civil, the penal, and the constitutional.

XXIV. *Expository matter, a great quantity of it exists everywhere, in no other form than that of common or judiciary law.* In countries, where a great part of the law exists in no other shape, than that of which in England is called *common* law but might be more expressively termed *judiciary,* there must be a great multitude of laws, the import of which cannot be sufficiently made out for practice, without referring to this common law, for more or less of the expository matter belonging to them. Thus in England the exposition of the word *title,* that basis of the whole fabric of the laws of property, is nowhere else to be found. And, as uncertainty is of the very essence of every particle of law so denominated (for the instant it is clothed in a certain authoritative form of words it changes its nature, and passes over to the other denomination) hence it is that a great part of the laws in being in such countries remain uncertain and incomplete. What are those countries? To this hour, every one on the surface of the globe.

XXV. *Hence the deplorable date of the science of legislation, considered in respect of its* form. Had the science of architecture no fixed nomenclature belonging to it— were there no settled names for distinguishing the different sorts of buildings, nor the different parts of the same building from each other—what would it be? It would be what the science of legislation, considered with respect to its *form,* remains at present.

Were there no architects who could distinguish a dwelling-house from a barn, or a side-wall from a ceiling, what would architects be? They would be what all legislators are at present.

XXVI. *Occasions affording an exemplification of the difficulty as well as importance of this branch of science;—attempts to limit the powers of supreme representative legislatures.* From this very slight and imperfect sketch, may be collected not an answer to the questions in the text but an intimation, and that but an imperfect one, of the course to be taken for giving such an answer; and, at any rate, some idea of the difficulty, as well as of the necessity, of the task.

If it were thought necessary to recur to experience for proofs of this difficulty, and this necessity, they need not be long wanting.

Take, for instance, so many well-meant endeavours on the part of popular bodies, and so many well-meant recommendations in ingenious books, to restrain supreme representative assemblies from making laws in such and such cases, or to such and such an effect. Such laws, to answer the intended purpose, require a perfect mastery in the science of law considered in respect of its form—in the sort of anatomy spoken of in the preface to this work: but a perfect, or even a moderate insight into that science, would prevent their being couched in those loose and inadequate terms, in which they may be observed so frequently to be conceived; as a perfect acquaintance with the dictates of utility on that head would, in many, if not in most, of those instances, discounsel the attempt. Keep to the letter, and in attempting to prevent the making of bad laws, you will find them prohibiting the making of the most necessary laws, perhaps even of all laws: quit the letter, and they express no more than if each man were to say, *Your laws shall become ipso facto void, as often as they contain any thing which is not to my mind.*

Of such unhappy attempts, examples may be met with in the legislation of many nations: but in none more frequently than in that newly-created nation, one of the most enlightened, if not the most enlightened, at this day on the globe.

XXVII. *Example: American declarations of rights.* Take for instance the *Declaration of Rights,* enacted by the State of North Carolina, in convention, in or about the month of September, 1788, and said to be copied, with a small exception, from one in like manner enacted by the State of Virginia [Recherches sur les Etats Unis, 8vo. 1788, vol. i. p. 158.].

The following, to go no farther, is the first and fundamental article:

'That there are certain natural rights, of which men, when they form a social compact, cannot deprive or divest their posterity, among which are the enjoyment of life and liberty, with the means of acquiring, possessing, and protecting property, and pursuing and obtaining happiness and safety.'

Not to dwell on the oversight of confining to posterity the benefit of the rights thus declared, what follows? That—as against those whom the protection, thus meant to be afforded, includes—every law, or other order, *divesting* a man of *the enjoyment of life or liberty,* is void.

Therefore this is the case, amongst others, with every coercive law.

Therefore, as against the persons thus protected, every order, for example, to pay money on the score of taxation, or of debt from individual to individual, or otherwise, is void: for the effect of it, if complied with, is 'to *deprive* and *divest him,'* *pro tanto,* of the enjoyment of liberty, viz. the liberty of paying or not paying as he thinks proper: not to mention the species opposed to imprisonment, in the event of such a mode of coercion's being resorted to: likewise of property, which is itself a *'means of acquiring, possessing, and protecting property, and of pursuing and obtaining happiness and safety.'*

Therefore also, as against such persons, every order to attack an armed enemy, in time of war, is also void: for, the necessary effect of such an order is *'to deprive* some of them of *the enjoyment of life.'*

The above-mentioned consequences may suffice for examples, amongst an endless train of similar ones.†

Leaning on his elbow, in an attitude of profound and solemn meditation, *'What a multitude of things there are'* (exclaimed the dancing-master Marcel) *'in a minuet!'—May* we now add?—*and in a law.*

---

† The Virginian Declaration of Rights, said, in the French work above quoted, to have been enacted the 1st of June, 1776, is not inserted in the publication entitled *'The Constitutions of the several independent states of America, &c.' Published by order of Congress. Philadelphia printed. Reprinted for Stockdale and Walker, London,* 1782: though that publication contains the form of government enacted in the same convention, between the 6th of May and the 5th of July in the same year.

But in that same publication is contained a *Declaration of Rights,* of the province of *Massachusetts,* dated in the year 1779 and 1780, which in its first article is a little similar: also one of the province of *Pennsylvania,* dated between July 15th and September 28th, in which the similarity is rather more considerable.

Moreover, the famous *Declaration of Independence,* published by Congress July 5th, 1776, after a preambular opening, goes on in these words: *'We hold these truths to be self-evident: that all men are created equal: that they are endued* by the creator *with certain unalienable rights: that amongst those are life, liberty, and the pursuit of happiness.'*

The Virginian Declaration of Rights is that, it seems, which claims the honour of having served as a model to those of the other Provinces; and in respect of the above leading article, at least, to the above-mentioned general Declaration of Independence. See Recherches, &c., i. 197

Who can help lamenting, that so rational a cause should be rested upon reasons, so much fitter to beget objections, than to remove them?

But with men, who are unanimous and hearty about *measures,* nothing so weak but may pass in the character of a *reason:* nor is this the first instance in the world, where the conclusion has supported the premises, instead of the premises the conclusion.

Index

Bentham on
"The Greatest Good for
the Greatest Number"

EXCERPT ON THE PHRASE
"Greatest Happiness of the Greatest Number"

[This passage is excerpted from Bentham's unpublished article on Utilitarianism, written to help James Mill in his famous controversy with Macaulay.]

Greatest happiness *of the greatest number.* Some years have now elapsed since, upon a closer scrutiny, reason, altogether incontestable, was found for discarding this appendage. On the surface, additional clearness and correctness given to the idea: at bottom, the opposite qualities. Be the community in question what it may, divide it into two unequal parts, call one of them the majority, the other minority, layout of the account the feelings of the minority, include in the account no feelings but those of the majority, the result you will find is that of this operation, that to the aggregate stock of the happiness of the community, loss not profit is the result of the operation. Of this proposition the truth will be the more palpable, the greater the ratio of the number of the minority to that of the majority: in other words, the less difference between the two unequal parts: and suppose the condivident part equal, the quantity of the error [evil?] will then be at its maximum.

Number of the majority, suppose 2001; number of the minority, 2000. Suppose in the first place the stock of happiness in such sort divided that by every one of the 4001, an equal portion of happiness shall be possessed. Take now from every one of the 2000 his share of happiness, and divide it anyhow among the 2001: instead of augmentation, vast is the diminution you will find to be the result. The feelings of the minority being by the supposition laid entirely out of the account (for such in the enlarged form is the import of the propositions), the vacuum thus left may, instead of remaining a *vacuum*, be filled with unhappiness, positive suffering, magnitude, intensity and duration taken together, the greatest which it is in the power of human nature to endure.

Take from your 2000 and give to your 2001 all the happiness you find your 2000 in possession of: insert in the room of the happiness you have taken out, unhappiness in as large a quantity as the receptacle will contain:

to the aggregate amount of the happiness possessed by the 4001 taken together will the result be net profit? on the contrary, the whole profit will
have given place to loss. How so? because so it is that such is the nature of
the receptacle, the quantity of unhappiness it is capable of containing during any given portion of time is greater than the quantity of happiness.

At the outset place your 4001 in a state of equal perfect equality in respect of the means or say instruments of happiness—and in particular
power and opulence: every one of them in a state of equal liberty—every
one independent of every other: every one of them possessing an equal
portion of money and money's worth: in this state it is that you find them.
Taking in hand now your 2000 reduce them to a state of slavery, and no
matter in what proportions of the slaves thus constituted divide the whole
number with such their property among your 2001: the operation performed, of the happiness of the whole number 4001, will an augmentation
be the result? The question answers itself.

Were it otherwise, note now the practical application that would be to
be made of it in the British Isles. In Great Britain take the whole body of
the Roman Catholics, make slaves of them and divide them in any proportion, them and their progeny, among the whole body of the Protestants. In
Ireland take the whole body of the Protestants and divide them in like
manner among the whole body of the Roman Catholics.

Bentham on
"Push–Pin versus Poetry"

(from *The Rationale of Reward*)

The utility of all these arts and sciences,—I speak both of those of amusement and curiosity,—the value which they possess, is exactly in proportion to the pleasure they yield. Every other species of preeminence which may be attempted to be established among them is altogether fanciful. Prejudice apart, the game of push-pin is of equal value with the arts and sciences of music and poetry. If the game of push-pin furnish more pleasure, it is more valuable than either. Everybody can play at push-pin: poetry and music are relished only by a few. The game of push-pin is always innocent: it were well could the same be always asserted of poetry. Indeed, between poetry and truth there is natural opposition: false morals and fictitious nature. The poet always stands in need of something false. When he pretends to lay his foundations in truth, the ornaments of his superstructure are fictions; his business consist in stimulating our passions, and exciting our prejudices. Truth, exactitude of every kind is fatal to poetry. The poet must see everything through coloured media, and strive to make every one else do the same. It is true, there have been noble spirits, to whom poetry and philosophy have been equally indebted; but these exceptions do not counteract the mischiefs which have resulted from this magic art. If poetry and music deserve to he preferred before a game of push-pin, it must be because they are calculated to gratify those individuals who are most difficult to be pleased.

Mill's
Utilitarianism

CHAPTER 1
General Remarks

There are few circumstances among those which make up the present condition of human knowledge more unlike what might have been expected, or more significant of the backward state in which speculation on the most important subjects still lingers, than the little progress which has been made in the decision of the controversy respecting the criterion of right and wrong. From the dawn of philosophy, the question concerning the *summum bonum*, or, what is the same thing, concerning the foundation of morality, has been accounted the main problem in speculative thought, has occupied the most gifted intellects and divided them into sects and schools carrying on a vigorous warfare against one another. And after more than two thousand years the same discussions continue, philosophers are still ranged under the same contending banners, and neither thinkers nor mankind at large seem nearer to being unanimous on the subject than when the youth Socrates listened to the old Protagoras and asserted (if Plato's dialogue be grounded on a real conversation) the theory of utilitarianism against the popular morality of the so-called sophist.

It is true that similar confusion and uncertainty and, in some cases, similar discordance exist respecting the first principles of all the sciences, not excepting that which is deemed the most certain of them—mathematics, without much impairing, generally indeed without impairing at all, the trustworthiness of the conclusions of those sciences. An apparent anomaly, the explanation of which is that the detailed doctrines of a science are not usually deduced from, nor depend for their evidence upon, what are called its first principles. Were it not so, there would be no science more precarious, or whose conclusions were more insufficiently made out, than algebra, which derives none of its certainty from what are commonly taught to learners as its elements, since these, as laid down by some of its most eminent teachers, are as full of fictions as English law, and of mysteries as theology. The truths which are ultimately accepted as the first principles of a science are really the last results of metaphysical analysis practiced on the elementary notions with which the science is conversant; and their relation to the science is not that of foundations to an edifice, but of roots to a tree, which may perform their office equally well though they be never dug down to and exposed to light. But though in science the particular truths precede the general theory, the contrary might be expected to be the case with a practical art, such as morals or legislation. All action is for the sake of some end, and rules of action, it seems natural to suppose, must take their whole character and color from the end to which they are subservient. When we engage in pursuit, a clear and precise conception of what we are pursuing would seem to be the first thing we need, instead of the last we are to look forward to. A test of right and wrong must be the means, one would think, of ascertaining what is right or wrong, and not a consequence of having already ascertained it.

The difficulty is not avoided by having recourse to the popular theory of a natural faculty, a sense of instinct, informing us of right and wrong. For—besides that the existence of such a moral instinct is itself one of the matters in dispute—those believers in it who have any pretensions to philosophy have been obliged to abandon the idea that it discerns what is right or wrong in the particular case in hand, as our other senses discern the sight or sound actually present. Our moral faculty, according to all those of its interpreters who are entitled to the name of thinkers, supplies us only with the general principles of moral judgments; it is a branch of our reason, not of our sensitive faculty, and must be looked to for the abstract doctrines of morality, not for perception of it in the concrete. The intuitive, no less than what may be termed the inductive, school of ethics insists on the necessity of general laws. They both agree that the morality of an individual action is not a question of direct perception, but of the application of a law to an individual case. They recognize also, to a great extent, the same moral laws, but differ as to their evidence and the source from which they derive their authority. According to the one opinion, the principles of morals are evident *a priori*, requiring nothing to command assent except that the meaning of the terms be understood. According to the other doctrine, right and wrong, as well as truth and falsehood, are questions of observation and experience. But both hold equally that morality must be deduced from principles; and the intuitive school affirm as strongly as the inductive that there is a science of morals. Yet they seldom attempt to make out a list of the *a priori* principles which are to serve as the premises of the science; still more rarely do they make any effort to reduce those various principles to one first principle or common ground of obligation. They either assume the ordinary precepts of morals as of *a priori* authority, or they lay down as the common groundwork of those maxims some generality much less obviously authoritative than the maxims themselves, and which has never succeeded in gaining popular acceptance. Yet to support their pretensions there ought either to be some one fundamental principle or law at the root of all morality, or, if there be several, there should be a determinate order of precedence among them; and the one principle, or the rule for deciding between the various principles when they conflict, ought to be self-evident.

To inquire how far the bad effects of this deficiency have been mitigated in practice, or to what extent the moral beliefs of mankind have been vitiated or made uncertain by the absence of any distinct recognition of an ultimate standard, would imply a complete survey and criticism of past and present ethical doctrine. It would, however, be easy to show that whatever steadiness or consistency these moral beliefs have attained has been mainly due to the tacit influence of a standard not recognized. Although the nonexistence of an acknowledged first principle has made ethics not so much a guide as a consecration of men's actual sentiments, still, as men's sentiments, both of favor and of aversion, are greatly influenced by what they suppose to be the effects of things upon their happiness, the principle of utility, or, as Bentham latterly called it, the greatest happiness principle, has had a large share in forming the moral doctrines even of those who most scornfully reject its authority. Nor is there any school of thought which refuses to admit that the influence of actions on happiness is a most material and even predominant consideration in many of the details of morals, however unwilling to acknowledge it as the fundamental principle of morality and the source of moral obligation. I might go much further and say that to all those *a priori* moralists who deem it necessary to argue at all, utilitarian arguments are indispensable. It is not my present purpose to criticize these thinkers; but I cannot help referring, for illustration, to a systematic treatise by one of the most illustrious of them, the *Metaphysics of Ethics* by Kant. This remarkable man, whose system of thought will long remain one of the landmarks in the history of philosophical speculation, does, in the treatise in question, lay down a universal first principle as the origin and ground of moral obligation; it is this: "So act that the rule on which thou actest would admit of being adopted as a law by all rational beings." But when he begins to deduce from this precept any of the actual duties of morality, he fails, almost grotesquely, to show that there would be any contradiction, any logical (not to say physical) impossibility, in the adoption by all rational beings of the most outrageously immoral rules of conduct. All he shows is that the *consequences* of their universal adoption would be such as no one would choose to incur.

On the present occasion, I shall, without further discussion of the other theories, attempt to contribute something toward the understanding and appreciation of the "utilitarian" or "happiness" theory, and toward such proof as it is susceptible of. It is evident that this cannot be proof in the ordinary and popular meaning of the term. Questions of ultimate ends are not amenable to direct proof. Whatever can be proved to be good must be

so by being shown to be a means to something admitted to be good without proof. The medical art is proved to be good by its conducing to health;
but how is it possible to prove that health is good? The art of music is
good, for the reason, among others, that it produces pleasure; but what
proof is it possible to give that pleasure is good? If, then, it is asserted that
there is a comprehensive formula, including all things which are in themselves good, and that whatever else is good is not so as an end but as a
means, the formula may be accepted or rejected, but is not a subject of
what is commonly understood by proof. We are not, however, to infer that
its acceptance or rejection must depend on blind impulse or arbitrary
choice. There is a larger meaning of the word "proof," in which this question is as amenable to it as any other of the disputed questions of philosophy. The subject is within the cognizance of the rational faculty; and
neither does that faculty deal with it solely in the way of intuition. Considerations may be presented capable of determining the intellect either to
give or withhold its assent to the doctrine; and this is equivalent to proof.

We shall examine presently of what nature are these considerations; in
what manner they apply to the case, and what rational grounds, therefore,
can be given for accepting or rejecting the utilitarian formula. But it is a
preliminary condition of rational acceptance or rejection that the formula
should be correctly understood. I believe that the very imperfect notion
ordinarily formed of its meaning is the chief obstacle which impedes its
reception, and that, could it be cleared even from only the grosser mis-
conceptions, the question would be greatly simplified and a large proportion of its difficulties removed. Before, therefore, I attempt to enter into
the philosophical grounds which can be given for assenting to the utilitarian standard, I shall offer some illustrations of the doctrine itself, with the
view of showing more clearly what it is, distinguishing it from what it is
not, and disposing of such of the practical objections to it as either originate in, or are closely connected with, mistaken interpretations of its
meaning. Having thus prepared the ground, I shall afterwards endeavor to
throw such light as I can upon the question considered as one of philosophical theory.

CHAPTER II
What Utilitarianism Is

A passing remark is all that needs be given to the ignorant blunder of supposing that those who stand up for utility as the test of right and wrong
use the term in that restricted and merely colloquial sense in which utility
is opposed to pleasure. An apology is due to the philosophical opponents
of utilitarianism for even the momentary appearance of confounding

them with anyone capable of so absurd a misconception; which is the more extraordinary, inasmuch as the contrary accusation, of referring everything to pleasure, and that, too, in its grossest form, is another of the common charges against utilitarianism: and, as has been pointedly remarked by an able writer, the same sort of persons, and often the very same persons, denounce the theory "as impracticably dry when the word 'utility' precedes the word 'pleasure,' and as too practicably voluptuous when the word 'pleasure' precedes the word 'utility.'" Those who know anything about the matter are aware that every writer, from Epicurus to Bentham, who maintained the theory of utility meant by it, not something to be contradistinguished from pleasure, but pleasure itself, together with exemption from pain; and instead of opposing the useful to the agreeable or the ornamental, have always declared that the useful means these, among other things. Yet the common herd, including the herd of writers, not only in newspapers and periodicals, but in books of weight and pretension, are perpetually falling into this shallow mistake. Having caught up the word "utilitarian," while knowing nothing whatever about it but its sound, they habitually express by it the rejection or the neglect of pleasure in some of its forms: of beauty, of ornament, or of amusement. Nor is the term thus ignorantly misapplied solely in disparagement, but occasionally in compliment, as though it implied superiority to frivolity and the mere pleasures of the moment. And this perverted use is the only one in which the word is popularly known, and the one from which the new generation are acquiring their sole notion of its meaning. Those who introduced the word, but who had for many years discontinued it as a distinctive appellation, may well feel themselves called upon to resume it if by doing so they can hope to contribute anything toward rescuing it from this utter degradation.[1]

The creed which accepts as the foundation of morals "utility" or the "greatest happiness principle" holds that actions are right in proportion as they tend to promote happiness; wrong as they tend to produce the reverse of happiness. By happiness is intended pleasure and the absence of pain; by unhappiness, pain and the privation of pleasure. To give a clear view of the moral standard set up by the theory, much more requires to be said; in particular, what things it includes in the ideas of pain and pleasure, and to what extent this is left an open question. But these supplementary explanations do not affect the theory of life on which this theory of morality is grounded—namely, that pleasure and freedom from pain are the only things desirable as ends; and that all desirable things (which are as numerous in the utilitarian as in any other scheme) are desirable either for pleasure inherent in themselves or as means to the promotion of pleasure and the prevention of pain.

Now such a theory of life excites in many minds, and among them in some of the most estimable in feeling and purpose, inveterate dislike. To suppose that life has (as they express it) no higher end than pleasure—no better and nobler object of desire and pursuit—they designate as utterly mean and groveling, as a doctrine worthy only of swine, to whom the followers of Epicurus were, at a very early period, contemptuously likened; and modern holders of the doctrine are occasionally made the subject of equally polite comparisons by its German, French, and English assailants.

When thus attacked, the Epicureans have always answered that it is not they, but their accusers, who represent human nature in a degrading light, since the accusation supposes human beings to be capable of no pleasures except those of which swine are capable. If this supposition were true, the charge could not be gainsaid, but would then be no longer an imputation; for if the sources of pleasure were precisely the same to human beings and to swine, the rule of life which is good enough for the one would be good enough for the other. The comparison of the Epicurean life to that of beasts is felt as degrading, precisely because a beast's pleasures do not satisfy a human being's conceptions of happiness. Human beings have faculties more elevated than the animal appetites and, when once made conscious of them, do not regard anything as happiness which does not include their gratification. I do not, indeed, consider the Epicureans to have been by any means faultless in drawing out their scheme of consequences from the utilitarian principle. To do this in any sufficient manner, many Stoic, as well as Christian, elements require to be included. But there is no known Epicurean theory of life which does not assign to the pleasures of the intellect, of the feelings and imagination, and of the moral sentiments a much higher value as pleasures than to those of mere sensation. It must be admitted, however, that utilitarian writers in general have placed the superiority of mental over bodily pleasures chiefly in the greater permanency, safety, uncostliness, etc., of the former—that is, in their circumstantial advantages rather than in their intrinsic nature. And on all these points utilitarians have fully proved their case; but they might have taken the other and, as it may be called, higher ground with entire consistency. It is quite compatible with the principle of utility to recognize the fact that some kinds of pleasure are more desirable and more valuable than others. It would be absurd that, while in estimating all other things quality is considered as well as quantity, the estimation of pleasure should be supposed to depend on quantity alone.

If I am asked what I mean by difference of quality in pleasures, or what makes one pleasure more valuable than another, merely as a pleasure, except its being greater in amount, there is but one possible answer. Of two pleasures, if there be one to which all or almost all who have experience of

both give a decided preference, irrespective of any feeling of moral obligation to prefer it, that is the more desirable pleasure. If one of the two is,
by those who are competently acquainted with both, placed so far above
the other that they prefer it, even though knowing it to be attended with a
greater amount of discontent, and would not resign it for any quantity of
the other pleasure which their nature is capable of, we are justified in as-
cribing to the preferred enjoyment a superiority in quality so far outweighing quantity as to render it, in comparison, of small account.

Now it is an unquestionable fact that those who are equally acquainted
with and equally capable of appreciating and enjoying both do give a most
marked preference to the manner of existence which employs their higher
faculties. Few human creatures would consent to be changed into any of
the lower animals for a promise of the fullest allowance of a beast's pleasures; no intelligent human being would consent to be a fool, no instructed person would be an ignoramus, no person of feeling and
conscience would be selfish and base, even though they should be persuaded that the fool, the dunce, or the rascal is better satisfied with his lot
than they are with theirs. They would not resign what they possess more
than he for the most complete satisfaction of all the desires which they
have in common with him. If they ever fancy they would, it is only in
cases of unhappiness so extreme that to escape from it they would exchange their lot for almost any other, however undesirable in their own
eyes. A being of higher faculties requires more to make him happy, is capable probably of more acute suffering, and certainly accessible to it at
more points, than one of an inferior type; but in spite of these liabilities,
he can never really wish to sink into what he feels to be a lower grade of
existence. We may give what explanation we please of this unwillingness;
we may attribute it to pride, a name which is given indiscriminately to
some of the most and to some of the least estimable feelings of which
mankind are capable; we may refer it to the love of liberty and personal independence, an appeal to which was with the Stoics one of the most effective means for the inculcation of it; to the love of power or to the love of
excitement, both of which do really enter into and contribute to it; but its
most appropriate appellation is a sense of dignity, which all human beings
possess in one form or other, and in some, though by no means in exact,
proportion to their higher faculties, and which is so essential a part of the
happiness of those in whom it is strong that nothing which conflicts with
it could be otherwise than momentarily an object of desire to them. Whoever supposes that this preference takes place at a sacrifice of happiness—
that the superior being, in anything like equal circumstances, is not
happier than the inferior —confounds the two very different ideas of happiness and content. It is indisputable that the being whose capacities of

enjoyment are low has the greatest chance of having them fully satisfied; and a highly endowed being will always feel that any happiness which he can look for, as the world is constituted, is imperfect. But he can learn to bear its imperfections, if they are at all bearable; and they will not make him envy the being who is indeed unconscious of the imperfections, but only because he feels not at all the good which those imperfections qualify. It is better to be a human being dissatisfied than a pig satisfied; better to be Socrates dissatisfied than a fool satisfied. And if the fool, or the pig, are of a different opinion, it is because they only know their own side of the question. The other party to the comparison knows both sides.

It may be objected that many who are capable of the higher pleasures occasionally, under the influence of temptation, postpone them to the lower. But this is quite compatible with a full appreciation of the intrinsic superiority of the higher. Men often, from infirmity of character, make their election for the nearer good, though they know it to be the less valuable; and this no less when the choice is between two bodily pleasures than when it is between bodily and mental. They pursue sensual indulgences to the injury of health, though perfectly aware that health is the greater good. It may be further objected that many who begin with youthful enthusiasm for everything noble, as they advance in years, sink into indolence and selfishness. But I do not believe that those who undergo this very common change voluntarily choose the lower description of pleasures in preference to the higher. I believe that, before they devote themselves exclusively to the one, they have already become incapable of the other. Capacity for other nobler feelings is in most natures a very tender plant, easily killed, not only by hostile influences, but by mere want of sustenance; and in the majority of young persons it speedily dies away if the occupations to which their position in life has devoted them, and the society into which it has thrown them, are not favorable to keeping that higher capacity in exercise. Men lose their high aspirations as they lose their intellectual tastes, because they have not time or opportunity for indulging them; and they addict themselves to inferior pleasures, not because they deliberately prefer them, but because they are either the only ones to which they have access or the only ones which they are any longer capable of enjoying. It may be questioned whether anyone who has remained equally susceptible to both classes of pleasures ever knowingly and calmly preferred the lower, though many, in all ages, have broken down in an ineffectual attempt to combine both.

From this verdict of the only competent judges, I apprehend there can be no appeal. On a question which is the best worth having of two pleasures, or which of two modes of existence is the most grateful to the feelings, apart from its moral attributes and from its consequences, the judgment of those who are qualified by knowledge of both, or, if they differ, that of the majority among them, must be admitted as final. And there needs be the less hesitation to accept this judgment respecting the quality of pleasures, since there is no other tribunal to be referred to even on the question of quantity. What means are there of determining which is the acutest of two pains, or the intensest of two pleasurable sensations, except the general suffrage of those who are familiar with both? Neither pains nor pleasures are homogeneous, and pain is always heterogeneous with pleasure. What is there to decide whether a particular pleasure is worth purchasing at the cost of a particular pain, except the feelings and judgment of the experienced? When, therefore, those feelings and judgment declare the pleasures derived from the higher faculties to be preferable *in kind,* apart from the question of intensity, to those of which the animal nature, disjoined from the higher faculties, is susceptible, they are entitled on this subject to the same regard.

I have dwelt on this point as being a necessary part of a perfectly just conception of utility or happiness considered as the directive rule of human conduct. But it is by no means an indispensable condition to the acceptance of the utilitarian standard; for that standard is not the agent's own greatest happiness, but the greatest amount of happiness altogether; and if it may possibly be doubted whether a noble character is always the happier for its nobleness, there can be no doubt that it makes other people happier, and that the world in general is immensely a gainer by it. Utilitarianism, therefore, could only attain its end by the general cultivation of nobleness of character, even if each individual were only benefited by the nobleness of others, and his own, so far as happiness is concerned, were a sheer deduction from the benefit. But the bare enunciation of such an absurdity as this last renders refutation superfluous.

According to the greatest happiness principle, as above explained, the ultimate end, with reference to and for the sake of which all other things are desirable—whether we are considering our own good or that of other people—is an existence exempt as far as possible from pain, and as rich as possible in enjoyments, both in point of quantity and quality; the test of quality and the rule of measuring it against quantity being the preference felt by those who, in their opportunities of experience, to which must be added their habits of self-consciousness and self-observation, are best furnished with the means of comparison. This, being according to the utilitarian opinion the end of human action, is necessarily also the standard of morality, which may accordingly be defined "the rules and precepts for human conduct," by the observance of which an existence such as has been described might be, to the greatest extent possible, secured to all mankind; and not to them only, but, so far as the nature of things admits, to the whole sentient creation.

Against this doctrine, however, arises another class of objectors who say that happiness, in any form, cannot be the rational purpose of human life and action; because, in the first place, it is unattainable; and they contemptuously ask, What right hast thou to be happy?— a question which Mr. Carlyle clinches by the addition, What right, a short time ago, hadst thou even *to be?* Next they say that men can do *without* happiness; that all noble human beings have felt this, and could not have become noble but by learning the lesson of *Entsagen,* or renunciation; which lesson, thoroughly learned and submitted to, they affirm to be the beginning and necessary condition of all virtue.

The first of these objections would go to the root of the matter were it well founded; for if no happiness is to be had at all by human beings, the attainment of it cannot be the end of morality or of any rational conduct. Though, even in that case, something might still be said for the utilitarian theory, since utility includes not solely the pursuit of happiness, but the prevention or mitigation of unhappiness; and if the former aim be chimerical, there will be all the greater scope and more imperative need for the latter, so long at least as mankind think fit to live and do not take refuge in the simultaneous act of suicide recommended under certain conditions by Novalis. When, however, it is thus positively asserted to be impossible that human life should be happy, the assertion, if not something like a verbal quibble, is at least an exaggeration. If by happiness be meant a continuity of highly pleasurable excitement, it is evident enough that this is impossible. A state of exalted pleasure lasts only moments or in some cases, and with some intermissions, hours or days, and is the occasional brilliant flash of enjoyment, not its permanent and steady flame. Of this the philosophers who have taught that happiness is the end of life were as fully aware as those who taunt them. The happiness which they meant was not a life of rapture, but moments of such, in an existence made up of few and transitory pains, many and various pleasures, with a decided predominance of the active over the passive, and having as the foundation of the whole not to expect more from life than it is capable of bestowing. A life thus composed, to those who have been fortunate enough to obtain it, has always appeared worthy of the name of happiness. And such an existence is even now the lot of many during some considerable portion of their lives. The present wretched education and wretched social arrangements are the only real hindrance to its being attainable by almost all.

The objectors perhaps may doubt whether human beings, if taught to consider happiness as the end of life, would be satisfied with such a moderate share of it. But great numbers of mankind have been satisfied with much less. The main constituents of a satisfied life appear to be two, either of which by itself is often found sufficient for the purpose: tranquillity and excitement. With much tranquillity, many find that they can be content with very little pleasure; with much excitement, many can reconcile themselves to a considerable quantity of pain. There is assuredly no inherent impossibility of enabling even the mass of mankind to unite both, since the two are so far from being incompatible that they are in natural alliance, the prolongation of either being a preparation for, and exciting a wish for, the other. It is only those in whom indolence amounts to a vice that do not desire excitement after an interval of repose; it is only those in whom the need of excitement is a disease that feel the tranquillity which follows excitement dull and insipid, instead of pleasurable in direct proportion to the excitement which preceded it. When people who are tolerably fortunate in their outward lot do not find in life sufficient enjoyment to make it valuable to them, the cause generally is caring for nobody but themselves. To those who have neither public nor private affections, the excitements of life are much curtailed, and in any case dwindle in value as the time approaches when all selfish interests must be terminated by death; while those who leave after them objects of personal affection, and especially those who have also cultivated a fellow-feeling with the collective interests of mankind, retain as lively an interest in life on the eve of death as in the vigor of youth and health. Next to selfishness, the principal cause which makes life unsatisfactory is want of mental cultivation. A cultivated mind—I do not mean that of a philosopher, but any mind to which the fountains of knowledge have been opened, and which has been taught, in any tolerable degree, to exercise its faculties—finds sources of inexhaustible interest in all that surrounds it: in the objects of nature, the achievements of art, the imaginations of poetry, the incidents of history, the ways of mankind, past and present, and their prospects in the future. It is possible, indeed, to become indifferent to all this, and that too without having exhausted a thousandth part of it, but only when one has had from the beginning no moral or human interest in these things and has sought in them only the gratification of curiosity.

Now there is absolutely no reason in the nature of things why an amount of mental culture sufficient to give an intelligent interest in these objects of contemplation should not be the inheritance of everyone born in a civilized country. As little is there an inherent necessity that any human being should be a selfish egotist, devoid of every feeling or care but those which center in his own miserable individuality. Something far superior to this is sufficiently common even now, to give ample earnest of what the human species may be made. Genuine private affections and a sincere interest in the public good are possible, though in unequal degrees, to every rightly brought up human being. In a world in which there is so much to interest, so much to enjoy, and so much also to correct and improve, everyone who has this moderate amount of moral and intellectual requisites is capable of an existence which may be called enviable; and unless such a person, through bad laws or subjection to the will of others, is denied the liberty to use the sources of happiness within his reach, he will not fail to find this enviable existence, if he escapes the positive evils of life, the great sources of physical and mental suffering—such as indigence, disease, and the unkindness, worthlessness, or premature loss of objects of affection. The main stress of the problem lies, therefore, in the contest with these calamities from which it is a rare good fortune entirely to escape; which, as things now are, cannot be obviated, and often cannot be in any material degree mitigated. Yet no one whose opinion deserves a moment's consideration can doubt that most of the great positive evils of the world are in themselves removable, and will, if human affairs continue to improve, be in the end reduced within narrow limits. Poverty, in any sense implying suffering, may be completely extinguished by the wisdom of society combined with the good sense and providence of individuals. Even that most intractable of enemies, disease, may be indefinitely reduced in dimensions by good physical and moral education and proper control of noxious influences, while the progress of science holds out a promise for the future of still more direct conquests over this detestable foe. And every advance in that direction relieves us from some, not only of the chances which cut short our own lives, but, what concerns us still more, which deprive us of those in whom our happiness is wrapt up. As for vicissitudes of fortune and other disappointments connected with worldly circumstances, these are principally the effect either of gross imprudence, of ill-regulated desires, or of bad or imperfect social institutions. All the grand sources, in short, of human suffering are in a great degree, many of them almost entirely, conquerable by human care and effort; and though their removal is grievously slow—though a long succession of generations will perish in the breach before the conquest is completed, and this world becomes all that, if will and knowledge were not wanting, it might easily be made—yet every mind sufficiently intelligent and generous to bear a part, however small and inconspicuous, in the endeavor will draw a noble enjoyment from the contest itself, which he would not for any bribe in the form of selfish indulgence consent to be without.

And this leads to the true estimation of what is said by the objectors concerning the possibility and the obligation of learning to do without happiness. Unquestionably it is possible to do without happiness; it is done involuntarily by nineteen-twentieths of mankind, even in those parts of our present world which are least deep in barbarism; and it often has to be done voluntarily by the hero or the martyr, for the sake of something which he prizes more than his individual happiness. But this something, what is it, unless the happiness of others or some of the requisites of happiness? It is noble to be capable of resigning entirely one's own portion of happiness, or chances of it; but, after all, this self-sacrifice must be for some end; it is not its own end; and if we are told that its end is not happiness but virtue, which is better than happiness, I ask, would the sacrifice be made if the hero or martyr did not believe that it would earn for others immunity from similar sacrifices? Would it be made if he thought that his renunciation of happiness for himself would produce no fruit for any of his fellow creatures, but to make their lot like his and place them also in the condition of persons who have renounced happiness? All honor to those who can abnegate for themselves the personal enjoyment of life when by such renunciation they contribute worthily to increase the amount of happiness in the world; but he who does it or professes to do it for any other purpose is no more deserving of admiration than the ascetic mounted on his pillar. He may be an inspiring proof of what men *can* do, but assuredly not an example of what they *should*.

Though it is only in a very imperfect state of the world's arrangements that anyone can best serve the happiness of others by the absolute sacrifice of his own, yet, so long as the world is in that imperfect state, I fully acknowledge that the readiness to make such a sacrifice is the highest virtue which can be found in man. I will add that in this condition of the world, paradoxical as the assertion may be, the conscious ability to do without happiness gives the best prospect of realizing such happiness as is attainable. For nothing except that consciousness can raise a person above the chances of life by making him feel that, let fate and fortune do their worst, they have not power to subdue him; which, once felt, frees him from excess of anxiety concerning the evils of life and enables him, like many a Stoic in the worst times of the Roman Empire, to cultivate in tranquillity the sources of satisfaction accessible to him, without concerning himself about the uncertainty of their duration any more than about their inevitable end.

Meanwhile, let utilitarians never cease to claim the morality of self-devotion as a possession which belongs by as good a right to them as either to the Stoic or to the Transcendentalist. The utilitarian morality does recognize in human beings the power of sacrificing their own greatest good for the good of others. It only refuses to admit that the sacrifice is itself a good. A sacrifice which does not increase or tend to increase the sum total of happiness, it considers as wasted. The only self-renunciation which it applauds is devotion to the happiness, or to some of the means of happiness, of others, either of mankind collectively or of individuals within the limits imposed by the collective interests of mankind.

I must again repeat what the assailants of utilitarianism seldom have the justice to acknowledge, that the happiness which forms the utilitarian standard of what is right in conduct is not the agent's own happiness but that of all concerned. As between his own happiness and that of others, utilitarianism requires him to be as strictly impartial as a disinterested and benevolent spectator. In the golden rule of Jesus of Nazareth, we read the complete spirit of the ethics of utility. "To do as you would be done by," and "to love your neighbor as yourself," constitute the ideal perfection of utilitarian morality. As the means of making the nearest approach to this ideal, utility would enjoin, first, that laws and social arrangements should place the happiness or (as, speaking practically, it may be called) the interest of every individual as nearly as possible in harmony with the interest of the whole; and, secondly, that education and opinion, which have so vast a power over human character, should so use that power as to establish in the mind of every individual an indissoluble association between his own happiness and the good of the whole, especially between his own happiness and the practice of such modes of conduct, negative and positive, as regard for the universal happiness prescribes; so that not only he may be unable to conceive the possibility of happiness to himself, consistently with conduct opposed to the general good, but also that a direct impulse to promote the general good may be in every individual one of the habitual motives of action, and the sentiments connected therewith may fill a large and prominent place in every human being's sentient existence. If the impugners of the utilitarian morality represented it to their own minds in this its true character, I know not what recommendation possessed by any other morality they could possibly affirm to be wanting to it; what more beautiful or more exalted developments of human nature any other ethical system can be supposed to foster, or what springs of action, not accessible to the utilitarian, such systems rely on for giving effect to their mandates.

The objectors to utilitarianism cannot always be charged with representing it in a discreditable light. On the contrary, those among them who entertain anything like a just idea of its disinterested character sometimes find fault with its standard as being too high for humanity. They say it is exacting too much to require that people shall always act from the inducement of promoting the general interests of society. But this is to mistake the very meaning of a standard of morals and confound the rule of action with the motive of it. It is the business of ethics to tell us what are our duties, or by what test we may know them; but no system of ethics requires that the sole motive of all we do shall be a feeling of duty; on the contrary, ninety-nine hundredths of all our actions are done from other motives, and rightly so done if the rule of duty does not condemn them. It is the more unjust to utilitarianism that this particular misapprehension should be made a ground of objection to it, inasmuch as utilitarian moralists have gone beyond almost all others in affirming that the motive has nothing to do with the morality of the action, though much with the worth of the agent. He who saves a fellow creature from drowning does what is morally right, whether his motive be duty or the hope of being paid for his trouble; he who betrays the friend that trusts him is guilty of a crime, even if his object be to serve another friend to whom he is under greater obligations.[2] But to speak only of actions done from the motive of duty, and in direct obedience to principle: it is a misapprehension of the utilitarian mode of thought to conceive it as implying that people should fix their minds upon so wide a generality as the world, or society at large. The great majority of good actions are intended not for the benefit of the world, but for that of individuals, of which the good of the world is made up; and the thoughts of the most virtuous man need not on these occasions travel beyond the particular persons concerned, except so far as is necessary to assure himself that in benefiting them he is not violating the rights, that is, the legitimate and authorized expectations, of anyone else. The multiplication of happiness is, according to the utilitarian ethics, the object of virtue: the occasions on which any person (except one in a thousand) has it in his power to do this on an extended scale— in other words, to be a public benefactor—are but exceptional; and on these occasions alone is he called on to consider public utility; in every other case, private utility, the interest or happiness of some few persons, is all he has to attend to. Those alone the influence of whose actions extends to society in general need concern themselves habitually about so large an object. In the case of abstinences indeed—of things which people forbear to do from moral considerations, though the consequences in the particular case might be beneficial—it would be unworthy of an intelligent agent not to be consciously aware that the action is of a class which, if practiced generally, would be generally injurious, and that this is the ground of the obligation to abstain from it. The amount of regard for the public interest implied in this recognition is no greater than is demanded by every system of morals, for they all enjoin to abstain from whatever is manifestly pernicious to society.

The same considerations dispose of another reproach against the doctrine of utility, founded on a still grosser misconception of the purpose of a standard of morality and of the very meaning of the words "right" and

"wrong." It is often affirmed that utilitarianism renders men cold and un-
sympathizing; that it chills their moral feelings toward individuals; that it
makes them regard only the dry and hard consideration of the consequences of actions, not taking into their moral estimate the qualities from
which those actions emanate. If the assertion means that they do not allow
their judgment respecting the rightness or wrongness of an action to be
influenced by their opinion of the qualities of the person who does it, this
is a complaint not against utilitarianism, but against any standard or
morality at all; for certainly no known ethical standard decides an action to
be good or bad because it is done by a good or bad man, still less because
done by an amiable, a brave, or a benevolent man, or the contrary. These
considerations are relevant, not to the estimation of actions, but of persons; and there is nothing in the utilitarian theory inconsistent with the
fact that there are other things which interest us in persons besides the
rightness and wrongness of their actions. The Stoics, indeed, with the
paradoxical misuse of language which was part of their system, and by
which they strove to raise themselves above all concern about anything but
virtue, were fond of saying that he who has that has everything; that he,
and only he, is rich, is beautiful, is a king. But no claim of this description
is made for the virtuous man by the utilitarian doctrine. Utilitarians are
quite aware that there are other desirable possessions and qualities besides
virtue, and are perfectly willing to allow to all of them their full worth.
They are also aware that a right action does not necessarily indicate a virtuous character, and that actions which are blamable often proceed from
qualities entitled to praise. When this is apparent in any particular case, it
modifies their estimation, not certainly of the act, but of the agent. I grant
that they are, notwithstanding, of opinion that in the long run the best
proof of a good character is good actions; and resolutely refuse to consider
any mental disposition as good of which the predominant tendency is to
produce bad conduct. This makes them unpopular with many people, but
it is an unpopularity which they must share with everyone who regards
the distinction between right and wrong in a serious light; and the reproach is not one which a conscientious utilitarian need be anxious to
repel.

If no more be meant by the objection than that many utilitarians look
on the morality of actions, as measured by the utilitarian standards, with
too exclusive a regard, and do not lay sufficient stress upon the other
beauties of character which go toward making a human being lovable or
admirable, this may be admitted. Utilitarians who have cultivated their
moral feelings, but not their sympathies, nor their artistic perceptions, do
fall into this mistake; and so do all other moralists under the same conditions. What can be said in excuse for other moralists is equally available for

them, namely, that, if there is to be any error, it is better that it should be on that side. As a matter of fact, we may affirm that among utilitarians, as among adherents of other systems, there is every imaginable degree of rigidity and of laxity in the application of their standard; some are even puritanically rigorous, while others are as indulgent as can possibly be desired by sinner or by sentimentalist. But on the whole, a doctrine which brings prominently forward the interest that mankind have in the repression and prevention of conduct which violates the moral law is likely to be inferior to no other in turning the sanctions of opinion against such violations. It is true, the question "What does violate the moral law?" is one on which those who recognize different standards of morality are likely now and then to differ. But difference of opinion on moral questions was not first introduced into the world by utilitarianism, while that doctrine does supply, if not always an easy, at all events a tangible and intelligible, mode of deciding such differences.

It may not be superfluous to notice a few more of the common misapprehensions of utilitarian ethics, even those which are so obvious and gross that it might appear impossible for any person of candor and intelligence to fall into them; since persons, even of considerable mental endowment, often give themselves so little trouble to understand the bearings of any opinion against which they entertain a prejudice, and men are in general so little conscious of this voluntary ignorance as a defect that the vulgarest misunderstandings of ethical doctrines are continually met with in the deliberate writings of persons of the greatest pretensions both to high principle and to philosophy. We not uncommonly hear the doctrine of utility inveighed against a *godless* doctrine. If it be necessary to say anything at all against so mere an assumption, we may say that the question depends upon what idea we have formed of the moral character of the Deity. If it be a true belief that God desires, above all things, the happiness of his creatures, and that this was his purpose in their creation, utility is not only not a godless doctrine, but more profoundly religious than any other. If it be meant that utilitarianism does not recognize the revealed will of God as the supreme law of morals, I answer that a utilitarian who believes in the perfect goodness and wisdom of *God* necessarily believes that whatever God has thought fit to reveal on the subject of morals must fulfill the requirements of utility in a supreme degree. But others besides utilitarians have been of opinion that the Christian revelation was intended, and is fitted, to inform the hearts and minds of mankind with a spirit which should enable them to find for themselves what is right, and incline them to do it when found, rather than to tell them, except in a very general way, what it is; and that we need a doctrine of ethics, carefully followed out, to *interpret* to us the will of God. Whether this opinion is correct or not, it is superfluous here to discuss; since whatever aid religion, either natural or revealed, can afford to ethical investigation is as open to the utilitarian moralist as to any other. He can use it as the testimony of God to the usefulness or hurtfulness of any given course of action by as good a right as others can use it for the indication of a transcendental law having no connection with usefulness or with happiness.

Again, utility is often summarily stigmatized as an immoral doctrine by giving it the name of "expediency," and taking advantage of the popular use of that term to contrast it with principle. But the expedient, in the sense in which it is opposed to the right, generally means that which is expedient for the particular interest of the agent himself; as when a minister sacrifices the interests of his country to keep himself in place. When it means anything better than this, it means that which is expedient for some immediate object, some temporary purpose, but which violates a rule whose observance is expedient in a much higher degree. The expedient, in this sense, instead of being the same thing with the useful, is a branch of the hurtful. Thus it would often be expedient, for the purpose of getting over some momentary embarrassment, or attaining some object immediately useful to ourselves or others, to tell a lie. But inasmuch as the cultivation in ourselves of a sensitive feeling on the subject of veracity is one of the most useful, and the enfeeblement of that feeling one of the most hurtful, things to which our conduct can be instrumental; and inasmuch as any, even unintentional, deviation from truth does that much toward weakening the trustworthiness of human assertion, which is not only the principal support of all present social well-being, but the insufficiency of which does more than any one thing that can be named to keep back civilization, virtue, everything on which human happiness on the largest scale depends—we feel that the violation, for a present advantage, of a rule of such transcendent expediency is not expedient, and that he who, for the sake of convenience to himself or to some other individual, does what depends on him to deprive mankind of the good, and inflict upon them the evil, involved in the greater or less reliance which they can place in each other's word, acts the part of one of their worst enemies. Yet that even this rule, sacred as it is, admits of possible exceptions is acknowledged by all moralists; the chief of which is when the withholding of some fact (as of information from a malefactor, or of bad news from a person dangerously ill) would save an individual (especially an individual other than oneself) from great and unmerited evil, and when the withholding can only be effected by denial. But in order that the exception may not extend itself beyond the need, and may have the least possible effect in weakening reliance on veracity, it ought to be recognized and, if possible, its limits defined; and, if the principle of utility is good for anything, it must be good for weighing these conflicting utilities against one another and marking out the region within which one or the other preponderates.

Again, defenders of utility often find themselves called upon to reply to such objections as this—that there is not time, previous to action, for calculating and weighing the effects of any line of conduct on the general happiness. This is exactly as if anyone were to say that it is impossible to guide our conduct by Christianity because there is not time, on every occasion on which anything has to be done, to read through the Old and New Testaments. The answer to the objection is that there has been ample time, namely, the whole past duration of the human species. During all that time mankind have been learning by experience the tendencies of actions; on which experience all the prudence as well as all the morality of life are dependent. People talk as if the commencement of this course of experience had hitherto been put off, and as if, at the moment when some man feels tempted to meddle with the property or life of another, he had to begin considering for the first time whether murder and theft are injurious to human happiness. Even then I do not think that he would find the question very puzzling; but, at all events, the matter is now done to his hand. It is truly a whimsical supposition that, if mankind were agreed in considering utility to be the test of morality, they would remain without any agreement as to what *is* useful, and would take no measures for having their notions on the subject taught to the young and enforced by law and opinion. There is no difficulty in proving any ethical standard whatever to work ill if we suppose universal idiocy to be conjoined with it; but on any hypothesis short of that, mankind must by this time have acquired positive beliefs as to the effects of some actions on their happiness; and the beliefs which have thus come down are the rules of morality for the multitude, and for the philosopher until he has succeeded in finding better. That philosophers might easily do this, even now, on many subjects; that the received code of ethics is by no means of divine right; and that mankind have still much to learn as to the effects of actions on the general happiness, I admit or rather earnestly maintain. The corollaries from the principle of utility, like the precepts of every practical art, admit of indefinite improvement, and, in a progressive state of the human mind, their improvement is perpetually going on. But to consider the rules of morality as improvable is one thing; to pass over the intermediate generalization entirely and endeavor to test each individual action directly by the first principle is another. It is a strange notion that the acknowledgment of a first principle is inconsistent with the admission of secondary ones. To inform a traveler respecting the place of his ultimate destination is not to forbid the use of landmarks and direction-posts on the way. The proposition that happiness is the end and aim of morality does not mean that no road ought to be laid down to that goal, or that persons going thither should not be advised to take one direction rather than another. Men really ought to leave off talking a kind of nonsense on this subject, which they would neither talk nor listen to on other matters of practical concernment. Nobody argues that the art of navigation is not founded on astronomy because sailors cannot wait to calculate the Nautical Almanac. Being rational creatures, they go to sea with it ready calculated; and all rational creatures go out upon the sea of life with their minds made up on the common questions of right and wrong, as well as on many of the far more difficult questions of wise and foolish. And this, as long as foresight is a human quality, it is to be presumed they will continue to do. Whatever we adopt as the fundamental principle of morality, we require subordinate principles to apply it by; the impossibility of doing without them, being common to all systems, can afford no argument against any one in particular; but gravely to argue as if no such secondary principles could be had, and as if mankind had remained till now, and always must remain, without drawing any general conclusions from the experience of human life is as high a pitch, I think, as absurdity has ever reached in philosophical controversy.

The remainder of the stock arguments against utilitarianism mostly consist in laying to its charge the common infirmities of human nature, and the general difficulties which embarrass conscientious persons in shaping their course through life. We are told that a utilitarian will be apt to make his own particular case an exception to moral rules, and, when under temptation, will see a utility in the breach of a rule, greater than he will see in its observance. But is utility the only creed which is able to furnish us with excuses for evil-doing and means of cheating our own conscience? They are afforded in abundance by all doctrines which recognize as a fact in morals the existence of conflicting considerations, which all doctrines do that have been believed by sane persons. It is not the fault of any creed, but of the complicated nature of human affairs, that rules of conduct cannot be so framed as to require no exceptions, and that hardly any kind of action can safely be laid down as either always obligatory or always condemnable. There is no ethical creed which does not temper the rigidity of its laws by giving a certain latitude, under the moral responsibility of the agent, for accommodation to peculiarities of circumstances; and under every creed, at the opening thus made, self-deception and dishonest casuistry get in. There exists no moral system under which there do not arise unequivocal cases of conflicting obligation. These are the real difficulties, the knotty points both in the theory of ethics and in the conscientious guidance of personal conduct. They are overcome practically, with greater or with less success, according to the intellect and virtue of the individual; but it can hardly be pretended that anyone will be the less qualified for dealing with them, from possessing an ultimate standard to which conflicting rights and duties can be referred. If utility is the ultimate source of moral obligations, utility may be invoked to decide between them when their demands are incompatible. Though the application of the standard may be difficult, it is better than none at all; while in other systems, the moral laws all claiming independent authority, there is no common umpire entitled to interfere between them; their claims to precedence one over another rest on little better than sophistry, and, unless determined, as they generally are, by the unacknowledged influence of consideration of utility, afford a free scope for the action of personal desires and partialities. We must remember that only in these cases of conflict between secondary principles is it requisite that first principles should be appealed to. There is no case of moral obligation in which some secondary principle is not involved; and if only one, there can seldom be any real doubt which one it is, in the mind of any person by whom the principle itself is recognized.

CHAPTER III
Of the Ultimate Sanction of the Principle of Utility

The question is often asked, and properly so, in regard to any supposed moral standard—What is its sanction? what are the motives to obey? or, more specifically, what is the source of its obligation? whence does it derive its binding force? It is a necessary part of moral philosophy to provide the answer to this question, which, though frequently assuming the shape of an objection to the utilitarian morality, as if it had some special applicability to that above others, really arises in regard to all standards. It arises, in fact, whenever a person is called on to *adopt* a standard, or refer morality to any basis on which he has not been accustomed to rest it. For the customary morality, that which education and opinion have consecrated, is the only one which presents itself to the mind with the feeling of being *in itself* obligatory; and when a person is asked to believe that this morality *derives* its obligation from some general principle round which custom has not thrown the same halo, the assertion is to him a paradox; the supposed corollaries seem to have a more binding force than the original theorem; the superstructure seems to stand better without than with what is represented as its foundation. He says to himself, I feel that I am bound not to rob or murder, betray or deceive; but why am I bound to promote the general happiness? If my own happiness lies in something else, why may I not give that the preference?

If the view adopted by the utilitarian philosophy of the nature of the moral sense be correct, this difficulty will always present itself until the influences which form moral character have taken the same hold of the principle which they have taken of some of the consequences—until, by the improvement of education, the feeling of unity with our fellow creatures shall be (what it cannot be denied that Christ intended it to be) as deeply rooted in our character, and to our own consciousness as completely a part of our nature, as the horror of crime is in an ordinarily well-brought up young person. In the meantime, however, the difficulty has no peculiar application to the doctrine of utility, but is inherent in every attempt to analyze morality and reduce it to principles; which, unless the principle is already in men's minds invested with as much sacredness as any of its applications, always seems to divest them of a part of their sanctity.

The principle of utility either has, or there is no reason why it might not have, all the sanctions which belong to any other system of morals. Those sanctions are either external or internal. Of the external sanctions it is not necessary to speak at any length. They are the hope of favor and the fear of displeasure from our fellow creatures or from the Ruler of the universe, along with whatever we may have of sympathy or affection for them, or of love and awe of Him, inclining us to do His will independently of selfish consequences. There is evidently no reason why all these motives for observance should not attach themselves to the utilitarian morality as completely and as powerfully as to any other. Indeed, those of them which refer to our fellow creatures are sure to do so, in proportion to the amount of general intelligence; for whether there be any other ground of moral obligation than the general happiness or not, men do desire happiness; and however imperfect may be their own practice, they desire and commend all conduct in others toward themselves by which they think their happiness is promoted. With regard to the religious motive, if men believe, as most profess to do, in the goodness of God, those who think that conduciveness to the general happiness is the essence or even only the criterion of good must necessarily believe that it is also that which God approves. The whole force therefore of external reward and punishment, whether physical or moral, and whether proceeding from God or from our fellow men, together with all that the capacities of human nature admit of disinterested devotion to either, become available to enforce the utilitarian morality, in proportion as that morality is recognized; and the more powerfully, the more the appliances of education and general cultivation are bent to the purpose.

So far as to external sanctions. The internal sanction of duty, whatever our standard of duty may be, is one and the same—a feeling in our own mind; a pain, more or less intense, attendant on violation of duty, which in properly cultivated moral natures rises, in the more serious cases, into shrinking from it as an impossibility. This feeling, when disinterested and connecting itself with the pure idea of duty, and not with some particular form of it, or with any of the merely accessory circumstances, is the essence of conscience; though in that complex phenomenon as it actually exists, the simple fact is in general all encrusted over with collateral associations derived from sympathy, from love, and still more from fear; from all the forms of religious feeling; from the recollections of childhood and of all our past life; from self-esteem, desire of the esteem of others, and occasionally even self-abasement. This extreme complication is, I apprehend, the origin of the sort of mystical character which, by a tendency of the human mind of which there are many other examples, is apt to be attributed to the idea of moral obligation, and which leads people to believe that the idea cannot possibly attach itself to any other objects than those which, by a supposed mysterious law, are found in our present experience to excite it. Its binding force, however, consists in the existence of a mass of feeling which must be broken through in order to do what violates our standard of right, and which, if we do nevertheless violate that standard, will probably have to be encountered afterwards in the form of remorse. Whatever theory we have of the nature or origin of conscience, this is what essentially constitutes it.

The ultimate sanction, therefore, of all morality (external motives apart) being a subjective feeling in our own minds, I see nothing embarrassing to those whose standard is utility in the question, What is the sanction of that particular standard? We may answer, the same as of all other moral standards—the conscientious feelings of mankind. Undoubtedly this sanction has no binding efficacy on those who do not possess the feelings it appeals to; but neither will these persons be more obedient to any other moral principle than to the utilitarian one. On them morality of any kind has no hold but through the external sanctions. Meanwhile the feelings exist, a fact in human nature, the reality of which, and the great power with which they are capable of acting on those in whom they have been duly cultivated, are proved by experience. No reason has ever been shown why they may not be cultivated to as great intensity in connection with the utilitarian as with any other rule of morals.

There is, I am aware, a disposition to believe that a person who sees in moral obligation a transcendental fact, an objective reality belonging to the province of "things in themselves," is likely to be more obedient to it than one who believes it to be entirely subjective, having its seat in human consciousness only. But whatever a person's opinion may be on this point of ontology, the force he is really urged by is his own subjective feeling, and is exactly measured by its strength. No one's belief that duty is an objective reality is stronger than the belief that God is so; yet the belief in God, apart from the expectation of actual reward and punishment, only operates on conduct through, and in proportion to, the subjective religious feeling. The sanction, so far as it is disinterested, is always in the mind itself; and the notion, therefore, of the transcendental moralists must be that this sanction will not exist *in* the mind unless it is believed to have its root out of the mind; and that if a person is able to say to himself, "That which is restraining me and which is called my conscience is only a feeling in my own mind," he may possibly draw the conclusion that when the feeling ceases the obligation ceases, and that if he find the feeling inconvenient, he may disregard it and endeavor to get rid of it. But is this danger confined to the utilitarian morality? Does the belief that moral obligation has its seat outside the mind make the feeling of it too strong to be got rid of? The fact is so far otherwise that all moralists admit and lament the ease with which, in the generality of minds, conscience can be silenced or stifled. The question, "Need I obey my conscience?" is quite as often put to themselves by persons who never heard of the principle of utility as by its adherents. Those whose conscientious feelings are so weak as to allow of their asking this question, if they answer it affirmatively, will not do so because they believe in the transcendental theory, but because of the external sanctions.

It is not necessary, for the present purpose, to decide whether the feeling of duty is innate or implanted. Assuming it to be innate, it is an open question to what objects it naturally attaches itself; for the philosophic supporters of that theory are now agreed that the intuitive perception is of principles of morality and not of the details. If there be anything innate in the matter, I see no reason why the feeling which is innate should not be that of regard to the pleasures and pains of others. If there is any principle of morals which is intuitively obligatory, I should say it must be that. If so, the intuitive ethics would coincide with the utilitarian, and there would be no further quarrel between them. Even as it is, the intuitive moralists, though they believe that there are other intuitive moral obligations, do already believe this to be one; for they unanimously hold that a large *portion* of morality turns upon the consideration due to the interests of our fellow creatures. Therefore, if the belief in the transcendental origin of moral obligation gives any additional efficacy to the internal sanction, it appears to me that the utilitarian principle has already the benefit of it.

On the other hand, if, as is my own belief, the moral feelings are not innate but acquired, they are not for that reason the less natural. It is natural to man to speak, to reason, to build cities, to cultivate the ground, though these are acquired faculties. The moral feelings are not indeed a part of our nature in the sense of being in any perceptible degree present in all of us; but this, unhappily, is a fact admitted by those who believe the most strenuously in their transcendental origin. Like the other acquired capacities above referred to, the moral faculty, if not a part of our nature, is a natural outgrowth from it; capable, like them, in a certain small degree, of springing up spontaneously; and susceptible of being brought by cultivation to a high degree of development. Unhappily it is also susceptible, by a sufficient use of the external sanctions and of the force of early impressions, of being cultivated in almost any direction, so that there is hardly anything so absurd or so mischievous that it may not, by means of these influences, be made to act on the human mind with all the authority of conscience. To doubt that the same potency might be given by the same means to the principle of utility, even if it had no foundation in human nature, would be flying in the face of all experience.

But moral associations which are wholly of artificial creation, when the intellectual culture goes on, yield by degrees to the dissolving force of analysis; and if the feeling of duty, when associated with utility, would appear equally arbitrary; if there were no leading department of our nature, no powerful class of sentiments, with which that association would harmonize, which would make us feel congenial and incline us not only to foster it in others (for which we have abundant interested motives), but also to cherish it in ourselves—if there were not, in short, a natural basis of sentiment for utilitarian morality, it might well happen that this association also, even after it had been implanted by education, might be analyzed away.

But there *is* this basis of powerful natural sentiment; and that it is which, when once the general happiness is recognized as the ethical standard, will constitute the strength of the utilitarian morality. This firm foundation is that of the social feelings of mankind—the desire to be in unity with our fellow creatures, which is already a powerful principle in human nature, and happily one of those which tend to become stronger, even without express inculcation, from the influences of advancing civilization. The social state is at once so natural, so necessary, and so habitual to man, that, except in some unusual circumstances or by an effort of voluntary abstraction, he never conceives himself otherwise than as a member of a body; and this association is riveted more and more, as mankind are further removed from the state of savage independence. Any condition, therefore, which is essential to a state of society becomes more and more an inseparable part of every person's conception of the state of things which he is born into, and which is the destiny of a human being. Now society between human beings, except in the relation of master and slave, is manifestly impossible on any other footing than that the interests of all are to be consulted. Society between equals can only exist on the understanding that the interests of all are to be regarded equally. And since in all states of civilization, every person, except an absolute monarch, has equals, everyone is obliged to live on these terms with somebody; and in every age some advance is made toward a state in which it will be impossible to live permanently on other terms with anybody. In this way people grow up unable to conceive as possible to them a state of total disregard of other people's interests. They are under a necessity of conceiving themselves as at least abstaining from all the grosser injuries, and (if only for their own protection) living in a state of constant protest against them. They are also familiar with the fact of co-operating with others and proposing to themselves a collective, not an individual, interest as the aim (at least for the time being) of their actions. So long as they are co-operating, their ends are identified with those of others; there is at least a temporary feeling that the interests of others are their own interests. Not only does all strengthening of social ties, and all healthy growth of society, give to each individual a stronger personal interest in practically consulting the welfare of others, it also leads him to identify his *feelings* more and more with their good, or at least with an even greater degree of practical consideration for it. He comes, as though instinctively, to be conscious of himself as a being who *of course* pays regard to others. The good of others becomes to him a thing naturally and necessarily to be attended to, like any of the physical conditions of our existence. Now, whatever amount of this feeling a person has, he is urged by the strongest motives both of interest and of sympathy to demonstrate it, and to the utmost of his power encourage it in others; and even if he has none of it himself, he is as greatly interested as anyone else that others should have it. Consequently, the smallest germs of the feeling are laid hold of and nourished by the contagion of sympathy and the influences of education; and a complete web of corroborative association is woven round it by the powerful agency of the external sanctions. This mode of conceiving ourselves and human life, as civilization goes on, is felt to be more and more natural. Every step in political improvement renders it more so, by removing the sources of opposition of interest and leveling those inequalities of legal privilege between individuals or classes, owing to which there are large portions of mankind whose happiness it is still practicable to disregard. In an improving state of the human mind, the influences are constantly on the increase which tend to generate in each individual a feeling of unity with all the rest; which, if perfect, would make him never think of, or desire, any beneficial condition for himself in the benefits of which they are not included. If we now suppose this feeling of unity to be taught as a religion, and the whole force of education, of institutions, and of opinion directed, as it once was in the case of religion, to make every person grow up from infancy surrounded on all sides both by the profession and the practice of it, I think that no one who can realize this conception will feel any misgiving about the sufficiency of the ultimate sanction for the happiness morality. To any ethical student who finds the realization difficult, I recommend, as a means of facilitating it, the second of M. Comte's two principal works, the *Traité de Politique Positive*. I entertain the strongest objections to the system of politics and morals set forth in that treatise, but I think it has superabundantly shown the possibility of giving to the service of humanity, even without the aid of belief in a Providence, both the psychological power and the social efficacy of a religion, making it take hold of human life, and color all thought, feeling, and action in a manner of which the greatest ascendancy ever exercised by any religion may be but a type and foretaste; and of which the danger is, not that it should be insufficient, but that it should be so excessive as to interfere unduly with human freedom and individuality.

Neither is it necessary to the feeling which constitutes the binding force of the utilitarian morality on those who recognize it to wait for those social influences which would make its obligation felt by mankind at large. In the comparatively early state of human advancement in which we now live, a person cannot, indeed, feel that entireness of sympathy with all others which would make any real discordance in the general direction of their conduct in life impossible, but already a person in whom the social feeling is at all developed cannot bring himself to think of the rest of his fellow creatures as struggling rivals with him for the means of happiness, whom he must desire to see defeated in their object in order that he may succeed in his. The deeply rooted conception which every individual even now has of himself as a social being tends to make him feel it one of his natural wants that there should be harmony between his feelings and aims and those of his fellow creatures. If differences of opinion and of mental culture make it impossible for him to share many of their actual feelings— perhaps make him denounce and defy those feelings—he still needs to be conscious that his real aim and theirs do not conflict; that he is not opposing himself to what they really wish for, namely, their own good, but is, on the contrary, promoting it. This feeling in most individuals is much inferior in strength to their selfish feelings, and is often wanting altogether. But to those who have it, it possesses all the characters of a natural feeling. It does not present itself to their minds as a superstition of education or a law despotically imposed by the power of society, but as an attribute which it would not be well for them to be without. This conviction is the ultimate sanction of the greatest happiness morality. This it is which makes any mind of well-developed feelings work with, and not against, the outward motives to care for others, afforded by what I have called the external sanctions; and, when those sanctions are wanting or act in an opposite direction, constitutes in itself a powerful internal binding force, in proportion to the sensitiveness and thoughtfulness of the character, since few but those whose mind is a moral blank could bear to lay out their course of life on the plan of paying no regard to others except so far as their own private interest compels.

CHAPTER IV

Of What Sort of Proof the Principle of Utility is Susceptible

It has already been remarked that questions of ultimate ends do not admit of proof, in the ordinary acceptation of the term. To be incapable of proof by reasoning is common to all first principles, to the first premises of our knowledge, as well as to those of our conduct. But the former, being matters of fact, may be the subject of a direct appeal to the faculties which judge of fact—namely, our senses and our internal consciousness. Can an appeal be made to the same faculties on questions of practical ends? Or by what other faculty is cognizance taken of them?

Questions about ends are, in other words, questions what things are desirable. The utilitarian doctrine is that happiness is desirable, and the only thing desirable, as an end; all other things being only desirable as means to that end. What ought to be required of this doctrine, what conditions is it requisite that the doctrine should fulfill—to make good its claim to be believed?

The only proof capable of being given that an object is visible is that people actually see it. The only proof that a sound is audible is that people hear it; and so of the other sources of our experience. In like manner, I apprehend, the sole evidence it is possible to produce that anything is desirable is that people do actually desire it. If the end which the utilitarian doctrine proposes to itself were not, in theory and in practice, acknowledged to be an end, nothing could ever convince any person that it was so. No reason can be given why the general happiness is desirable, except that each person, so far as he believes it to be attainable, desires his own happiness. This, however, being a fact, we have not only all the proof which the case admits of, but all which it is possible to require, that happiness is a good: that each person's happiness is a good to that person, and the general happiness, therefore, a good to the aggregate of all persons. Happiness has made out its title as *one* of the ends of conduct and, consequently, one of the criteria of morality.

But it has not, by this alone, proved itself to be the sole criterion. To do that, it would seem, by the same rule, necessary to show, not only that people desire happiness, but that they never desire anything else. Now it is palpable that they do desire things which, in common language, are decidedly distinguished from happiness. They desire, for example, virtue and the absence of vice no less really than pleasure and the absence of pain. The desire of virtue is not as universal, but it is as authentic a fact as the desire of happiness. And hence the opponents of the utilitarian standard deem that they have a right to infer that there are other ends of human action besides happiness, and that happiness is not the standard of approbation and disapprobation.

But does the utilitarian doctrine deny that people desire virtue, or maintain that virtue is not a thing to be desired? The very reverse. It maintains not only that virtue is to be desired, but that it is to be desired disinterestedly, for itself. Whatever may be the opinion of utilitarian moralists as to the original conditions by which virtue is made virtue, however they may believe (as they do) that actions and dispositions are only virtuous because they promote another end than virtue, yet this being granted, and it having been decided, from considerations of this description, what *is* virtuous, they not only place virtue at the very head of the things which are good as means to the ultimate end, but they also recognize as a psychological fact the possibility of its being, to the individual, a good in itself, without looking to any end beyond it; and hold that the mind is not in a right state, not in a state conformable to utility, not in the state most conducive to the general happiness, unless it does love virtue in this manner—as a thing desirable in itself, even although, in the individual instance, it should not produce those other desirable consequences which it tends to produce, and on account of which it is held to be virtue. This opinion is not, in the smallest degree, a departure from the happiness principle. The ingredients of happiness are very various, and each of them is desirable in itself, and not merely when considered as swelling an aggregate. The principle of utility does not mean that any given pleasure, as music, for instance, or any given exemption from pain, as for example health, is to be looked upon as means to a collective something termed happiness, and to be desired on that account. They are desired and desirable in and for themselves; besides being means, they are a part of the end. Virtue, according to the utilitarian doctrine, is not naturally and originally part of the end, but it is capable of becoming so; and in those who live it disinterestedly it has become so, and is desired and cherished, not as a means to happiness, but as a part of their happiness.

To illustrate this further, we may remember that virtue is not the only thing originally a means, and which if it were not a means to anything else would be and remain indifferent, but which by association with what it is a means to comes to be desired for itself, and that too with the utmost intensity. What, for example, shall we say of the love of money? There is nothing originally more desirable about money than about any heap of glittering pebbles. Its worth is solely that of the things which it will buy;

the desires for other things than itself, which it is a means of gratifying. Yet the love of money is not only one of the strongest moving forces of human life, but money is, in many cases, desired in and for itself; the desire to possess it is often stronger than the desire to use it, and goes on increasing when all the desires which point to ends beyond it, to be compassed by it, are falling off. It may, then, be said truly that money is desired not for the sake of an end, but as part of the end. From being a means to happiness, it has come to be itself a principal ingredient of the individual's conception of happiness. The same may be said of the majority of the great objects of human life: power, for example, or fame, except that to each of these there is a certain amount of immediate pleasure annexed, which has at least the semblance of being naturally inherent in them—a thing which cannot be said of money. Still, however, the strongest natural attraction, both of power and of fame, is the immense aid they give to the attainment of our other wishes; and it is the strong association thus generated between them and all our objects of desire which gives to the direct desire of them the intensity it often assumes, so as in some characters to surpass in strength all other desires. In these cases the means have become a part of the end, and a more important part of it than any of the things which they are means to. What was once desired as an instrument for the attainment of happiness has come to be desired for its own sake. In being desired for its own sake it is, however, desired as *part* of happiness. The person is made, or thinks he would be made, happy by its mere possession; and is made unhappy by failure to obtain it. The desire of it is not a different thing from the desire of happiness any more than the love of music or the desire of health. They are included in happiness. They are some of the elements of which the desire of happiness is made up. Happiness is not an abstract idea but a concrete whole; and these are some of its parts. And the utilitarian standard sanctions and approves their being so. Life would be a poor thing, very ill provided with sources of happiness, if there were not this provision of nature by which things originally indifferent, but conducive to, or otherwise associated with, the satisfaction of our primitive desires, become in themselves sources of pleasure more valuable than the primitive pleasures, both in permanency, in the space of human existence that they are capable of covering, and even in intensity.

Virtue, according to the utilitarian conception, is a good of this description. There was no original desire of it, or motive to it, save its conduciveness to pleasure, and especially to protection from pain. But through the association thus formed it may be felt a good in itself, and desired as such with as great intensity as any other good; and with this difference between it and the love of money, of power, or of fame—that all of these may, and often do, render the individual noxious to the other members of the society to which he belongs, whereas there is nothing which makes him so much a blessing to them as the cultivation of the disinterested love of virtue. And consequently, the utilitarian standard, while it tolerates and approves those other acquired desires, up to the point beyond which they would be more injurious to the general happiness than promotive of it, enjoins and requires the cultivation of the love of virtue up to the greatest strength possible, as being above all things important to the general happiness.

It results from the preceding considerations that there is in reality nothing desired except happiness. Whatever is desired otherwise than as a means to some end beyond itself, and ultimately to happiness, is desired as itself a part of happiness, and is not desired for itself until it has become so. Those who desire virtue for its own sake desire it either because the consciousness of it is a pleasure, or because the consciousness of being without it is a pain, or for both reasons united; as in truth the pleasure and pain seldom exist separately, but almost always together—the same person feeling pleasure in the degree of virtue attained, and pain in not having attained more. If one of these gave him no pleasure, and the other no pain, he would not love or desire virtue, or would desire it only for the other benefits which it might produce to himself or to persons whom he cared for.

We have now, then, an answer to the question, of what sort of proof the principle of utility is susceptible. If the opinion which I have now stated is psychologically true—if human nature is so constituted as to desire nothing which is not either a part of happiness or a means of happiness—we can have no other proof, and we require no other, that these are the only things desirable. If so, happiness is the sole end of human action, and the promotion of it the test by which to judge of all human conduct; from whence it necessarily follows that it must be the criterion of morality, since a part is included in the whole.

And now to decide whether this is really so, whether mankind do desire nothing for itself but that which is a pleasure to them, or of which the absence is a pain, we have evidently arrived at a question of fact and experience, dependent, like all similar questions, upon evidence. It can only be determined by practiced self-consciousness and self-observation, assisted by observation of others. I believe that these sources of evidence, impartially consulted, will declare that desiring a thing and finding it pleasant, aversion to it and thinking of it as painful, are phenomena entirely inseparable or, rather, two parts of the same phenomenon—in strictness of language, two different modes of naming the same psychological fact; that to think of an object as desirable (unless for the sake of its consequences) and to think of it as pleasant are one and the same thing; and that to desire anything except in proportion as the idea of it is pleasant is a physical and metaphysical impossibility.

So obvious does this appear to me that I expect it will hardly be disputed; and the objection made will be, not that desire can possibly be directed to anything ultimately except pleasure and exemption from pain, but that the will is a different thing from desire; that a person of confirmed virtue or any other person whose purposes are fixed carries out his purposes without any thought of the pleasure he has in contemplating them or expects to derive from their fulfillment, and persists in acting on them, even though these pleasures are much diminished by changes in his character or decay of his passive sensibilities, or are outweighed by the pains which the pursuit of the purposes may bring upon him. All this I fully admit and have stated it elsewhere as positively and emphatically as anyone. Will, the active phenomenon, is a different thing from desire, the state of passive sensibility, and, though originally an offshoot from it, may in time take root and detach itself from the parent stock, so much so that in the case of a habitual purpose, instead of willing the thing because we desire it, we often desire it only because we will it. This, however, is but an instance of that familiar fact, the power of habit, and is nowise confined to the case of virtuous actions. Many indifferent things which men originally did from a motive of some sort they continue to do from habit. Sometimes this is done unconsciously, the consciousness coming only after the action; at other times with conscious volition, but volition which has become habitual and is put in operation by the force of habit, in opposition perhaps to the deliberate preference, as often happens with those who have contracted habits of vicious or hurtful indulgence. Third and last comes the case in which the habitual act of will in the individual instance is not in contradiction to the general intention prevailing at other times, but in fulfillment of it, as in the case of the person of confirmed virtue and of all who pursue deliberately and consistently any determinate end. The distinction between will and desire thus understood is an authentic and highly important psychological fact; but the fact consists solely in this— that will, like all other parts of our constitution, is amenable to habit, and that we may will from habit what we no longer desire for itself, or desire only because we will it. It is not the less true that will, in the beginning, is entirely produced by desire, including in that term the repelling influence of pain as well as the attractive one of pleasure. Let us take into consideration no longer the person who has a confirmed will to do right, but him in whom that virtuous will is still feeble, conquerable by temptation, and not to be fully relied on; by what means can it be strengthened? How can the will to be virtuous, where it does not exist in sufficient force, be implanted or awakened? Only by making the person *desire* virtue—by making him think of it in a pleasurable light, or of its absence in a painful one. It is by associating the doing right with pleasure, or the doing wrong with pain, or by eliciting and impressing and bringing home to the person's experience the pleasure naturally involved in the one or the pain in the other, that it is possible to call forth that will to be virtuous which, when confirmed, acts without any thought of either pleasure or pain. Will is the child of desire, and passes out of the dominion of its parent only to come under that of habit. That which is the result of habit affords no presumption of being intrinsically good; and there would be no reason for wishing that the purpose of virtue should become independent of pleasure and pain were it not that the influence of the pleasurable and painful associations which prompt to virtue is not sufficiently to be depended on for unerring constancy of action until it has acquired the support of habit. Both in feeling and in conduct, habit is the only thing which imparts certainty; and it is because of the importance to others of being able to rely absolutely on one's feelings and conduct, and to oneself of being able to rely on one's own, that the will to do right ought to be cultivated into this habitual independence. In other words, this state of the will is a means to good, not intrinsically a good; and does not contradict the doctrine that nothing is a good to human beings but in so far as it is either itself pleasurable or a means of attaining pleasure or averting pain.

But if this doctrine be true, the principle of utility is proved. Whether it is so or not must now be left to the consideration of the thoughtful reader.

CHAPTER V
On the Connection Between Justice and Utility

In all ages of speculation one of the strongest obstacles to the reception of the doctrine that utility or happiness is the criterion of right and wrong has been drawn from the idea of justice. The powerful sentiment and apparently clear perception which that word recalls with a rapidity and certainty resembling an instinct have seemed to the majority of thinkers to point to an inherent quality in things; to show that the just must have an existence in nature as something absolute, generically distinct from every variety of the expedient and, in idea, opposed to it, though (as is commonly acknowledged) never, in the long run, disjoined from it in fact.

In the case of this, as of our other moral sentiments, there is no necessary connection between the question of its origin and that of its binding force. That a feeling is bestowed on us by nature does not necessarily legitimate all its promptings. The feeling of justice might be a peculiar instinct, and might yet require, like our other instincts, to be controlled and enlightened by a higher reason. If we have intellectual instincts leading us to judge in a particular way, as well as animal instincts that prompt us to act in a particular way, there is no necessity that the former should be more infallible in their sphere than the latter in theirs; it may as well happen that wrong judgments are occasionally suggested by those, as wrong actions by these. But though it is one thing to believe that we have natural feelings of justice, and another to acknowledge them as an ultimate criterion of conduct, these two opinions are very closely connected in point of fact. Mankind are always predisposed to believe that any subjective feeling, not otherwise accounted for, is a revelation of some objective reality. Our present object is to determine whether the reality to which the feeling of justice corresponds is one which needs any such special revelation, whether the justice or injustice of an action is a thing intrinsically peculiar and distinct from all its other qualities or only a combination of certain of those qualities presented under a peculiar aspect. For the purpose of this inquiry it is practically important to consider whether the feeling itself, of justice and injustice, is *sui generis* like our sensations of color and taste or a derivative feeling formed by a combination of others. And this it is the more essential to examine, as people are in general willing enough to allow that objectively the dictates of justice coincide with a part of the field of general expediency; but inasmuch as the subjective mental feeling of justice is different from that which commonly attaches to simple expediency, and, except in the extreme cases of the latter, is far more imperative in its demands, people find it difficult to see in justice only a particular kind or branch of general utility, and think that its superior binding force requires a totally different origin.

To throw light upon this question, it is necessary to attempt to ascertain what is the distinguishing character of justice, or of injustice; what is the quality, or whether there is any quality, attributed in common to all modes of conduct designated as unjust (for justice, like many other moral attributes, is best defined by its opposite), and distinguishing them from such modes of conduct as are disapproved, but without having that particular epithet of disapprobation applied to them. If in everything which men are accustomed to characterize as just or unjust some one common attribute or collection of attributes is always present, we may judge whether this particular attribute or combination of attributes would be capable of gathering round it a sentiment of that peculiar character and intensity by virtue of the general laws of our emotional constitution, or whether the sentiment is inexplicable and requires to be regarded as a special provision of nature. If we find the former to be the case, we shall, in resolving this question, have resolved also the main problem; if the latter, we shall have to seek for some other mode of investigating it.

To find the common attributes of a variety of objects, it is necessary to begin by surveying the objects themselves in the concrete. Let us therefore advert successively to the various modes of action and arrangements of human affairs which are classed, by universal or widely spread opinion, as just or as unjust. The things well known to excite the sentiments associated with those names are of a very multifarious character. I shall pass them rapidly in review, without studying any particular arrangement.

In the first place, it is mostly considered unjust to deprive anyone of his personal liberty, his property, or any other thing which belongs to him by law. Here, therefore, is one instance of the application of the terms "just" and "unjust" in a perfectly definite sense, namely, that it is just to respect, unjust to violate, the *legal rights* of anyone. But this judgment admits of several exceptions, arising from the other forms in which the notions of justice and injustice present themselves. For example, the person who suffers the deprivation may (as the phrase is) have *forfeited* the rights which he is so deprived of—a case to which we shall return presently. But also—

Secondly, the legal rights of which he is deprived may be rights which *ought* not to have belonged to him; in other words, the law which confers on him these rights may be a bad law. When it is so or when (which is the same thing for our purpose) it is supposed to be so, opinions will differ as to the justice or injustice of infringing it. Some maintain that no law, however bad, ought to be disobeyed by an individual citizen; that his opposition to it, if shown at all, should only be shown in endeavoring to get it altered by competent authority. This opinion (which condemns many of the most illustrious benefactors of mankind, and would often protect pernicious institutions against the only weapons which, in the state of things existing at the time, have any chance of succeeding against them) is defended by those who hold it on grounds of expediency, principally on that of the importance to the common interest of mankind, of maintaining inviolate the sentiment of submission to law. Other persons, again, hold the directly contrary opinion that any law, judged to be bad, may blamelessly be disobeyed, even though it be not judged to be unjust but only inexpedient, while others would confine the license of disobedience to the case of unjust laws; but, again, some say that all laws which are inexpedient are unjust, since every law imposes some restriction on the natural liberty of mankind, which restriction is an injustice unless legitimated by tending to their good. Among these diversities of opinion it seems to be universally admitted that there may be unjust laws, and that law, consequently, is not the ultimate criterion of justice, but may give to one person a benefit, or impose on another an evil, which justice condemns. When, however, a law is thought to be unjust, it seems always to be regarded as being so in the same way in which a breach of law is unjust, namely, by infringing somebody's right, which, as it cannot in this case be a legal right, receives a different appellation and is called a moral right. We may say, therefore, that a second case of injustice consists in taking or withholding from any person that to which he has a *moral right*.

Thirdly, it is universally considered just that each person should obtain that (whether good or evil) which he *deserves,* and unjust that he should obtain a good or be made to undergo an evil which he does not deserve. This is, perhaps, the clearest and most emphatic form in which the idea of justice is conceived by the general mind. As it involves the notion of desert, the question arises what constitutes desert? Speaking in a general way, a person is understood to deserve good if he does right, evil if he does wrong; and in a more particular sense, to deserve good from those to whom he does or has done good, and evil from those to whom he does or has done evil. The precept of returning good for evil has never been regarded as a case of the fulfillment of justice, but as one in which the claims of justice are waived, in obedience to other considerations.

Fourthly, it is confessedly unjust to *break faith* with anyone: to violate an engagement, either express or implied, or disappoint expectations raised by our own conduct, at least if we have raised those expectations knowingly and voluntarily. Like the other obligations of justice already spoken of, this one is not regarded as absolute, but as capable of being overruled by a stronger obligation of justice on the other side, or by such conduct on the part of the person concerned as is deemed to absolve us from our obligation to him and to constitute a *forfeiture* of the benefit which he has been led to expect.

Fifthly, it is, by universal admission, inconsistent with justice to be *partial*—to show favor or preference to one person over another in matters to which favor and preference do not properly apply. Impartiality, however, does not seem to be regarded as a duty in itself, but rather as instrumental to some other duty; for it is admitted that favor and preference are not always censurable, and, indeed, the cases in which they are condemned are rather the exception than the rule. A person would be more likely to be blamed than applauded for giving his family or friends no superiority in good offices over strangers when he could do so without violating any other duty; and no one thinks it unjust to seek one person in preference to another as a friend, connection, or companion. Impartiality where rights are concerned is of course obligatory, but this is involved in the more general obligation of giving to everyone his right. A tribunal, for example, must be impartial because it is bound to award, without regard to any other consideration, a disputed object to the one of two parties who has the right to it. There are other cases in which impartiality means being solely influenced by desert, as with those who, in the capacity of judges, preceptors, or parents, administer reward and punishment as such. There are cases, again, in which it means being solely influenced by consideration for the public interest, as in making a selection among candidates for a government employment. Impartiality, in short, as an obligation of justice, may be said to mean being exclusively influenced by the considerations which it is supposed ought to influence the particular case in hand, and resisting solicitation of any motives which prompt to conduct different from what those considerations would dictate.

Nearly allied to the idea of impartiality is that of *equality*, which often enters as a component part both into the conception of justice and into the practice of it, and, in the eyes of many persons, constitutes its essence. But in this, still more than in any other case, the notion of justice varies in different persons, and always conforms in its variations to their notion of utility. Each person maintains that equality is the dictate of justice, except where he thinks that expediency requires inequality. The justice of giving equal protection to the rights of all is maintained by those who support the most outrageous inequality in the rights themselves. Even in slave countries it is theoretically admitted that the rights of the slave, such as they are, ought to be as sacred as those of the master, and that a tribunal which fails to enforce them with equal strictness is wanting in justice; while, at the same time, institutions which leave to the slave scarcely any rights to enforce are not deemed unjust because they are not deemed inexpedient. Those who think that utility requires distinctions of rank do not consider it unjust that riches and social privileges should be unequally dispensed; but those who think this inequality inexpedient think it unjust also. Whoever thinks that government is necessary sees no injustice in as much inequality as is constituted by giving to the magistrate powers not granted to other people. Even among those who hold leveling doctrines, there are differences of opinion about expediency. Some communists consider it unjust that the produce of the labor of the community should be shared on any other principle than that of exact equality; others think it just that those should receive most whose needs are greatest; while others hold that those who work harder, or who produce more, or whose services are more valuable to the community, may justly claim a larger quota in the division of the produce. And the sense of natural justice may be plausibly appealed to in behalf of every one of these opinions.

Among so many diverse applications of the term "justice," which yet is not regarded as ambiguous, it is a matter of some difficulty to seize the mental link which holds them together, and on which the moral sentiment adhering to the term essentially depends. Perhaps, in this embarrassment, some help may be derived from the history of the word, as indicated by its etymology.

In most if not in all languages, the etymology of the word which corresponds to "just" points distinctly to an origin connected either with positive law, or with that which was in most cases the primitive form of law—authoritative custom. *Justum* is a form of *jussum,* that which has been ordered. *Jus* is of the same origin. Δίκαιον comes from δικη, of which the principal meaning, at least in the historical ages of Greece, was a suit at law. Originally, indeed, it meant only the mode or *manner* of doing things, but it early came to mean the *prescribed* manner, that which the recognized authorities, patriarchal, judicial, or political, would enforce. *Recht,* from which came *right* and *righteous,* is synonymous with law. The original meaning indeed of *recht* did not point to law, but to physical straightness, as *wrong* and its Latin equivalents meant twisted or *tortuous*; and from this it is argued that right did not originally mean law, but on the contrary law meant right. But however this may be, the fact that *recht* and *droit* became restricted in their meaning to positive law, although much which is not required by law is equally necessary to moral straightness or rectitude, is as significant of the original character of moral ideas as if the derivation had been the reverse way.

It is true that mankind consider the idea of justice and its obligations as applicable to many things which neither are, nor is it desired that they should be, regulated by law. Nobody desires that laws should interfere with the whole detail of private life; yet everyone allows that in all daily conduct a person may and does show himself to be either just or unjust. But even here, the idea of the breach of what ought to be law still lingers in a modified shape. It would always give us pleasure, and chime in with our feelings of fitness, that acts which we deem unjust should be punished, though we do not always think it expedient that this should be done by the tribunals. We forego that gratification on account of incidental inconveniences. We should be glad to see just conduct enforced and injustice repressed, even in the minutest details, if we were not, with reason, afraid of trusting the magistrate with so unlimited an amount of power over individuals. When we think that a person is bound in justice to do a thing, it is an ordinary form of language to say that he ought to be compelled to do it. We should be gratified to see the obligation enforced by anybody who had the power. If we see that its enforcement by law would be inexpedient, we lament the impossibility, we consider the impunity given to injustice as an evil, and strive to make amends for it by bringing a strong expression of our own and the public disapprobation to bear upon the offender. Thus the idea of legal constraint is still the generating idea of the notion of justice, though undergoing several transformations before that notion as it exists in an advanced state of society becomes complete.

The above is, I think, a true account, as far as it goes, of the origin and progressive growth of the idea of justice. But we must observe that it contains as yet nothing to distinguish that obligation from moral obligation in general. For the truth is that the idea of penal sanction, which is the essence of law, enters not only into the conception of injustice, but into that of any kind of wrong. We do not call anything wrong unless we mean to imply that a person ought to be punished in some way or other for doing it—if not by law, by the opinion of his fellow creatures; if not by opinion, by the reproaches of his own conscience. This seems the real turning point of the distinction between morality and simple expediency. It is a part of the notion of duty in every one of its forms that a person may rightfully be compelled to fulfill it. Duty is a thing which may be *exacted* from a person, as one exacts a debt. Unless we think that it may be exacted from him, we do not call it his duty. Reasons of prudence, or the interest of other people, may militate against actually exacting it, but the person himself, it is clearly understood, would not be entitled to complain. There are other things, on the contrary, which we wish that people should do, which we like or admire them for doing, perhaps dislike or despise them for not doing, but yet admit that they are not bound to do; it is not a case of moral obligation; we do not blame them, that is, we do not think that they are proper objects of punishment. How we come by these ideas of deserving and not deserving punishment will appear, perhaps, in the sequel; but I think there is no doubt that this distinction lies at the bottom of the notions of right and wrong; that we call any conduct wrong, or employ, instead, some other term of dislike or disparagement, according as we think that the person ought, or ought not, to be punished for it; and we say it would be right to do so and so, or merely that it would be desirable or laudable, according as we would wish to see the person whom it concerns compelled, or only persuaded and exhorted, to act in that manner.[1]

This, therefore, being the characteristic difference which marks off, not justice, but morality in general from the remaining provinces of expediency and worthiness, the character is still to be sought which distinguishes justice from other branches of morality. Now it is known that ethical writers divide moral duties into two classes, denoted by the ill-chosen expressions, duties of perfect and of imperfect obligation; the latter being those in which, though the act is obligatory, the particular occasions of performing it are left to our choice, as in the case of charity or beneficence, which we are indeed bound to practice but not toward any definite person, nor at any prescribed time. In the more precise language of philosophic jurists, duties of perfect obligation are those duties in virtue of which a correlative *right* resides in some person or persons; duties of imperfect obligation are those moral obligations which do not give birth to any right. I think it will be found that this distinction exactly coincides with that which exists between justice and the other obligations of morality. In our survey of the various popular acceptations of justice, the term appeared generally to involve the idea of a personal right—a claim on the part of one or more individuals, like that which the law gives when it confers a proprietary or other legal right. Whether the injustice consists in depriving a person of a possession, or in breaking faith with him, or in treating him worse than he deserves, or worse than other people who have no greater claims—in each case the supposition implies two things: a wrong done, and some assignable person who is wronged. Injustice may also be done by treating a person better than others; but the wrong in this case is to his competitors, who are also assignable persons. It seems to me that this feature in the case—a right in some person, correlative to the moral obligation—constitutes the specific difference between justice and generosity or beneficence. Justice implies something which it is not only right to do, and wrong not to do, but which some individual person can claim from us as his moral right. No one has a moral right to our generosity or beneficence because we are not morally bound to practice those virtues toward any given individual. And it will be found with respect to this as to every correct definition that the instances which seem to conflict with it are those which most confirm it. For if a moralist attempts, as some have done, to make out that mankind generally, though not any given individual, have a right to all the good we can do them, he at once, by that thesis, includes generosity and beneficence within the category of justice. He is obliged to say that our utmost exertions are *due* to our fellow creatures, thus assimilating them to a debt; or that nothing less can be a sufficient *return* for what society does for us, thus classing the case as one of gratitude; both of which are acknowledged cases of justice, and not of the virtue of beneficence; and whoever does not place the distinction between justice and morality in general, where we have now placed it, will be found to make no distinction between them at all, but to merge all morality in justice.

Having thus endeavored to determine the distinctive elements which enter into the composition of the idea of justice, we are ready to enter on the inquiry whether the feeling which accompanies the idea is attached to it by a special dispensation of nature, or whether it could have grown up, by any known laws, out of the idea itself; and, in particular, whether it can have originated in considerations of general expediency.

I conceive that the sentiment itself does not arise from anything which would commonly or correctly be termed an idea of expediency, but that, though the sentiment does not, whatever is moral in it does.

We have seen that the two essential ingredients in the sentiment of justice are the desire to punish a person who has done harm and the knowledge or belief that there is some definite individual or individuals to whom harm has been done.

Now it appears to me that the desire to punish a person who has done harm to some individual is a spontaneous outgrowth from two sentiments, both in the highest degree natural and which either are or resemble instincts: the impulse of self-defense and the feeling of sympathy.

It is natural to resent and to repel or retaliate any harm done or attempted against ourselves or against those with whom we sympathize. The origin of this sentiment it is not necessary here to discuss. Whether it be an instinct or a result of intelligence, it is, we know, common to all animal nature; for every animal tries to hurt those who have hurt, or who it thinks are about to hurt, itself or its young. Human beings, on this point, only differ from other animals in two particulars. First, in being capable of sympathizing, not solely with their offspring, or, like some of the more noble animals, with some superior animal who is kind to them, but with all human, and even with all sentient, beings; secondly, in having a more developed intelligence, which gives a wider range to the whole of their sentiments, whether self-regarding or sympathetic. By virtue of his superior intelligence, even apart from his superior range of sympathy, a human being is capable of apprehending a community of interest between himself and the human society of which he forms a part, such that any conduct which threatens the security of the society generally is threatening to his own, and calls forth his instinct (if instinct it be) of self-defense. The same superiority of intelligence, joined to the power of sympathizing with human beings generally, enables him to attach himself to the collective idea of his tribe, his country, or mankind in such a manner that any act hurtful to them raises his instinct of sympathy and urges him to resistance.

The sentiment of justice, in that one of its elements which consists of the desire to punish, is thus, I conceive, the natural feeling of retaliation or vengeance, rendered by intellect and sympathy applicable to those injuries, that is, to those hurts, which wound us through, or in common with, society at large. This sentiment, in itself, has nothing moral in it; what is moral is the exclusive subordination of it to the social sympathies, so as to wait on and obey their call. For the natural feeling would make us resent indiscriminately whatever anyone does that is disagreeable to us; but, when moralized by the social feeling, it only acts in the directions conformable to the general good: just persons resenting a hurt to society, though not otherwise a hurt to themselves, and not resenting a hurt to themselves, however painful, unless it be of the kind which society has a common interest with them in the repression of.

It is no objection against this doctrine to say that, when we feel our sentiment of justice outraged, we are not thinking of society at large or of any collective interest, but only of the individual case. It is common enough, certainly, though the reverse of commendable, to feel resentment merely because we have suffered pain; but a person whose resentment is really a moral feeling, that is, who considers whether an act is blamable before he allows himself to resent it—such a person, though he may not say expressly to himself that he is standing up for the interest of society, certainly does feel that he is asserting a rule which is for the benefit of others as well as for his own. If he is not feeling this, if he is regarding the act solely as it affects him individually, he is not consciously just; he is not concerning himself about the justice of his actions. This is admitted even by anti–utilitarian moralists. When Kant (as before remarked) propounds as the fundamental principle of morals, "So act that thy rule of conduct might be adopted as a law by all rational beings," he virtually acknowledges that the interest of mankind collectively, or at least of mankind indiscriminately, must be in the mind of the agent when conscientiously deciding on the morality of the act. Otherwise he uses words without a meaning; for that a rule even of utter selfishness could not *possibly* be adopted by all rational beings—that there is any insuperable obstacle in the nature of things to its adoption—cannot be even plausibly maintained. To give any meaning to Kant's principle, the sense put upon it must be that we ought to shape our conduct by a rule which all rational beings might adopt *with benefit to their collective interest*.

To recapitulate: the idea of justice supposes two things—a rule of conduct and a sentiment which sanctions the rule. The first must be supposed common to all mankind and intended for their good. The other (the sentiment) is a desire that punishment may be suffered by those who infringe the rule. There is involved, in addition, the conception of some definite person who suffers by the infringement, whose rights (to use the expression appropriated to the case) are violated by it. And the sentiment of justice appears to me to be the animal desire to repel or retaliate a hurt or damage to oneself or to those with whom one sympathizes, widened so as to include all persons, by the human capacity of enlarged sympathy and the human conception of intelligent self-interest. From the latter elements the feeling derives its morality; from the former, its peculiar impressiveness and energy of self-assertion.

I have, throughout, treated the idea of a *right* residing in the injured person and violated by the injury, not as a separate element in the composition of the idea and sentiment, but as one of the forms in which the other two elements clothe themselves. These elements are a hurt to some assignable person or persons, on the one hand, and a demand for punishment, on the other. An examination of our own minds, I think, will show that these two things include all that we mean when we speak of violation of a right. When we call anything a person's right, we mean that he has a valid claim on society to protect him in the possession of it, either by the force of law or by that of education and opinion. If he has what we consider a sufficient claim, on whatever account, to have something guaranteed to him by society, we say that he has a right to it. If we desire to prove that anything does not belong to him by right, we think this done as soon as it is admitted that society ought not to take measure for securing it to him, but should leave him to chance or to his own exertions. Thus a person is said to have a right to what he can earn in fair professional competition, because society ought not to allow any other person to hinder him from endeavoring to earn in that manner as much as he can. But he has not a right to three hundred a year, though he may happen to be earning it; because society is not called on to provide that he shall earn that sum. On the contrary, if he owns ten thousand pounds three-percent stock, he *has* a right to three hundred a year because society has come under an obligation to provide him with an income of that amount.

To have a right, then, is, I conceive, to have something which society ought to defend me in the possession of. If the objector goes on to ask why it ought, I can give him no other reason than general utility. If that expression does not seem to convey a sufficient feeling of the strength of the obligation, nor to account for the peculiar energy of the feeling, it is because there goes to the composition of the sentiment, not a rational only but also an animal element—the thirst for retaliation; and this thirst derives its intensity, as well as its moral justification, from the extraordinarily important and impressive kind of utility which is concerned. The interest involved is that of security, to everyone's feelings the most vital of all interests. All other earthly benefits are needed by one person, not needed by another; and many of them can, if necessary, be cheerfully foregone or replaced by something else; but security no human being can possibly do without; on it we depend for all our immunity from evil and for the whole value of all and every good, beyond the passing moment, since nothing but the gratification of the instant could be of any worth to us if we could be deprived of everything the next instant by whoever was momentarily stronger than ourselves. Now this most indispensable of all necessaries, after physical nutriment, cannot be had, unless the machinery for providing it is kept unintermittedly in active play. Our notion, therefore, of the claim we have on our fellow creatures to join in making safe for us the very groundwork of our existence gathers feelings around it so much more intense than those concerned in any of the more common cases of utility that the difference in degree (as is often the case in psychology) becomes a real difference in kind. The claim assumes that character of absoluteness, that apparent infinity and incommensurability with all other considerations which constitute the distinction between the feeling of right and wrong and that of ordinary expediency and inexpediency. The feelings concerned are so powerful, and we count so positively on finding a responsive feeling in others (all being alike interested) that *ought* and *should* grow into *must,* and recognized indispensability becomes a moral necessity, analogous to physical, and often not inferior to it in binding force.

If the preceding analysis, or something resembling it, be not the correct account of the notion of justice—if justice be totally independent of utility, and be a standard *per se,* which the mind can recognize by simple introspection of itself—it is hard to understand why that internal oracle is so ambiguous, and why so many things appear either just or unjust, according to the light in which they are regarded.

We are continually informed that utility is an uncertain standard, which every different person interprets differently, and that there is no safety but in the immutable, ineffaceable, and unmistakable dictates of justice, which carry their evidence in themselves and are independent of the fluctuations of opinion. One would suppose from this that on questions of justice there could be no controversy; that, if we take that for our rule, its application to any given case could leave us in as little doubt as a mathematical demonstration. So far is this from being the fact that there is as fierce difference of opinion, and as much discussion, about what is just as about what is useful to society. Not only have different nations and individuals different notions of justice, but in the mind of one and the same individual, justice is not some one rule, principle, or maxim, but many which do not always coincide in their dictates, and, in choosing between which, he is guided either by some extraneous standard or by his own personal predilections.

For instance, there are some who say that it is unjust to punish anyone for the sake of example to others, that punishment is just only when intended for the good of the sufferer himself. Others maintain the extreme reverse, contending that to punish persons who have attained years of discretion, for their own benefit, is despotism and injustice, since, if the matter at issue is solely their own good, no one has a right to control their own judgment of it; but that they may justly be punished to prevent evil to others, this being the exercise of the legitimate right of self-defense. Mr. Owen, again, affirms that it is unjust to punish at all, for the criminal did not make his own character; his education and the circumstances which surrounded him have made him a criminal, and for these he is not responsible. All these opinions are extremely plausible; and so long as the question is argued as one of justice simply, without going down to the principles which lie under justice and are the source of its authority, I am unable to see how any of these reasoners can be refuted. For in truth every one of the three builds upon rules of justice confessedly true. The first appeals to the acknowledged injustice of singling out an individual and making him a sacrifice, without his consent, for other people's benefit. The second relies on the acknowledged justice of self-defense and the admitted injustice of forcing one person to conform to another's notions of what constitutes his good. The Owenite invokes the admitted principle that it is unjust to punish anyone for what he cannot help. Each is triumphant so long as he is not compelled to take into consideration any other maxims of justice than the one he has selected; but as soon as their several maxims are brought face to face, each disputant seems to have exactly as much to say for himself as the others. No one of them can carry out his own notion of justice without trampling upon another equally binding. These are difficulties; they have always been felt to be such; and many devices have been invented to turn rather than to overcome them. As a refuge from the last of the three, men imagined what they called the freedom of the will— fancying that they could not justify punishing a man whose will is in a thoroughly hateful state unless it be supposed to have come into that state through no influence of anterior circumstances. To escape from the other difficulties, a favorite contrivance has been the fiction of a contract whereby at some unknown period all the members of society engaged to obey the laws and consented to be punished for any disobedience to them, thereby giving to their legislators the right, which it is assumed they would not otherwise have had, of punishing them, either for their own good or for that of society. This happy thought was considered to get rid of the whole difficulty and to legitimate the infliction of punishment, in virtue of another received maxim of justice, *volenti non fit injuria*—that is not unjust which is done with the consent of the person who is supposed to be hurt by it. I need hardly remark that, even if the consent were not mere fiction, this maxim is not superior in authority to the others which it is brought in to supersede. It is, on the contrary, an instructive specimen of the loose and irregular manner in which supposed principles of justice grow up. This particular one evidently came into use as a help to the coarse exigencies of courts of law, which are sometimes obliged to be content with very uncertain presumptions, on account of the greater evils which would often arise from any attempt on their part to cut finer. But even courts of law are not able to adhere consistently to the maxim, for they allow voluntary engagements to be set aside on the ground of fraud, and sometimes on that of mere mistake or misinformation.

Again, when the legitimacy of inflicting punishment is admitted, how many conflicting conceptions of justice come to light in discussing the proper apportionment of punishments to offenses. No rule on the subject recommends itself so strongly to the primitive and spontaneous sentiment of justice as the *lex talionis,* an eye for an eye and a tooth for a tooth. Though this principle of the Jewish and of the Mohammedan law has been generally abandoned in Europe as a practical maxim, there is, I suspect, in most minds, a secret hankering after it; and when retribution accidentally falls on an offender in that precise shape, the general feeling of satisfaction evinced bears witness how natural is the sentiment to which this repayment in kind is acceptable. With many, the test of justice in penal infliction is that the punishment should be proportioned to the offense, meaning that it should be exactly measured by the moral guilt of the culprit (whatever be their standard for measuring moral guilt), the consideration what amount of punishment is necessary to deter from the offense having nothing to do with the question of justice, in their estimation; while there are others to whom that consideration is all in all, who maintain that it is not just, at least for man, to inflict on a fellow creature, whatever may be his offenses, any amount of suffering beyond the least that will suffice to prevent him from repeating, and others from imitating, his misconduct.

To take another example from a subject already once referred to. In cooperative industrial associations, is it just or not that talent or skill should give a title to superior remuneration? On the negative side of the question it is argued that whoever does the best he can deserves equally well, and ought not in justice to be put in a position of inferiority for no fault of his own; that superior abilities have already advantages more than enough, in the admiration they excite, the personal influence they command, and the internal sources of satisfaction attending them, without adding to these a superior share of the world's goods; and that society is bound in justice rather to make compensation to the less favored for this unmerited inequality of advantages than to aggravate it. On the contrary side it is contended that society receives more from the efficient laborer; that, his services being more useful, society owes him a larger return for them; that a greater share of the joint result is actually his work, and not to allow his claim to it is a kind of robbery; that, if he is only to receive as much as others, he can only be justly required to produce as much, and to give a smaller amount of time and exertion, proportioned to his superior efficiency. Who shall decide between these appeals to conflicting principles of justice? Justice has in this case two sides to it, which it is impossible to bring into harmony, and the two disputants have chosen opposite sides; the one looks to what it is just that the individual should receive, the other to what it is just that the community should give. Each, from his own point of view, is unanswerable; and any choice between them, on grounds of justice, must be perfectly arbitrary. Social utility alone can decide the preference.

How many, again, and how irreconcilable are the standards of justice to which reference is made in discussing the repartition of taxation. One opinion is that payment to the state should be in numerical proportion to pecuniary means. Others think that justice dictates what they term graduated taxation—taking a higher percentage from those who have more to spare. In point of natural justice a strong case might be made for disregarding means altogether, and taking the same absolute sum (whenever it could be got) from everyone; as the subscribers to a mess or to a club all pay the same sum for the same privileges, whether they can all equally afford it or not. Since the protection (it might be said) of law and government is afforded to and is equally required by all, there is no injustice in making all buy it at the same price. It is reckoned justice, not injustice, that a dealer should charge to all customers the same price for the same article, not a price varying according to their means of payment. This doctrine, as applied to taxation, finds no advocates because it conflicts so strongly with man's feelings of humanity and of social expediency; but the principle of justice which it invokes is as true and as binding as those which can be appealed to against it. Accordingly it exerts a tacit influence on the line of defense employed for other modes of assessing taxation. People feel obliged to argue that the state does more for the rich man than for the poor, as a justification for its taking more from them, though this is in reality not true, for the rich would be far better able to protect themselves, in the absence of law or government, than the poor, and indeed would probably be successful in converting the poor into their slaves. Others, again, so far defer to the same conception of justice as to maintain that all should pay an equal capitation tax for the protection of their persons (these being of equal value to all), and an unequal tax for the protection of their property, which is unequal. To this others reply that the all of one man is as valuable to him as the all of another. From these confusions there is no other mode of extrication than the utilitarian.

Is, then, the difference between the just and the expedient a merely imaginary distinction? Have mankind been under a delusion in thinking that justice is a more sacred thing than policy, and that the latter ought only to be listened to after the former has been satisfied? By no means. The exposition we have given of the nature and origin of the sentiment recognizes a real distinction; and no one of those who profess the most sublime contempt for the consequences of actions as an element in their morality attaches more importance to the distinction than I do. While I dispute the pretensions of any theory which sets up an imaginary standard of justice not grounded on utility, I account the justice which is grounded on utility to be the chief part, and incomparably the most sacred and binding part, of all morality. Justice is a name for certain classes of moral rules which concern the essentials of human well-being more nearly, and are therefore of more absolute obligation, than any other rules for the guidance of life; and the notion which we have found to be of the essence of the idea of justice—that of a right residing in an individual—implies and testifies to this more binding obligation.

The moral rules which forbid mankind to hurt one another (in which we must never forget to include a wrongful interference with each other's freedom) are more vital to human well-being than any maxims, however important, which only point out the best mode of managing some department of human affairs. They have also the peculiarity that they are the main element in determining the whole of the social feelings of mankind. It is their observance which alone preserves peace among human beings; if obedience to them were not the rule, and disobedience the exception, everyone would see in everyone else an enemy against whom he must be perpetually guarding himself. What is hardly less important, these are the precepts which mankind have the strongest and the most direct inducements for impressing upon one another. By merely giving to each other prudential instruction or exhortation, they may gain, or think they gain, nothing; in inculcating on each other the duty of positive beneficence, they have an unmistakable interest, but far less in degree; a person may possibly not need the benefits of others, but he always needs that they should not do him hurt. Thus the moralities which protect every individual from being harmed by others, either directly or by being hindered in his freedom of pursuing his own good, are at once those which he himself has most at heart and those which he has the strongest interest in publishing and enforcing by word and deed. It is by a person's observance of these that his fitness to exist as one of the fellowship of human beings is tested and decided; for on that depends his being a nuisance or not to those with whom he is in contact. Now it is these moralities primarily which compose the obligation of justice. The most marked cases of injustice, and those which give the tone to the feeling of repugnance which characterizes the sentiment, are acts of wrongful aggression or wrongful exercise of power over someone; the next are those which consist in wrongfully withholding from him something which is his due—in both cases inflicting on him a positive hurt, either in the form of direct suffering or of the privation of some good which he had reasonable ground, either of a physical or of a social kind, for counting upon.

The same powerful motives which command the observance of these primary moralities enjoin the punishment of those who violate them; and as the impulses of self-defense, of defense of others, and of vengeance are all called forth against such persons, retribution, or evil for evil, becomes closely connected with the sentiment of justice, and is universally included in the idea. Good for good is also one of the dictates of justice; and this, though its social utility is evident, and though it carries with it a natural human feeling, has not at first sight that obvious connection with hurt or injury which, existing in the most elementary cases of just and unjust, is the source of the characteristic intensity of the sentiment. But the connection, though less obvious, is not less real. He who accepts benefits and denies a return of them when needed inflicts a real hurt by disappointing one of the most natural and reasonable of expectations, and one which he must at least tacitly have encouraged, otherwise the benefits would seldom have been conferred. The important rank, among human evils and wrongs, of the disappointment of expectation is shown in the fact that it constitutes the principal criminality of two such highly immoral acts as a breach of friendship and a breach of promise. Few hurts which human beings can sustain are greater, and none wound more, than when that on which they habitually and with full assurance relied fails them in the hour of need; and few wrongs are greater than this mere withholding of good; none excite more resentment, either in the person suffering or in a sympathizing spectator. The principle, therefore, of giving to each what they deserve, that is, good for good as well as evil for evil, is not only included within the idea of justice as we have defined it, but is a proper object of that intensity of sentiment which places the just human estimation above the simply expedient.

Most of the maxims of justice current in the world, and commonly appealed to in its transactions, are simply instrumental to carrying into effect the principles of justice which we have now spoken of. That a person is only responsible for what he has done voluntarily, or could voluntarily have avoided, that it is unjust to condemn any person unheard; that the punishment ought to be proportioned to the offense, and the like, are maxims intended to prevent the just principle of evil for evil from being perverted to the infliction of evil without that justification. The greater part of these common maxims have come into use from the practice of courts of justice, which have been naturally led to a more complete recognition and elaboration than was likely to suggest itself to others, of the rules necessary to enable them to fulfill their double function—of inflicting punishment when due, and of awarding to each person his right.

That first of judicial virtues, impartiality, is an obligation of justice, partly for the reason last mentioned, as being a necessary condition of the fulfillment of other obligations of justice. But this is not the only source of the exalted rank, among human obligations, of those maxims of equality and impartiality, which, both in popular estimation and in that of the most enlightened, are included among the precepts of justice. In one point of view, they may be considered as corollaries from the principles already laid down. If it is a duty to do to each according to his deserts, returning good for good, as well as repressing evil by evil, it necessarily follows that we should treat all equally well (when no higher duty forbids) who have deserved equally well of *us,* and that society should treat all equally well who have deserved equally well of *it,* that is, who have deserved equally well absolutely. This is the highest abstract standard of social and distributive justice, toward which all institutions and the efforts of all virtuous citizens should be made in the utmost possible degree to converge. But this great moral duty rests upon a still deeper foundation, being a direct emanation from the first principle of morals, and not a mere logical corollary from secondary or derivative doctrines. It is involved in the very meaning of utility, or the greatest happiness principle. That principle is a mere form of words without rational signification unless one person's happiness, supposed equal in degree (with the proper allowance made for kind), is counted for exactly as much as another's. Those conditions being supplied, Bentham's dictum "everybody to count for one, nobody for more than one," might be written under the principle of utility as an explanatory commentary.[2] The equal claim of everybody to happiness, in the estimation of the moralist and of the legislator, involves an equal claim to all the means of happiness except in so far as the inevitable conditions of human life and the general interest in which that of every individual is included set limits to the maxim; and those limits ought to be strictly construed. As every other maxim of justice, so this is by no means applied or held applicable universally; on the contrary, as I have already remarked, it bends to every person's ideas of social expediency. But in whatever case it is deemed applicable at all, it is held to be the dictate of justice. All persons are deemed to have a *right* to equality of treatment, except when some recognized social expediency requires the reverse. And hence all social inequalities which have ceased to be considered expedient assume the character, not of simple inexpediency, but of injustice, and appear so tyrannical that people are apt to wonder how they ever could have been tolerated—forgetful that they themselves, perhaps, tolerate other inequalities under an equally mistaken notion of expediency, the correction of which would make that which they approve seem quite as monstrous as what they have at last learned to condemn. The entire history of social improvement has been a series of transitions by which one custom or institution after another, from being a supposed primary necessity of social existence, has passed into the rank of a universally stigmatized injustice and tyranny. So it has been with the distinctions of slaves and freemen, nobles and serfs, patricians and plebeians; and so it will be, and in part already is, with the aristocracies of color, race, and sex.

It appears from what has been said that justice is a name for certain moral requirements which, regarded collectively, stand higher in the scale of social utility, and are therefore of more paramount obligation, than any others, though particular cases may occur in which some other social duty is so important as to overrule any one of the general maxims of justice. Thus, to save a life, it may not only be allowable, but a duty, to steal or take by force the necessary food or medicine, or to kidnap and compel to officiate the only qualified medical practitioner. In such cases, as we do not call anything justice which is not a virtue, we usually say, not that justice must give way to some other moral principle, but that what is just in ordinary cases is, by reason of that other principle, not just in the particular case. By this useful accommodation of language, the character of indefeasibility attributed to justice is kept up, and we are saved from the necessity of maintaining that there can be laudable injustice.

The considerations which have now been adduced resolve, I conceive, the only real difficulty in the utilitarian theory of morals. It has always been evident that all cases of justice are also cases of expediency; the difference is in the peculiar sentiment which attaches to the former, as contradistinguished from the latter. If this characteristic sentiment has been sufficiently accounted for; if there is no necessity to assume for it any peculiarity of origin; if it is simply the natural feeling of resentment, moralized by being made coextensive with the demands of social good; and if this feeling not only does but ought to exist in all the classes of cases to which the idea of justice corresponds—that idea no longer presents itself as a stumbling block to the utilitarian ethics. Justice remains the appropriate name for certain social utilities which are vastly more important, and therefore more absolute and imperative, than any others are as a class (though not more so than others may be in particular cases); and which, therefore, ought to be, as well as naturally are, guarded by a sentiment, not only different in degree, but also in kind; distinguished from the milder feeling which attaches to the mere idea of promoting human pleasure or convenience at once by the more definite nature of its commands and by the sterner character of its sanctions.

NOTES

CHAPTER II

[1]The author of this essay has reason for believing himself to be the first person who brought the word "utilitarian" into use. He did not invent it, but adopted it from a passing expression in Mr. Galt's *Annals of the Parish*. After using it as a designation for several years, he and others abandoned it from a growing dislike to anything resembling a badge or watchword of sectarian distinction. But as a name for one single opinion, not a set of opinions—to denote the recognition of utility as a standard, not any particular way of applying it—the term supplies a want in

the language, and offers, in many cases, a convenient mode of avoiding tiresome circumlocutions.

[2]An opponent, whose intellectual and moral fairness it is a pleasure to acknowledge (the Rev. J. Llewellyn Davies), has objected to this passage, saying, "Surely the rightness or wrongness of saving a man from drowning does depend very much upon the motive with which it is done. Suppose that a tyrant, when his enemy jumped into the sea to escape from him, saved him from drowning simply in order that he might inflict upon him more exquisite tortures, would it tend to clearness to speak of that rescue as 'a morally right action'? Or suppose again, according to one of the stock illustrations of ethical inquiries, that a man betrayed a trust received from a friend, because the discharge of it would fatally injure that friend himself or someone belonging to him, would utilitarianism compel one to call the betrayal 'a crime' as much as if it had been done from the meanest motive?"

I submit that he who saves another from drowning in order to kill him by torture afterwards does not differ only in motive from him who does the same thing from duty or benevolence; the act itself is different. The rescue of the man is, in the case supposed, only the necessary first step of an act far more atrocious than leaving him to drown would have been. Had Mr. Davies said, "The rightness or wrongness of saving a man from drowning does depend very much"—not upon the motive, but—"upon the *intention*," no utilitarian would have differed from him. Mr. Davies, by an oversight too common not to be quite venial, has in this case confounded the very different ideas of Motive and Intention. There is no point which utilitarian thinkers (and Bentham preeminently) have taken more pains to illustrate than this. The morality of the action depends entirely upon the intention—that is, upon what the agent *wills to do*. But the motive, that is, the feeling which makes him will so to do, if it makes no difference in the act, makes none in the morality: though it makes a great difference in our moral estimation of the agent, especially if it indicates a good or a bad habitual *disposition*—a bent of character from which useful, or from which hurtful actions are likely to arise.

CHAPTER V

[1]See this point enforced and illustrated by Professor Bain, in an admirable chapter (entitled "The Ethical Emotions, or the Moral Sense"), of the second of the two treatises composing his elaborate and profound work on the Mind.

[2]This implication, in the first principle of the utilitarian scheme, of perfect impartiality between persons is regarded by Mr. Herbert Spencer (in his *Social Statics*) as a disproof of the pretensions of utility to be a sufficient guide to right; since (he says) the principle of utility presupposes the anterior principle that everybody has an equal right to happiness. It may be more correctly described as supposing that equal amounts of happiness are equally desirable, whether felt by the same or different persons. This, however, is not a *pre*supposition, not a premise needful to support the principle of utility, but the very principle itself; for what is the principle of utility if it be not that "happiness" and "desirable" are synonymous terms? If there is any anterior principle implied, it can be no other than this, that the

truths of arithmetic are applicable to the valuation of happiness, as of all other measurable quantities.

[Mr. Herbert Spencer, in a private communication on the subject of the preceding note, objects to being considered an opponent of utilitarianism and states that he regards happiness as the ultimate end of morality; but deems that end only partially attainable by empirical generalizations from the observed results of conduct, and completely attainable only by deducing, from the laws of life and the conditions of existence, what kinds of action necessarily tend to produce happiness, and what kinds to produce unhappiness. With the exception of the word "necessarily," I have no dissent to express from this doctrine; and (omitting that word) I am not aware that any modern advocate of utilitarianism is of a different opinion. Bentham, certainly, to whom in the *Social Statics* Mr. Spencer particularly referred, is, least of all writers, chargeable with unwillingness to deduce the effect of actions on happiness from the laws of human nature and the universal conditions of human life. The common charge against him is of relying too exclusively upon such deductions and declining altogether to be bound by the generalizations from specific experience which Mr. Spencer thinks that utilitarians generally confine themselves to. My own opinion (and, as I collect, Mr. Spencer's) is that in ethics, as in all other branches of scientific study, the consilience of the results of both these processes, each corroborating and verifying the other, is requisite to give to any general proposition the kind and degree of evidence which constitutes scientific proof.]

INDEX

Mill's

On Liberty

The grand, leading principle, towards which every argument
unfolded in these pages directly converges, is the absolute and
essential importance of human development in its richest diversity.

—Wilhelm von Humboldt,
Sphere and Duties of Government

To the beloved and deplored memory of her who was the inspirer, and in part the author, of all that is best in my writings—the friend and wife whose exalted sense of truth and right was my strongest incitement, and whose approbation was my chief reward—I dedicate this volume. Like all that I have written for many years, it belongs as much to her as to me; but the work as it stands has had, in a very insufficient degree, the inestimable advantage of her revision; some of the most important portions having been reserved for a more careful re-examination, which they are now never destined to receive. Were I but capable of interpreting to the world one half the great thoughts and noble feelings which are buried in her grave, I should be the medium of a greater benefit to it, than is ever likely to arise from anything that I can write, unprompted and unassisted by her all but unrivaled wisdom.

On Liberty

Chapter I
Introductory

The subject of this essay is not the so-called "liberty of the will," so unfortunately opposed to the misnamed doctrine of philosophical necessity; but civil, or social liberty: the nature and limits of the power which can be legitimately exercised by society over the individual. A question seldom stated, and hardly ever discussed in general terms, but which profoundly influences the practical controversies of the age by its latent presence, and is likely soon to make itself recognized as the vital question of the future. It is so far from being new that, in a certain sense, it has divided mankind almost from the remotest ages; but in the stage of progress into which the more civilized portions of the species have now entered, it presents itself under new conditions and requires a different and more fundamental treatment.

The struggle between liberty and authority is the most conspicuous feature in the portions of history with which we are earliest familiar, particularly in that of Greece, Rome, and England. But in old times this contest was between subjects, or some classes of subjects, and the government. By liberty was meant protection against the tyranny of the political rulers. The rulers were conceived (except in some of the popular governments of Greece) as in a necessarily antagonistic position to the people whom they ruled. They consisted of a governing One, or a governing tribe or caste, who derived their authority from inheritance or conquest, who, at all events, did not hold it at the pleasure of the governed, and whose supremacy men did not venture, perhaps did not desire, to contest, whatever precautions might be taken against its oppressive exercise. Their power was regarded as necessary, but also as highly dangerous; as a weapon which they would attempt to use against their subjects, no less than against external enemies. To prevent the weaker members of the community from being preyed upon by innumerable vultures, it was needful that there should be an animal of prey stronger than the rest, commissioned to keep them down. But as the king of the vultures would be no less bent upon preying on the flock than any of the minor harpies, it was indispensable to be in a perpetual attitude of defense against his beak and claws. The aim, therefore, of patriots was to set limits to the power which the ruler should be suffered to exercise over the community; and this limitation was what they meant by liberty. It was attempted in two ways. First, by obtaining a recognition of certain immunities, called political liberties or rights, which it was to be regarded as a breach of duty in the ruler to infringe, and which if he did infringe, specific resistance or general rebellion was held to be justifiable. A second, and generally a later, expedient was the establishment of constitutional checks by which the consent of the community, or of a body of some sort, supposed to represent its interests, was made a necessary condition to some of the more important acts of the governing power. To the first of these mode of limitation, the ruling power, in most European countries, was compelled, more or less, to submit. It was not so with the second; and, to attain this, or, when already in some degree possessed, to attain it more completely, became everywhere the principal object of the lovers of liberty. And so long as mankind were content to combat one enemy by another, and to be ruled by a master on condition of being guaranteed more or less efficaciously against his tyranny, they did not carry their aspirations beyond this point.

A time, however, came, in the progress of human affairs, when men ceased to think it a necessity of nature that their governors should be an independent power opposed in interest to themselves. It appeared to them much better that the various magistrates of the state should be their tenants or delegates, revocable at their pleasure. In that way alone, it seemed, could they have complete security that the powers of government would never be abused to their disadvantage. By degrees this new demand for elective and temporary rulers became the prominent object of the exertions of the popular party wherever any such party existed, and superseded, to a considerable extent, the previous efforts to limit the power of rulers. As the struggle proceeded for making the ruling power emanate from the periodical choice of the ruled, some persons began to think that too much importance had been attached to the limitation of the power itself. *That* (it might seem) was a resource against rulers whose interests were habitually opposed to those of the people. What was now wanted was that the rulers should be identified with the people, that their interest and will should be the interest and will of the nation. The nation did not need to be protected against its own will. There was no fear of its tyrannizing over itself. Let the rulers be effectually responsible to it, promptly removable by it, and it could afford to trust them with power of which it could itself dictate the use to be made. Their power was but the nation's own power, concentrated and in a form convenient for exercise. This mode of thought, or rather perhaps of feeling, was common among the last generation of European liberalism, in the Continental section of which it still apparently predominates. Those who admit any limit to what a government may do, except in the case of such governments as they think ought not to exist, stand out as brilliant exceptions among the political thinkers of the Continent. A similar tone of sentiment might by this time have been prevalent in our own country if the circumstances which for a time encouraged it had continued unaltered.

But, in political and philosophical theories as well as in persons, success discloses faults and infirmities which failure might have concealed from observation. The notion that the people have no need to limit their power over themselves might seem axiomatic, when popular government was a thing only dreamed about, or read of as having existed at some distant period of the past. Neither was that notion necessarily disturbed by such temporary aberrations as those of the French Revolution, the worst of which were the work of a usurping few, and which, in any case, belonged, not to the permanent working of popular institutions, but to a sudden and convulsive outbreak against monarchical and aristocratic despotism. In time, however, a democratic republic came to occupy a large portion of the earth's surface and made itself felt as one of the most powerful members of the community of nations, and elective and responsible government became subject to the observations and criticisms which wait upon a great existing fact. It was now perceived that such phrases as "self-government," and "the power of the people over themselves," do not express the true state of the case. The "people" who exercise the power are not always the same people with those over whom it is exercised; and the "self-government" spoken of is not the government of each by himself, but of each by all the rest. The will of the people, moreover, practically means the will of the most numerous or the most active part of the people—the majority, or those who succeed in making themselves accepted as the majority; the people, consequently, *may* desire to oppress a part of their number, and precautions are as much needed against this as against any other abuse of power. The limitation, therefore, of the power of government over individuals loses none of its importance when the holders of power are regularly accountable to the community, that is, to the strongest party therein. This view of things, recommending itself equally to the intelligence of thinkers and to the inclination of those important classes in European society to whose real or supposed interests democracy is adverse, has had no difficulty in establishing itself, and in political speculations "the tyranny of the majority" is now generally included among the evils against which society requires to be on its guard.

Like other tyrannies, the tyranny of the majority was at first, and is still vulgarly, held in dread, chiefly as operating through the acts of the public authorities. But reflecting persons perceived that when society is itself the tyrant—society collectively over the separate individuals who compose it—its means of tyrannizing are not restricted to the acts which it may do by the hands of its political functionaries. Society can and does execute its own mandates; and if it issues wrong mandates instead of right, or any mandates at all in things with which it ought not to meddle, it practices a social tyranny more formidable than many kinds of political oppression, since, though not usually upheld by such extreme penalties, it leaves fewer means of escape, penetrating much more deeply into the details of life, and enslaving the soul itself. Protection, therefore, against the tyranny of the magistrate is not enough; there needs protection also against the tyranny of the prevailing opinion and feeling, against the tendency of society to impose, by other means than, civil penalties, its own ideas and practices as rules of conduct on those who dissent from them; to fetter the development and, if possible, prevent the formation of any individuality not in harmony with its ways, and compel all characters to fashion themselves upon the model of its own. There is a limit to the legitimate interference of collective opinion with individual independence; and to find that limit, and maintain it against encroachment, is as indispensable to a good condition of human affairs as protection against political despotism.

But though this proposition is not likely to be contested in general terms, the practical question where to place the limit—how to make the fitting adjustment between individual independence and social control—is a subject on which nearly everything remains to be done. All that makes existence valuable to anyone depends on the enforcement of restraints upon the actions of other people. Some rules of conduct, therefore, must be imposed—by law in the first place, and by opinion on many things which are not fit subjects for the operation of law. What these rules should be is the principal question in human affairs; but if we except a few of the most obvious cases, it is one of those which least progress has been made in resolving. No two ages, and scarcely any two countries, have decided it alike; and the decision of one age or country is a wonder to another. Yet the people of any given age and country no more suspect any difficulty in it than if it were a subject on which mankind had always been agreed. The rules which obtain among themselves appear to them self-evident and self-justifying. This all but universal illusion is one of the examples of the magical influence of custom, which is not only, as the proverb says, a second nature but is continually mistaken for the first. The effect of custom, in preventing any misgiving respecting the rules of conduct which mankind impose on one another, is all the more complete because the subject is one on which it is not generally considered necessary that reasons should be given, either by one person to others or by each to himself. People are accustomed to believe, and have been encouraged in the belief by some who aspire to the character of philosophers, that their feelings on subjects of this nature are better than reasons and render reasons unnecessary. The practical principle which guides them to their opinions on the regulation of human conduct is the feeling in each person's mind that everybody should be required to act as he, and those with whom he sympathizes, would like them to act. No one, indeed, acknowledges to himself that his standard of judgment is his own liking; but an opinion on a point of conduct, not supported by reasons, can only count as one person's preference; and if the reasons, when given, are a mere appeal to a similar preference felt by other people, it is still only many people's liking instead of one. To an ordinary man, however, his own preference, thus supported, is not only a perfectly satisfactory reason but the only one he generally has for any of his notions of morality, taste, or propriety, which are not expressly written in his religious creed, and his chief guide in the interpretation even of that. Men's opinions, accordingly, on what is laudable or blamable are affected by all the multifarious causes which influence their wishes in regard to the conduct of others, and which are as numerous as those which determine their wishes on any other subject. Sometimes their reason; at other times their prejudices or superstitions; often their social affections, not seldom their antisocial ones, their envy or jealousy, their arrogance or contemptuousness; but most commonly their desires or fears for themselves—their legitimate or illegitimate self-interest. Wherever there is an ascendant class, a large portion of the morality of the country emanates from its class interests and its feelings of class superiority. The morality between Spartans and Helots, between planters and Negroes, between princes and subjects, between nobles and roturiers, between men and women has been for the most part the creation of these class interests and feelings; and the sentiments thus generated react in turn upon the moral feelings of the members of the ascendant class, in their relations among themselves. Where, on the other hand, a class, formerly ascendant, has lost its ascendancy, or where its ascendancy is unpopular, the prevailing moral sentiments frequently bear the impress of an impatient dislike of superiority. Another grand determining principle of the rules of conduct, both in act and forbearance, which have been enforced by law or opinion, has been the servility of mankind toward the supposed preferences or aversions of their temporal masters or of their gods. This servility, though essentially selfish, is not hypocrisy; it gives rise to perfectly genuine sentiments of abhorrence; it made men burn magicians and heretics. Among so many baser influences, the general and obvious interests of society have, of course, had a share, and a large one, in the direction of the moral sentiments; less, however, as a matter of reason, and on their own account, than as a consequence of the sympathies and antipathies which grew out of them; and sympathies and antipathies which had little or nothing to do with the interests of society have made themselves felt in the establishment of moralities with quite as great force.

The likings and dislikings of society, or of some powerful portion of it, are thus the main thing which has practically determined the rules laid down for general observance, under the penalties of law or opinion. And in general, those who have been in advance of society in thought and feeling have left this condition of things unassailed in principle, however they may have come into conflict with it in some of its details. They have occupied themselves rather in inquiring what things society ought to like or dislike than in questioning whether its likings or dislikings should be a law to individuals. They preferred endeavoring to alter the feelings of mankind on the particular points on which they were themselves heretical rather than make common cause in defense of freedom with heretics generally. The only case in which the higher ground has been taken on principle and maintained with consistency, by any but an individual here and there, is that of religious belief: a case instructive in many ways, and not least so as forming a most striking instance of the fallibility of what is called the moral sense; for the *odium theologicum*, in a sincere bigot, is one of the most unequivocal cases of moral feeling. Those who first broke the yoke of what called itself the Universal Church were in general as little willing to permit difference of religious opinion as that church itself. But when the heat of the conflict was over, without giving a complete victory to any party, and each church or sect was reduced to limit its hopes to retaining possession of the ground it already occupied, minorities, seeing that they had no chance of becoming majorities, were under the necessity of pleading to those whom they could not convert for permission to differ.

It is accordingly on this battlefield, almost solely, that the rights of the individual against society have been asserted on broad grounds of principle, and the claim of society to exercise authority over dissentients openly controverted. The great writers to whom the world owes what religious liberty it possesses have mostly asserted freedom of conscience as an indefeasible right, and denied absolutely that a human being is accountable to others for his religious belief. Yet so natural to mankind is intolerance in whatever they really care about that religious freedom has hardly anywhere been practically realized, except where religious indifference, which dislikes to have its peace disturbed by theological quarrels, has added its weight to the scale. In the minds of almost all religious persons, even in the most tolerant countries, the duty of toleration is admitted with tacit reserves. One person will bear with dissent in matters of church government, but not of dogma; another can tolerate everybody, short of a Papist or a Unitarian; another, everyone who believes in revealed religion; a few extend their charity a little further, but stop at the belief in a God and in a future state. Wherever the sentiment of the majority is still genuine and intense, it is found to have abated little of its claim to be obeyed.

In England, from the peculiar circumstances of our political history, though the yoke of opinion is perhaps heavier, that of law is lighter than in most other countries of Europe; and there is considerable jealousy of direct interference by the legislative or the executive power with private conduct, not so much from any just regard for the independence of the individual as from the still subsisting habit of looking on the government as representing an opposite interest to the public. The majority have not yet learned to feel the power of the government their power, or its opinions their opinions. When they do so, individual liberty will probably be as much exposed to invasion from the government as it already is from public opinion. But, as yet, there is a considerable amount of feeling ready to be called forth against any attempt of the law to control individuals in things in which they have not hitherto been accustomed to be controlled by it; and this with very little discrimination as to whether the matter is, or is not, within the legitimate sphere of legal control; insomuch that the feeling, highly salutary on the whole, is perhaps quite as often misplaced as well grounded in the particular instances of its application. There is, in fact, no recognized principle by which the propriety or impropriety of government interference is customarily tested. People decide according to their personal preferences. Some, whenever they see any good to be done, or evil to be remedied, would willingly instigate the government to undertake the business, while others prefer to bear almost any amount of social evil rather than add one to the departments of human interests amenable to governmental control. And men range themselves on one or the other side in any particular case, according to this general direction of their sentiments, or according to the degree of interest which they feel in the particular thing which it is proposed that the government should do, or according to the belief they entertain that the government would, or would not, do it in the manner they prefer; but very rarely on account of any opinion to which they consistently adhere, as to what things are fit to be done by a government. And it seems to me that in consequence of this absence of rule or principle, one side is at present as often wrong as the other; the interference of government is, with about equal frequency, improperly invoked and improperly condemned.

The object of this essay is to assert one very simple principle, as entitled to govern absolutely the dealings of society with the individual in the way of compulsion and control, whether the means used be physical force in the form of legal penalties or the moral coercion of public opinion. That principle is that the sole end for which mankind are warranted, individually or collectively, in interfering with the liberty of action of any of their number is self-protection. That the only purpose for which power can be rightfully exercised over any member of a civilized community, against his will, is to prevent harm to others. His own good, either physical or moral, is not a sufficient warrant. He cannot rightfully be compelled to do or forbear because it will be better for him to do so, because it will make him happier, because, in the opinions of others, to do so would be wise or even right. These are good reasons for remonstrating with him, or reasoning with him, or persuading him, or entreating him, but not for compelling him or visiting him with any evil in case he do otherwise. To justify that, the conduct from which it is desired to deter him must be calculated to produce evil to someone else. The only part of the conduct of anyone for which he is amenable to society is that which concerns others. In the part which merely concerns himself, his independence is, of right, absolute. Over himself, over his own body and mind, the individual is sovereign.

It is, perhaps, hardly necessary to say that this doctrine is meant to apply only to human beings in the maturity of their faculties. We are not speaking of children or of young persons below the age which the law may fix as that of manhood or womanhood. Those who are still in a state to require being taken care of by others must be protected against their own actions as well as against external injury. For the same reason we may leave out of consideration those backward states of society in which the race itself may be considered as in its nonage. The early difficulties in the way of spontaneous progress are so great that there is seldom any choice of means for overcoming them; and a ruler full of the spirit of improvement is warranted in the use of any expedients that will attain an end perhaps otherwise unattainable. Despotism is a legitimate mode of government in dealing with barbarians, provided the end be their improvement and the means justified by actually effecting that end. Liberty, as a principle, has no application to any state of things anterior to the time when mankind have become capable of being improved by free and equal discussion. Until then, there is nothing for them but implicit obedience to an Akbar or a Charlemagne if they are so fortunate as to find one. But as soon as mankind have attained the capacity of being guided to their own improvement by conviction or persuasion (a period long since reached in all nations with whom we need here concern ourselves), compulsion, either in the direct form or in that of pains and penalties for noncompliance, is no longer admissible as a means to their own good, and justifiable only for the security of others.

It is proper to state that I forego any advantage which could be derived to my argument from the idea of abstract right as a thing independent of utility. I regard utility as the ultimate appeal on all ethical questions; but it must be utility in the largest sense, grounded on the permanent interests of man as a progressive being. Those interests, I contend, authorize the subjection of individual spontaneity to external control only in respect to those actions of each which concern the interest of other people. If anyone does an act hurtful to others, there is a *prima facie* case for punishing him by law or, where legal penalties are not safely applicable, by general disapprobation. There are also many positive acts for the benefit of others which he may rightfully be compelled to perform, such as to give evidence in a court of justice, to bear his fair share in the common defense or in any other joint work necessary to the interest of the society of which he enjoys the protection, and to perform certain acts of individual beneficence, such as saving a fellow creature's life or interposing to protect the defenseless against ill usage—things which whenever it is obviously a man's duty to do he may rightfully be made responsible to society for not doing. A person may cause evil to others not only by his actions but by his inaction, and in either case he is justly accountable to them for the injury. The latter case, it is true, requires a much more cautious exercise of compulsion than the former. To make anyone answerable for doing evil to others is the rule; to make him answerable for not preventing evil is, comparatively speaking, the exception. Yet there are many cases clear enough and grave enough to justify that exception. In all things which regard the external relations of the individual, he is *de jure* amenable to those whose interests are concerned, and, if need be, to society as their protector. There are often good reasons for not holding him to the responsibility; but these reasons must arise from the special expediencies of the case: either because it is a kind of case in which he is on the whole likely to act better when left to his own discretion than when controlled in any way in which society have it in their power to control him; or because the attempt to exercise control would produce other evils, greater than those which it would prevent. When such reasons as these preclude the enforcement of responsibility, the conscience of the agent himself should step into the vacant judgment seat and protect those interests of others which have no external protection; judging himself all the more rigidly, because the case does not admit of his being made accountable to the judgment of his fellow creatures.

But there is a sphere of action in which society, as distinguished from the individual, has, if any, only an indirect interest: comprehending all that portion of a person's life and conduct which affects only himself or, if it also affects others, only with their free, voluntary, and undeceived consent and participation. When I say only himself, I mean directly and in the first instance; for whatever affects himself may affect others through himself: and the objection which may be grounded on this contingency will receive consideration in the sequel. This, then, is the appropriate region of human liberty. It comprises, first, the inward domain of consciousness, demanding liberty of conscience in the most comprehensive sense, liberty of thought and feeling, absolute freedom of opinion and sentiment on all subjects, practical or speculative, scientific, moral, or theological. The liberty of expressing and publishing opinions may seem to fall under a different principle, since it belongs to that part of the conduct of an individual which concerns other people, but, being almost of as much importance as the liberty of thought itself and resting in great part on the same reasons, is practically inseparable from it. Secondly, the principle requires liberty of tastes and pursuits, of framing the plan of our life to suit our own character, of doing as we like, subject to such consequences as may follow, without impediment from our fellow creatures, so long as what we do does not harm them, even though they should think our conduct foolish, perverse, or wrong. Thirdly, from this liberty of each individual follows the liberty, within the same limits, of combination among individuals; freedom to unite for any purpose not involving harm to others: the persons combining being supposed to be of full age and not forced or deceived.

No society in which these liberties are not, on the whole, respected is free, whatever may be its form of government; and none is completely free in which they do not exist absolute and unqualified. The only freedom which deserves the name is that of pursuing our own good in our own way, so long as we do not attempt to deprive others of theirs or impede their efforts to obtain it. Each is the proper guardian of his own health, whether bodily *or* mental and spiritual. Mankind are greater gainers by suffering each other to live as seems good to themselves than by compelling each to live as seems good to the rest.

Though this doctrine is anything but new and, to some persons, may have the air of a truism, there is no doctrine which stands more directly opposed to the general tendency of existing opinion and practice. Society has expended fully as much effort in the attempt (according to its lights) to compel people to conform to its notions of personal as of social excellence. The ancient commonwealths thought themselves entitled to practice, and the ancient philosophers countenanced, the regulation of every part of private conduct by public authority, on the ground that the State had a deep interest in the whole bodily and mental discipline of every one of its citizens—a mode of thinking which may have been admissible in small republics surrounded by powerful enemies, in constant peril of being subverted by foreign attack or internal commotion, and to which even a short interval of relaxed energy and self-command might so easily be fatal that they could not afford to wait for the salutary permanent effects of freedom. In the modern world, the greater size of political communities and, above all, the separation between spiritual and temporal authority (which placed the direction of men's consciences in other hands than those which controlled their worldly affairs) prevented so great an interference by law in the details of private life; but the engines of moral repression have been wielded more strenuously against divergence from the reigning opinion in self-regarding than even in social matters; religion, the most powerful of the elements which have entered into the formation of moral feeling, having almost always been governed either by the ambition of a hierarchy seeking control over every department of human conduct, or by the spirit of Puritanism. And some of those modern reformers who have placed themselves in strongest opposition to the religions of the past have been noway behind either churches or sects in their assertion of the right of spiritual domination: M. Comte, in particular, whose social system, as unfolded in his *Système de Politique Positive,* aims at establishing (though by moral more than by legal appliances) a despotism of society over the individual surpassing anything contemplated in the political ideal of the most rigid disciplinarian among the ancient philosophers.

Apart from the peculiar tenets of individual thinkers, there is also in the world at large an increasing inclination to stretch unduly the powers of society over the individual both by the force of opinion and even by that of legislation; and as the tendency of all the changes taking place in the world is to strengthen society and diminish the power of the individual, this encroachment is not one of the evils which tend spontaneously to disappear, but, on the contrary, to grow more and more formidable. The dis-

position of mankind, whether as rulers or as fellow citizens, to impose
their own opinions and inclinations as a rule of conduct on others is so en-
ergetically supported by some of the best and by some of the worst feelings incident to human nature that it is hardly ever kept under restraint by
anything but want of power; and as the power is not declining, but growing, unless a strong barrier of moral conviction can be raised against the
mischief, we must expect, in the present circumstances of the world, to
see it increase.

It will be convenient for the argument if, instead of at once entering
upon the general thesis, we confine ourselves in the first instance to a single branch of it on which the principle here stated is, if not fully, yet to a
certain point, recognized by the current opinions. This one branch is the
Liberty of Thought, from which it is impossible to separate the cognate
liberty of speaking and of writing. Although these liberties, to some considerable amount, form part of the political morality of all countries
which profess religious toleration and free institutions, the grounds, both
philosophical and practical, on which they rest are perhaps not so familiar
to the general mind, nor so thoroughly appreciated by many, even of the
leaders of opinion, as might have been expected. Those grounds, when
rightly understood, are of much wider application than to only one division of the subject, and a thorough consideration of this part of the question will be found the best introduction to the remainder. Those to whom
nothing which I am about to say will be new may therefore, I hope, excuse
me if on a subject which for now three centuries has been so often discussed I venture on one discussion more.

CHAPTER II
Of the Liberty of Thought and Discussion

The time, it is to be hoped, is gone by when any defense would be necessary of the "liberty of the press" as one of the securities against corrupt or
tyrannical government. No argument, we may suppose, can now be
needed against permitting a legislature or an executive, not identified in
interest with the people, to prescribe opinions to them and determine
what doctrines or what arguments they shall be allowed to hear. This aspect of the question, besides, has been so often and so triumphantly enforced by preceding writers that it needs not be specially insisted on in
this place. Though the law of England, on the subject of the press, is as
servile to this day as it was in the time of the Tudors, there is little danger
of its being actually put in force against political discussion except during
some temporary panic when fear of insurrection drives ministers and
judges from their propriety;[1] and, speaking generally, it is not, in consti-

tutional countries, to be apprehended that the government, whether completely responsible to the people or not, will often attempt to control the
expression of opinion, except when in doing so it makes itself the organ of
the general intolerance of the public. Let us suppose, therefore, that the
government is entirely at one with the people, and never thinks of exerting
any power of coercion unless in agreement with what it conceives to be
their voice. But I deny the right of the people to exercise such coercion, either by themselves or by their government. The power itself is illegitimate. The best government has no more title to it than the worst. It is as
noxious, or more noxious, when exerted in accordance with public opinion
than when in opposition to it. If all mankind minus one were of one opinion, and only one person were of the contrary opinion, mankind would be
no more justified in silencing that one person than he, if he had the power,
would be justified in silencing mankind. Were an opinion a personal possession of no value except to the owner, if to be obstructed in the enjoyment of it were simply a private injury, it would make some difference
whether the injury was inflicted only on a few persons or on many. But the
peculiar evil of silencing the expression of an opinion is that it is robbing
the human race, posterity as well as the existing generation—those who
dissent from the opinion, still more than those who hold it. If the opinion
is right, they are deprived of the opportunity of exchanging error for truth;
if wrong, they lose, what is almost as great a benefit, the clearer perception
and livelier impression of truth produced by its collision with error.

It is necessary to consider separately these two hypotheses, each of
which has a distinct branch of the argument corresponding to it. We can
never be sure that the opinion we are endeavoring to stifle is a false opinion; and if we were sure, stifling it would be an evil still.

First, the opinion which it is attempted to suppress by authority may
possibly be true. Those who desire to suppress it, of course, deny its truth;
but they are not infallible. They have no authority to decide the question
for all mankind and exclude every other person from the means of judging. To refuse a hearing to an opinion because they are sure that it is false
is to assume that *their* certainty is the same thing as *absolute* certainty. All
silencing of discussion is an assumption of infallibility. Its condemnation
may be allowed to rest on this common argument, not the worse for being
common.

Unfortunately for the good sense of mankind, the fact of their fallibility
is far from carrying the weight in their practical judgment which is always
allowed to it in theory; for while everyone well knows himself to be fallible, few think it necessary to take any precautions against their own fallibility, or admit the supposition that any opinion of which they feel very
certain may be one of the examples of the error to which they acknowl-

edge themselves to be liable. Absolute princes, or others who are accustomed to unlimited deference, usually feel this complete confidence in
their own opinions on nearly all subjects. People more happily situated,
who sometimes hear their opinions disputed and are not wholly unused to
be set right when they are wrong, place the same unbounded reliance only
on such of their opinions as are shared by all who surround them, or to
whom they habitually defer; for in proportion to a man's want of confidence in his own solitary judgment does he usually repose, with implicit
trust, on the infallibility of "the world" in general. And the world, to each
individual, means the part of it with which he comes in contact: his party,
his sect, his church, his class of society; the man may be called, by comparison, almost liberal and large-minded to whom it means anything so
comprehensive as his own country or his own age. Nor is his faith in this
collective authority at all shaken by his being aware that other ages, countries, sects, churches, classes, and parties have thought, and even now
think, the exact reverse. He devolves upon his own world the responsibility of being in the right against the dissentient worlds of other people; and
it never troubles him that mere accident has decided which of these numerous worlds is the object of his reliance, and that the same causes which
make him a churchman in London would have made him a Buddhist or a
Confucian in Peking. Yet it is as evident in itself, as any amount of argument can make it, that ages are no more infallible than individuals—every
age having held many opinions which subsequent ages have deemed not
only false but absurd; and it is as certain that many opinions, now general,
will be rejected by future ages, as it is that many, once general, are rejected
by the present.

The objection likely to be made to this argument would probably take
some such form as the following. There is no greater assumption of infallibility in forbidding the propagation of error than in any other thing
which is done by public authority on its own judgment and responsibility.
Judgment is given to men that they may use it. Because it may be used er-
roneously, are men to be told that they ought not to use it at all? To prohibit what they think pernicious is not claiming exemption from error, but
fulfilling the duty incumbent on them, although fallible, of acting on their
conscientious conviction. If we were never to act on our opinions, because
those opinions may be wrong, we should leave all our interests uncared
for, and all our duties unperformed. An objection which applies to all conduct can be no valid objection to any conduct in particular. It is the duty
of governments, and of individuals, to form the truest opinions they can;
to form them carefully, and never impose them upon others unless they
are quite sure of being right. But when they are sure (such reasoners may
say), it is not conscientiousness but cowardice to shrink from acting on

their opinions and allow doctrines which they honestly think dangerous to the welfare of mankind, either in this life or in another, to be scattered abroad without restraint, because other people, in less enlightened times, have persecuted opinions now believed to be true. Let us take care, it may be said, not to make the same mistake; but governments and nations have made mistakes in other things which are not denied to be fit subjects for the exercise of authority: they have laid on bad taxes, made unjust wars. Ought we therefore to lay on no taxes and, under whatever provocation, make no wars? Men and governments must act to the best of their ability. There is no such thing as absolute certainty, but there is assurance sufficient for the purposes of human life. We may, and must, assume our opinion to be true for the guidance of our own conduct; and it is assuming no more when we forbid bad men to pervert society by the propagation of opinions which we regard as false and pernicious.

I answer, that it is assuming very much more. There is the greatest difference between presuming an opinion to be true because, with every opportunity for contesting it, it has not been refuted, and assuming its truth for the purpose of not permitting its refutation. Complete liberty of contradicting and disproving our opinion is the very condition which justifies us in assuming its truth for purposes of action; and on no other terms can a being with human faculties have any rational assurance of being right.

When we consider either the history of opinion or the ordinary conduct of human life, to what is it to be ascribed that the one and the other are no worse than they are? Not certainly to the inherent force of the human understanding, for on any matter not self-evident there are ninety-nine persons totally incapable of judging of it for one who is capable; and the capacity of the hundredth person is only comparative, for the majority of the eminent men of every past generation held many opinions now known to be erroneous, and did or approved numerous things which no one will now justify. Why is it, then, that there is on the whole a preponderance among mankind of rational opinions and rational conduct? If there really is this preponderance—which there must be unless human affairs are, and have always been, in an almost desperate state—it is owing to a quality of the human mind, the source of everything respectable in man either as an intellectual or as a moral being, namely, that his errors are corrigible. He is capable of rectifying his mistakes by discussion and experience. Not by experience alone. There must be discussion to show how experience is to be interpreted. Wrong opinions and practices gradually yield to fact and argument; but facts and arguments, to produce any effect on the mind, must be brought before it. Very few facts are able to tell their own story, without comments to bring out their meaning. The whole strength and value, then, of human judgment depending on the one property, that it can be set right when it is wrong, reliance can be placed on it only when the means of setting it right are kept constantly at hand. In the case of any person whose judgment is really deserving of confidence, how has it become so? Because he has kept his mind open to criticism of his opinions and conduct. Because it has been his practice to listen to all that could be said against him; to profit by as much of it as was just, and expound to himself, and upon occasion to others, the fallacy of what was fallacious. Because he has felt that the only way in which a human being can make some approach to knowing the whole of a subject is by hearing what can be said about it by persons of every variety of opinion, and studying all modes in which it can be looked at by every character of mind. No wise man ever acquired his wisdom in any mode but this; nor is it in the nature of human intellect to become wise in any other manner. The steady habit of correcting and completing his own opinion by collating it with those of others, so far from causing doubt and hesitation in carrying it into practice, is the only stable foundation for a just reliance on it; for, being cognizant of all that can, at least obviously, be said against him, and having taken up his position against all gainsayers—knowing that he has sought for objections and difficulties instead of avoiding them, and has shut out no light which can be thrown upon the subject from any quarter—he has a right to think his judgment better than that of any person, or any multitude, who have not gone through a similar process.

It is not too much to require that what the wisest of mankind, those who are best entitled to trust their own judgment, find necessary to warrant their relying on it, should be submitted to by that miscellaneous collection of a few wise and many foolish individuals called the public. The most intolerant of churches, the Roman Catholic Church, even at the canonization of a saint admits, and listens patiently to, a "devil's advocate." The holiest of men, it appears, cannot be admitted to posthumous honors until all that the devil could say against him is known and weighed. If even the Newtonian philosophy were not permitted to be questioned, mankind could not feel as complete assurance of its truth as they now do. The beliefs which we have most warrant for have no safeguard to rest on but a standing invitation to the whole world to prove them unfounded. If the challenge is not accepted, or is accepted and the attempt fails, we are far enough from certainty still, but we have done the best that the existing state of human reason admits of: we have neglected nothing that could give the truth a chance of reaching us; if the lists are kept open, we may hope that, if there be a better truth, it will be found when the human mind is capable of receiving it; and in the meantime we may rely on having attained such approach to truth as is possible in our own day. This is the amount of certainty attainable by a fallible being, and this the sole way of attaining it.

Strange it is that men should admit the validity of the arguments for free discussion, but object to their being "pushed to an extreme," not seeing that unless the reasons are good for an extreme case, they are not good for any case. Strange that they should imagine that they are not assuming infallibility when they acknowledge that there should be free discussion on all subjects which can possibly be *doubtful,* but think that some particular principle or doctrine should be forbidden to be questioned because it is so *certain,* that is, because *they are certain* that it is certain. To call any proposition certain, while there is anyone who would deny its certainty if permitted, but who is not permitted, is to assume that we ourselves, and those who agree with us, are the judges of certainty, and judges without hearing the other side.

In the present age—which has been described as "destitute of faith, but terrified at skepticism"—in which people feel sure, not so much that their opinions are true as that they should not know what to do without them—the claims of an opinion to be protected from public attack are rested not so much on its truth as on its importance to society. There are, it is alleged, certain beliefs so useful, not to say indispensable, to well-being that it is as much the duty of governments to uphold those beliefs as to protect any other of the interests of society. In a case of such necessity, and so directly in the line of their duty, something less than infallibility may, it is maintained, warrant, and even bind, governments to act on their own opinion confirmed by the general opinion of mankind. It is also often argued, and still oftener thought, that none but bad men would desire to weaken these salutary beliefs; and there can be nothing wrong, it is thought, in restraining bad men and prohibiting what only such men would wish to practice. This mode of thinking makes the justification of restraints on discussion not a question of the truth of doctrines but of their usefulness, and flatters itself by that means to escape the responsibility of claiming to be an infallible judge of opinions. But those who thus satisfy themselves do not perceive that the assumption of infallibility is merely shifted from one point to another. The usefulness of an opinion is itself matter of opinion—as disputable, as open to discussion, and requiring discussion as much as the opinion itself. There is the same need of an infallible judge of opinions to decide an opinion to be noxious as to decide it to be false, unless the opinion condemned has full opportunity of defending itself. And it will not do to say that the heretic may be allowed to maintain the utility or harmlessness of his opinion, though forbidden to maintain its truth. The truth of an opinion is part of its utility. If we would know whether or not it is desirable that a proposition should be believed, is it possible to exclude the consideration of whether or not it is true? In the opinion, not of bad men, but of the best men, no belief which

is contrary to truth can be really useful; and can you prevent such men
from urging that plea when they are charged with culpability for denying
some doctrine which they are told is useful, but which they believe to be
false? Those who are on the side of received opinions never fail to take all
possible advantage of this plea; you do not find *them* handling the question
of utility as if it could be completely abstracted from that of truth; on the
contrary, it is, above all, because their doctrine is "the truth" that the
knowledge or the belief of it is held to be so indispensable. There can be
no fair discussion of the question of usefulness when an argument so vital
may be employed on one side, but not on the other. And in point of fact,
when law or public feeling do not permit the truth of an opinion to be disputed, they are just as little tolerant of a denial of its usefulness. The utmost they allow is an extenuation of its absolute necessity, or of the
positive guilt of rejecting it.

In order more fully to illustrate the mischief of denying a hearing to
opinions because we, in our own judgment, have condemned them, it
will be desirable to fix down the discussion to a concrete case; and I
choose, by preference, the cases which are least favorable to me—in
which the argument against freedom of opinion, both on the score of
truth and on that of utility, is considered the strongest. Let the opinions
impugned be the belief in a God and in a future state, or any of the commonly received doctrines of morality. To fight the battle on such ground
gives a great advantage to an unfair antagonist, since he will be sure to
say (and many who have no desire to be unfair will say it internally), Are
these the doctrines which you do not deem sufficiently certain to be
taken under the protection of law? Is the belief in a God one of the opinions to feel sure of which you hold to be assuming infallibility? But I
must be permitted to observe that it is not the feeling sure of a doctrine
(be it what it may) which I call an assumption of infallibility. It is the undertaking to decide that question, *for others*, without allowing them to
hear what can be said on the contrary side. And I denounce and reprobate this pretension not the less if put forth on the side of my most
solemn convictions. However positive anyone's persuasion may be, not
only of the falsity but of the pernicious consequences—not only of the
pernicious consequences, but (to adopt expressions which I altogether
condemn) the immorality and impiety of an opinion—yet if, in pursuance
of that private judgment, though backed by the public judgment of his
country or his contemporaries, he prevents the opinion from being heard
in its defense, he assumes infallibility. And so far from the assumption
being less objectionable or less dangerous because the opinion is called
immoral or impious, this is the case of all others in which it is most fatal.
These are exactly the occasions on which the men of one generation com-

mit those dreadful mistakes which excite the astonishment and horror of posterity. It is among such that we find the instances memorable in history, when the arm of the law has been employed to root out the best men and the noblest doctrines; with deplorable success as to the men, though some of the doctrines have survived to be (as if in mockery) invoked in defense of similar conduct toward those who dissent from *them,* or from their received interpretation.

Mankind can hardly be too often reminded that there was once a man named Socrates, between whom and the legal authorities and public opinion of his time there took place a memorable collision. Born in an age and country abounding in individual greatness, this man has been handed down to us by those who best knew both him and the age as the most virtuous man in it; while *we* know him as the head and prototype of all subsequent teachers of virtue, the source equally of the lofty inspiration of Plato and the judicious utilitarianism of Aristotle, *"i maestri di color che sanno,"* the two headsprings of ethical as of all other philosophy. This acknowledged master of all the eminent thinkers who have since lived— whose fame, still growing after more than two thousand years, all but outweighs the whole remainder of the names which make his native city illustrious—was put to death by his countrymen, after a judicial conviction, for impiety and immorality. Impiety, in denying the gods recognized by the State; indeed, his accuser asserted (see the *Apologia*) that he believed in no gods at all. Immorality, in being, by his doctrines and instructions, a "corruptor of youth." Of these charges the tribunal, there is every ground for believing, honestly found him guilty, and condemned the man who probably of all then born had deserved best of mankind to be put to death as a criminal.

To pass from this to the only other instance of judicial iniquity, the mention of which, after the condemnation of Socrates, would not be an anticlimax: the event which took place on Calvary rather more than eighteen hundred years ago. The man who left on the memory of those who witnessed his life and conversation such an impression of his moral grandeur that eighteen subsequent centuries have done homage to him as the Almighty in person, was ignominiously put to death, as what? As a blasphemer. Men did not merely mistake their benefactor, they mistook him for the exact contrary of what he was and treated him as that prodigy of impiety which they themselves are now held to be for their treatment of him. The feelings with which mankind now regard these lamentable transactions, especially the later of the two, render them extremely unjust in their judgment of the unhappy actors. These were, to all appearance, not bad men—not worse than men commonly are, but rather the contrary; men who possessed in a full, or somewhat more than a full measure, the religious, moral, and patriotic feelings of their time and people: the very kind of men who, in all times, our own included, have every chance of passing through life blameless and respected. The high priest who rent his garments when the words were pronounced, which, according to all the ideas of his country, constituted the blackest guilt, was in all probability quite as sincere in his horror and indignation as the generality of respectable and pious men now are in the religious and moral sentiments they profess; and most of those who now shudder at his conduct, if they had lived in his time, and been born Jews, would have acted precisely as he did. Orthodox Christians who are tempted to think that those who stoned to death the first martyrs must have been worse men than they themselves are ought to remember that one of those persecutors was Saint Paul.

Let us add one more example, the most striking of all, if the impressiveness of an error is measured by the wisdom and virtue of him who falls into it. If ever anyone possessed of power had grounds for thinking himself the best and most enlightened among his contemporaries, it was the Emperor Marcus Aurelius. Absolute monarch of the whole civilized world, he preserved through life not only the most unblemished justice, but what was less to be expected from his Stoical breeding, the tenderest heart. The few failings which are attributed to him were all on the side of indulgence, while his writings, the highest ethical product of the ancient mind, differ scarcely perceptibly, if they differ at all, from the most characteristic teachings of Christ. This man, a better Christian in all but the dogmatic sense of the word than almost any of the ostensibly Christian sovereigns who have since reigned, persecuted Christianity. Placed at the summit of all the previous attainments of humanity, with an open, unfettered intellect, and a character which led him of himself to embody in his moral writings the Christian ideal, he yet failed to see that Christianity was to be a good and not an evil to the world, with his duties to which he was so deeply penetrated. Existing society he knew to be in a deplorable state. But such as it was, he saw, or thought he saw, that it was held together, and prevented from being worse, by belief and reverence of the received divinities. As a ruler of mankind, he deemed it his duty not to suffer society to fall in pieces; and saw not how, if its existing ties were removed, any others could be formed which could again knit it together. The new religion openly aimed at dissolving these ties; unless, therefore, it was his duty to adopt that religion, it seemed to be his duty to put it down. Inasmuch then as the theology of Christianity did·not appear to him true or of divine origin, inasmuch as this strange history of a crucified God was not credible to him, and a system which purported to rest entirely upon a foundation to him so wholly unbelievable, could not be foreseen by him to be that renovating agency which, after all abatements, it has in fact proved to be; the gentlest and most amiable of philosophers and rulers, under a solemn sense of duty, authorized the persecution of Christianity. To my mind this is one of the most tragical facts in all history. It is a bitter thought how different a thing the Christianity of the world might have been if the Christian faith had been adopted as the religion of the empire under the auspices of Marcus Aurelius instead of those of Constantine. But it would be equally unjust to him and false to truth to deny that no one plea which can be urged for punishing anti-Christian teaching was wanting to Marcus Aurelius for punishing, as he did, the propagation of Christianity. No Christian more firmly believes that atheism is false and tends to the dissolution of society than Marcus Aurelius believed the same things of Christianity; he who, of all men then living, might have been thought the most capable of appreciating it. Unless anyone who approves of punishment for the promulgation of opinions flatters himself that he is a wiser and better man than Marcus Aurelius—more deeply versed in the wisdom of his time, more elevated in his intellect above it, more earnest in his search for truth, or more single-minded in his devotion to it when found—let him abstain from that assumption of the joint infallibility of himself and the multitude which the great Antoninus [Aurelius] made with so unfortunate a result.

Aware of the impossibility of defending the use of punishment for restraining irreligious opinions by any argument which will not justify Marcus Antoninus, the enemies of religious freedom, when hard pressed, occasionally accept this consequence and say, with Dr. Johnson, that the persecutors of Christianity were in the right, that persecution is an ordeal through which truth ought to pass, and always passes successfully, legal penalties being, in the end, powerless against truth, though sometimes beneficially effective against mischievous errors. This is a form of the argument for religious intolerance sufficiently remarkable not to be passed without notice.

A theory which maintains that truth may justifiably be persecuted because persecution cannot possibly do it any harm cannot be charged with being intentionally hostile to the reception of new truths; but we cannot commend the generosity of its dealing with the persons to whom mankind are indebted for them. To discover to the world something which deeply concerns it, and of which it was previously ignorant, to prove to it that it had been mistaken on some vital point of temporal or spiritual interest, is as important a service as a human being can render to his fellow creatures, and in certain cases, as in those of the early Christians and of the Reformers, those who think with Dr. Johnson believe it to have been the most precious gift which could be bestowed on mankind. That the authors of such splendid benefits should be requited by martyrdom, that their reward should be to be dealt with as the vilest of criminals, is not, upon this theory, a deplorable error and misfortune for which humanity should mourn in sackcloth and ashes, but the normal and justifiable state of things. The propounder of a new truth, according to this doctrine, should stand, as stood, in the legislation of the Locrians, the proposer of a new law, with a halter round his neck, to be instantly tightened if the public assembly did not, on hearing his reasons, then and there adopt his proposition. People who defend this mode of treating benefactors cannot be supposed to set much value on the benefit; and I believe this view of the subject is mostly confined to the sort of persons who think that new truths may have been desirable once, but that we have had enough of them now.

But, indeed, the dictum that truth always triumphs over persecution is one of those pleasant falsehoods which men repeat after one another till they pass into commonplaces, but which all experience refutes. History teems with instances of truth put down by persecution. If not suppressed forever, it may be thrown back for centuries. To speak only of religious opinions: the Reformation broke out at least twenty times before Luther, and was put down. Arnold of Brescia was put down. Fra Dolcino was put down. Savonarola was put down. The Albigeois were put down. The Vaudois were put down. The Lollards were put down. The Hussites were put down. Even after the era of Luther, wherever persecution was persisted in, it was successful. In Spain, Italy, Flanders, the Austrian empire, Protestantism was rooted out; and, most likely, would have been so in England had Queen Mary lived or Queen Elizabeth died. Persecution has always succeeded save where the heretics were too strong a party to be effectually persecuted. No reasonable person can doubt that Christianity might have been extirpated in the Roman Empire. It spread and became predominant because the persecutions were only occasional, lasting but a short time, and separated by long intervals of almost undisturbed propagandism. It is a piece of idle sentimentality that truth, merely as truth, has any inherent power denied to error of prevailing against the dungeon and the stake. Men are not more zealous for truth than they often are for error, and a sufficient application of legal or even of social penalties will generally succeed in stopping the propagation of either. The real advantage which truth has consists in this, that when an opinion is true, it may be extinguished once, twice, or many times, but in the course of ages there will generally be found persons to rediscover it, until some one of its reappearances falls on a time when from favorable circumstances it escapes persecution until it has made such head as to withstand all subsequent attempts to suppress it.

It will be said that we do not now put to death the introducers of new opinions: we are not like our fathers who slew the prophets; we even build sepulchers to them. It is true we no longer put heretics to death; and the amount of penal infliction which modern feeling would probably tolerate, even against the most obnoxious opinions, is not sufficient to extirpate them. But let us not flatter ourselves that we are yet free from the stain even of legal persecution. Penalties for opinion, or at least for its expression, still exist by law; and their enforcement is not, even in these times, so unexampled as to make it at all incredible that they may some day be revived in full force. In the year 1857, at the summer assizes of the county of Cornwall, an unfortunate man,[2] said to be of unexceptionable conduct in all relations of life, was sentenced to twenty-one months' imprisonment for uttering, and writing on a gate, some offensive words concerning Christianity. Within a month of the same time, at the Old Bailey, two persons, on two separate occasions,[3] were rejected as jurymen, and one of them grossly insulted by the judge and by one of the counsel, because they honestly declared that they had no theological belief; and a third, a foreigner,[4] for the same reason, was denied justice against a thief. This refusal of redress took place in virtue of the legal doctrine that no person can be allowed to give evidence in a court of justice who does not profess belief in a God (any god is sufficient) and in a future state, which is equivalent to declaring such persons to be outlaws, excluded from the protection of the tribunals; who may not only be robbed or assaulted with impunity, if no one but themselves, or persons of similar opinions, be present, but anyone else may be robbed or assaulted with impunity if the proof of the fact depends on their evidence. The assumption on which this is grounded is that the oath is worthless of a person who does not believe in a future state—a proposition which betokens much ignorance of history in those who assent to it (since it is historically true that a large proportion of infidels in all ages have been persons of distinguished integrity and honor), and would be maintained by no one who had the smallest conception how many of the persons in greatest repute with the world, both for virtues and for attainments, are well known, at least to their intimates, to be unbelievers. The rule, besides, is suicidal and cuts away its own foundation. Under pretense that atheists must be liars, it admits the testimony of all atheists who are willing to lie, and rejects only those who brave the obloquy of publicly confessing a detested creed rather than affirm a falsehood. A rule thus self-convicted of absurdity so far as regards its professed purpose can be kept in force only as a badge of hatred, a relic of persecution—a persecution, too, having the peculiarity that the qualification for undergoing it is the being clearly proved not to deserve it. The rule and the theory it implies are hardly less insulting to believers than to infidels. For if he who does not believe in a future state necessarily lies, it follows that they who do believe are only prevented from lying, if prevented they are, by the fear of hell. We will not do the authors and abettors of the rule the injury of supposing that the conception which they have formed of Christian virtue is drawn from their own consciousness.

These, indeed, are but rags and remnants of persecution, and may be thought to be not so much an indication of the wish to persecute, as an example of that very frequent infirmity of English minds, which makes them take a preposterous pleasure in the assertion of a bad principle, when they are no longer bad enough to desire to carry it really into practice. But unhappily there is no security in the state of the public mind that the suspension of worse forms of legal persecution, which his lasted for about the space of a generation, will continue. In this age the quiet surface of routine is as often ruffled by attempts to resuscitate past evils as to introduce new benefits. What is boasted of at the present time as the revival of religion is always, in narrow and uncultivated minds, at least as much the revival of bigotry; and where there is the strong permanent leaven of intolerance in the feelings of a people, which at all times abides in the middle classes of this country, it needs but little to provoke them into actively persecuting those whom they have never ceased to think proper objects of persecution.[5] For it is this—it is the opinions men entertain, and the feelings they cherish, respecting those who disown the beliefs they deem important which makes this country not a place of mental freedom. For a long time past, the chief mischief of the legal penalties is that they strengthen the social stigma. It is that stigma which is really effective, and so effective is it that the profession of opinions which are under the ban of society is much less common in England than is, in many other countries, the avowal of those which incur risk of judicial punishment. In respect to all persons but those whose pecuniary circumstances make them independent of the good will of other people, opinion, on this subject, is as efficacious as law; men might as well be imprisoned as excluded from the means of earning their bread. Those whose bread is already secured, and who desire no favors from men in power, or from bodies of men, or from the public, have nothing to fear from the open avowal of any opinions but to be ill-thought of and ill-spoken of, and this it ought not to require a very heroic mold to enable them to bear. There is no room for any appeal *ad misericordiam* in behalf of such persons. But though we do not now inflict so much evil on those who think differently from us as it was formerly our custom to do, it may be that we do ourselves as much evil as ever by our treatment of them. Socrates was put to death, but the Socratic philosophy rose like the sun in heaven and spread its illumination over the whole intellectual firmament. Christians were cast to the lions, but the Christian church grew up a stately and spreading tree, overtopping the older and less vigorous growths, and stifling them by its shade. Our merely social intolerance kills no one, roots out no opinions, but induces men to disguise them or to abstain from any active effort for their diffusion. With us, heretical opinions do not perceptibly gain, or even lose, ground in each decade or generation; they never blaze out far and wide, but continue to smolder in the narrow circles of thinking and studious persons among whom they originate, without ever lighting up the general affairs of mankind with either a true or a deceptive light. And thus is kept up a state of things very satisfactory to some minds, because, without the unpleasant process of fining or imprisoning anybody, it maintains all prevailing opinions outwardly undisturbed, while it does not absolutely interdict the exercise of reason by dissentients afflicted with the malady of thought. A convenient plan for having peace in the intellectual world, and keeping all things going on therein very much as they do already. But the price paid for this sort of intellectual pacification is the sacrifice of the entire moral courage of the human mind. A state of things in which a large portion of the most active and inquiring intellects find it advisable to keep the general principles and grounds of their convictions within their own breasts, and attempt, in what they address to the public, to fit as much as they can of their own conclusions to premises which they have internally renounced, cannot send forth the open, fearless characters and logical, consistent intellects who once adorned the thinking world. The sort of men who can be looked for under it are either mere conformers to commonplace, or timeservers for truth, whose arguments on all great subjects are meant for their hearers, and are not those which have convinced themselves. Those who avoid this alternative do so by narrowing their thoughts and interest to things which can be spoken of without venturing within the region of principles, that is, to small practical matters which would come right of themselves, if but the minds of mankind were strengthened and enlarged, and which will never be made effectually right until then, while that which would strengthen and enlarge men's minds—free and daring speculation on the highest subjects—is abandoned

Those in whose eyes this reticence on the part of heretics is no evil should consider, in the first place, that in consequence of it there is never any fair and thorough discussion of heretical opinions; and that such of them as could not stand such a discussion, though they may be prevented from spreading, do not disappear. But it is not the minds of heretics that are deteriorated most by the ban placed on all inquiry which does not end in the orthodox conclusions. The greatest harm done is to those who are not heretics, and whose whole mental development is cramped and their reason cowed by the fear of heresy. Who can compute what the world loses in the multitude of promising intellects combined with timid characters, who dare not follow out any bold, vigorous, independent train of thought, lest it should land them in something which would admit of being considered irreligious or immoral? Among them we may occasionally see some man of deep conscientiousness and subtle and refined understanding, who spends a life in sophisticating with an intellect which he cannot silence, and exhausts the resources of ingenuity in attempting to reconcile the promptings of his conscience and reason with orthodoxy, which yet he does not, perhaps, to the end succeed in doing. No one can be a great thinker who does not recognize that as a thinker it is his first duty to follow his intellect to whatever conclusions it may lead. Truth gains more even by the errors of one who, with due study and preparation, thinks for himself than by the true opinions of those who only hold them because they do not suffer themselves to think. Not that it is solely, or chiefly, to form great thinkers that freedom of thinking is required. On the contrary, it is as much and even more indispensable to enable average human beings to attain the mental stature which they are capable of. There have been, and may again be, great individual thinkers in a general atmosphere of mental slavery. But there never has been, nor ever will be, in that atmosphere an intellectually active people. When any people has made a temporary approach to such a character, it has been because the dread of heterodox speculation was for a time suspended. Where there is a tacit convention that principles are not to be disputed, where the discussion of the greatest questions which can occupy humanity is considered to be closed, we cannot hope to find that generally high scale of mental activity which has made some periods of history so remarkable. Never when controversy avoided the subjects which are large and important enough to kindle enthusiasm was the mind of a people stirred up from its foundations, and the impulse given which raised even persons of the most ordinary intellect to something of the dignity of thinking beings. Of such we have had an example in the condition of Europe during the times immediately following the Reformation; another, though limited to the Continent and to a more cultivated class, in the speculative movement of the latter half of the eighteenth century; and a third, of still briefer duration, in the intellectual fermentation of Germany during the Goethian and Fichtean period. These periods differed widely in the particular opinions which they developed, but were alike in this, that during all three the yoke of authority was broken. In each, an old mental despotism had been thrown off, and no new one had yet taken its place. The impulse given at these three periods has made Europe what it now is. Every single improvement which has taken place either in the human mind or in institutions may be traced distinctly to one or other of them. Appearances have for some time indicated that all three impulses are well-nigh spent; and we can expect no fresh start until we again assert our mental freedom.

Let us now pass to the second division of the argument, and dismissing the supposition that any of the received opinions may be false, let us assume them to be true and examine into the worth of the manner in which they are likely to be held when their truth is not freely and openly canvassed. However unwillingly a person who has a strong opinion may admit the possibility that his opinion may be false, he ought to be moved by the consideration that, however true it may be, if it is not fully, frequently, and fearlessly discussed, it will be held as a dead dogma, not a living truth.

There is a class of persons (happily not quite so numerous as formerly) who think it enough if a person assents undoubtingly to what they think true, though he has no knowledge whatever of the grounds of the opinion and could not make a tenable defense of it against the most superficial objections. Such persons, if they can once get their creed taught from authority, naturally think that no good, and some harm, comes of its being allowed to be questioned. Where their influence prevails, they make it nearly impossible for the received opinion to be rejected wisely and considerately, though it may still be rejected rashly and ignorantly; for to shut out discussion entirely is seldom possible, and when it once gets in, beliefs not grounded on conviction are apt to give way before the slightest semblance of an argument. Waiving, however, this possibility—assuming that the true opinion abides in the mind, but abides as a prejudice, a belief independent of, and proof against, argument—this is not the way in which truth ought to be held by a rational being. This is not knowing the truth. Truth, thus held, is but one superstition the more, accidentally clinging to the words which enunciate a truth.

If the intellect and judgment of mankind ought to be cultivated, a thing which Protestants at least do not deny, on what can these faculties be more appropriately exercised by anyone than on the things which concern him so much that it is considered necessary for him to hold opinions on them? If the cultivation of the understanding consists in one thing more than in another, it is surely in learning the grounds of one's own opinions. Whatever people believe, on subjects on which it is of the first importance to believe rightly, they ought to be able to defend against at least the common objections. But, someone may say, "Let them be *taught* the grounds of their opinions. It does not follow that opinions must be merely parroted because they are never heard controverted. Persons who learn geometry do not simply commit the theorems to memory, but understand and learn likewise the demonstrations; and it would be absurd to say that they remain ignorant of the grounds of geometrical truths because they never hear anyone deny and attempt to disprove them." Undoubtedly: and such teaching suffices on a subject like mathematics, where there is nothing at all to be said on the wrong side of the question. The peculiarity of the evidence of mathematical truths is that all the argument is on one side. There are no objections, and no answers to objections. But on every subject on which difference of opinion is possible, the truth depends on a balance to be struck between two sets of conflicting reasons. Even in natural philosophy, there is always some other explanation possible of the same facts; some geocentric theory instead of heliocentric, some phlogiston instead of oxygen; and it has to be shown why that other theory cannot be the true one; and until this is shown, and until we know how it is shown, we do not understand the grounds of our opinion. But when we turn to subjects infinitely more complicated, to morals, religion, politics, social relations, and the business of life, three-fourths of the arguments for every disputed opinion consist in dispelling the appearances which favor some opinion different from it. The greatest orator, save one, of antiquity, has left it on record that he always studied his adversary's case with as great, if not with still greater, intensity than even his own. What Cicero practiced as the means of forensic success requires to be imitated by all who study any subject in order to arrive at the truth. He who knows only his own side of the case knows little of that. His reasons may be good, and no one may have been able to refute them. But if he is equally unable to refute the reasons on the opposite side, if he does not so much as know what they are, he has no ground for preferring either opinion. The rational position for him would be suspension of judgment, and unless he contents himself with that, he is either led by authority or adopts, like the generality of the world, the side to which he feels most inclination. Nor is it enough that he should hear the arguments of adversaries from his own teachers, presented as they state them, and accompanied by what they offer as refutations. That is not the way to do justice to the arguments or bring them into real contact with his own mind. He must be able to hear them from persons who actually believe them, who defend them in earnest and do their very utmost for them. He must know them in their most plausible and persuasive form; he must feel the whole force of the difficulty which the true view of the subject has to encounter and dispose of, else he will never really possess himself of the portion of truth which meets and removes that difficulty. Ninety-nine in a hundred of what are called educated men are in this condition, even of those who can argue fluently for their opinions. Their conclusion may be true, but it might be false for anything they know; they have never thrown themselves into the mental position of those who think differently from them, and considered what such persons may have to say; and, consequently, they do not, in any proper sense of the word, know the doctrine which they themselves profess. They do not know those parts of it which explain and justify the remainder—the considerations which show that a fact which seemingly conflicts with another is reconcilable with it, or that, of two apparently strong reasons, one and not the other ought to be preferred. All that part of the truth which turns the scale and decides the judgment of a completely informed mind, they are strangers to; nor is it ever really known but to those who have attended equally and impartially to both sides and endeavored to see the reasons of both in the strongest light. So essential is this discipline to a real understanding of moral and human subjects that, if opponents of all-important truths do not exist, it is indispensable to imagine them and supply them with the strongest arguments which the most skillful devil's advocate can conjure up.

To abate the force of these considerations, an enemy of free discussion may be supposed to say that there is no necessity for mankind in general to know and understand all that can be said against or for their opinions by philosophers and theologians. That it is not needful for common men to be able to expose all the misstatements or fallacies of an ingenious opponent. That it is enough if there is always somebody capable of answering them, so that nothing likely to mislead uninstructed persons remains unrefuted. That simple minds, having been taught the obvious grounds of the truths inculcated on them, may trust to authority for the rest and, being aware that they have neither knowledge nor talent to resolve every difficulty which can be raised, may repose in the assurance that all those which have been raised have been or can be answered by those who are specially trained to the task.

Conceding to this view of the subject the utmost that can be claimed for it by those most easily satisfied with the amount of understanding of truth which ought to accompany the belief of it, even so, the argument for free discussion is noway weakened. For even this doctrine acknowledges that mankind ought to have a rational assurance that all objections have been satisfactorily answered; and how are they to be answered if that which requires to be answered is not spoken? Or how can the answer be known to be satisfactory if the objectors have no opportunity of showing that it is unsatisfactory? If not the public, at least the philosophers and theologians who are to resolve the difficulties must make themselves familiar with those difficulties in their most puzzling form; and this cannot be accomplished unless they are freely stated and placed in the most advantageous light which they admit of. The Catholic Church has its own way of dealing with this embarrassing problem. It makes a broad separation between those who can be permitted to receive its doctrines on conviction and those who must accept them on trust. Neither, indeed, are allowed any choice as to what they will accept; but the clergy, such at least as can be fully confided in, may admissibly and meritoriously make themselves acquainted with the arguments of opponents, in order to answer them, and may, therefore, read heretical books; the laity, not unless by special permission, hard to be obtained. This discipline recognizes a knowledge of the enemy's case as beneficial to the teachers, but finds means, consistent with this, of denying it to the rest of the world, thus giving to the *élite* more mental culture, though not more mental freedom, than it allows to the mass. By this device it succeeds in obtaining the kind of mental superiority which its purposes require; for though culture without freedom never made a large and liberal mind, it can make a clever *nisi prius* advocate of a cause. But in countries professing Protestantism, this resource is denied, since Protestants hold, at least in theory, that the responsibility for the choice of a religion must be borne by each for himself and cannot be thrown off upon teachers. Besides, in the present state of the world, it is practically impossible that writings which are read by the instructed can be kept from the uninstructed. If the teachers of mankind are to be cognizant of all that they ought to know, everything must be free to be written and published without restraint.

If, however, the mischievous operation of the absence of free discussion, when the received opinions are true, were confined to leaving men ignorant of the grounds of those opinions, it might be thought that this, if an intellectual, is no moral evil and does not affect the worth of the opinions, regarded in their influence on the character. The fact, however, is that not only the grounds of the opinion are forgotten in the absence of discussion, but too often the meaning of the opinion itself. The words which convey it cease to suggest ideas, or suggest only a small portion of those they were originally employed to communicate. Instead of a vivid conception and a living belief, there remain only a few phrases retained by rote; or, if any part, the shell and husk only of the meaning is retained, the finer essence being lost. The great chapter in human history which this fact occupies and fills cannot be too earnestly studied and meditated on.

It is illustrated in the experience of almost all ethical doctrines and religious creeds. They are all full of meaning and vitality to those who originate them, and to the direct disciples of the originators. Their meaning continues to be felt in undiminished strength, and is perhaps brought out into even fuller consciousness, so long as the struggle lasts to give the doctrine or creed an ascendancy over other creeds. At last it either prevails and becomes the general opinion, or its progress stops; it keeps possession of the ground it has gained, but ceases to spread further. When either of these results has become apparent, controversy on the subject flags, and gradually dies away. The doctrine has taken its place, if not as a received opinion, as one of the admitted sects or divisions of opinion; those who hold it have generally inherited, not adopted it; and conversion from one of these doctrines to another, being now an exceptional fact, occupies little place in the thoughts of their professors. Instead of being, as at first, constantly on the alert either to defend themselves against the world or to bring the world over to them, they have subsided into acquiescence and neither listen, when they can help it, to arguments against their creed, nor trouble dissentients (if there be such) with arguments in its favor. From this time may usually be dated the decline in the living power of the doctrine. We often hear the teachers of all creeds lamenting the difficulty of keeping up in the minds of believers a lively apprehension of the truth which they nominally recognize, so that it may penetrate the feelings and acquire a real mastery over the conduct. No such difficulty is complained of while the creed is still fighting for its existence; even the weaker combatants then know and feel what they are fighting for, and the difference between it and other doctrines; and in that period of every creed's existence not a few persons may be found who have realized its fundamental principles in all the forms of thought, have weighed and considered them in all their important bearings, and have experienced the full effect on the character which belief in that creed ought to produce in a mind thoroughly imbued with it. But when it has come to be an hereditary creed, and to be received passively, not actively—when the mind is no longer compelled, in the same degree as at first, to exercise its vital powers on the questions which its belief presents to it, there is a progressive tendency to forget all of the belief except the formularies, or to give it a dull and torpid assent, as if accepting it on trust dispensed with the necessity of realizing it in consciousness, or testing it by personal experience, until it almost ceases to connect itself at all with the inner life of the human being. Then are seen the cases, so frequent in this age of the world as almost to form the majority, in which the creed remains as it were outside the mind, incrusting and petrifying it against all other influences addressed to the higher parts of our nature; manifesting its power by not suffering any fresh and living conviction to get in, but itself doing nothing for the mind or heart except standing sentinel over them to keep them vacant.

To what an extent doctrines intrinsically fitted to make the deepest impression upon the mind may remain in it as dead beliefs, without being ever realized in the imagination, the feelings, or the understanding, is exemplified by the manner in which the majority of believers hold the doctrines of Christianity. By Christianity, I here mean what is accounted such by all churches and sects—the maxims and precepts contained in the New Testament. These are considered sacred, and accepted as laws, by all professing Christians. Yet it is scarcely too much to say that not one Christian in a thousand guides or tests his individual conduct by reference to those laws. The standard to which he does refer it is the custom of his nation, his class, or his religious profession. He has thus, on the one hand, a collection of ethical maxims which he believes to have been vouchsafed to him by infallible wisdom as rules for his government; and, on the other, a set of everyday judgments and practices which go a certain length with some of those maxims, not so great a length with others, stand in direct opposition to some, and are, on the whole, a compromise between the Christian creed and the interests and suggestions of worldly life. To the first of these standards he gives his homage; to the other his real allegiance. All Christians believe that the blessed are the poor and humble, and those who are ill-used by the world; that it is easier for a camel to pass through the eye of a needle than for a rich man to enter the kingdom of heaven; that they should judge not, lest they be judged; that they should swear not at all; that they should love their neighbor as themselves; that if one take their cloak, they should give him their coat also; that they should take no thought for the morrow; that if they would be perfect they should sell all that they have and give it to the poor. They are not insincere when they say that they believe these things. They do believe them, as people believe what they have always heard lauded and never discussed. But in the sense of that living belief which regulates conduct, they believe these doctrines just up to the point to which it is usual to act upon them. The doctrines in their integrity are serviceable to pelt adversaries with; and it is understood that they are to be put forward (when possible) as the reasons for whatever people do that they think laudable. But anyone who reminded them that the maxims require an infinity of things which they never even think of doing would gain nothing but to be classed among those very unpopular characters who affect to be better than other people. The doctrines have no hold on ordinary believers—are not a power in their minds. They have an habitual respect for the sound of them, but no feeling which spreads from the words to the things signified and forces the mind to take *them* in and make them conform to the formula. Whenever conduct is concerned, they look round for Mr. A and B to direct them how far to go in obeying Christ.

Now we may be well assured that the case was not thus, but far otherwise, with the early Christians. Had it been thus, Christianity never would have expanded from an obscure sect of the despised Hebrews into the religion of the Roman empire. When their enemies said, "See how these Christians love one another" (a remark not likely to be made by anybody now), they assuredly had a much livelier feeling of the meaning of their creed than they have ever had since. And to this cause, probably, it is chiefly owing that Christianity now makes so little progress in extending its domain, and after eighteen centuries is still nearly confined to Europeans and the descendants of Europeans. Even with the strictly religious, who are much in earnest about their doctrines and attach a greater amount of meaning to many of them than people in general, it commonly happens that the part which is thus comparatively active in their minds is that which was made by Calvin, or Knox, or some such person much nearer in character to themselves. The sayings of Christ coexist passively in their minds, producing hardly any effect beyond what is caused by mere listening to words so amiable and bland. There are many reasons, doubtless, why doctrines which are the badge of a sect retain more of their vitality than those common to all recognized sects, and why more pains are taken by teachers to keep their meaning alive; but one reason certainly is that the peculiar doctrines are more questioned and have to be oftener defended against open gainsayers. Both teachers and learners go to sleep at their post as soon as there is no enemy in the field.

The same thing holds true, generally speaking, of all traditional doctrines—those of prudence and knowledge of life as well as of morals or religion. All languages and literatures are full of general observations on life, both as to what it is and how to conduct oneself in it—observations which everybody knows, which everybody repeats or hears with acquiescence, which are received as truisms, yet of which most people first truly learn the meaning when experience, generally of a painful kind, has made it a reality to them. How often, when smarting under some unforeseen misfortune or disappointment, does a person call to mind some proverb or common saying, familiar to him all his life, the meaning of which, if he had ever before felt it as he does now, would have saved him from the calamity. There are indeed reasons for this, other than the absence of discussion; there are many truths of which the full meaning *cannot* be realized until personal experience has brought it home. But much more of the meaning even of these would have been understood, and what was understood would have been far more deeply impressed on the mind, if the man had been accustomed to hear it argued *pro* and *con* by people who did understand it. The fatal tendency of mankind to leave off thinking about a thing when it is no longer doubtful is the cause of half their errors. A contemporary author has well spoken of "the deep slumber of a decided opinion."

But what! (it may be asked), Is the absence of unanimity an indispensable condition of true knowledge? Is it necessary that some part of mankind should persist in error to enable any to realize the truth? Does a belief cease to be real and vital as soon as it is generally received—and is a proposition never thoroughly understood and felt unless some doubt of it remains? As soon as mankind have unanimously accepted a truth, does the truth perish within them? The highest aim and best result of improved intelligence, it has hitherto been thought, is to unite mankind more and more in the acknowledgment of all important truths; and does the intelligence only last as long as it has not achieved its object? Do the fruits of conquest perish by the very completeness of the victory?

I affirm no such thing. As mankind improve, the number of doctrines which are no longer disputed or doubted will be constantly on the increase; and the well-being of mankind may almost be measured by the number and gravity of the truths which have reached the point of being uncontested. The cessation, on one question after another, of serious controversy is one of the necessary incidents of the consolidation of opinion—a consolidation as salutary in the case of true opinions as it is dangerous and noxious when the opinions are erroneous. But though this gradual narrowing of the bounds of diversity of opinion is necessary in both senses of the term, being at once inevitable and indispensable, we are not therefore obliged to conclude that all its consequences must be beneficial. The loss of so important an aid to the intelligent and living apprehension of a truth as is afforded by the necessity of explaining it to, or defending it against, opponents, though not sufficient to outweigh, is no trifling drawback from the benefit of its universal recognition. Where this advantage can no longer be had, I confess I should like to see the teachers of mankind endeavoring to provide a substitute for it—some contrivance for making the difficulties of the question as present to the learner's consciousness as if they were pressed upon him by a dissentient champion, eager for his conversion.

But instead of seeking contrivances for this purpose, they have lost those they formerly had. The Socratic dialectics, so magnificently exemplified in the dialogues of Plato, were a contrivance of this description. They were essentially a negative discussion of the great questions of philosophy and life, directed with consummate skill to the purpose of convincing anyone who had merely adopted the commonplaces of received opinion that he did not understand the subject—that he as yet attached no definite meaning to the doctrines he professed; in order that, becoming aware of his ignorance, he might be put in the way to obtain a stable belief, resting on a clear apprehension both of the meaning of doctrines and of their evidence. The school disputations of the Middle Ages had a somewhat similar object. They were intended to make sure that the pupil understood his own opinion, and (by necessary correlation) the opinion opposed to it, and could enforce the grounds of the one and confute those of the other. These last-mentioned contests had indeed the incurable defect that the premises appealed to were taken from authority, not from reason; and, as a discipline to the mind, they were in every respect inferior to the powerful dialectics which formed the intellects of the *"Socratici viri"*; but the modern mind owes far more to both than it is generally willing to admit, and the present modes of education contain nothing which in the smallest degree supplies the place either of the one or of the other. A person who derives all his instruction from teachers or books, even if he escape the besetting temptation of contenting himself with cram, is under no compulsion to hear both sides; accordingly it is far from a frequent accomplishment, even among thinkers, to know both sides; and the weakest part of what everybody says in defense of his opinion is what he intends as a reply to antagonists. It is the fashion of the present time to disparage negative logic—that which points out weaknesses in theory or errors in practice without establishing positive truths. Such negative criticism would indeed be poor enough as an ultimate result, but as a means to attaining any positive knowledge or conviction worthy the name it cannot be valued too highly; and until people are again systematically trained to it, there will be few great thinkers and a low general average of intellect in any but the mathematical and physical departments of speculation. On any other subject no one's opinions deserve the name of knowledge, except so far as he has either had forced upon him by others or gone through of himself the same mental process which would have been required of him in carrying on an active controversy with opponents. That, therefore, which, when absent, it is so indispensable, but so difficult, to create, how worse than absurd it is to forego when spontaneously offering itself! If there are any persons who contest a received opinion, or who will do so if law or opinion will let them, let us thank them for it, open our minds to listen to them, and rejoice that there is someone to do for us what we otherwise ought, if we have any regard for either the certainty or the vitality of our convictions, to do with much greater labor for ourselves.

It still remains to speak of one of the principal causes which make diversity of opinion advantageous, and will continue to do so until mankind shall have entered a stage of intellectual advancement which at present seems at an incalculable distance. We have hitherto considered only two possibilities: that the received opinion may be false, and some other opinion, consequently, true; or that, the received opinion being true, a conflict with the opposite error is essential to a clear apprehension and deep feeling of its truth. But there is a commoner case than either of these: when the conflicting doctrines, instead of being one true and the other false, share the truth between them, and the nonconforming opinion is needed to supply the remainder of the truth of which the received doctrine embodies only a part. Popular opinions, on subjects not palpable to sense, are often true, but seldom or never the whole truth. They are a part of the truth, sometimes a greater, sometimes a smaller part, but exaggerated, distorted, and disjoined from the truths by which they ought to be accompanied and limited. Heretical opinions, on the other hand, are generally some of these suppressed and neglected truths, bursting the bonds which kept them down, and either seeking reconciliation with the truth contained in the common opinion, or fronting it as enemies, and setting themselves up, with similar exclusiveness, as the whole truth. The latter case is hitherto the most frequent, as, in the human mind, one-sidedness has always been the rule, and many-sidedness the exception. Hence, even in revolutions of opinion, one part of the truth usually sets while another rises. Even progress, which ought to superadd, for the most part only substitutes one partial and incomplete truth for another; improvement consisting chiefly in this, that the new fragment of truth is more wanted, more adapted to the needs of the time than that which it displaces. Such being the partial character of prevailing opinions, even when resting on a true foundation, every opinion which embodies somewhat of the portion of truth which the common opinion omits ought to be considered precious, with whatever amount of error and confusion that truth may be blended. No sober judge of human affairs will feel bound to be indignant because those who force on our notice truths which we should otherwise have overlooked, overlook some of those which we see. Rather, he will think that so long as popular truth is one-sided, it is more desirable than otherwise that unpopular truth should have one-sided assertors, too, such being usually the most energetic and the most likely to compel reluctant attention to the fragment of wisdom which they proclaim as if it were the whole.

Thus, in the eighteenth century, when nearly all the instructed, and all those of the uninstructed who were led by them, were lost in admiration of what is called civilization, and of the marvels of modern science, literature, and philosophy, and while greatly overrating the amount of unlikeness between the men of modern and those of ancient times, indulged the belief that the whole of the difference was in their own favor; with what a salutary shock did the paradoxes of Rousseau explode like bombshells in the midst, dislocating the compact mass of one-sided opinion and forcing its elements to recombine in a better form and with additional ingredients. Not that the current opinions were on the whole farther from the truth than Rousseau's were; on the contrary, they were nearer to it; they contained more of positive truth, and very much less of error. Nevertheless there lay in Rousseau's doctrine, and has floated down the stream of opinion along with it, a considerable amount of exactly those truths which the popular opinion wanted; and these are the deposit which was left behind them when the flood subsided. The superior worth of simplicity of life, the enervating and demoralizing effect of the trammels and hypocrisies of artificial society are ideas which have never been entirely absent from cultivated minds since Rousseau wrote; and they will in time produce their due effect, though at present needing to be asserted as much as ever, and to be asserted by deeds; for words, on this subject, have nearly exhausted their power.

In politics, again, it is almost a commonplace that a party of order or stability and a party of progress or reform are both necessary elements of a healthy state of political life, until the one or the other shall have so enlarged its mental grasp as to be a party equally of order and of progress, knowing and distinguishing what is fit to be preserved from what ought to be swept away. Each of these modes of thinking derives its utility from the deficiencies of the other; but it is in a great measure the opposition of the other that keeps each within the limits of reason and sanity. Unless opinions favorable to democracy and to aristocracy, to property and to equality, to co-operation and to competition, to luxury and to abstinence, to sociality and individuality, to liberty and discipline, and all the other standing antagonisms of practical life, are expressed with equal freedom and enforced and defended with equal talent and energy, there is no chance of both elements obtaining their due; one scale is sure to go up, and the other down. Truth, in the great practical concerns of life, is so much a question of the reconciling and combining of opposites that very few have minds sufficiently capacious and impartial to make the adjustment with an approach to correctness, and it has to be made by the rough process of a struggle between combatants fighting under hostile banners. On any of the great open questions just enumerated, if either of the two opinions has a better claim than the other, not merely to be tolerated, but to be encouraged and countenanced, it is the one which happens at the particular time and place to be in a minority. That is the opinion which, for the time being, represents the neglected interests, the side of human well-being which is in danger of obtaining less than its share. I am aware that there is not, in this country, any intolerance of differences of opinion on most of these topics. They are adduced to show, by admitted and multiplied examples, the universality of the fact that only through diversity of opinion is there, in the existing state of human intellect, a chance of fair play to all sides of the truth. When there are persons to be found who form an exception to the apparent unanimity of the world on any subject, even if the world is in the right, it is always probable that dissentients have something worth hearing to say for themselves, and that truth would lose something by their silence.

It may be objected, "But *some* received principles, especially on the highest and most vital subjects, are more than half-truths. The Christian morality, for instance, is the whole truth on that subject, and if anyone teaches a morality which varies from it, he is wholly in error." As this is of all cases the most important in practice, none can be fitter to test the general maxim. But before pronouncing what Christian morality is or is not, it would be desirable to decide what is meant by Christian morality. If it means the morality of the New Testament, I wonder that any one who derives his knowledge of this from the book itself can suppose that it was announced, or intended, as a complete doctrine of morals. The Gospel always refers to a preexisting morality and confines its precepts to the particulars in which that morality was to be corrected or superseded by a wider and higher, expressing itself, moreover, in terms most general, often impossible to be interpreted literally, and possessing rather the impressiveness of poetry or eloquence than the precision of legislation. To extract from it a body of ethical doctrine has never been possible without eking it out from the Old Testament, that is, from a system elaborate indeed, but in many respects barbarous, and intended only for a barbarous people. St. Paul, a declared enemy to this Judaical mode of interpreting the doctrine and filling up the scheme of his Master, equally assumes a pre-existing morality, namely that of the Greeks and Romans; and his advice to Christians is in a great measure a system of accommodation to that, even to the extent of giving an apparent sanction to slavery. What is called Christian, but should rather be termed theological, morality was not the work of Christ or the Apostles, but is of much later origin, having been gradually built up by the Catholic Church of the first five centuries, and though not implicitly adopted by moderns and Protestants, has been much less modified by them than might have been expected. For the most part, indeed, they have contented themselves with cutting off the additions which had been made to it in the Middle Ages, each sect supplying the place by fresh additions, adapted to its own character and tendencies. That mankind owe a great debt to this morality, and to its early teachers, I should be the last person to deny, but I do not scruple to say of it that it is, in many important points, incomplete and one-sided, and that, unless ideas and feelings not sanctioned by it had contributed to the formation of European life and character, human affairs would have been in a worse condition than they now are. Christian morality (so called) has all the characters of a reaction; it is, in great part, a protest against paganism. Its ideal is negative rather than positive; passive rather than active; innocence rather than nobleness; abstinence from evil rather than energetic pursuit of good; in its precepts (as has been well said) "thou shalt not" predominates unduly over "though shalt." In its horror of sensuality, it made an idol of asceticism which has been gradually compromised away into one of legality. It holds out the hope of heaven and the threat of hell as the appointed and appropriate motives to a virtuous life: in this falling far below the best of the ancients, and doing what lies in it to give to human morality an essentially selfish character, by disconnecting each man's feelings of duty from the interests of his fellow creatures, except so far as a self-interested inducement is offered to him for consulting them. It is essentially a doctrine of passive obedience; it inculcates submission to all authorities found established; who indeed are not to be actively obeyed when they command what religion forbids, but who are not to be resisted, far less rebelled against, for any amount of wrong to ourselves. And while, in the morality of the best pagan nations, duty to the State holds even a disproportionate place, infringing on the just liberty of the individual, in purely Christian ethics that grand department of duty is scarcely noticed or acknowledged. It is in the Koran, not the New Testament, that we read the maxim: "A ruler who appoints any man to an office, when there is in his dominions another man better qualified for it, sins against God and against the State." What little recognition the idea of obligation to the public obtains in modem morality is derived from Greek and Roman sources, not from Christian; as, even in the morality of private life, whatever exists of magnanimity, high-mindedness, personal dignity, even the sense of honor, is derived from the purely human, not the religious part of our education, and never could have grown out of a standard of ethics in which the only worth, professedly recognized, is that of obedience.

I am as far as anyone from pretending that these defects are necessarily inherent in the Christian ethics in every manner in which it can be conceived, or that the many requisites of a complete moral doctrine which it does not contain do not admit of being reconciled with it. Far less would I insinuate this out of the doctrines and precepts of Christ himself. I believe that the sayings of Christ are all that I can see any evidence of their having been intended to be; that they are irreconcilable with nothing which a comprehensive morality requires; that everything which is excellent in ethics may be brought within them, with no greater violence to their language than has been done to it by all who have attempted to deduce from them any practical system of conduct whatever. But it is quite consistent with this to believe that they contain, and were meant to contain, only a part of the truth; that many essential elements of the highest morality are among the things which are not provided for, nor intended to be provided for, in the recorded deliverances of the Founder of Christianity, and which have been entirely thrown aside in the system of ethics erected on the basis of those deliverances by the Christian Church. And this being so, I think it a great error to persist in attempting to find in the Christian doctrine that complete rule for our guidance which its Author intended it to sanction and enforce, but only partially to provide. I believe, too, that this narrow theory is becoming a grave practical evil, detracting greatly from the value of the moral training and instruction which so many well-meaning persons are now at length exerting themselves to promote. I

much fear that by attempting to form the mind and feelings on an exclusively religious type, and discarding those secular standards (as for want of
a better name they may be called) which heretofore coexisted with and
supplemented the Christian ethics, receiving some of its spirit, and infus-
ing into it some of theirs, there will result, and is even now resulting, a
low, abject, servile type of character which, submit itself as it may to what
it deems the Supreme Will, is incapable of rising to or sympathizing in the
conception of Supreme Goodness. I believe that other ethics than any
which can be evolved from exclusively Christian sources must exist side
by side with Christian ethics to produce the moral regeneration of
mankind; and that the Christian system is no exception to the rule that in
an imperfect state of the human mind the interests of truth require a diversity of opinions. It is not necessary that in ceasing to ignore the moral
truths not contained in Christianity men should ignore any of those which
it does contain. Such prejudice or oversight, when it occurs, is altogether
an evil, but it is one from which we cannot hope to be always exempt, and
must be regarded as the price paid for an inestimable good. The exclusive
pretension made by a part of the truth to be the whole must and ought to
be protested against; and if a reactionary impulse should make the protes-
tors unjust in their turn, this one-sidedness, like the other, may be
lamented but must be tolerated. If Christians would teach infidels to be
just to Christianity, they should themselves be just to infidelity. It can do
truth no service to blink the fact, known to all who have the most ordinary
acquaintance with literary history, that a large portion of the noblest and
most valuable moral teaching has been the work, not only of men who did
not know, but of men who knew and rejected, the Christian faith.

I do not pretend that the most unlimited use of the freedom of enunciating all possible opinions would put an end to the evils of religious or
philosophical sectarianism. Every truth which men of narrow capacity are
in earnest about is sure to be asserted, inculcated, and in many ways even
acted on, as if no other truth existed in the world, or at all events none that
could limit or qualify the first. I acknowledge that the tendency of all
opinions to become sectarian is not cured by the freest discussion, but is
often heightened and exacerbated thereby; the truth which ought to have
been, but was not, seen, being rejected all the more violently because proclaimed by persons regarded as opponents. But it is not on the impassioned partisan, it is on the calmer and more disinterested bystander, that
this collision of opinions works its salutary effect. Not the violent conflict
between parts of the truth, but the quiet suppression of half of it, is the
formidable evil; there is always hope when people are forced to listen to
both sides; it is when they attend only to one that errors harden into prejudices, and truth itself ceases to have the effect of truth by being exagger-

ated into falsehood. And since there are few mental attributes more rare than that judicial faculty which can sit in intelligent judgment between two sides of a question, of which only one is represented by an advocate before it, truth has no chance but in proportion as every side of it, every opinion which embodies any fraction of the truth, not only finds advocates, but is so advocated as to be listened to.

We have now recognized the necessity to the mental well-being of mankind (on which all their other well-being depends) of freedom of opinion, and freedom of the expression of opinion, on four distinct grounds, which we will now briefly recapitulate:

First, if any opinion is compelled to silence, that opinion may, for aught we can certainly know, be true. To deny this is to assume our own infallibility.

Secondly, though the silenced opinion be an error, it may, and very commonly does, contain a portion of truth; and since the general or prevailing opinion on any subject is rarely or never the whole truth, it is only by the collision of adverse opinions that the remainder of the truth has any chance of being supplied.

Thirdly, even if the received opinion be not only true, but the whole truth; unless it is suffered to be, and actually is, vigorously and earnestly contested, it will, by most of those who receive it, be held in the manner of a prejudice, with little comprehension or feeling of its rational grounds. And not only this, but, fourthly, the meaning of the doctrine itself will be in danger of being lost or enfeebled, and deprived of its vital effect on the character and conduct: the dogma becoming a mere formal profession, inefficacious for good, but cumbering the ground and preventing the growth of any real and heartfelt conviction from reason or personal experience.

Before quitting the subject of freedom of opinion, it is fit to take some notice of those who say that the free expression of all opinions should be permitted on condition that the manner be temperate, and do not pass the bounds of fair discussion. Much might be said on the impossibility of fixing where these supposed bounds are to be placed; for if the test be offense to those whose opinion is attacked, I think experience testifies that this offense is given whenever the attack is telling and powerful, and that every opponent who pushes them hard, and whom they find it difficult to answer, appears to them, if he shows any strong feeling on the subject, an intemperate opponent. But this, though an important consideration in a practical point of view, merges in a more fundamental objection. Undoubtedly, the manner of asserting an opinion, even though it be a true one, may be very objectionable and may justly incur severe censure. But the principal offenses of the kind are such as it is mostly impossible, un-

less by accidental self-betrayal, to bring home to conviction. The gravest
of them is, to argue sophistically, to suppress facts or arguments, to mis-
state the elements of the case, or misrepresent the opposite opinion. But
all this, even to the most aggravated degree, is so continually done in perfect good faith by persons who are not considered, and in many other respects may not deserve to be considered, ignorant or incompetent, that it
is rarely possible, on adequate grounds, conscientiously to stamp the mis-
representation as morally culpable, and still less could law presume to interfere with this kind of controversial misconduct. With regard to what is
commonly meant by intemperate discussion, namely invective, sarcasm,
personality, and the like, the denunciation of these weapons would deserve
more sympathy if it were ever proposed to interdict them equally to both
sides; but it is only desired to restrain the employment of them against the
prevailing opinion; against the unprevailing they may not only be used
without general disapproval, but will be likely to obtain for him who uses
them the praise of honest zeal and righteous indignation. Yet whatever
mischief arises from their use is greatest when they are employed against
the comparatively defenseless; and whatever unfair advantage can be derived by any opinion from this mode of asserting it accrues almost exclusively to received opinions. The worst offense of this kind which can be
committed by a polemic is to stigmatize those who hold the contrary
opinion as bad and immoral men. To calumny of this sort, those who hold
any unpopular opinion are peculiarly exposed, because they are in general
few and uninfluential, and nobody but themselves feels much interested
in seeing justice done them; but this weapon is, from the nature of the
case, denied to those who attack a prevailing opinion: they can neither use
it with safety to themselves, nor, if they could, would it do anything but
recoil on their own cause. In general, opinions contrary to those commonly received can only obtain a hearing by studied moderation of language and the most cautious avoidance of unnecessary offense, from
which they hardly ever deviate even in a slight degree without losing
ground, while unmeasured vituperation employed on the side of the prevailing opinion really does deter people from professing contrary opinions
and from listening to those who profess them. For the interest, therefore,
of truth and justice it is far more important to restrain this employment of
vituperative language than the other; and, for example, if it were necessary
to choose, there would be much more need to discourage offensive attacks
on infidelity than on religion. It is, however, obvious that law and authority have no business with restraining either, while opinion ought, in every
instance, to determine its verdict by the circumstances of the individual
case—condemning everyone, on whichever side of the argument he
places himself, in whose mode of advocacy either want of candor, or

malignity, bigotry, or intolerance of feeling manifest themselves; but not inferring these vices from the side which a person takes, though it be the contrary side of the question to our own; and giving merited honor to everyone, whatever opinion he may hold, who has calmness to see and honesty to state what his opponents and their opinions really are, exaggerating nothing to their discredit, keeping nothing back which tells, or can be supposed to tell, in their favor. This is the real morality of public discussion; and if often violated, I am happy to think that there are many controversialists who to a great extent observe it, and a still greater number who conscientiously strive toward it.

CHAPTER III
Of Individuality, as One of the Elements of Well-Being

Such being the reasons which make it imperative that human beings should be free to form opinions and to express their opinions without reserve; and such the baneful consequences to the intellectual, and through that to the moral nature of man, unless this liberty is either conceded or asserted in spite of prohibition; let us next examine whether the same reasons do not require that men should be free to act upon their opinions—to carry these out in their lives without hindrance, either physical or moral, from their fellow men, so long as it is at their own risk and peril. This last proviso is of course indispensable. No one pretends that actions should be as free as opinions. On the contrary, even opinions lose their immunity when the circumstances in which they are expressed are such as to constitute their expression a positive instigation to some mischievous act. An opinion that corn dealers are starvers of the poor, or that private property is robbery, ought to be unmolested when simply circulated through the press, but may justly incur punishment when delivered orally to an excited mob assembled before the house of a corn dealer, or when handed about among the same mob in the form of a placard. Acts, of whatever kind, which without justifiable cause do harm to others may be, and in the more important cases absolutely require to be, controlled by the unfavorable sentiments, and, when needful, by the active interference of mankind. The liberty of the individual must be thus far limited; he must not make himself a nuisance to other people. But if he refrains from molesting others in what concerns them, and merely acts according to his own inclination and judgment in things which concern himself, the same reasons which show that opinion should be free prove also that he should be allowed, without molestation, to carry his opinions into practice at his own cost. That mankind are not infallible; that their truths, for the most part, are only half-truths; that unity of opinion, unless resulting from the fullest and freest comparison of opposite opinions, is not desirable, and diversity not an evil, but a good, until mankind are much more capable than at present of recognizing all sides of the truth, are principles applicable to men's modes of action not less than to their opinions. As it is useful that while mankind are imperfect there should be different opinions, so is it that there should be different experiments of living; that free scope should be given to varieties of character, short of injury to others; and that the worth of different modes of life should be proved practically, when anyone thinks fit to try them. It is desirable, in short, that in things which do not primarily concern others individuality should assert itself. Where not the person's own character but the traditions or customs of other people are the rule of conduct, there is wanting one of the principal ingredients of human happiness, and quite the chief ingredient of individual and social progress.

In maintaining this principle, the greatest difficulty to be encountered does not lie in the appreciation of means toward an acknowledged end, but in the indifference of persons in general to the end itself. If it were felt that the free development of individuality is one of the leading essentials of well-being; that it is not only a co-ordinate element with all that is designated by the terms civilization, instruction, education, culture, but is itself a necessary part and condition of all those things, there would be no danger that liberty should be undervalued, and the adjustment of the boundaries between it and social control would present no extraordinary difficulty. But the evil is that individual spontaneity is hardly recognized by the common modes of thinking as having any intrinsic worth, or deserving any regard on its own account. The majority, being satisfied with the ways of mankind as they now are (for it is they who make them what they are), cannot comprehend why those ways should not be good enough for everybody; and what is more, spontaneity forms no part of the ideal of the majority of moral and social reformers, but is rather looked on with jealousy, as a troublesome and perhaps rebellious obstruction to the general acceptance of what these reformers, in their own judgment, think would be best for mankind. Few persons, out of Germany, even comprehend the meaning of the doctrine which Wilhelm von Humboldt, so eminent both as a *savant* and as a politician, made the text of a treatise—that "the end of man, or that which is prescribed by the eternal or immutable dictates of reason, and not suggested by vague and transient desires, is the highest and most harmonious development of his powers to a complete and consistent whole"; that, therefore, the object "toward which every human being must ceaselessly direct his efforts, and on which especially those who design to influence their fellow men must ever keep their eyes, is the individuality of power and development"; that for this there are two requisites, "freedom, and variety of situations"; and that from the union of these arise "individual vigor and manifold diversity," which combine themselves in "originality."[6]

Little, however, as people are accustomed to a doctrine like that of von Humboldt, and surprising as it may be to them to find so high a value attached to individuality, the question, one must nevertheless think, can only be one of degree. No one's idea of excellence in conduct is that people should do absolutely nothing but copy one another. No one would assert that people ought not to put into their mode of life, and into the conduct of their concerns, any impress whatever of their own judgment or of their own individual character. On the other hand, it would be absurd to pretend that people ought to live as if nothing whatever had been known in the world before they came into it; as if experience had as yet done nothing toward showing that one mode of existence, or of conduct, is preferable to another. Nobody denies that people should be so taught and trained in youth as to know and benefit by the ascertained results of human experience. But it is the privilege and proper condition of a human being, arrived at the maturity of his faculties, to use and interpret experience in his own way. It is for him to find out what part of recorded experience is properly applicable to his own circumstances and character. The traditions and customs of other people are, to a certain extent, evidence of what their experience has taught *them*—presumptive evidence, and as such, have a claim to his deference: but, in the first place, their experience may be too narrow, or they may not have interpreted it rightly. Secondly, their interpretation of experience may be correct, but unsuitable to him. Customs are made for customary circumstances and customary characters; and his circumstances or his character may be uncustomary. Thirdly, though the customs be both good as customs and suitable to him, yet to conform to custom merely as custom does not educate or develop in him any of the qualities which are the distinctive endowment of a human being. The human faculties of perception, judgment, discriminative feeling, mental activity, and even moral preference are exercised only in making a choice. He who does anything because it is the custom makes no choice. He gains no practice either in discerning or in desiring what is best. The mental and moral, like the muscular, powers are improved only by being used. The faculties are called into no exercise by doing a thing merely because others do it, no more than by believing a thing only because others believe it. If the grounds of an opinion are not conclusive to the person's own reason, his reason cannot be strengthened, but is likely to be weakened, by his adopting it: and if the inducements to an act are not such as are consentaneous to his own feelings and character (where affection, or the rights of others, are not concerned), it is so much done toward rendering his feelings and character inert and torpid instead of active and energetic.

He who lets the world, or his own portion of it, choose his plan of life for him has no need of any other faculty than the ape-like one of imitation. He who chooses his plan for himself employs all his faculties. He must use observation to see, reasoning and judgment to foresee, activity to gather materials for decision, discrimination to decide, and when he has decided, firmness and self-control to hold to his deliberate decision. And these qualities he requires and exercises exactly in proportion as the part of his conduct which he determines according to his own judgment and feelings is a large one. It is possible that he might be guided in some good path, and kept out of harm's way, without any of these things. But what will be his comparative worth as a human being? It really is of importance, not only what men do, but also what manner of men they are that do it. Among the works of man which human life is rightly employed in perfecting and beautifying, the first in importance surely is man himself. Supposing it were possible to get houses built, corn grown, battles fought, causes tried, and even churches erected and prayers said by machinery— by automatons in human form—it would be a considerable loss to exchange for these automatons even the men and women who at present inhabit the more civilized parts of the world, and who assuredly are but starved specimens of what nature can and will produce. Human nature is not a machine to be built after a model, and set to do exactly the work prescribed for it, but a tree, which requires to grow and develop itself on all sides, according to the tendency of the inward forces which make it a living thing.

It will probably be conceded that it is desirable people should exercise their understandings, and that an intelligent following of custom, or even occasionally an intelligent deviation from custom, is better than a blind and simply mechanical adhesion to it. To a certain extent it is admitted that our understanding should be our own; but there is not the same willingness to admit that our desires and impulses should be our own likewise, or that to possess impulses of our own, and of any strength, is anything but a peril and a snare. Yet desires and impulses are as much a part of a perfect human being as beliefs and restraints; and strong impulses are only perilous when not properly balanced, when one set of aims and inclinations is developed into strength, while others, which ought to coexist with them, remain weak and inactive. It is not because men's desires are strong that they act ill; it is because their consciences are weak. There is no natural connection between strong impulses and a weak conscience. The natural connection is the other way. To say that one person's desires and feelings are stronger and more various than those of another is merely to say that he has more of the raw material of human nature and is therefore capable, perhaps of more evil, but certainly of more good. Strong impulses are but another name for energy. Energy may be turned to bad uses; but more good may always be made of an energetic nature than of an indolent and impassive one. Those who have most natural feeling are always those whose cultivated feelings may be made the strongest. The same strong susceptibilities which make the personal impulses vivid and powerful are also the source from whence are generated the most passionate love of virtue and the sternest self-control. It is through the cultivation of these that society both does its duty and protects its interests, not by rejecting the stuff of which heroes are made, because it knows not how to make them. A person whose desires and impulses are his own—are the expression of his own nature, as it has been developed and modified by his own culture—is said to have a character. One whose desires and impulses are not his own has no character, no more than a steam engine has a character. If, in addition to being his own, his impulses are strong and are under the government of a strong will, he has an energetic character. Whoever thinks that individuality of desires and impulses should not be encouraged to unfold itself must maintain that society has no need of strong natures—is not the better for containing many persons who have much character—and that a high general average of energy is not desirable.

In some early states of society, these forces might be, and were, too much ahead of the power which society then possessed of disciplining and controlling them. There has been a time when the element of spontaneity and individuality was in excess, and the social principle had a hard struggle with it. The difficulty then was to induce men of strong bodies or minds to pay obedience to any rules which required them to control their impulses. To overcome this difficulty, law and discipline, like the Popes struggling against the Emperors, asserted a power over the whole man, claiming to control all his life in order to control his character—which society had not found any other sufficient means of binding. But society has now fairly got the better of individuality; and the danger which threatens human nature is not the excess, but the deficiency, of personal impulses and preferences. Things are vastly changed since the passions of those who were strong by station or by personal endowment were in a state of habitual rebellion against laws and ordinances, and required to be rigorously chained up to enable the persons within their reach to enjoy any particle of security. In our times, from the highest class of society down to the lowest, everyone lives as under the eye of a hostile and dreaded censorship. Not only in what concerns others, but in what concerns only themselves, the individual or the family do not ask themselves, what do I prefer? or, what would suit my character and disposition? or, what would allow the best and highest in me to have fair play and enable it to grow and thrive? They ask themselves, what is suitable to my position? what is usually done by persons of my station and pecuniary circumstances? or (worse still) what is usually done by persons of a station and circumstances superior to mine? I do not mean that they choose what is customary in preference to what suits their own inclination. It does not occur to them to have any inclination except for what is customary. Thus the mind itself is bowed to the yoke: even in what people do for pleasure, conformity is the first thing thought of; they like in crowds; they exercise choice only among things commonly done; peculiarity of taste, eccentricity of conduct are shunned equally with crimes, until by dint of not following their own nature they have no nature to follow: their human capacities are withered and starved; they become incapable of any strong wishes or native pleasures, and are generally without either opinions or feelings of home growth, or properly their own. Now is this, or is it not, the desirable condition of human nature?

It is so, on the Calvinistic theory. According to that, the one great offense of man is self-will. All the good of which humanity is capable is comprised in obedience. You have no choice; thus you must do, and no otherwise: "Whatever is not a duty is a sin." Human nature being radically corrupt, there is no redemption for anyone until human nature is killed within him. To one holding this theory of life, crushing out any of the human faculties, capacities, and susceptibilities is no evil: man needs no capacity but that of surrendering himself to the will of God; and if he uses any of his faculties for any other purpose but to do that supposed will more effectually, he is better without them. This is the theory of Calvinism; and it is held, in a mitigated form, by many who do not consider themselves Calvinists; the mitigation consisting in giving a less ascetic interpretation to the alleged will of God, asserting it to be his will that mankind should gratify some of their inclinations, of course not in the manner they themselves prefer, but in the way of obedience, that is, in a way prescribed to them by authority, and, therefore, by the necessary condition of the case, the same for all.

In some such insidious form there is at present a strong tendency to this narrow theory of life, and to the pinched and hidebound type of human character which it patronizes. Many persons, no doubt, sincerely think that human beings thus cramped and dwarfed are as their Maker designed them to be, just as many have thought that trees are a much finer thing when clipped into pollards, or cut out into figures of animals, than as nature made them. But if it be any part of religion to believe that man was made by a good Being, it is more consistent with that faith to believe that this Being gave all human faculties that they might be cultivated and unfolded, not rooted out and consumed, and that he takes delight in every nearer approach made by his creatures to the ideal conception embodied in them, every increase in any of their capabilities of comprehension, of action, or of enjoyment. There is a different type of human excellence from the Calvinistic: a conception of humanity as having its nature bestowed on it for other purposes than merely to be abnegated. "Pagan self-assertion" is one of the elements of human worth, as well as "Christian self-denial."[7] There is a Greek ideal of self-development, which the Platonic and Christian ideal of self-government blends with, but does not supersede. It may be better to be a John Knox than an Alcibiades, but it is better to be a Pericles than either, nor would a Pericles, if we had one in these days, be without anything good which belonged to John Knox.

It is not by wearing down into uniformity all that is individual in themselves, but by cultivating it and calling it forth, within the limits imposed by the rights and interests of others, that human beings become a noble and beautiful object of contemplation; and as the works partake the character of those who do them, by the same process human life also becomes rich, diversified, and animating, furnishing more abundant aliment to high thoughts and elevating feelings, and strengthening the tie which binds every individual to the race, by making the race infinitely better worth belonging to. In proportion to the development of his individuality, each person becomes more valuable to himself, and is, therefore, capable of being more valuable to others. There is a greater fullness of life about his own existence, and when there is more life in the units there is more in the mass which is composed of them. As much compression as is necessary to prevent the stronger specimens of human nature from encroaching on the rights of others cannot be dispensed with; but for this there is ample compensation even in the point of view of human development. The means of development which the individual loses by being prevented from gratifying his inclinations to the injury of others are chiefly obtained at the expense of the development of other people. And even to himself there is a full equivalent in the better development of the social part of his nature, rendered possible by the restraint put upon the selfish part. To be held to rigid rules of justice for the sake of others develops the feelings and capacities which have the good of others for their object. But to be restrained in things not affecting their good, by their mere displeasure, develops nothing valuable except such force of character as may unfold itself in resisting the restraint. If acquiesced in, it dulls and blunts the whole nature. To give any fair play to the nature of each, it is essential that different persons should be allowed to lead different lives. In proportion as this latitude has been exercised in any age has that age been noteworthy to posterity. Even despotism does not produce its worst effects so long as individuality exists under it; and whatever crushes individuality is despotism, by whatever name it may be called and whether it professes to be enforcing the will of God or the injunctions of men.

Having said that Individuality is the same thing with development, and that it is only the cultivation of individuality which produces, or can produce, well-developed human beings, I might here close the argument; for what more or better can be said of any condition of human affairs than that it brings human beings themselves nearer to the best thing they can be? Or what worse can be said of any obstruction to good than that it prevents this? Doubtless, however, these considerations will not suffice to convince those who most need convincing; and it is necessary farther to show that these developed human beings are of some use to the undeveloped—to point out to those who do not desire liberty, and would not avail themselves of it, that they may be in some intelligible manner rewarded for allowing other people to make use of it without hindrance.

In the first place, then, I would suggest that they might possibly learn something from them. It will not be denied by anybody that originality is a valuable element in human affairs. There is always need of persons not only to discover new truths and point out when what were once truths are true no longer, but also to commence new practices and set the example of more enlightened conduct and better taste and sense in human life. This cannot well be gainsaid by anybody who does not believe that the world has already attained perfection in all its ways and practices. It is true that this benefit is not capable of being rendered by everybody alike; there are but few persons, in comparison with the whole of mankind, whose experiments, if adopted by others, would be likely to be any improvement on established practice. But these few are the salt of the earth; without them, human life would become a stagnant pool. Not only is it they who introduce good things which did not before exist; it is they who keep the life in those which already existed. If there were nothing new to be done, would human intellect cease to be necessary? Would it be a reason why those who do the old things should forget why they are done, and do them like cattle, not like human beings? There is only too great a tendency in the best beliefs and practices to degenerate into the mechanical; and unless there were a succession of persons whose ever-recurring originality prevents the grounds of those beliefs and practices from becoming merely traditional, such dead matter would not resist the smallest shock from anything really alive, and there would be no reason why civilization should not die out, as in the Byzantine Empire. Persons of genius, it is true, are, and are always likely to be, a small minority; but in order to have them, it is necessary to preserve the soil in which they grow. Genius can only breathe freely in an *atmosphere* of freedom. Persons of genius are, *ex vi ter-*

mini, more individual than any other people—less capable, consequently, of fitting themselves, without hurtful compression, into any of the small number of molds which society provides in order to save its members the trouble of forming their own character. If from timidity they consent to be forced into one of these molds, and to let all that part of themselves which cannot expand under the pressure remain unexpanded, society will be little the better for their genius. If they are of a strong character and break their fetters, they become a mark for the society which has not succeeded in reducing them to commonplace, to point at with solemn warning as "wild," "erratic," and the like—much as if one should complain of the Niagara river for not flowing smoothly between its banks like a Dutch canal.

I insist thus emphatically on the importance of genius and the necessity of allowing it to unfold itself freely both in thought and in practice, being well aware that no one will deny the position in theory, but knowing also that almost everyone, in reality, is totally indifferent to it. People think genius a fine thing if it enables a man to write an exciting poem or paint a picture. But in its true sense, that of originality in thought and action, though no one says that it is not a thing to be admired, nearly all, at heart, think that they can do very well without it. Unhappily this is too natural to be wondered at. Originality is the one thing which unoriginal minds cannot feel the use of. They cannot see what it is to do for them: how should they? If they could see what it would do for them, it would not be originality. The first service which originality has to render them is that of opening their eyes: which being once fully done, they would have a chance of being themselves original. Meanwhile, recollecting that nothing was ever yet done which someone was not the first to do, and that all good things which exist are the fruits of originality, let them be modest enough to believe that there is something still left for it to accomplish, and assure themselves that they are more in need of originality, the less they are conscious of the want.

In sober truth, whatever homage may be professed, or even paid, to real or supposed mental superiority, the general tendency of things throughout the world is to render mediocrity the ascendant power among mankind. In ancient history, in the Middle Ages, and in a diminishing degree through the long transition from feudality to the present time, the individual was a power in himself; and if he had either great talents or a high social position, he was a considerable power. At present individuals are lost in the crowd. In politics it is almost a triviality to say that public opinion now rules the world. The only power deserving the name is that of masses, and of governments while they make themselves the organ of the tendencies and instincts of masses. This is as true in the moral and social relations of private life as in public transactions. Those whose opinions go by the name of public opinion are not always the same sort of public: in America, they are the whole white population; in England, chiefly the middle class. But they are always a mass, that is to say, collective mediocrity. And what is a still greater novelty, the mass do not now take their opinions from dignitaries in Church or State, from ostensible leaders, or from books. Their thinking is done for them by men much like themselves, addressing them or speaking in their name, on the spur of the moment, through the newspapers. I am not complaining of all this. I do not assert that anything better is compatible, as a general rule, with the present low state of the human mind. But that does not hinder the government of mediocrity from being mediocre government. No government by a democracy or a numerous aristocracy, either in its political acts or in the opinions, qualities, and tone of mind which it fosters, ever did or could rise above mediocrity except in so far as the sovereign. Many have let themselves be guided (which in their best times they always have done) by the counsels and influence of a more highly gifted and instructed *one* or *few*. The initiation of all wise or noble things comes and must come from individuals; generally at first from some one individual. The honor and glory of the average man is that he is capable of following that initiative; that he can respond internally to wise and noble things, and be led to them with his eyes open. I am not countenancing the sort of "hero-worship" which applauds the strong man of genius for forcibly seizing on the government of the world and making it do his bidding in spite of itself. All he can claim is freedom to point out the way. The power of compelling others into it is not only inconsistent with the freedom and development of all the rest, but corrupting to the strong man himself. It does seem, however, that when the opinions of masses of merely average men are everywhere become or becoming the dominant power, the counterpoise and corrective to that tendency would be the more and more pronounced individuality of those who stand on the higher eminences of thought. It is in these circumstances most especially that exceptional individuals, instead of being deterred, should be encouraged in acting differently from the mass. In other times there was no advantage in their doing so, unless they acted not only differently but better. In this age, the mere example of nonconformity, the mere refusal to bend the knee to custom, is itself a service. Precisely because the tyranny of opinion is such as to make eccentricity a reproach, it is desirable, in order to break through that tyranny, that people should be eccentric. Eccentricity has always abounded when and where strength of character has abounded; and the amount of eccentricity in a society has generally been proportional to the amount of genius, mental vigor, and moral courage which it contained. That so few now dare to be eccentric marks the chief danger of the time.

I have said that it is important to give the freest scope possible to un-customary things, in order that it may in time appear which of these are fit to be converted into customs. But independence of action and disregard of custom are not solely deserving of encouragement for the chance they afford that better modes of action, and customs more wordly of general adoption, may be struck out; nor is it only persons of decided mental su-periority who have a just claim to carry on their lives in their own way. There is no reason that all human existence should be constructed on some one or some small number of patterns. If a person possesses any tol-erable amount of common sense and experience, his own mode of laying out his existence is the best, not because it is the best in itself, but because it is his own mode. Human beings are not like sheep; and even sheep are not undistinguishably alike. A man cannot get a coat or a pair of boots to fit him unless they are either made to his measure or he has a whole ware-houseful to choose from; and is it easier to fit him with a life than with a coat, or are human beings more like one another in their whole physical and spiritual conformation than in the shape of their feet? If it were only that people have diversities of taste, that is reason enough for not attempt-ing to shape them all after one model. But different persons also require different conditions for their spiritual development; and can no more exist healthily in the same moral than all the variety of plants can in the same physical, atmosphere and climate. The same things which are helps to one person toward the cultivation of his higher nature are hindrances to another. The same mode of life is a healthy excitement to one, keeping all his faculties of action and enjoyment in their best order, while to another it is a distracting burden which suspends or crushes all internal life. Such are the differences among human beings in their sources of pleasure, their susceptibilities of pain, and the operation on them of different physical and moral agencies that, unless there is a corresponding diversity in their modes of life, they neither obtain their fair share of happiness, nor grow up to the mental, moral, and aesthetic stature of which their nature is capa-ble. Why then should tolerance, as far as the public sentiment is concerned, extend only to tastes and modes of life which extort acquiescence by the multitude of their adherents? Nowhere (except in some monastic institu-tions) is diversity of taste entirely unrecognized; a person may, without blame, either like or dislike rowing, or smoking, or music, or athletic exer-cises, or chess, or cards, or study, because both those who like each of these things and those who dislike them are too numerous to be put down. But the man, and still more the woman, who can be accused either of doing "what nobody does," or of not doing "what everybody does," is the subject of as much depreciatory remark as if he or she had committed some grave moral delinquency. Persons require to possess a title, or some other badge of rank, or of the consideration of people of rank, to be able to indulge somewhat in the luxury of doing as they like without detriment to their estimation. To indulge somewhat, I repeat: for whoever allow themselves much of that indulgence incur the risk of something worse than disparaging speeches—they are in peril of a commission *de lunatico* and of having their property taken from them and given to their relations.[8]

There is one characteristic of the present direction of public opinion peculiarly calculated to make it intolerant of any marked demonstration of individuality. The general average of mankind are not only moderate in intellect, but also moderate in inclinations; they have no tastes or wishes strong enough to incline them to do anything unusual, and they consequently do not understand those who have, and class all such with the wild and intemperate whom they are accustomed to look down upon. Now, in addition to this fact which is general, we have only to suppose that a strong movement has set in toward the improvement of morals, and it is evident what we have to expect. In these days such a movement has set in; much has actually been effected in the way of increased regularity of conduct and discouragement of excesses; and there is a philanthropic spirit abroad for the exercise of which there is no more inviting field than the moral and prudential improvement of our fellow creatures. These tendencies of the times cause the public to be more disposed than at most former periods to prescribe general rules of conduct and endeavor to make everyone conform to the approved standard. And that standard, express or tacit, is to desire nothing strongly. Its ideal of character is to be without any marked character—to maim by compression, like a Chinese lady's foot, every part of human nature which stands out prominently and tends to make the person markedly dissimilar in outline to commonplace humanity.

As is usually the case with ideals which exclude one-half of what is desirable, the present standard of approbation produces only an inferior imitation of the other half. Instead of great energies guided by vigorous reason and strong feelings strongly controlled by a conscientious will, its result is weak feelings and weak energies, which therefore can be kept in outward conformity to rule without any strength either of will or of reason. Already energetic characters on any large scale are becoming merely traditional. There is now scarcely any outlet for energy in this country except business. The energy expended in this may still be regarded as considerable. What little is left from that employment is expended on some hobby, which may be a useful, even a philanthropic, hobby, but is always some one thing, and generally a thing of small dimensions. The greatness of England is now all collective; individually small, we only appear capable of anything great by our habit of combining; and with this our moral and religious philanthropists are perfectly contented. But it was men of another stamp than this that made England what it has been; and men of another stamp will be needed to prevent its decline.

The despotism of custom is everywhere the standing hindrance to human advancement, being in unceasing antagonism to that disposition to aim at something better than customary, which is called, according to circumstances, the spirit of liberty, or that of progress or improvement. The spirit of improvement is not always a spirit of liberty, for it may aim at forcing improvements on an unwilling people; and the spirit of liberty, in so far as it resists such attempts, may ally itself locally and temporarily with the opponents of improvement; but the only unfailing and permanent source of improvement is liberty, since by it there are as many possible independent centers of improvement as there are individuals. The progressive principle, however, in either shape, whether as the love of liberty or of improvement, is antagonistic to the sway of custom, involving at least emancipation from that yoke; and the contest between the two constitutes the chief interest of the history of mankind. The greater part of the world has, properly speaking, no history, because the despotism of Custom is complete. This is the case over the whole East. Custom is there, in all things, the final appeal; justice and right mean conformity to custom; the argument of custom no one, unless some tyrant intoxicated with power, thinks of resisting. And we see the result. Those nations must once have had originality; they did not start out of the ground populous, lettered, and versed in many of the arts of life; they made themselves all this, and were then the greatest and most powerful nations of the world. What are they now? The subjects or dependents of tribes whose forefathers wandered in the forests when theirs had magnificent palaces and gorgeous temples, but over whom custom exercised only a divided rule with liberty and progress. A people, it appears, may be progressive for a certain length of time, and then stop: when does it stop? When it ceases to possess individuality. If a similar change should befall the nations of Europe, it will not be in exactly the same shape: the despotism of custom with which these nations are threatened is not precisely stationariness. It proscribes singularity, but it does not preclude change, provided all change together. We have discarded the fixed costumes of our forefathers; everyone must still dress like other people, but the fashion may change once or twice a year. We thus take care that when there is change, it shall be for change's sake, and not from any idea of beauty or convenience; for the same idea of beauty or convenience would not strike all the world at the same moment, and be simultaneously thrown aside by all at another moment. But we are progressive as well as changeable: we continually make new inventions in mechanical things, and keep them until they are again superseded by better; we are eager for improvement in politics, in education, even in morals, though in this last our idea of improvement chiefly consists in persuading or forcing other people to be as good as ourselves. It is not progress that we object to; on the contrary, we flatter ourselves that we are the most progressive people who ever lived. It is individuality that we war against: we should think we had done wonders if we had made ourselves all alike, forgetting that the unlikeness of one person to another is generally the first thing which draws the attention of either to the imperfection of his own type and the superiority of another, or the possibility, by combining the advantages of both, of producing something better than either. We have a warning example in China—a nation of much talent and, in some respects, even wisdom, owing to the rare good fortune of having been provided at an early period with a particularly good set of customs, the work, in some measure, of men to whom even the most enlightened European must accord, under certain limitations, the title of sages and philosophers. They are remarkable, too, in the excellence of their apparatus for impressing, as far as possible, the best wisdom they possess upon every mind in the community, and securing that those who have appropriated most of it shall occupy the posts of honor and power. Surely the people who did this have discovered the secret of human progressiveness and must have kept themselves steadily at the head of the movement of the world. On the contrary, they have become stationary—have remained so for thousands of years; and if they are ever to be further improved, it must be by foreigners. They have succeeded beyond all hope in what English philanthropists are so industriously working, at—in making a people all alike, all governing their thoughts and conduct by the same maxims and rules; and these are the fruits. The modern *régime* of public opinion is, in an unorganized form, what the Chinese educational and political systems are in an organized; and unless individuality shall be able successfully to assert itself against this yoke, Europe, notwithstanding its noble antecedents and its professed Christianity, will tend to become another China.

What is it that has hitherto preserved Europe from this lot? What has made the European family of nations an improving, instead of a stationary, portion of mankind? Not any superior excellence in them, which, when it exists, exists as the effect, not as the cause, but their remarkable diversity of character and culture. Individuals, classes, nations have been extremely unlike one another: they have struck out a great variety of paths, each leading to something valuable; and although at every period those who traveled in different paths have been intolerant of one another, and each would have thought it an excellent thing if all the rest could have been compelled to travel his road, their attempts to thwart each other's development have rarely had any permanent success, and each has in time endured to receive the good which the others have offered. Europe is, in my judgment, wholly indebted to this plurality of paths for its progressive and many-sided development. But it already begins to possess this benefit in a considerably less degree. It is decidedly advancing toward the Chinese ideal of making all people alike. M. de Tocqueville, in his last important work, remarks how much more the Frenchmen of the present day resemble one another than did those even of the last generation. The same remark might be made of Englishmen in a far greater degree. In a passage already quoted from Wilhelm von Humboldt, he points out two things as necessary conditions of human development—because necessary to render people unlike one another—namely, freedom and variety of situations. The second of these two conditions is in this country every day diminishing. The circumstances which surround different classes and individuals, and shape their characters, are daily becoming more assimilated. Formerly, different ranks, different neighborhoods, different trades and professions lived in what might be called different worlds; at present, to a great degree in the same. Comparatively speaking, they now read the. same things, listen to the same things, see the same things, go to the same places, have their hopes and fears directed to the same objects, have the same rights and liberties, and the same means of asserting them. Great as are the differences of position which remain, they are nothing to those which have ceased. And the assimilation is still proceeding. All the political changes of the age promote it, since they all tend to raise the low and to lower the high. Every extension of education promotes it, because education brings people under common influences and gives them access to the general stock of facts and sentiments. Improvements in the means of communication promote it, by bringing the inhabitants of distant places into personal contact, and keeping up a rapid flow of changes of residence between one place and another. The increase of commerce and manufactures promotes it, by diffusing more widely the advantages of easy circumstances and opening all objects of ambition, even the highest, to general competition, whereby the desire of rising becomes no longer the character of a particular class, but of all classes. A more powerful agency than even all these, in bringing about a general similarity among mankind, is the complete establishment, in this and other free countries, of the ascendancy of public opinion in the State. As the various social eminences which enabled persons entrenched on them to disregard the opinion of the multitude gradually become leveled; as the very idea of resisting the will of the public, when it is positively known that they have a will, disappears more and more from the minds of practical politicians, there ceases to be any social support for nonconformity—any substantive power in society which, itself opposed to the ascendancy of numbers, is interested in taking under its protection opinions and tendencies at variance with those of the public.

The combination of all these causes forms so great a mass of influences hostile to individuality that it is not easy to see how it can stand its ground. It will do so with increasing difficulty unless the intelligent part of the public can be made to feel its value—to see that it is good there should be differences, even though not for the better, even though, as it may appear to them, some should be for the worse. If the claims of individuality are ever to be asserted, the time is now while much is still wanting to complete the enforced assimilation. It is only in the earlier stages that any stand can be successfully made against the encroachment. The demand that all other people shall resemble ourselves grows by what it feeds on. If resistance waits till life is reduced *nearly* to one uniform type, all deviations from that type will come to be considered impious, immoral, even monstrous and contrary to nature. Mankind speedily become unable to conceive diversity when they have been for some time unaccustomed to see it.

CHAPTER IV
Of the Limits to the Authority of
Society over the Individual

What, then, is the rightful limit to the sovereignty of the individual over himself? Where does the authority of society begin? How much of human life should be assigned to individuality, and how much to society?

Each will receive its proper share if each has that which more particularly concerns it. To individuality should belong the part of life in which it is chiefly the individual that is interested; to society, the part which chiefly interests society.

Though society is not founded on a contract, and though no good purpose is answered by inventing a contract in order to deduce social obligations from it, everyone who receives the protection of society owes a return for the benefit, and the fact of living in society renders it indispensable that each should be bound to observe a certain line of conduct toward the rest. This conduct consists, first, in not injuring the interests of one another, or rather certain interests which, either by express legal provision or by tacit understanding, ought to be considered as rights; and secondly, in each person's bearing his share (to be fixed on some equitable principle) of the labors and sacrifices incurred for defending the society or its members from injury and molestation. These conditions society is justified in enforcing at all costs to those who endeavor to withhold fulfillment. Nor is this all that society may do. The acts of an individual may be hurtful to others or wanting in due consideration for their welfare, without going to the length of violating any of their constituted rights. The offender may then be justly punished by opinion, though not by law. As soon as any part of a person's conduct affects prejudicially the interests of others, society has jurisdiction over it, and the question whether the general welfare will or will not be promoted by interfering with it becomes open to discussion. But there is no room for entertaining any such question when a person's conduct affects the interests of no persons besides himself, or needs not affect them unless they like (all the persons concerned being of full age and the ordinary amount of understanding). In all such cases, there should be perfect freedom, legal and social, to do the action and stand the consequences.

It would be a great misunderstanding of this doctrine to suppose that it is one of selfish indifference which pretends that human beings have no business with each other's conduct in life, and that they should not concern themselves about the well-doing or well-being of one another, unless their own interest is involved. Instead of any diminution, there is need of a great increase of disinterested exertion to promote the good of others. But disinterested benevolence can find other instruments to persuade people to their good than whips and scourges, either of the literal or the metaphorical sort. I am the last person to undervalue the self-regarding virtues; they are only second in importance, if even second, to the social. It is equally the business of education to cultivate both. But even education works by conviction and persuasion as well as by compulsion, and it is by the former only that, when the period of education is past, the self-regarding virtues should be inculcated. Human beings owe to each other help to distinguish the better from the worse, and encouragement to choose the former and avoid the latter. They should be forever stimulating each other to increased exercise of their higher faculties and increased direction of their feelings and aims toward wise instead of foolish, elevating instead of degrading, objects and contemplations. But neither one person, nor any number of persons, is warranted in saying to another human creature of ripe years that he shall not do with his life for his own benefit what he chooses to do with it. He is the person most interested in his own well-being: the interest which any other person, except in cases of strong personal attachment, can have in it is trifling compared with that which he himself has; the interest which society has in him individually (except as to his conduct to others) is fractional and altogether indirect, while with respect to his own feelings and circumstances the most ordinary man or woman has means of knowledge immeasurably surpassing those that can be possessed by anyone else. The interference of society to overrule his judgment and purposes in what only regards himself must be grounded on general presumptions which may be altogether wrong and, even if right, are as likely as not to be misapplied to individual cases, by persons no better acquainted with the circumstances of such cases than those are who look at them merely from without. In this department, therefore, of human affairs, individuality has its proper field of action. In the conduct of human beings toward one another it is necessary that general rules should for the most part be observed in order that people may know what they have to expect; but in each person's own concerns his individual spontaneity is entitled to free exercise. Considerations to aid his judgment, exhortations to strengthen his will may be offered to him, even obtruded on him, by others; but he himself is the final judge. All errors which he is likely to commit against advice and warning are far outweighed by the evil of allowing others to constrain him to what they deem his good.

I do not mean that the feelings with which a person is regarded by others ought not to be in any way affected by his self-regarding qualities or deficiencies. This is neither possible nor desirable. If he is eminent in any of the qualities which conduce to his own good, he is, so far, a proper object of admiration. He is so much the nearer to the ideal perfection of human nature. If he is grossly deficient in those qualities, a sentiment the opposite of admiration will follow. There is a degree of folly, and a degree of what may be called (though the phrase is not unobjectionable) lowness or depravation of taste, which, though it cannot justify doing harm to the person who manifests it, renders him necessarily and properly a subject of distaste, or, in extreme cases, even of contempt: a person could not have the opposite qualities in due strength without entertaining these feelings. Though doing no wrong to anyone, a person may so act as to compel us to judge him, and feel to him, as a fool or as a being of an inferior order; and since this judgment and feeling are a fact which he would prefer to avoid, it is doing him a service to warn him of it beforehand, as of any other disagreeable consequence to which he exposes himself. It would be well, indeed, if this good office were much more freely rendered than the common notions of politeness at present permit, and if one person could honestly point out to another that he thinks him in fault, without being considered unmannerly or presuming. We have a right, also, in various ways, to act upon our unfavorable opinion of anyone, not to the oppression of his individuality, but in the exercise of ours. We are not bound, for example, to seek his society; we have a right to avoid it (though not to parade the avoidance), for we have a right to choose the society most acceptable to us. We have a right, and it may be our duty, to caution others against him if we think his example or conversation likely to have a pernicious effect on those with whom he associates. We may give others a preference over him in optional good offices, except those which tend to his improvement. In these various modes a person may suffer very severe penalties at the hands of others for faults which directly concern only himself; but he suffers these penalties only in so far as they are the natural and, as it were, the spontaneous consequences of the faults themselves, not because they are purposely inflicted on him for the sake of punishment. A person who shows rashness, obstinacy, self-conceit—who cannot live within moderate means; who cannot restrain himself from hurtful indulgence; who pursues animal pleasures at the expense of those of feeling and intellect—must expect to be lowered in the opinion of others, and to have a less share of their favorable sentiments; but of this he has no right to complain unless he has merited their favor by special excellence in his social relations and has thus established a title to their good offices, which is not affected by his demerits toward himself.

What I contend for is that the inconveniences which are strictly inseparable from the unfavorable judgment of others are the only ones to which a person should ever be subjected for that portion of his conduct and character which concerns his own good, but which does not affect the interest of others in their relations with him. Acts injurious to others require a totally different treatment. Encroachment on their rights; infliction on them of any loss or damage not justified by his own rights; falsehood or duplicity in dealing with them; unfair or ungenerous use of advantages over them; even selfish abstinence from defending them against injury—these are fit objects of moral reprobation and, in grave cases, of moral retribution and punishment. And not only these acts, but the dispositions which lead to them, are properly immoral and fit subjects of disapprobation which may rise to abhorrence. Cruelty of disposition; malice and ill-nature; that most antisocial and odious of all passions, envy; dissimulation and insincerity, irascibility on insufficient cause, and resentment disproportioned to the provocation; the love of domineering over others; the desire to engross more than one's share of advantages (the *pleonexia* of the Greeks); the pride which derives gratification from the abasement of others; the egotism which thinks self and its concerns more important than everything else, and decides all doubtful questions in its own favor—these are moral vices and constitute a bad and odious moral character; unlike the self-regarding faults previously mentioned, which are not properly immoralities and, to whatever pitch they may be carried, do not constitute wickedness. They may be proofs of any amount of folly or want of personal dignity and self-respect, but they are only a subject of moral reprobation when they involve a breach of duty to others, for whose sake the individual is bound to have care for himself. What are called duties to ourselves are not socially obligatory unless circumstances render them at the same time duties to others. The term duty to oneself, when it means anything more than prudence, means self-respect or self-development, and for none of these is anyone accountable to his fellow creatures, because for none of them is it for the good of mankind that he be held accountable to them.

The distinction between the loss of consideration which a person may rightly incur by defect of prudence or of personal dignity, and the reprobation which is due to him for an offense against the rights of others, is not a merely nominal distinction. It makes a vast difference both in our feelings and in our conduct toward him whether he displeases us in things in which we think we have a right to control him or in things in which we know that we have not. If he displeases us, we may express our distaste, and we may stand aloof from a person as well as from a thing that displeases us; but we shall not therefore feel called on to make his life uncomfortable. We shall reflect that he already bears, or will bear, the whole penalty of his error; if he spoils his life by mismanagement, we shall not, for that reason, desire to spoil it still further; instead of wishing to punish him, we shall rather endeavor to alleviate his punishment by showing him how he may avoid or cure the evils his conduct tends to bring upon him. He may be to us an object of pity, perhaps of dislike, but not of anger or resentment; we shall not treat him like an enemy of society; the worst we shall think ourselves justified in doing is leaving him to himself, if we do not interfere benevolently by showing interest or concern for him. It is far otherwise if he has infringed the rules necessary for the protection of his fellow creatures, individually or collectively. The evil consequences of his acts do not then fall on himself, but on others; and society, as the protector of all its members, must retaliate on him, must inflict pain on him for the express purpose of punishment, and must take care that it be sufficiently severe. In the one case, he is an offender at our bar, and we are called on not only to sit in judgment on him, but, in one shape or another, to execute our own sentence; in the other case, it is not our part to inflict any suffering on him, except what may incidentally follow from our using the same liberty in the regulation of our own affairs which we allow to him in his.

The distinction here pointed out between the part of a person's life which concerns only himself and that which concerns others, many persons will refuse to admit. How (it may be asked) can any part of the conduct of a member of society be a matter of indifference to the other members? No person is an entirely isolated being; it is impossible for a person to do anything seriously or permanently hurtful to himself without mischief reaching at least to his near connections, and often far beyond them. If he injures his property, he does harm to those who directly or indirectly derived support from it, and usually diminishes, by a greater or less amount, the general resources of the community. If he deteriorates his bodily or mental faculties, he not only brings evil upon all who depended on him for any portion of their happiness, but disqualifies himself for rendering the services which he owes to his fellow creatures generally, perhaps becomes a burden on their affection or benevolence; and if such conduct were very frequent hardly any offense that is committed would detract more from the general sum of good. Finally, if by his vices or follies a person does no direct harm to others, he is nevertheless (it may be said) injurious by his example, and ought to be compelled to control himself for the sake of those whom the sight or knowledge of his conduct might corrupt or mislead.

And even (it will be added) if the consequences of misconduct could be confined to the vicious or thoughtless individual, ought society to abandon to their own guidance those who are manifestly unfit for it? If protection against themselves is confessedly due to children and persons under age, is not society equally bound to afford it to persons of mature years who are equally incapable of self-government? If gambling, or drunkenness, or incontinence, or idleness, or uncleanliness are as injurious to happiness, and as great a hindrance to improvement, as many or most of the acts prohibited by law, why (it may be asked) should not law, so far as is consistent with practicability and social convenience, endeavor to repress these also? And as a supplement to the unavoidable imperfections of law, ought not opinion at least to organize a powerful police against these vices and visit rigidly with social penalties those who are known to practice them? There is no question here (it may be said) about restricting individuality, or impeding the trial of new and original experiments in living. The only things it is sought to prevent are things which have been tried and condemned from the beginning of the world until now—things which experience has shown not to be useful or suitable to any person's individuality. There must be some length of time and amount of experience after which a moral or prudential truth may be regarded as established; and it is merely desired to prevent generation after generation from falling over the same precipice which has been fatal to their predecessors.

I fully admit that the mischief which a person does to himself may seriously affect, both through their sympathies and their interests, those nearly connected with him and, in a minor degree, society at large. When, by conduct of this sort, a person is led to violate a distinct and assignable obligation to any other person or persons, the case is taken out of the self-regarding class and becomes amenable to moral disapprobation in the proper sense of the term. If, for example, a man, through intemperance or extravagance, becomes unable to pay his debts, or, having undertaken the moral responsibility of a family, becomes from the same cause incapable of supporting or educating them, he is deservedly reprobated and might be justly punished; but it is for the breach of duty to his family or creditors, not for the extravagance. If the resources which ought to have been devoted to them had been diverted from them for the most prudent investment, the moral culpability would have been the same. George Barnwell murdered his uncle to get money for his mistress, but if he had done it to set himself up in business, he would equally have been hanged. Again, in the frequent case of a man who causes grief to his family by addiction to bad habits, he deserves reproach for his unkindness or ingratitude; but so he may for cultivating habits not in themselves vicious, if they are painful to those with whom he passes his life, or who from personal ties are dependent on him for their comfort. Whoever fails in the consideration generally due to the interests and feelings of others, not being compelled by some more imperative duty, or justified by allowable self-preference, is a subject of moral disapprobation for that failure, but not for the cause of it, nor for the errors, merely personal to himself, which may have remotely led to it. In like manner, when a person disables himself, by conduct purely self-regarding, from the performance of some definite duty incumbent on him to the public, he is guilty of a social offense. No person ought to be punished simply for being drunk; but a soldier or a policeman should be punished for being drunk on duty. Whenever, in short, there is a definite damage, or a definite risk of damage, either to an individual or to the public, the case is taken out of the province of liberty and placed in that of morality or law.

But with regard to the merely contingent or, as it may be called, constructive injury which a person causes to society by conduct which neither violates any specific duty to the public, nor occasions perceptible hurt to any assignable individual except himself, the inconvenience is one which society can afford to bear, for the sake of the greater good of human freedom. If grown persons are to be punished for not taking proper care of themselves, I would rather it were for their own sake than under pretense of preventing them from impairing their capacity of rendering to society benefits which society does not pretend it has a right to exact. But I cannot consent to argue the point as if society had no means of bringing its weaker members up to its ordinary standard of rational conduct, except waiting till they do something irrational, and then punishing them, legally or morally, for it. Society has had absolute power over them during all the early portion of their existence; it has had the whole period of childhood and nonage in which to try whether it could make them capable of rational conduct in life. The existing generation is master both of the training and the entire circumstances of the generation to come; it cannot indeed make them perfectly wise and good, because it is itself so lamentably deficient in goodness and wisdom; and its best efforts are not always, in individual cases, its most successful ones; but it is perfectly well able to make the rising generation, as a whole, as good as, and a little better than, itself. If society lets any considerable number of its members grow up mere children, incapable of being acted on by rational consideration of distant motives, society has itself to blame for the consequences. Armed not only with all the powers of education, but with the ascendency which the authority of a received opinion always exercises over the minds who are least fitted to judge for themselves, and aided by the *natural* penalties which cannot be prevented from falling on those who incur the distaste or the contempt of those who know them—let not society pretend that it needs, besides all this, the power to issue commands and enforce obedience in the personal concerns of individuals in which, on all principles of justice and policy, the decision ought to rest with those who are to abide the consequences. Nor is there anything which tends more to discredit and frustrate the better means of influencing conduct than a resort to the worse. If there be among those whom it is attempted to coerce into prudence or temperance any of the material of which vigorous and independent characters are made, they will infallibly rebel against the yoke. No such person will ever feel that others have a right to control him in his concerns, such as they have to prevent him from injuring them in theirs; and it easily comes to be considered a mark of spirit and courage to fly in the face of such usurped authority and do with ostentation the exact opposite of what it enjoins, as in the fashion of grossness which succeeded, in the time of Charles II, to the fanatical moral intolerance of the Puritans. With respect to what is said of the necessity of protecting society from the bad example set to others by the vicious or the self-indulgent, it is true that bad example may have a pernicious effect, especially the example of doing wrong to others with impunity to the wrongdoer. But we are now speaking of conduct which, while it does no wrong to others, is supposed to do great harm to the agent himself; and I do not see how those who believe this can think otherwise than that the example, on the whole, must be more salutary than hurtful, since, if it displays the misconduct, it displays also the painful or degrading consequences which, if the conduct is justly censured, must be supposed to be in all or most cases attendant on it.

But the strongest of all the arguments against the interference of the public with purely personal conduct is that, when it does interfere, the odds are that it interferes wrongly and in the wrong place. On questions of social morality, of duty to others, the opinion of the public, that is, of an overruling majority, though often wrong, is likely to be still oftener right, because on such questions they are only required to judge of their own interests, of the manner in which some mode of conduct, if allowed to be practiced, would affect themselves. But the opinion of a similar majority, imposed as a law on the minority, on questions of self-regarding conduct is quite as likely to be wrong as right, for in these cases public opinion means, at the best, some people's opinion of what is good or bad for other people, while very often it does not even mean that—the public, with the most perfect indifference, passing over the pleasure or convenience of those whose conduct they censure and considering only their own preference. There are many who consider as an injury to themselves any conduct which they have a distaste for, and resent it as an outrage to their feelings; as a religious bigot, when charged with disregarding the religious feelings of others, has been known to retort that they disregard his feelings by persisting in their abominable worship or creed. But there is no parity between the feeling of a person for his own opinion and the feeling of another who is offended at his holding it, no more than between the desire of a thief to take a purse and the desire of the right owner to keep it. And a person's taste is as much his own peculiar concern as his opinion or his purse. It is easy for anyone to imagine an ideal public which leaves the freedom and choice of individuals in all uncertain matters undisturbed and only requires them to abstain from modes of conduct which universal experience has condemned. But where has there been seen a public which set any such limit to its censorship? Or when does the public trouble itself about universal experience? In its interferences with personal conduct it is seldom thinking of anything but the enormity of acting or feeling differently from itself; and this standard of judgment, thinly disguised, is held up to mankind as the dictate of religion and philosophy by nine-tenths of all moralists and speculative writers. These teach that things are right because they are right; because we feel them to be so. They tell us to search in our own minds and hearts for laws of conduct binding on ourselves and on all others. What can the poor public do but apply these instructions and make their own personal feelings of good and evil, if they are tolerably unanimous in them, obligatory on all the world?

The evil here pointed out is not one which exists only in theory; and it may perhaps be expected that I should specify the instances in which the public of this age and country improperly invests its own preferences with the character of moral laws. I am not writing an essay on the aberrations of existing moral feeling. That is too weighty a subject to be discussed parenthetically, and by way of illustration. Yet examples are necessary to show that the principle I maintain is of serious and practical moment, and that I am not endeavoring to erect a barrier against imaginary evils. And it is not difficult to show, by abundant instances, that to extend the bounds of what may be called moral police until it encroaches on the most unquestionably legitimate liberty of the individual is one of the most universal of all human propensities.

As a first instance, consider the antipathies which men cherish on no better grounds than that persons whose religious opinions are different from theirs do not practice their religious observances, especially their religious abstinences. To cite a rather trivial example, nothing in the creed or practice of Christians does more to envenom the hatred of Mohammedans against them than the fact of their eating pork. There are few acts which Christians and Europeans regard with more unaffected disgust than Mussulmans regard this particular mode of satisfying hunger. It is in the first place, an offense against their religion; but this circumstance by no means explains either the degree or the kind of their repugnance; for wine also is forbidden by their religion, and to partake of it is by all Mussulmans accounted wrong, but not disgusting. Their aversion to the flesh of the "unclean beast" is, on the contrary, of that peculiar character, resembling an instinctive antipathy, which the idea of uncleanness, when once it thoroughly sinks into the feelings, seems always to excite even in those whose personal habits are anything but scrupulously cleanly, and of which the sentiment of religious impurity, so intense in the Hindus, is a remarkable example. Suppose now that in a people of whom the majority were Mussulmans, that majority should insist upon not permitting pork to be eaten within the limits of the country. This would be nothing new in Mohammedan countries.[9] Would it be a legitimate exercise of the moral authority of public opinion, and if not, why not? The practice is really revolting to such a public. They also sincerely think that it is forbidden and abhorred by the Deity. Neither could the prohibition be censured as religious persecution. It might be religious in its origin, but it would not be persecution for religion, since nobody's religion makes it a duty to eat pork. The only tenable ground of condemnation would be that with the personal tastes and self-regarding concerns of individuals the public has no business to interfere.

To come somewhat nearer home: the majority of Spaniards consider it a gross impiety, offensive in the highest degree to the Supreme Being, to worship him in any other manner than the Roman Catholic; and no other public worship is lawful on Spanish soil. The people of all southern Europe look upon a married clergy as not only irreligious, but unchaste, indecent, gross, disgusting. What do Protestants think of these perfectly sincere feelings, and of the attempt to enforce them against non-Catholics? Yet, if mankind are justified in interfering with each other's liberty in things which do not concern the interests of others, on what principle is it possible consistently to exclude these cases? Or who can blame people for desiring to suppress what they regard as a scandal in the

sight of God and man? No stronger case can be shown for prohibiting
anything which is regarded as a personal immorality than is made out for
suppressing these practices in the eyes of those who regard them as impi-
eties; and unless we are willing to adopt the logic of persecutors, and to
say that we may persecute others because we are right, and that they must
not persecute us because they are wrong, we must beware of admitting a
principle of which we should resent as a gross injustice the application to
ourselves.

The preceding instances may be objected to, although unreasonably, as
drawn from contingencies impossible among us—opinion, in this country, not being likely to enforce abstinence from meats or to interfere with
people for worshiping and for either marrying or not marrying, according
to their creed or inclination. The next example, however, shall be taken
from an interference with liberty which we have by no means passed all
danger of. Wherever the Puritans have been sufficiently powerful, as in
New England, and in Great Britain at the time of the Commonwealth,
they have endeavored, with considerable success, to put down all public,
and nearly all private, amusements: especially music, dancing, public
games, or other assemblages for purposes of diversion, and the theater.
There are still in this country large bodies of persons by whose notions of
morality and religion these recreations are condemned; and those persons
belonging chiefly to the middle class, who are the ascendant power in the
present social and political condition of the kingdom, it is by no means
impossible that persons of these sentiments may at some time or other
command a majority in Parliament. How will the remaining portion of the
community like to have the amusements that shall be permitted to them
regulated by the religious and moral sentiments of the stricter Calvinists
and Methodists? Would they not, with considerable peremptoriness, desire these intrusively pious members of society to mind their own business? This is precisely what should be said to every government and every
public who have the pretension that no person shall enjoy any pleasure
which they think wrong. But if the principle of the pretension be admitted, no one can reasonably object to its being acted on in the sense of the
majority, or other preponderating power in the country; and all persons
must be ready to conform to the idea of a Christian commonwealth as understood by the early settlers in New England, if a religious profession
similar to theirs should ever succeed in regaining its lost ground, as religions supposed to be declining have so often been known to do.

To imagine another contingency, perhaps more likely to be realized
than the one last mentioned. There is confessedly a strong tendency in the
modern world toward a democratic constitution of society, accompanied
or not by popular political institutions. It is affirmed that in the country

where this tendency is most completely realized—where both society and the government are most democratic: the United States—the feeling of the majority, to whom any appearance of a more showy or costly style of living than they can hope to rival is disagreeable, operates as a tolerably effectual sumptuary law, and that in many parts of the Union it is really difficult for a person possessing a very large income to find any mode of spending it which will not incur popular disapprobation. Though such statements as these are doubtless much exaggerated as a representation of existing facts, the state of things they describe is not only a conceivable and possible, but a probable result of democratic feeling combined with the notion that the public has a right to a veto on the manner in which individuals shall spend their incomes. We have only further to suppose a considerable diffusion of Socialist opinions, and it may become infamous in the eyes of the majority to possess more property than some very small amount, or any income not earned by manual labor. Opinions similar in principle to these already prevail widely among the artisan class and weigh oppressively on those who are amenable to the opinion chiefly of that class, namely, its own members. It is known that the bad workmen who form the majority of the operatives in many branches of industry are decidedly of opinion that bad workmen ought to receive the same wages as good, and that no one ought to be allowed, through piecework or otherwise, to earn by superior skill or industry more than others can without it. And they employ a moral police, which occasionally becomes a physical one, to deter skillful workmen from receiving, and employers from giving, a larger remuneration for a more useful service. If the public have any jurisdiction over private concerns, I cannot see that these people are in fault, or that any individual's particular public can be blamed for asserting the same authority over his individual conduct which the general public asserts over people in general.

But, without dwelling upon supposititious cases, there are, in our own day, gross usurpations upon the liberty of private life actually practiced, and still greater ones threatened with some expectation of success, and opinions propounded which assert an unlimited right in the public not only to prohibit by law everything which it thinks wrong, but, in order to get at what it thinks wrong, to prohibit any number of things which it admits to be innocent.

Under the name of preventing intemperance, the people of one English colony, and of nearly half the United States, have been interdicted by law from making any use whatever of fermented drinks, except for medical purposes, for prohibition of their sale is in fact, as it is intended to be, prohibition of their use. And though the impracticability of executing the law has caused its repeal in several of the States which had adopted it, including the one from which it derives its name, an attempt has notwithstanding been commenced, and is prosecuted with considerable zeal by many of the professed philanthropists, to agitate for a similar law in this country. The association, or "Alliance," as it terms itself, which has been formed for this purpose, has acquired some notoriety through the publicity given to a correspondence between its secretary and one of the very few English public men who hold that a politician's opinions ought to be founded on principles. Lord Stanley's share in this correspondence is calculated to strengthen the hopes already built on him by those who know how rare such qualities as are manifested in some of his public appearances unhappily are among those who figure in political life. The organ of the Alliance, who would "deeply deplore the recognition of any principle which could be wrested to justify bigotry and persecution," undertakes to point out the "broad and impassable barrier" which divides such principles from those of the association. "All matters relating to thought, opinion, conscience, appear to me," he says, "to be without the sphere of legislation; all pertaining to social act, habit, relation, subject only to a discretionary power vested in the State itself, and not in the individual, to be within it." No mention is made of a third class, different from either of these, viz., acts and habits which are not social, but individual; although it is to this class, surely that the act of drinking fermented liquors belongs. Selling fermented liquors, however, is trading, and trading is a social act. But the infringement complained of is not on the liberty of the seller, but on that of the buyer and consumer; since the State might just as well forbid him to drink wine as purposely make it impossible for him to obtain it. The secretary, however, says, "I claim, as a citizen, a right to legislate whenever my social rights are invaded by the social act of another." And now for the definition of these "social rights": "If anything invades my social rights, certainly the traffic in strong drink does. It destroys my primary right of security by constantly creating and stimulating social disorder. It invades my right of equality by deriving a profit from the creation of a misery I am taxed to support. It impedes my right to free moral and intellectual development by surrounding my path with dangers and by weakening and demoralizing society, from which I have a right to claim mutual aid and intercourse." A theory of "social rights" the like of which probably never before found its way into distinct language: being nothing short of this—that it is the absolute social right of every individual that every other individual shall act in every respect exactly as he ought; that whosoever fails thereof in the smallest particular violates my social right and entitles me to demand from the legislature the removal of the grievance. So monstrous a principle is far more dangerous than any single interference with liberty; there is no violation of liberty which it would not justify; it acknowledges no right to any freedom whatever, except perhaps to that of holding opinions in secret, without ever disclosing them; for the moment an opinion which I consider noxious passes anyone's lips, it invades all the "social rights" attributed to me by the Alliance. The doctrine ascribes to all mankind a vested interest in each other's moral, intellectual, and even physical perfection, to be defined by each claimant according to his own standard.

Another important example of illegitimate interference with the rightful liberty of the individual, not simply threatened, but long since carried into triumphant effect, is Sabbatarian legislation. Without doubt, abstinence on one day in the week, so far as the exigencies of life permit, from the usual daily occupation, though in no respect religiously binding on any except Jews, is a highly beneficial custom. And inasmuch as this custom cannot be observed without a general consent to that effect among the industrious classes, therefore, in so far as some persons by working may impose the same necessity on others, it may be allowable and right that the law should guarantee to each the observance by others of the custom, by suspending the greater operations of industry on a particular day. But this justification, grounded on the direct interest which others have in each individual's observance of the practice, does not apply to the self-chosen occupations in which a person may think fit to employ his leisure, nor does it hold good, in the smallest degree, for legal restrictions on amusements. It is true that the amusement of some is the day's work of others; but the pleasure, not to say the useful recreation, of many is worth the labor of a few, provided the occupation is freely chosen and can be freely resigned. The operatives are perfectly right in thinking that if all worked on Sunday, seven days' work would have to be given for six days' wages; but so long as the great mass of employments are suspended, the small number who for the enjoyment of others must still work obtain a proportional increase of earnings; and they are not obliged to follow those occupations if they prefer leisure to emolument. If a further remedy is sought, it might be found in the establishment by custom of a holiday on some other day of the week for those particular classes of persons. The only ground, therefore, on which restrictions on Sunday amusements can be defended must be that they are religiously wrong—a motive of legislation which never can be too earnestly protested against. *"Deorum injuriae Diis curae."* It remains to be proved that society or any of its officers holds a commission from on high to avenge any supposed offense to Omnipotence which is not also a wrong to our fellow creatures. The notion that it is one man's duty that another should be religious was the foundation of all the religious persecutions ever perpetrated, and, if admitted, would fully justify them. Though the feeling which breaks out in the repeated attempts to stop railway traveling on Sunday, in the resistance to the opening of museums, and the like, has not the cruelty of the old persecutors, the state of mind indicated by it is fundamentally the same. It is a determination not to tolerate others in doing what is permitted by their religion, because it is not permitted by the persecutor's religion. It is a belief that God not only abominates the act of the misbeliever, but will not hold us guiltless if we leave him unmolested.

I cannot refrain from adding to these examples of the little account commonly made of human liberty the language of downright persecution which breaks out from the press of this country whenever it feels called on to notice the remarkable phenomenon of Mormonism. Much might be said on the unexpected and instructive fact that an alleged new revelation and a religion founded on it—the product of palpable imposture, not even supported by the *prestige* of extraordinary qualities in its founder—is believed by hundreds of thousands, and has been made the foundation of a society in the age of newspapers, railways, and the electric telegraph. What here concerns us is that this religion, like other and better religions, has its martyrs: that its prophet and founder was, for his teaching, put to death by a mob; that others of its adherents lost their lives by the same lawless violence; that they were forcibly expelled, in a body, from the country in which they first grew up, while, now that they have been chased into a solitary recess in the midst of a desert, many in this country openly declare that it would be right (only that it is not convenient) to send an expedition against them and compel them by force to conform to the opinions of other people. The article of the Mormonite doctrine which is the chief provocative to the antipathy which thus breaks through the ordinary restraints of religious tolerance is its sanction of polygamy; which, though permitted to Mohammedans, and Hindus, and Chinese, seems to excite unquenchable animosity when practiced by persons who speak English and profess to be a kind of Christians. No one has a deeper disapprobation than I have of this Mormon institution; both for other reasons and because, far from being in any way countenanced by the principle of liberty, it is a direct infraction of that principle, being a mere riveting of the chains of one half of the community, and an emancipation of the other from reciprocity of obligation toward them. Still, it must be remembered that this relation is as much voluntary on the part of the women concerned in it, and who may be deemed the sufferers by it, as is the case with any other form of the marriage institution; and however surprising this fact may appear, it has its explanation in the common ideas and customs of the world, which, teaching women to think marriage the one thing needful, make it intelligible that many a woman should prefer being one of several wives to not being a wife at all. Other countries are not asked to recognize such unions, or release any portion of their inhabitants from their own laws on the score of Mormonite opinions. But when the dissentients have conceded to the hostile sentiments of others far more than could justly be demanded; when they have left the countries to which their doctrines were unacceptable and established themselves in a remote corner of the earth, which they have been the first to render habitable to human beings, it is difficult to see on what principles but those of tyranny they can be prevented from living there under what laws they please, provided they commit no aggression on other nations and allow perfect freedom of departure to those who are dissatisfied with their ways. A recent writer, in some respects of considerable merit, proposes (to use his own words) not a crusade, but a *civilizade,* against this polygamous community, to put an end to what seems to him a retrograde step in civilization. It also appears so to me, but I am not aware that any community has a right to force another to be civilized. So long as the sufferers by the bad law do not invoke assistance from other communities, I cannot admit that persons entirely unconnected with them ought to step in and require that a condition of things with which all who are directly interested appear to be satisfied should be put an end to because it is a scandal to persons some thousands of miles distant who have no part or concern in it. Let them send missionaries, if they please, to preach against it; and let them, by any fair means (of which silencing the teachers is not one), oppose the progress of similar doctrines among their own people. If civilization has got the better of barbarism when barbarism had the world to itself, it is too much to profess to be afraid lest barbarism, after having been fairly got under, should revive and conquer civilization. A civilization that can thus succumb to its vanquished enemy must first have become so degenerate that neither its appointed priests and teachers, nor anybody else, has the capacity, or will take the trouble, to stand up for it. If this be so, the sooner such a civilization receives notice to quit, the better. It can only go on from bad to worse until destroyed and regenerated (like the Western Empire) by energetic barbarians.

Chapter V
Applications

The principles asserted in these pages must be more generally admitted as the basis for discussion of details before a consistent application of them to all the various departments of government and morals can be attempted with any prospect of advantage. The few observations I propose to make on questions of detail are designed to illustrate the principles rather than to follow them out to their consequences. I offer not so much applications as specimens of application, which may serve to bring into greater clearness the meaning and limits of the two maxims which together form the entire doctrine of this essay, and to assist the judgment in holding the balance between them in the cases where it appears doubtful which of them is applicable to the case.

The maxims are, first, that the individual is not accountable to society for his actions in so far as these concern the interests of no person but himself. Advice, instruction, persuasion, and avoidance by other people, if thought necessary by them for their own good, are the only measures by which society can justifiably express its dislike or disapprobation of his conduct. Secondly, that for such actions as are prejudicial to the interests of others, the individual is accountable and may be subjected either to social or to legal punishment if society is of opinion that the one or the other is requisite for its protection.

In the first place, it must by no means be supposed, because damage, or probability of damage, to the interests of others can alone justify the interference of society, that therefore it always does justify such interference. In many cases an individual, in pursuing a legitimate object, necessarily and therefore legitimately causes pain or loss to others, or intercepts a good which they had a reasonable hope of obtaining. Such oppositions of interest between individuals often arise from bad social institutions, but are unavoidable while those institutions last; and some would be unavoidable under any institutions. Whoever succeeds in an overcrowded profession or in a competitive examination, whoever is preferred to another in any contest for an object which both desire, reaps benefit from the loss of others, from their wasted exertion and their disappointment. But it is, by common admission, better for the general interest of mankind that persons should pursue their objects undeterred by this sort of consequences. In other words, society admits no right, either legal or moral, in the disappointed competitors to immunity from this kind of suffering, and feels called on to interfere only when means of success have been employed which it is contrary to the general interest to permit—namely, fraud or treachery, and force.

Again, trade is a social act. Whoever undertakes to sell any description of goods to the public does what affects the interest of other persons, and of society in general; and thus his conduct, in principle, comes within the jurisdiction of society; accordingly, it was once held to be the duty of governments, in all cases which were considered of importance, to fix prices and regulate the processes of manufacture. But it is now recognized, though not till after a long struggle, that both the cheapness and the good quality of commodities are most effectually provided for by leaving the producers and sellers perfectly free, under the sole check of equal freedom to the buyers for supplying themselves elsewhere. This is the so-called doctrine of "free trade," which rests on grounds different from, though equally solid with, the principle of individual liberty asserted in this essay. Restrictions on trade, or on production for purposes of trade, are indeed restraints; and all restraint, *qua* restraint, is an evil; but the restraints in question affect only that part of conduct which society is competent to restrain, and are wrong solely because they do not really produce the results which it is desired to produce by them. As the principle of individual liberty is not involved in the doctrine of free trade, so neither is it in most of the questions which arise respecting the limits of that doctrine, as, for example, what amount of public control is admissible for the prevention of fraud by adulteration; how far sanitary precautions, or arrangements to protect workpeople employed in dangerous occupations, should be enforced on employers. Such questions involve considerations of liberty only in so far as leaving people to themselves is always better, *caeteris paribus,* than controlling them; but that they may be legitimately controlled for these ends is in principle undeniable. On the other hand, there are questions relating to interference with trade which are essentially questions of liberty, such as the Maine Law, already touched upon; the prohibition of the importation of opium into China; the restriction of the sale of poisons—all cases, in short, where the object of the interference is to make it impossible or difficult to obtain a particular commodity. These interferences are objectionable, not as infringements on the liberty of the producer or seller, but on that of the buyer.

One of these examples, that of the sale of poisons, opens a new question: the proper limits of what may be called the functions of police; how far liberty may legitimately be invaded for the prevention of crime, or of accident. It is one of the undisputed functions of government to take precautions against crime before it has been committed, as well as to detect and punish it afterwards. The preventive function of government, however, is far more liable to be abused, to the prejudice of liberty, than the punitory function; for there is hardly any part of the legitimate freedom of action of a human being which would not admit of being represented, and fairly, too, as increasing the facilities for some form or other of delinquency. Nevertheless, if a public authority, or even a private person, sees anyone evidently preparing to commit a crime, they are not bound to look on inactive until the crime is committed, but may interfere to prevent it. If poisons were never bought or used for any purpose except the commission of murder, it would be right to prohibit their manufacture and sale. They may, however, be wanted not only for innocent but for useful purposes, and restrictions cannot be imposed in the one case without operating in the other. Again, it is a proper office of public authority to guard against accidents. If either a public officer or anyone else saw a person attempting to cross a bridge which had been ascertained to be unsafe, and there were no time to warn him of his danger, they might seize him and turn him back, without any real infringement of his liberty; for liberty consists in doing what one desires, and he does not desire to fall into the river. Nevertheless, when there is not a certainty, but only a danger of mischief, no one but the person himself can judge of the sufficiency of the motive which may prompt him to incur the risk; in this case, therefore (unless he is a child, or delirious, or in some state of excitement or absorption incompatible with the full use of the reflecting faculty), he ought, I conceive, to be only warned of the danger; not forcibly prevented from exposing himself to it. Similar considerations, applied to such a question as the sale of poisons, may enable us to decide which among the possible modes of regulation are or are not contrary to principle. Such a precaution, for example, as that of labeling the drug with some word expressive of its dangerous character may be enforced without violation of liberty: the buyer cannot wish not to know that the thing he possesses has poisonous qualities. But to require in all cases the certificate of a medical practitioner would make it sometimes impossible, always expensive, to obtain the article for legitimate uses. The only mode apparent to me, in which difficulties may be thrown in the way of crime committed through this means, without any infringement worth taking into account upon the liberty of those who desire the poisonous substance for other purposes, consists in providing what, in the apt language of Bentham, is called "preappointed evidence." This provision is familiar to everyone in the case of contracts. It is usual and right that the law, when a contract is entered into, should require as the condition of its enforcing performance that certain formalities should be observed, such as signatures, attestation of witnesses, and the like, in order that in case of subsequent dispute there may be evidence to prove that the contract was really entered into, and that there was nothing in the circumstances to render it legally invalid, the effect being to throw great obstacles in the way of fictitious contracts, or contracts made in circumstances which, if known, would destroy their validity. Precautions of a similar nature might be enforced in the sale of articles adapted to be instruments of crime. The seller, for example, might be required to enter in a register the exact time of the transaction, the name and address of the buyer, the precise quality and quantity sold; to ask the purpose for which it was wanted, and record the answer he received. When there was no medical prescription, the presence of some third person might be required to bring home the fact to the purchaser, in case there should afterwards be reason to believe that the article had been applied to criminal purposes. Such regulations would in general be no material impediment to obtaining the article, but a very considerable one to making an improper use of it without detection.

The right inherent in society to ward off crimes against itself by antecedent precautions suggests the obvious limitations to the maxim that purely self-regarding misconduct cannot properly be meddled with in the way of prevention or punishment. Drunkenness, for example, in ordinary cases, is not a fit subject for legislative interference, but I should deem it perfectly legitimate that a person who had once been convicted of any act of violence to others under the influence of drink should be placed under a special legal restriction, personal to himself; that if he were afterwards found drunk, he should be liable to a penalty, and that if, when in that state, he committed another offense, the punishment to which he would be liable for that other offense should be increased in severity. The making himself drunk, in a person whom drunkenness excites to do harm to others, is a crime against others. So, again, idleness, except in a person receiving support from the public, or except when it constitutes a breach of contract, cannot without tyranny be made a subject of legal punishment; but if, either from idleness or from any other avoidable cause, a man fails to perform his legal duties to others, as for instance to support his children, it is no tyranny to force him to fulfill that obligation by compulsory labor if no other means are available.

Again, there are many acts which, being directly injurious only to the agents themselves, ought not to be legally interdicted, but which, if done publicly, are a violation of good manners and, coming thus within the category of offenses against others, may rightly be prohibited. Of this kind are offenses against decency; on which it is unnecessary to dwell, the rather as they are only connected indirectly with our subject, the objection to publicity being equally strong in the case of many actions not in themselves condemnable, nor supposed to be so.

There is another question to which an answer must be found, consistent with the principles which have been laid down. In cases of personal conduct supposed to be blamable, but which respect for liberty precludes society from preventing or punishing because the evil directly resulting falls wholly on the agent; what the agent is free to do, ought other persons to be equally free to counsel or instigate? This question is not free from difficulty. The case of a person who solicits another to do an act is not strictly a case of self-regarding conduct. To give advice or offer inducements to anyone is a social act and may, therefore, like actions in general which affect others, be supposed amenable to social control. But a little reflection corrects the first impression, by showing that if the case is not strictly within the definition of individual liberty, yet the reasons on which the principle of individual liberty is grounded are applicable to it.

If people must be allowed, in whatever concerns only themselves, to act as seems best to themselves, at their own peril, they must equally be free to consult with one another about what is fit to be so done; to exchange opinions, and give and receive suggestions. Whatever it is permitted to do, it must be permitted to advise to do. The question is doubtful only when the instigator derives a personal benefit from his advice, when he makes it his occupation, for subsistence or pecuniary gain, to promote what society and the State consider to be an evil. Then, indeed, a new element of complication is introduced—namely, the existence of classes of persons with an interest opposed to what is considered as the public weal, and whose mode of living is grounded on the counteraction of it. Ought this to be interfered with, or not? Fornication, for example, must be tolerated, and so must gambling; but should a person be free to be a pimp, or to keep a gambling house? The case is one of those which lie on the exact boundary line between two principles, and it is not at once apparent to which of the two it properly belongs. There are arguments on both sides. On the side of toleration it may be said that the fact of following anything as an occupation, and living or profiting by the practice of it, cannot make that criminal which would otherwise be admissible; that the act should either be consistently permitted or consistently prohibited; that if the principles which we have hitherto defended are true, society has no business, *as* society, to decide anything to be wrong which concerns only the individual; that it cannot go beyond dissuasion, and that one person should be as free to persuade as another to dissuade. In opposition to this it may be contended that, although the public, or the State, are not warranted in authoritatively deciding, for purposes of repression or punishment, that such or such conduct affecting only the interests of the individual is good or bad, they are fully justified in assuming, if they regard it as bad, that its being so or not is at least a disputable question: that, this being supposed, they cannot be acting wrongly in endeavoring to exclude the influence of solicitations which are not disinterested, of instigators who cannot possibly be impartial—who have a direct personal interest on one side, and that side the one which the State believes to be wrong, and who confessedly promote it for personal objects only. There can surely, it may be urged, be nothing lost, no sacrifice of good, by so ordering matters that persons shall make their election, either wisely or foolishly, on their own prompting, as free as possible from the arts of persons who stimulate their inclinations for interested purposes of their own. Thus (it may be said), though the statutes respecting unlawful games are utterly indefensible—though all persons should be free to gamble in their own or each other's houses, or in any place of meeting established by their own subscriptions and open only to the members and their visitors—yet public gambling houses should not be permitted. It is true that the prohibition is never effectual, and that, whatever amount of tyrannical power may be given to the police, gambling houses can always be maintained under other pretenses; but they may be compelled to conduct their operations with a certain degree of secrecy and mystery, so that nobody knows anything about them but those who seek them; and more than this society ought not to aim at. There is considerable force in these arguments. I will not venture to decide whether they are sufficient to justify the moral anomaly of punishing the accessory when the principal is (and must be) allowed to go free; of fining or imprisoning the procurer, but not the fornicator—the gambling-house keeper, but not the gambler. Still less ought the common operations of buying and selling to be interfered with on analogous grounds. Almost every article which is bought and sold may be used in excess, and the sellers have a pecuniary interest in encouraging that excess; but no argument can be founded on this in favor, for instance, of the Maine Law; because the class of dealers in strong drinks, though interested in their abuse, are indispensably required for the sake of their legitimate use. The interest, however, of these dealers in promoting intemperance is a real evil and justifies the State in imposing restrictions and requiring guarantees which, but for that justification, would be infringements of legitimate liberty.

A further question is whether the State, while it permits, should nevertheless indirectly discourage conduct which it deems contrary to the best interests of the agent; whether, for example, it should take measures to render the means of drunkenness more costly, or add to the difficulty of procuring them by limiting the number of the places of sale. On this, as on most other practical questions, many distinctions require to be made. To tax stimulants for the sole purpose of making them more difficult to be obtained is a measure differing only in degree from their entire prohibition, and would be justifiable only if that were justifiable. Every increase of cost is a prohibition to those whose means do not come up to the augmented price; and to those who do, it is a penalty laid on them for gratifying a particular taste. Their choice of pleasures and their mode of expending their income, after satisfying their legal and moral obligations to the State and to individuals, are their own concern and must rest with their own judgment. These considerations may seem at first sight to condemn the selection of stimulants as special subjects of taxation for purposes of revenue. But it must be remembered that taxation for fiscal purposes is absolutely inevitable; that in most countries it is necessary that a considerable part of that taxation should be indirect; that the State, therefore, cannot help imposing penalties, which to some persons may be prohibitory, on the use of some articles of consumption. It is hence the duty of the State to consider, in the imposition of taxes, what commodities the consumers can best spare; and *a fortiori*, to select in preference those of which it deems the use, beyond a very moderate quantity, to be positively injurious. Taxation, therefore, of stimulants up to the point which produces the largest amount of revenue (supposing that the State needs all the revenue which it yields) is not only admissible, but to be approved of.

The question of making the sale of these commodities a more or less exclusive privilege must be answered differently, according to the purposes to which the restriction is intended to be subservient. All places of public resort require the restraint of a police, and places of this kind peculiarly, because offenses against society are especially apt to originate there. It is, therefore, fit to confine the power of selling these commodities (at least for consumption on the spot) to persons of known or vouched-for respectability of conduct; to make such regulations respecting hours of opening and closing as may be requisite for public surveillance, and to withdraw the license if breaches of the peace repeatedly take place through the connivance or incapacity of the keeper of the house, or if it becomes a rendezvous for concocting and preparing offenses against the law. Any further restriction I do not conceive to be, in principle, justifiable. The limitation in number, for instance, of beer and spirit houses, for the express purpose of rendering them more difficult of access and diminishing the occasions of temptation, not only exposes all to an inconvenience because there are some by whom the facility would be abused, but is suited only to a state of society in which the laboring classes are avowedly treated as children or savages, and placed under an education of restraint, to fit them for future admission to the privileges of freedom. This is not the principle on which the laboring classes are professedly governed in any free country; and no person who sets due value on freedom will give his adhesion to their being so governed, unless after all efforts have been exhausted to educate them for freedom and govern them as freemen, and it has been definitively proved that they can only be governed as children. The bare statement of the alternative shows the absurdity of supposing that such efforts have been made in any case which needs be considered here. It is only because the institutions of this country are a mass of inconsistencies, that things find admittance into our practice which belong to the system of despotic, or what is called paternal, government, while the general freedom of our institutions precludes the exercise of the amount of control necessary to render the restraint of any real efficacy as a moral education.

It was pointed out in an early part of this essay that the liberty of the individual, in things wherein the individual is alone concerned, implies a corresponding liberty in any number of individuals to regulate by mutual agreement such things as regard them jointly, and regard no persons but themselves. This question presents no difficulty so long as the will of all the persons implicated remains unaltered; but since that will may change it is often necessary, even in things in which they alone are concerned, that they should enter into engagements with one another; and when they do, it is fit, as a general rule, that those engagements should be kept. Yet, in the laws, probably, of every country, this general rule has some exceptions. Not only persons are not held to engagements which violate the rights of third parties, but it is sometimes considered a sufficient reason for releasing them from an engagement that it is injurious to themselves. In this and most other civilized countries, for example, an engagement by which a person should sell himself, or allow himself to be sold, as a slave would be null and void, neither enforced by law nor by opinion. The ground for thus limiting his power of voluntarily disposing of his own lot in life is apparent, and is very clearly seen in this extreme case. The reason for not interfering, unless for the sake of others, with a person's voluntary acts is consideration for his liberty. His voluntary choice is evidence that what he so chooses is desirable, or at least endurable, to him, and his good is on the whole best provided for by allowing him to take his own means of pursuing it. But by selling himself for a slave, he abdicates his liberty; he foregoes any future use of it beyond that single act. He therefore defeats, in his own case, the very purpose which is the justification of allowing him to dispose of himself. He is no longer free, but is thenceforth in a position which has no longer the presumption in its favor that would be afforded by his voluntarily remaining in it. The principle of freedom cannot require that he should be free not to be free. It is not freedom to be allowed to alienate his freedom. These reasons, the force of which is so conspicuous in this peculiar case, are evidently of far wider application, yet a limit is everywhere set to them by the necessities of life, which continually require, not indeed that we should resign our freedom, but that we should consent to this and the other limitation of it. The principle, however, which demands uncontrolled freedom of action in all that concerns only the agents themselves requires that those who have become bound to one another, in things which concern no third party, should be able to release one another from the engagement; and even without such voluntary release there are perhaps no contracts or engagements, except those that relate to money or money's worth, of which one can venture to say that there ought to be no liberty whatever of retractation. Baron Wilhelm von Humboldt, in the excellent essay from which I have already quoted, states it as his conviction that engagements which involve personal relations or services should never be legally binding beyond a limited duration of time; and that the most important of these engagements, marriage, having the peculiarity that its objects are frustrated unless the feelings of both the parties are in harmony with it, should require nothing more than the declared will of either party to dissolve it. This subject is too important and too complicated to be discussed in a parenthesis, and I touch on it only so far as is necessary for purposes of illustration. If the conciseness and generality of Baron Humboldt's dissertation had not obliged him in this instance to content himself with enunciating his conclusion without discussing the premises, he would doubtless have recognized that the question cannot be decided on grounds so simple as those to which he confines himself. When a person, either by express promise or by conduct, has encouraged another to rely upon his continuing to act in a certain way—to build expectations and calculations, and stake any part of his plan of life upon that supposition—a new series of moral obligations arises on his part toward that person, which may possibly be overruled, but cannot be ignored. And again, if the relation between two contracting parties has been followed by consequences to others; if it has placed third parties in any peculiar position, or, as in the case of marriage, has even called third parties into existence, obligations arise on the part of both the contracting parties toward those third persons, the fulfillment of which, or at all events the mode of fulfillment, must be greatly affected by the continuance or disruption of the relation between the original parties to the contract. It does not follow, nor can I admit, that these obligations extend to requiring the fulfillment of the contract at all costs to the happiness of the reluctant party; but they are a necessary element in the question; and, even if, as von Humboldt maintains, they ought to make no difference in the *legal* freedom of the parties to release themselves from the engagement (and I also hold that they ought not to make *much* difference), they necessarily make a great difference in the *moral* freedom. A person is bound to take all these circumstances into account before resolving on a step which may affect such important interests of others; and if he does not allow proper weight to those interests, he is morally responsible for the wrong. I have made these obvious remarks for the better illustration of the general principle of liberty, and not because they are at all needed on the particular question, which, on the contrary, is usually discussed as if the interest of children was everything, and that of grown persons nothing.

I have already observed that, owing to the absence of any recognized general principles, liberty is often granted where it should be withheld, as well as withheld where it should be granted; and one of the cases in which, in the modern European world, the sentiment of liberty is the strongest is a case where, in my view, it is altogether misplaced. A person should be free to do as he likes in his own concerns, but he ought not to be free to do as he likes in acting for another, under the pretext that the affairs of the other are his own affairs. The State, while it respects the liberty of each in what specially regards himself, is bound to maintain a vigilant control over his exercise of any power which it allows him to possess over others. This obligation is almost entirely disregarded in the case of the family relations—a case, in its direct influence on human happiness, more important than all others taken together. The almost despotic power of husbands over wives needs not be enlarged upon here, because nothing more is needed for the complete removal of the evil than that wives should have the same rights and should receive the protection of law in the same manner as all other persons; and because, on this subject, the defenders of established injustice do not avail themselves of the plea of liberty but stand forth openly as the champions of power. It is in the case of children that misapplied notions of liberty are a real obstacle to the fulfillment by the State of its duties. One would almost think that a man's children were supposed to be literally, and not metaphorically, a part of himself, so jealous is opinion of the smallest interference of law with his absolute and exclusive control over them, more jealous than of almost any interference with his own freedom of action: so much less do the generality of mankind value liberty than power. Consider, for example, the case of education. Is it not almost a self-evident axiom that the State should require and compel the education, up to a certain standard, of every human being who is born its citizen? Yet who is there that is not afraid to recognize and assert this truth? Hardly anyone, indeed, will deny that it is one of the most sacred duties of the parents (or, as law and usage now stand, the father), after summoning a human being into the world, to give to that being an education fitting him to perform his part well in life toward others and toward himself. But while this is unanimously declared to be the father's duty, scarcely anybody, in this country, will bear to hear of obliging him to perform it. Instead of his being required to make any exertion or sacrifice for securing education to his child, it is left to his choice to accept it or not when it is provided gratis! It still remains unrecognized that to bring a child into existence without a fair prospect of being able, not only to provide food for its body, but instruction and training for its mind is a moral crime, both against the unfortunate offspring and against society; and that if the parent does not fulfill this obligation, the State ought to see it fulfilled at the charge, as far as possible, of the parent.

Were the duty of enforcing universal education once admitted there would be an end to the difficulties about what the State should teach, and how it should teach, which now convert the subject into a mere battlefield for sects and parties, causing the time and labor which should have been spent in educating to be wasted in quarreling about education. If the government would make up its mind to require for every child a good education, it might save itself the trouble of providing one. It might leave to parents to obtain the education where and how they pleased, and content itself with helping to pay the school fees of the poorer classes of children, and defraying the entire school expenses of those who have no one else to pay for them. The objections which are urged with reason against State education do not apply to the enforcement of education by the State, but to the State's taking upon itself to direct that education; which is a totally different thing. That the whole or any large part of the education of the people should be in State hands, I go as far as anyone in deprecating. All that has been said of the importance of individuality of character, and diversity in opinions and modes of conduct, involves, as of the same unspeakable importance, diversity of education. A general State education is a mere contrivance for molding people to be exactly like one another; and as the mold in which it casts them is that which pleases the predominant power in the government—whether this be a monarch, a priesthood, an aristocracy, or the majority of the existing generation—in proportion as it is efficient and successful, it establishes a despotism over the mind, leading by natural tendency to one over the body. An education established and controlled by the State should only exist, if it exist at all, as one among many competing experiments, carried on for the purpose of example and stimulus to keep the others up to a certain standard of excellence. Unless, indeed, when society in general is in so backward a state that it could not or would not provide for itself any proper institutions of education unless the government undertook the task, then, indeed, the government may, as the less of two great evils, take upon itself the business of schools and universities, as it may that of joint stock companies when private enterprise in a shape fitted for undertaking great works of industry does not exist in the country. But in general, if the country contains a sufficient number of persons qualified to provide education under government auspices, the same persons would be able and willing to give an equally good education on the voluntary principle, under the assurance of remuneration afforded by a law rendering education compulsory, combined with State aid to those unable to defray the expense.

The instrument for enforcing the law could be no other than public examinations, extending to all children and beginning at an early age. An age might be fixed at which every child must be examined, to ascertain if he (or she) is able to read. If a child proves unable, the father, unless he has some sufficient ground of excuse, might be subjected to a moderate fine, to be worked out, if necessary, by his labor, and the child might be put to school at his expense. Once in every year the examination should be renewed, with a gradually extending range of subjects, so as to make the universal acquisition and, what is more, retention of a certain minimum of general knowledge virtually compulsory. Beyond that minimum there should be voluntary examinations on all subjects, at which all who come up to a certain standard of proficiency might claim a certificate. To prevent the State from exercising, through these arrangements, an improper influence over opinion, the knowledge required for passing an examination (beyond the merely instrumental parts of knowledge, such as languages and their use) should, even in the higher classes of examinations, be confined to facts and positive science exclusively. The examinations on religion, politics, or other disputed topics should not turn on the truth or falsehood of opinions, but on the matter of fact that such and such an opinion is held, on such grounds, by such authors, or schools, or churches. Under this system, the rising generation would be no worse off in regard to all disputed truths than they are at present; they would be brought up either churchmen or dissenters as they now are, the State merely taking care that they should be instructed churchmen, or instructed dissenters. There would be nothing to hinder them from being taught religion, if their parents chose, at the same schools where they were taught other things. All attempts by the State to bias the conclusions of its citizens on disputed subjects are evil; but it may very properly offer to ascertain and certify that a person possesses the knowledge requisite to make his conclusions on any given subject worth attending to. A student of philosophy would be the better for being able to stand an examination both in Locke and in Kant, whichever of the two he takes up with, or even if with neither: and there is no reasonable objection to examining an atheist in the evidences of Christianity, provided he is not required to profess a belief in them. The examinations, however, in the higher branches of knowledge should, I conceive, be entirely voluntary. It would be giving too dangerous a power to governments were they allowed to exclude anyone from professions, even from the profession of teacher, for alleged deficiency of qualifications; and I think, with Wilhelm von Humboldt, that degrees or other public certificates of scientific or professional acquirements should be given to all who present themselves for examination and stand the test, but that such certificates should confer no advantage over competitors other than the weight which may be attached to their testimony by public opinion.

It is not in the matter of education only that misplaced notions of liberty prevent moral obligations on the part of parents from being recognized, and legal obligations from being imposed, where there are the strongest grounds for the former always, and in many cases for the latter also. The fact itself, of causing the existence of a human being, is one of the most responsible actions in the range of human life. To undertake this responsibility—to bestow a life which may be either a curse or a blessing—unless the being on whom it is to be bestowed will have at least the ordinary chances of a desirable existence, is a crime against that being. And in a country, either overpeopled or threatened with being so, to produce children, beyond a very small number, with the effect of reducing the reward of labor by their competition is a serious offense against all who live by the remuneration of their labor. The laws which, in many countries on the Continent, forbid marriage unless the parties can show that they have the means of supporting a family do not exceed the legitimate powers of the State; and whether such laws be expedient or not (a question mainly dependent on local circumstances and feelings), they are not objectionable as violations of liberty. Such laws are interferences of the State to prohibit a mischievous act—an act injurious to others, which ought to be a subject of reprobation and social stigma, even when it is not deemed expedient to superadd legal punishment. Yet the current ideas of liberty, which bend so easily to real infringements of the freedom of the individual in things which concern only himself, would repel the attempt to put any restraint upon his inclinations when the consequence of their indulgence is a life or lives of wretchedness and depravity to the offspring, with manifold evils to those sufficiently within reach to be in any way affected by their actions. When we compare the strange respect of mankind for liberty with their strange want of respect for it, we might imagine that a man had an indispensable right to do harm to others, and no right at all to please himself without giving pain to anyone.

I have reserved for the last place a large class of questions respecting the limits of government interference, which, though closely connected with the subject of this essay, do not, in strictness, belong to it. These are cases in which the reasons against interference do not turn upon the principle of liberty: the question is not about restraining the actions of individuals, but about helping them; it is asked whether the government should do, or cause to be done, something for their benefit instead of leaving it to be done by themselves, individually or in voluntary combination.

The objections to government interference, when it is not such as to involve infringement of liberty, may be of three kinds:

The first is when the thing to be done is likely to be better done by individuals than by the government. Speaking generally, there is no one so fit to conduct any business, or to determine how or by whom it shall be conducted, as those who are personally interested in it. This principle condemns the interferences, once so common, of the legislature, or the officers of government, with the ordinary processes of industry. But this part of the subject has been sufficiently enlarged upon by political economists, and is not particularly related to the principles of this essay.

The second objection is more nearly allied to our subject. In many cases, though individuals may not do the particular thing so well, on the average, as the officers of government, it is nevertheless desirable that it should be done by them, rather than by the government, as a means to their own mental education—a mode of strengthening their active faculties, exercising their judgment, and giving them a familiar knowledge of the subjects with which they are thus left to deal. This is a principal, though not the sole, recommendation of jury trial (in cases not political); of free and popular local and municipal institutions; of the conduct of industrial and philanthropic enterprises by voluntary associations. These are not questions of liberty, and are connected with that subject only by remote tendencies, but they are questions of development. It belongs to a different occasion from the present to dwell on these things as parts of national education, as being, in truth, the peculiar training of a citizen, the practical part of the political education of a free people, taking them out of the narrow circle of personal and family selfishness, and accustoming them to the comprehension of joint interests, the management of joint concerns—habituating them to act from public or semi-public motives, and guide their conduct by aims which unite instead of isolating them from one another. Without these habits and powers, a free constitution can neither be worked nor preserved, as is exemplified by the too-often transitory nature of political freedom in countries where it does not rest upon a sufficient basis of local liberties. The management of purely local business by the localities, and of the great enterprises of industry by the union of those who voluntarily supply the pecuniary means, is further recommended by all the advantages which have been set forth in this essay as belonging to individuality of development and diversity of modes of action. Government operations tend to be everywhere alike. With individuals and voluntary associations, on the contrary, there are varied experiments and endless diversity of experience. What the State can usefully do is to make itself a central depository, and active circulator and diffuser, of the experience resulting from many trials. Its business is to enable each experimentalist to benefit by the experiments of others, instead of tolerating no experiments but its own.

The third and most cogent reason for restricting the interference of government is the great evil of adding unnecessarily to its power. Every function superadded to those already exercised by the government causes its influence over hopes and fears to be more widely diffused, and converts, more and more, the active and ambitious part of the public into hangers-on of the government, or of some party which aims at becoming the government. If the roads, the railways, the banks, the insurance offices, the great joint-stock companies, the universities, and the public charities were all of them branches of the government; if, in addition, the municipal corporations and local boards, with all that now devolves on them, became departments of the central administration; if the employees of all these different enterprises were appointed and paid by the government and looked to the government for every rise in life, not all the freedom of the press and popular constitution of the legislature would make this or any other country free otherwise than in name. And the evil would be greater, the more efficiently and scientifically the administrative machinery was constructed—the more skillful the arrangements for obtaining the best qualified hands and heads with which to work it. In England it has of late been proposed that all the members of the civil service of government should be selected by competitive examination, to obtain for those employments the most intelligent and instructed persons procurable; and much has been said and written for and against this proposal. One of the arguments most insisted on by its opponents is that the occupation of a permanent official servant of the State does not hold out sufficient prospects of emolument and importance to attract the highest talents, which will always be able to find a more inviting career in the professions or in the service of companies and other public bodies. One would not have been surprised if this argument had been used by the friends of the proposition as an answer to its principal difficulty. Coming from the opponents it is strange enough. What is urged as an objection is the safety valve of the proposed system. If, indeed, all the high talent of the country *could* be drawn into the service of the government, a proposal tending to bring about that result might well inspire uneasiness. If every part of the business of society which required organized concert, or large and comprehensive views, were in the hands of the government, and if government offices were universally filled by the ablest men, all the enlarged culture and practiced intelligence in the country, except the purely speculative, would be concentrated in a numerous bureaucracy, to whom alone the rest of the community would look for all things—the multitude for direction and dictation in all they had to do; the able and aspiring for personal advancement. To be admitted into the ranks of this bureaucracy, and when admitted, to rise therein, would be the sole objects of ambition. Under this *régime* not only is the outside public ill-qualified, for want of practical experience, to criticize or check the mode of operation of the bureaucracy, but even if the accidents of despotic or the natural working of popular institutions occasionally raise to the summit a ruler or rulers of reforming inclinations, no reform can be effected which is contrary to the interest of the bureaucracy. Such is the melancholy condition of the Russian empire, as shown in the accounts of those who have had sufficient opportunity of observation. The Czar himself is powerless against the bureaucratic body; he can send any one of them to Siberia, but he cannot govern without them, or against their will. On every decree of his they have a tacit veto, by merely refraining from carrying it into effect. In countries of more advanced civilization and of a more insurrectionary spirit, the public, accustomed to expect everything to be done for them by the State, or at least to do nothing for themselves without asking from the State not only leave to do it, but even how it is to be done, naturally hold the State responsible for all evil which befalls them, and when the evil exceeds their amount of patience, they rise against the government and make what is called a revolution; whereupon somebody else, with or without legitimate authority from the nation, vaults into the seat, issues his orders to the bureaucracy, and everything goes on much as it did before; the bureaucracy being unchanged, and nobody else being capable of taking their place.

A very different spectacle is exhibited among a people accustomed to transact their own business. In France, a large part of the people, having been engaged in military service, many of whom have held at least the rank of noncommissioned officers, there are in every popular insurrection several persons competent to take the lead and improvise some tolerable plan of action. What the French are in military affairs, the Americans are in every kind of civil business; let them be left without a government, every body of Americans is able to improvise one and to carry on that or any other public business with a sufficient amount of intelligence, order, and decision. This is what every free people ought to be; and a people capable of this is certain to be free; it will never let itself be enslaved by any man or body of men because these are able to seize and pull the reins of the central administration. No bureaucracy can hope to make such a people as this do or undergo anything that they do not like. But where everything is done through the bureaucracy, nothing to which the bureaucracy is really adverse can be done at all. The constitution of such countries is an organization of the experience and practical ability of the nation into a disciplined body for the purpose of governing the rest; and the more perfect that organization is in itself, the more successful in drawing to itself and educating for itself the persons of greatest capacity from all ranks of the community, the more complete is the bondage of all, the members of the bureaucracy included. For the governors are as much the slaves of their organization and discipline as the governed are of the governors. A Chinese mandarin is as much the tool and creature of a despotism as the humblest cultivator. An individual Jesuit is to the utmost degree of abasement the slave of his order, though the order itself exists for the collective power and importance of its members.

It is not, also, to be forgotten that the absorption of all the principal ability of the country into the governing body is fatal, sooner or later, to the mental activity and progressiveness of the body itself. Banded together as they are—working a system which, like all systems, necessarily proceeds in a great measure by fixed rules—the official body are under the constant temptation of sinking into indolent routine, or, if they now and then desert that mill-horse round, of rushing into some half-examined crudity which has struck the fancy of some leading member of the corps; and the sole check to these closely allied, though seemingly opposite, tendencies, the only stimulus which can keep the ability of the body itself up to a high standard, is liability to the watchful criticism of equal ability outside the body. It is indispensable, therefore, that the means should exist, independently of the government, of forming such ability and furnishing it with the opportunities and experience necessary for a correct judgment of great practical affairs. If we would possess permanently a skillful and efficient body of functionaries—above all a body able to originate and willing to adopt improvements—if we would not have our bureaucracy degenerate into a pedantocracy, this body must not engross all the occupations which form and cultivate the faculties required for the government of mankind.

To determine the point at which evils, so formidable to human freedom and advancement, begin, or rather at which they begin to predominate over the benefits attending the collective application of the force of society, under its recognized chiefs, for the removal of the obstacles which stand in the way of its well-being; to secure as much of the advantages of centralized power and intelligence as can be had without turning into governmental channels too great a proportion of the general activity—is one of the most difficult and complicated questions in the art of government. It is, in a great measure, a question of detail in which many and various considerations must be kept in view, and no absolute rule can be laid down. But I believe that the practical principle in which safety resides, the ideal to be kept in view, the standard by which to test all arrangements intended for overcoming the difficulty, may be conveyed in these words: the greatest dissemination of power consistent with efficiency; but the greatest possible centralization of information and diffusion of it from the center. Thus, in municipal administration, there would be, as in the New England states, a very minute division among separate officers, chosen by the localities, of all business which is not better left to the persons directly interested; but besides this, there would be, in each department of local affairs, a central superintendence, forming a branch of the general government. The organ of this superintendence would concentrate, as in a focus, the variety of information and experience derived from the conduct of that branch of public business in all the localities, from everything analogous which is done in foreign countries, and from the general principles of political science. This central organ should have a right to know all that is done, and its special duty should be that of making the knowledge acquired in one place available for others. Emancipated from the petty prejudices and narrow views of a locality by its elevated position and comprehensive sphere of observation, its advice would naturally carry much authority; but its actual power, as a permanent institution, should, I conceive, be limited to compelling the local officers to obey the laws laid down for their guidance. In all things not provided for by general rules, those officers should be left to their own judgment, under responsibility to their constituents. For the violation of rules, they should be responsible to law, and the rules themselves should be laid down by the legislature; the central administrative authority only watching over their execution and, if they were not properly carried into effect, appealing, according to the nature of the case, to the tribunals to enforce the law, or to the constituencies to dismiss the functionaries who had not executed it according to its spirit. Such, in its general conception, is the central superintendence which the Poor Law Board is intended to exercise over the administrators of the Poor Rate throughout the country. Whatever powers the Board exercises beyond this limit were right and necessary in that peculiar case, for the cure of rooted habits of maladministration in matters deeply affecting not the localities merely, but the whole community; since no locality has a moral right to make itself by mismanagement a nest of pauperism, necessarily overflowing into other localities and impairing the moral and physical condition of the whole laboring community. The powers of administrative coercion and subordinate legislation possessed by the Poor Law Board (but which, owing to the state of opinion on the subject, are very scantily exercised by them), though perfectly justifiable in a case of first-rate national interest, would be wholly out of place in the superintendence of interests purely local. But a central organ of information and instruction for all the localities would be equally valuable in all departments of administration. A government cannot have too much of the kind of activity which does not impede, but aids and stimulates, individual exertion and development. The mischief begins when, instead of calling forth the activity and powers of individuals and bodies, it substitutes its own activity for theirs; when, instead of informing, advising, and, upon occasion, denouncing, it makes them work in fetters, or bids them stand aside and does their work instead of them. The worth of a State, in the long run, is the worth of the individuals composing it; and a State which postpones the interests of *their* mental expansion and elevation to a little more of administrative skill, or of that semblance of it which practice gives in the details of business; a State which dwarfs its men, in order that they may be more docile instruments in its hands even for beneficial purposes—will find that with small men no great thing can really be accomplished; and that the perfection of machinery to which it has sacrificed everything will in the end avail it nothing, for want of the vital power which, in order that the machine might work more smoothly, it has preferred to banish.

NOTES

CHAPTER II

[1]These words had scarcely been written when, as if to give them an emphatic contradiction, occurred the Government Press Prosecutions of 1858. That ill-judged interference with the liberty of public discussion has not, however, induced me to alter a single word in the text, nor has it at all weakened my conviction that, moments of panic excepted, the era of pains and penalties for political discussion has, in our own country, passed away. For, in the first place, the prosecutions were not persisted in; and, in the second, they were never, properly speaking, political prosecutions. The offense charged was not that of criticizing institutions or the acts or persons of rulers, but of circulating what was deemed an immoral doctrine, the lawfulness of tyrannicide.

If the arguments of the present chapter are of any validity, there ought to exist the fullest liberty of professing and discussing, as a matter of ethical conviction, any doctrine, however immoral it may be considered. It would, therefore, be irrelevant and out of place to examine here whether the doctrine of tyrannicide deserves that title. I shall content myself with saying that the subject has been at all times one of the open questions of morals; that the act of a private citizen in striking down a criminal who, by raising himself above the law, has placed himself beyond the reach of legal punishment or control has been accounted by whole nations, and by some of the best and wisest of men, not a crime but an act of exalted virtue; and that, right or wrong, it is not of the nature of assassination, but of civil war. As such, I hold that the instigation to it, in a specific case, may be a proper subject of punishment, but only if an overt act has followed, and at least a probable connection can be established between the act and the instigation. Even then it is not a foreign government but the very government assailed which alone, in the exercise of self-defense, can legitimately punish attacks directed against its own existence.

[2]Thomas Pooley, Bodmin Assizes, July 31, 1857. In December following, he received a free pardon from the crown.

[3]George Jacob Holyoake, August 17, 1857; Edward Truelove, July, 1857.

[4]Baron de Gleichen, Marlborough Street Police Court, August 4, 1857.

[5]Ample warning may be drawn from the large infusion of the passions of a persecutor, which mingled with the general display of the worst parts of our national character on the occasion of the Sepoy insurrection. The ravings of fanatics or charlatans from the pulpit may be unworthy of notice; but the heads of the Evangelical party have announced as their principle for the government of Hindus and

Mohammedans that no schools be supported by public money in which the Bible is not taught, and by necessary consequence that no public employment be given to any but real or pretended Christians. An Undersecretary of State, in a speech delivered to his constituents on the 12th of November, 1857, is reported to have said: "Toleration of their faith" (the faith of a hundred millions of British subjects), "the superstition which they called religion, by the British Government, had had the effect of retarding the ascendance of the British name, and preventing the salutary growth of Christianity. . . . Toleration was the great cornerstone of the religious liberties of this country; but do not let them abuse that precious word 'toleration.' As he understood it, it meant the complete liberty to all, freedom of worship, *among Christians, who worshiped upon the same foundation.* It meant toleration of all sects and denominations of *Christians who believed in the one mediation.*" I desire to call attention to the fact that a man who has been deemed fit to fill a high office in the government of this country under a liberal ministry maintains the doctrine that all who do not believe in the divinity of Christ are beyond the pale of toleration. Who, after this imbecile display, can indulge the illusion that religious persecution has passed away, never to return?

CHAPTER III

[6] *The Sphere and Duties of Government,* from the German of Baron Wilhelm von Humboldt, pp. 11–13.

[7] Sterling's *Essays.*

[8] There is something both contemptible and frightful in the sort of evidence on which, of late years, any person can be judicially declared unfit for the management of his affairs; and after his death, his disposal of his property can be set aside if there is enough of it to pay the expenses of litigation—which are charged on the property itself. All the minute details of his daily life are pried into, and whatever is found which, seen through the medium of the perceiving and describing faculties of the lowest of the low, bears an appearance unlike absolute commonplace, is laid before the jury as evidence of insanity, and often with success; the jurors being little, if at all, less vulgar and ignorant than the witnesses, while the judges, with that extraordinary want of knowledge of human nature and life which continually astonishes us in English lawyers, often help to mislead them. These trials speak volumes as to the state of feeling and opinion among the vulgar with regard to human liberty. So far from setting any value on individuality—so far from respecting the right of each individual to act, in things indifferent, as seems good to his own judgement and inclinations, judges and juries cannot even conceive that a person in a state of sanity can desire such freedom. In former days, when it was proposed to burn atheists, charitable people used to suggest putting them in a madhouse instead; it would be nothing surprising nowadays were we to see this done, and the doers applauding themselves because, instead of persecuting for religion, they had adopted so humane and Christian a mode of treating these unfortunates, not without a silent satisfaction at their having thereby obtained their deserts.

CHAPTER IV

[9]The case of the Bombay Parsees is a curious instance in point. When this industrious and enterprising tribe, the descendants of the Persian fire-worshipers, flying from their native country before the Caliphs, arrived in western India, they were admitted to toleration by the Hindu sovereigns, on condition of not eating beef. When those regions afterward fell under the dominion of Mohammedan conquerors, the Parsees obtained from them a continuance of indulgence, on condition of refraining from pork. What was at first obedience to authority became a second nature, and the Parsees to this day abstain both from beef and pork. Though not required by their religion, the double abstinence has had time to grow into a custom of their tribe; and custom, in the East, is a religion.

INDEX

Chapter XII of Book VI of Mill's
A System of Logic

Of the Logic of Practice, or Art;
Including Morality and Policy

1. *Morality not a Science, but an Art.* In the preceding chapters we have endeavoured to characterize the present state of those among the branches of knowledge called Moral, which are sciences in the only proper sense of the term, that is, inquiries into the course of nature. It is customary, however, to include under the term moral knowledge, and even (though improperly) under that of moral science, an inquiry the results of which do not express themselves in the indicative, but in the imperative mood, or in periphrases equivalent to it; what is called the knowledge of duties; practical ethics or morality.

Now, the imperative mood is the characteristic of art, as distinguished from science. Whatever speaks in rules, or precepts, not in assertions respecting matters of fact, is art: and ethics, or morality, is properly a portion of the art corresponding to the sciences of human nature and society.

The Method, therefore, of Ethics, can be no other than that of Art, or Practice, in general: and the portion yet uncompleted, of the task which we proposed to ourselves in the concluding Book, is to characterize the general Method of Art, as distinguished from Science.

2. *Relation between rules of art and the theorems of the corresponding science.* In all branches of practical business, there are cases in which individuals are bound to conform their practice to a preestablished rule, while there are others in which it is part of their task to find or construct the rule by which they are to govern their conduct. The first, for example, is the case of a judge, under a definite written code. The judge is not called upon to determine what course would be intrinsically the most advisable in the particular case in hand, but only within what rule of law it falls; what the legislature has ordained to be done in the kind of case, and must therefore be presumed to have intended in the individual case. The method must here be wholly and exclusively one of ratiocination, or syllogism; and the process is obviously, what in our analysis of the syllogism we showed that all ratiocination is, namely the interpretation of a formula.

In order that our illustration of the opposite case may be taken from the same class of subjects as the former, we will suppose, in contrast with the situation of the judge, the position of the legislator. As the judge has laws for his guidance, so the legislator has rules, and maxims of policy; but it would be a manifest error to suppose that the legislator is bound by these maxims in the same manner as the judge is bound by the laws, and that all he has to do is to argue down from them to the particular case, as the judge does from the laws. The legislator is bound to take into consideration the reasons or grounds of the maxim; the judge has nothing to do with those of the law, except so far as a consideration of them may throw light upon the intention of the lawmaker, where his words have left it doubtful. To the judge, the rule, once positively ascertained, is final; but the legislator, or other practitioner, who goes by rules rather than by their reasons, like the old-fashioned German tacticians who were vanquished by Napoleon, or the physician who preferred that his patients should die by rule rather than recover contrary to it, is rightly judged to be a mere pedant, and the slave of his formulas.

Now, the reasons of a maxim of policy, or of any other rule of art, can be no other than the theorems of the corresponding science.

The relation in which rules of art stand to doctrines of science may be thus characterized. The art proposes to itself an end to be attained, defines the end, and hands it over to the science. The science receives it, considers it as a phenomenon or effect to be studied, and having investigated its causes and conditions, sends it back to art with a theorem of the combinations of circumstances by which it could be produced. Art then examines these combinations of circumstances, and according as any of them are or are not in human power, pronounces the end attainable or not. The only one of the premises, therefore, which Art supplies, is the original major premise, which asserts that the attainment of the given end is desirable. Science then lends to Art the proposition (obtained by a series of inductions or of deductions) that the performance of certain actions will attain the end. From these premises Art concludes that the performance of these actions is desirable, and finding it also practicable, converts the theorem into a rule or precept.

3. *What is the proper function of rules of art?* It deserves particular notice, that the theorem or speculative truth is not ripe for being turned into a precept, until the whole, and not a part merely, of the operation which belongs to science, has been performed. Suppose that we have completed the scientific process only up to a certain point; have discovered that a particular cause will produce the desired effect, but have not ascertained all the negative conditions which are necessary, that is, all the circumstances which, if present, would prevent its production. If, in this imperfect state of the scientific theory, we attempt to frame a rule of art, we perform that operation prematurely. Whenever any counteracting cause, overlooked by the theorem, takes place, the rule will be at fault: we shall

employ the means and the end will not follow. No arguing from or about the rule itself will then help us through the difficulty: there is nothing for it but to turn back and finish the scientific process which should have preceded the formation of the rule. We must re-open the investigation, to inquire into the remainder of the conditions on which the effect depends; and only after we have ascertained the whole of these, are we prepared to transform the completed law of the effect into a precept, in which those circumstances or combinations of circumstances which the science exhibits as conditions, are prescribed as means.

It is true that, for the sake of convenience, rules must be formed from something less than this ideally perfect theory; in the first place, because the theory can seldom be made ideally perfect; and next, because, if all the counteracting contingencies, whether of frequent or of rare occurrence, were included, the rules would be too cumbrous to be apprehended and remembered by ordinary capacities, on the common occasions of life. The rules of art do not attempt to comprise more conditions than require to be attended to in ordinary cases; and are therefore always imperfect. In the manual arts, where the requisite conditions are not numerous, and where those which the rules do not specify are generally either plain to common observation or speedily learnt from practice, rules may often be safely acted on by persons who know nothing more than the rule. But in the complicated affairs of life, and still more in those of states and societies, rules cannot be relied on, without constantly referring back to the scientific laws on which they are founded. To know what are the practical contingencies which require a modification of the rule, or which are altogether exceptions to it, is to know what combinations of circumstances would interfere with, or entirely counteract, the consequences of those laws: and this can only be learnt by a reference to the theoretic grounds of the rule.

By a wise practitioner, therefore, rules of conduct will only be considered as provisional. Being made for the most numerous cases, or for those of most ordinary occurrence, they point out the manner in which it will be least perilous to act, where time or means do not exist for analysing the actual circumstances of the case, or where we cannot trust our judgement in estimating them. But they do not at all supersede the propriety of going through (when circumstances permit) the scientific process requisite for framing a rule from the data of the particular case before us. At the same time, the common rule may very properly serve as an admonition that a certain mode of action has been found by ourselves and others to be well adapted to the cases of most common occurrence; so that if it be unsuitable to the case in hand, the reason of its being so will be likely to arise from some unusual circumstance.

4. *Art cannot be deductive.* The error is therefore apparent, of those who would deduce the line of conduct proper to particular cases, from supposed universal practical maxims; overlooking the necessity of constantly referring back to the principles of the speculative science, in order to be sure of attaining even the specific end which the rules have in view. How much greater still, then, must the error be, of setting up such unbending principles, not merely as universal rules for attaining a given end, but as rules of conduct generally; without regard to the possibility, not only that some modifying cause may prevent the attainment of the given end by the means which the rule prescribes, but that success itself may conflict with some other end, which may possibly chance to be more desirable.

This is the habitual error of many of the political speculators whom I have characterized as the geometrical school; especially in France, where ratiocination from rules of practice forms the staple commodity of journalism and political oratory; a misapprehension of the functions of Deduction which has brought much discredit, in the estimation of other countries, upon the spirit of generalization so honourably characteristic of the French mind. The commonplaces of politics, in France, are large and sweeping practical maxims, from which, as ultimate premises, men reason downwards to particular applications, and this they call being logical and consistent. For instance, they are perpetually arguing that such and such a measure ought to be adopted, because it is a consequence of the principle on which the form of government is founded; of the principle of legitimacy, or the principle of the sovereignty of the people. To which it may be answered, that if these be really practical principles, they must rest on speculative grounds; the sovereignty of the people (for example) must be a right foundation for government, because a government thus constituted tends to produce certain beneficial effects. Inasmuch, however, as no government produces all possible beneficial effects, but all are attended with more or fewer inconveniences; and since these cannot usually be combated by means drawn from the very causes which produce them; it would be often a much stronger recommendation of some practical arrangement, that it does not follow from what is called the general principle of the government, than that it does. Under a government of legitimacy, the presumption is far rather in favour of institutions of popular origin; and in a democracy, in favour of arrangements tending to check the impetus of popular will. The line of argumentation so commonly mistaken in France for political philosophy, tends to the practical conclusion that we should exert our utmost efforts to aggravate, instead of alleviating, whatever are the characteristic imperfections of the system of institutions which we prefer, or under which we happen to live.

5. *Every Art consists of truths of Science, arranged in the order suitable for*

some practical use. The grounds, then, of every rule of art, are to be found in the theorems of science. An art, or a body of art, consists of the rules, together with as much of the speculative propositions as comprises the justification of those rules. The complete art of any matter, includes a selection of such a portion from the science, as is necessary to show on what conditions the effects, which the art aims at producing, depend. And Art in general, consists of the truths of Science, arranged in the most convenient order for practice, instead of the order which is the most convenient for thought. Science groups and arranges its truths, so as to enable us to take in at one view as much as possible of the general order of the universe. Art, though it must assume the same general laws, follows them only into such of their detailed consequences as have led to the formation of rules of conduct; and brings together from parts of the field of science most remote from one another, the truths relating to the production of the different and heterogeneous conditions necessary to each effect which the exigencies of practical life require to be produced.

Science, therefore, following one cause to its various effects, while art traces one effect to its multiplied and diversified causes and conditions; there is need of a set of intermediate scientific truths, derived from the higher generalities of science, and destined to serve as the generalia or first principles of the various arts. The scientific operation of framing these intermediate principles, M. Comte characterizes as one of those results of philosophy which are reserved for futurity. The only complete example which he points out as actually realized, and which can be held up as a type to be imitated in more important matters, is the general theory of the art of Descriptive Geometry, as conceived by M. Monge. It is not, however, difficult to understand what the nature of these intermediate principles must generally be. After framing the most comprehensive possible conception of the end to be aimed at, that is, of the effect to be produced, and determining in the same comprehensive manner the set of conditions on which that effect depends; there remains to be taken, a general survey of the resources which can be commanded for realizing this set of conditions; and when the result of this survey has been embodied in the fewest and most extensive propositions possible, those propositions will express the general relation between the available means and the end, and will constitute the general scientific theory of the art; from which its practical methods will follow as corollaries.

6. *Teleology, or the Doctrine of Ends.* But though the reasonings which connect the end or purpose of every art with its means, belong to the domain of Science, the definition of the end itself belongs exclusively to Art, and forms its peculiar province. Every art has one first principle, or general major premise, not borrowed from science; that which enunciates the

object aimed at, and affirms it to be a desirable object. The builder's art assumes that it is desirable to have buildings; architecture (as one of the fine arts), that it is desirable to have them beautiful or imposing. The hygienic and medical arts assume, the one that the preservation of health, the other that the cure of disease, are fitting and desirable ends. These are not propositions of science. Propositions of science assert a matter of fact: an existence, a coexistence, a succession, or a resemblance. The propositions now spoken of do not assert that anything is, but enjoin or recommend that something should be. They are a class by themselves. A proposition of which the predicate is expressed by the words *ought* or *should be*, is generically different from one which is expressed by *is*, or *will be*. It is true, that in the largest sense of the words, even these propositions assert something as a matter of fact. The fact affirmed in them is, that the conduct recommended excites in the speaker's mind the feeling of approbation. This, however, does not go to the bottom of the matter; for the speaker's approbation is no sufficient reason why other people should approve; nor ought it to be a conclusive reason even with himself. For the purposes of practice, every one must be required to justify his approbation: and for this there is need of general premises, determining what are the proper objects of approbation, and what the proper order of precedence among those objects.

These general premises, together with the principal conclusions which may be deduced from them, form (or rather might form) a body of doctrine, which is properly the Art of Life, in its three departments, Morality, Prudence or Policy, and Aesthetics; the Right, the Expedient, and the Beautiful or Noble, in human conduct and works. To this art (which, in the main, is unfortunately still to be created), all other arts are subordinate; since its principles are those which must determine whether the special aim of any particular art is worthy and desirable, and what is its place in the scale of desirable things. Every art is thus a joint result of laws of nature disclosed by science, and of the general principles of what has been called Teleology, or the Doctrine of Ends; which, borrowing the language of the German metaphysicians, may also be termed, not improperly, the principles of Practical Reason.

A scientific observer or reasoner, merely as such, is not an adviser for practice. His part is only to show that certain consequences follow from certain causes, and that to obtain certain ends, certain means are the most effectual. Whether the ends themselves are such as ought to be pursued, and if so, in what cases and to how great a length, it is no part of his business as a cultivator of science to decide, and science alone will never qualify him for the decision. In purely physical science, there is not much temptation to assume this ulterior office; but those who treat of human nature and society invariably claim it; they always undertake to say, not merely what is, but what ought to be. To entitle them to do this, a complete doctrine of Teleology is indispensable. A scientific theory, however perfect, of the subject matter, considered merely as part of the order of nature, can in no degree serve as a substitute. In this respect the various subordinate arts afford a misleading analogy. In them there is seldom any visible necessity for justifying the end, since in general its desirableness is denied by nobody, and it is only when the question of precedence is to be decided between that end and some other, that the general principles of Telology have to be called in: but a writer on Morals and Politics requires those principles at every step. The most elaborate and well-digested exposition of the laws of succession and coexistence among mental or social phenomena, and of their relation to one another as causes and effects, will be of no avail towards the art of Life or of Society, if the ends to be aimed at by that art are left to the vague suggestions of the *intellectus sibi permissus*, or are taken for granted without analysis or questioning.

7. *Necessity of an ultimate standard, or first principle of Teleology.* There is, then, a Philosophia Prima peculiar to Art, as there is one which belongs to Science. There are not only first principles of Knowledge, but first principles of Conduct. There must be some standard by which to determine the goodness or badness, absolute and comparative, of ends, or objects of desire. And whatever that standard is, there can be but one: for if there were several ultimate principles of conduct, the same conduct might be approved by one of those principles and condemned by another; and there would be needed some more general principle, as umpire between them.

Accordingly, writers on moral philosophy have mostly felt the necessity not only of referring all rules of conduct, and all judgements of praise and blame, to principles, but of referring them to some one principle; some rule, or standard, with which all other rules of conduct were required to be consistent, and from which by ultimate consequence they could all be deduced. Those who have dispensed with the assumption of such an universal standard, have only been enabled to do so by supposing that a moral sense, or instinct, inherent in our constitution, informs us, both what principles of conduct we are bound to observe, and also in what order these should be subordinated to one another.

The theory of the foundations of morality is a subject which it would be out of place, in a work like this, to discuss at large, and which could not to any useful purpose be treated incidentally. I shall content myself therefore with saying, that the doctrine of intuitive moral principles, even if true, would provide only for that portion of the field of conduct which is properly called moral. For the remainder of the practice of life some general principle, or standard, must still be sought; and if that principle be rightly chosen, it will be found, I apprehend, to serve quite as well for the ultimate principle of Morality, as for that of Prudence, Policy or Taste.

Without attempting in this place to justify my opinion, or even to define the kind of justification which it admits of, I merely declare my conviction, that the general principle to which all rules of practice ought to conform, and the test by which they should be tried, is that of conduciveness to the happiness of mankind, or rather, of all sentient beings: in other words, that the promotion of happiness is the ultimate principle of Teleology.

I do not mean to assert that the promotion of happiness should be itself the end of all actions, or even of all rules of action. It is the justification, and ought to be the controller, of all ends, but is not itself the sole end. There are many virtuous actions, and even virtuous in modes of action (though the cases are, I think, less frequent than is often supposed) by which happiness in the particular instance is sacrificed, more pain being produced than pleasure. But conduct of which this can be truly asserted, admits of justification only because it can be shown that on the whole more happiness will exist in the world, if feelings are cultivated which will make people, in certain cases, regardless of happiness. I fully admit that this is true: that the cultivation of an ideal nobleness of will and conduct, should be to individual human beings an end, to which the specific pursuit either of their own happiness or of that of others (except so far as included in that idea) should, in any case of conflict, give way. But I hold that the very question, what constitutes this elevation of character, is itself to be decided by a reference to happiness as the standard. The character itself should be, to the individual, a paramount end, simply because the existence of this ideal nobleness of character, or of a near approach to it, in any abundance, would go further than all things else towards making human life happy; both in the comparatively humble sense, of pleasure and freedom from pain, and in the higher meaning, of rendering life, not what it now is almost universally, puerile and insignificant—but such as human beings with highly developed faculties can care to have.

Mill's
"Remarks on Bentham's Philosophy"

It is no light task to give an abridged view of the philosophical opinions of one, who attempted to place the vast subjects of morals and legislation upon a scientific basis: a mere outline is all that can be attempted.

The first principles of Mr. Bentham's philosophy are these—that happiness, meaning by that term pleasure and exemption from pain, is the only thing desirable in itself; that all other things are desirable solely as means to that end; that the production, therefore, of the greatest possible happiness is the only fit purpose of all human thought and action, and consequently of all morality and government; and moreover, that pleasure and pain are the sole agencies by which the conduct of mankind is in fact governed, whatever circumstances the individual may be placed in, and whether he is aware of it or not.

Mr. Bentham does not appear to have entered very deeply into the metaphysical grounds of these doctrines; he seems to have taken those grounds very much upon the showing of the metaphysicians who preceded him. The principle of utility, or as he afterward called it, "the greatest-happiness principle," stands no otherwise demonstrated in his writings than by an enumeration of the phrases of a different description which have been commonly employed to denote the rule of life, and the rejection of them all, as having no intelligible meaning, further than as they may involve a tacit reference to considerations of utility. Such are the phrases "law of nature," "right reason," "natural rights," "moral sense." All these Mr. Bentham regarded as mere covers for dogmatism, excuses for setting up one's own *ipse dixit* as a rule to bind other people. "They consist, all of them," says he, "in so many contrivances for avoiding the obligation of appealing to any external standard, and for prevailing upon the reader to accept the author's sentiment or opinion as a reason for itself."

This, however, is not fair treatment of the believers in other moral principles than that of utility. All modes of speech are employed in an ignorant manner, by ignorant people; but no one who had thought deeply and systematically enough to be entitled to the name of a philosopher, ever supposed that his *own* private sentiments of approbation and disapprobation must necessarily be well- founded, and needed not to be compared with any external standard. The answer of such persons to Mr. Bentham would be, that by an inductive and analytical examination of the human mind, they had satisfied themselves that what we call our moral sentiments (that is, the feelings of complacency and aversion we experience when we compare actions of our own or of other people with our standard of right and wrong), are as much part of the original constitution of man's nature as the desire of happiness and the fear of suffering; that those sentiments do not indeed attach themselves to the same actions under all circumstances, but neither do they, in attaching themselves to actions, follow the law of utility; but certain other general laws, which are the same in all mankind, naturally, though education or external circumstances may counteract them, by creating artificial associations stronger than they. No *proof* indeed can be given that we ought to abide by these laws, but neither can any *proof* be given that we ought to regulate our conduct by utility. All that can be said is that the pursuit of happiness is natural to us; and so, it is contended, is the reverence for, and the inclination to square our actions by, certain general laws of morality.

Any one who is acquainted with the ethical doctrines either of the Reid and Stewart school, or of the German metaphysicians (not to go further back), knows that such would be the answer of those philosophers to Mr. Bentham; and it is an answer of which Mr. Bentham's writings furnish no sufficient refutation. For it is evident, that these views of the origin of moral distinctions are *not* what he says all such views are, destitute of any precise and tangible meaning; nor chargeable with setting up as a standard the feelings of the particular person. They set up as a standard what are assumed (on grounds which are considered sufficient) to be the instincts of the species, or principles of our common nature as universal and inexplicable as instincts.

To pass judgment on these doctrines belongs to a profounder and subtler metaphysics than Mr. Bentham possessed. I apprehend it will be the judgment of posterity that in his views of what in the felicitous expression of Hobbes may be called the *philosophia prima*, it has for the most part, even when he was most completely in the right, been reserved for others to *prove* him so. The greatest of Mr. Bentham's defects, his insufficient knowledge and appreciation of the thoughts of other men, shows itself constantly in his grappling with some delusive shadow of an adversary's opinions, and leaving the actual substance unharmed.

After laying down the principle of utility, Mr. Bentham is occupied, through the most voluminous and the most permanently valuable part of his works, in constructing the outlines of practical ethics and legislation, and filling up some portions of the latter science (or rather art) in great detail; by the uniform and unflinching application of his own greatest-happiness principle, from which the eminently consistent and systematic character of his intellect prevented him from ever swerving. In the writings of no philosopher, probably, are to be detected so few contradictions—so few instances of even momentary deviation from the principles he himself has laid down.

It is perhaps fortunate that Mr. Bentham devoted a much larger share of his time and labor to the subject of legislation, than to that of morals; for the mode in which he understood and applied the principle of utility appears to me far more conducive to the attainment of true and valuable results in the former, than in the latter of these two branches of inquiry. The recognition of happiness as the only thing desirable in itself, and of the production of the state of things most favorable to happiness as the only rational end both of morals and policy, by no means necessarily leads to the doctrine of expediency as professed by Paley: the ethical canon which judges of the morality of an act or a class of actions, solely by the probable *consequences* of that particular kind of act, supposing it to be generally practised. This is a very small part indeed of what a more enlarged understanding of the "greatest-happiness principle" would require us to take into the account. A certain kind of action, as for example, theft, or lying, would, if commonly practised, occasion certain evil consequences to society, but those evil consequences are far from constituting the entire moral bearings of the vices of theft or lying. We shall have a very imperfect view of the relation of those practises to the general happiness, if we suppose them to exist singly, and insulated. All acts suppose certain dispositions, and habits of mind and heart, which may be in themselves states of enjoyment or of wretchedness, and which must be fruitful in *other* consequences besides those particular acts. No person can be a thief or a liar without being much else, and if our moral judgments and feelings with respect to a person convicted of either vice were grounded solely upon the pernicious tendency of thieving and of lying, they would be partial and incomplete; many considerations would be omitted, which are at least equally "germane to the matter"; many which, by leaving them out of our general views, we may indeed teach ourselves a habit of overlooking, but which it is impossible for any of us not to be influenced by, in particular cases, in proportion as they are forced upon our attention.

Now, the great fault I have to find with Mr. Bentham as a moral philosopher, and the source of the chief part of the temporary mischief which, in that character, along with a vastly greater amount of permanent good, he must be allowed to have produced, is this: that he has practically, to a very great extent, confounded the principle of utility with the principle of specific consequences, and has habitually made up his estimate of the approbation or blame due to a particular kind of action, from a calculation solely of the consequences to which that very action, if practised generally, would itself lead. He has largely exemplified, and contributed very widely to diffuse, a tone of thinking, according to which any kind of action or any habit, which in its own specific consequences cannot be proved to be necessarily or probably productive of unhappiness to the agent himself or to others, is supposed to be fully justified; and any disapprobation or aversion entertained towards the individual by reason of it, is set down from that time forward as prejudice and superstition. It is not considered (at least not habitually considered) whether the act or habit in question, though not in itself necessarily pernicious, may not form part of a *character* essentially pernicious, or at least essentially deficient in some quality eminently conducive to the "greatest happiness." To apply such a standard as this would indeed often require a much deeper insight into the formation of character, and knowledge of the internal workings of human nature, than Mr. Bentham possessed. But, in a greater or less degree, he, and every one else, judges by this standard: even those who are warped, by some partial view, into the omission of all such elements from their general speculations.

When the moralist thus overlooks the relation of an act to a certain state of mind as its cause, and its connexion through that common cause with large classes and groups of actions apparently very little resembling itself, his estimation even of the consequences of the very act itself is rendered imperfect. For it may be affirmed with few exceptions, that any act whatever has a tendency to fix and perpetuate the state or character of mind in which itself has originated. And if that important element in the moral relations of the action, be not taken into account by the moralist as a cause, neither probably will it be taken into account as a consequence.

Mr. Bentham is far from having altogether overlooked this side of the subject. Indeed, those most original and instructive, though, as I conceive, in their spirit, partially erroneous chapters, on *motives* and on *dispositions,* in his first great work, the Introduction to the Principles of Morals and Legislation, open up a direct and broad path to these most important topics. It is not the less true that Mr. Bentham, and many others following his example, when they came to discuss particular questions of ethics, have commonly, in the superior stress which they laid upon the specific consequences of a class of acts, rejected all contemplation of the action in its general bearings upon the entire moral being of the agent, or have, to say the least, thrown those considerations so far into the background as to be almost out of sight. And by so doing they have not only marred the value of many of their speculations, considered as mere philosophical inquiries, but have always run the risk of incurring, and in many cases have in my opinion actually incurred, serious practical errors.

This incompleteness, however, in Mr. Bentham's general views, was not of a nature materially to diminish the value of his speculations through the greater part of the field of legislation. Those of the bearings of an action, upon which Mr. Bentham bestowed almost exclusive attention, were also those with which almost alone legislation is conversant. The legislator enjoins or prohibits an action, with very little regard to the general moral excellence or turpitude which it implies; he looks to the consequences to society of the particular kind of action; his object is not to render people incapable of *desiring* a crime, but to deter them from actually *committing* it. Taking human beings as he finds them, he endeavors to supply such inducements as will constrain even persons of the dispositions the most at variance with the general happiness, to practise as great a degree of regard to it in their actual conduct, as can be obtained from them by such means without preponderant inconvenience. A theory, therefore, which considers little in an action besides that action's *own* consequences, will generally be sufficient to serve the purposes of a philosophy of legislation. Such a philosophy will be most apt to fail in the consideration of the greater social question: the theory of organic institutions and general forms of policy; for those (unlike the details of legislation) to be duly estimated, must be viewed as the great instruments of forming the national character, of carrying forward the members of the community toward perfection, or preserving them from degeneracy. This, as might in some measure be expected, is a point of view in which, except for some partial or limited purpose, Mr. Bentham seldom contemplates these questions. And this signal omission is one of the greatest of the deficiencies by which his speculations on the theory of government, though full of valuable ideas, are rendered, in my judgment, altogether inconclusive in their general results.

To these we shall advert more fully hereafter. As yet I have not acquitted myself of the more agreeable task of setting forth some part of the services which the philosophy of legislation owes to Mr. Bentham.

The greatest service of all, that for which posterity will award most honor to his name, is one that is his exclusively, and can be shared by no man present or to come; it is the service which can be performed only once for any science, that of pointing out by what method of investigation it may be *made* a science. What Bacon did for physical knowledge, Mr. Bentham has done for philosophical legislation. Before Bacon's time, many physical facts had been ascertained, and previously to Mr. Bentham, mankind were in possession of many just and valuable detached observations on the making of laws. But he was the first who attempted regularly to deduce all the secondary and intermediate principles of law, by direct and systematic inference from the one great axiom or principle of general utility. In all existing systems of law, those secondary principles or dicta in which the essence of the systems resided, had grown up in detail, and even when founded in views of utility, were not the result of any scientific and comprehensive course of inquiry, but more frequently were purely technical; that is, they had grown out of circumstances purely *historical*, and not having been altered when those circumstances changed, had nothing left to rest upon but fictions, and unmeaning forms. Take for instance the law of real property, the whole of which continues to this very day to be founded on the doctrine of feudal tenures, when those tenures have long ceased to exist except in the phraseology of Westminster Hall. Nor was the *theory* of law in a better state than the practical systems; speculative jurists having dared little more than to refine somewhat upon the technical maxims of the particular body of jurisprudence which they happened to have studied. Mr. Bentham was the first who had the genius and courage to conceive the idea of bringing back the science to first principles. This could not be done, could scarcely even be attempted, without, as a necessary consequence, making obvious the utter worthlessness of many, and the crudity and want of precision of almost all, the maxims which had previously passed everywhere for principles of law.

Mr. Bentham, moreover, has warred against the errors of existing systems of jurisprudence, in a more direct manner than by merely presenting the contrary truths. The force of argument with which he rent asunder the fantastic and illogical maxims on which the various technical systems are founded, and exposed the flagrant evils which they practically produce, is only equaled by the pungent sarcasm and exquisite humor with which he has derided their absurdities, and the eloquent declamation which he continually pours forth against them, sometimes in the form of lamentation, and sometimes of invective.

This then was the first, and perhaps the grandest achievement of Mr. Bentham: the entire discrediting of all technical systems, and the example which he set of treating law as no peculiar mystery, but a simple piece of practical business, wherein means were to be adapted to ends, as in any of the other arts of life. To have accomplished this, supposing him to have done nothing else, is to have equaled the glory of the greatest scientific benefactors of the human race.

But Mr. Bentham, unlike Bacon, did not merely prophesy a science; he made large strides towards the creation of one. He was the first who conceived, with anything approaching to precision, the idea of a Code or complete body of law, and the distinctive characters of its essential parts—the Civil Law, the Penal Law, and the Law of Procedure. On the first two of these three departments he rendered valuable service; the third he actually created. Conformably to the habits of his mind, he set about investigating, *ab initio,* a philosophy or science for each of the three branches. He did with the received principles of each, what a good code would do with the laws themselves—extirpated the bad, substituting others; reenacted the good, but in so much clearer and more methodical a form that those who were most familiar with them before scarcely recognized them as the same. Even upon old truths, when they pass through his hands, he leaves so many of his marks, that often he almost seems to claim the discovery of what he has only systematized.

In creating the philosophy of Civil Law, he proceeded not much beyond establishing on the proper basis some of its most general principles, and cursorily discussing some of the most interesting of its details. Nearly the whole of what he has published on this branch of law is contained in the *Traités de Législation,* edited by M. Dumont. To the most difficult part, and that which most needed a master-hand to clear away its difficulties, the nomenclature and arrangement of the Civil Code, he contributed little, except detached observations and criticisms upon the errors of his predecessors. The *"Vue Générale d'un Corps Complet de Législation,"* included in the work just cited, contains almost all which he has given to us on this subject.

In the department of Penal Law, he is the author of the best attempt yet made toward a philosophical classification of offenses. The theory of punishments (for which however more had been done by his predecessors than for any other part of the science of law) he left nearly complete.

The theory of Procedure (including that of the constitution of the courts of justice) he found in a more utterly barbarous state than even either of the other branches, and he left it incomparably the most perfect. There is scarcely a question of practical importance in this most important department, which he has not settled. He has left next to nothing for his successors.

He has shown with the force of demonstration, and has enforced and illustrated the truth in a hundred ways, that by sweeping away the greater part of the artificial rules and forms which obtain in all the countries called civilized, and adopting the simple and direct modes of investigation which all men employ in endeavoring to ascertain facts for their own private knowledge, it is possible to get rid of at least nine tenths of the expense, and ninety-nine hundredths of the delay, of law proceedings, not only with no increase, but with an almost incredible diminution of the chances of erroneous decision. He has also established irrefragably the principles of a good judicial establishment: a division of the country into districts, with *one* judge in each, appointed only for a limited period, and deciding all sorts of cases, with a deputy under him, appointed and removable by himself; an appeal lying in all cases whatever, but by the transmission of papers only, to a supreme court or courts, consisting each of only *one* judge, and stationed in the metropolis.

It is impossible within the compass of this sketch, to attempt any further statement of Mr. Bentham's principles and views on the great science which first became a science in his hands.

As an analyst of human nature (the faculty in which above all it is necessary that an ethical philosopher should excel) I cannot rank Mr. Bentham very high. He has done little in this department, beyond introducing what appears to me a very deceptive phraseology, and furnishing a catalog of the "springs of action," from which some of the most important are left out.

That the actions of sentient beings are wholly determined by pleasure and pain, is the fundamental principle from which he starts; and thereupon Mr. Bentham creates a *motive,* and an *interest,* corresponding to each pleasure or pain, and affirms that our actions are determined by our *interests,* by the *preponderant* interest, by the *balance* of motives. Now if this only means what was before asserted, that our actions are determined by pleasure and pain, that simple and unambiguous mode of stating the proposition is preferable. But under cover of the obscurer phrase a meaning creeps in, both to the author's mind and the reader's, which goes much further, and is entirely false: that all our acts are determined by pains and pleasures *in prospect,* pains and pleasures to which we look forward as the *consequences* of our acts. This, as a universal truth, can in no way be maintained. The pain or pleasure which determines our conduct is as frequently one which *precedes* the moment of action as one which follows it. A man *may,* it is true, be deterred in circumstances of temptation, from perpetrating a crime, by his dread of the punishment, or of the remorse, which he fears he may have to endure *after* the guilty act; and in that case we may say, with some kind of propriety, that his conduct is swayed by the balance of motives, or if you will, of interests. But the case *may* be, and is to the full as likely to be, that he recoils from the very thought of committing the act; the idea of placing himself in such a situation is so painful, that he cannot dwell upon it long enough to have even the physical power of perpetrating the crime. His conduct is determined by pain; but by a pain which precedes the act, not by one which is expected to follow it. Not only *may* this be so, but unless it be so, the man is not really virtuous. The fear of pain *consequent* upon the act, cannot arise, unless there be *deliberation;* and the man as well as "the woman who deliberates" is in imminent danger of being lost. With what propriety shrinking from an action without deliberation can be called yielding to an *interest,* I cannot see. *Interest* surely conveys, and is intended to convey, the idea of an *end,* to which the conduct (whether it be act or forbearance) is designed as the *means.* Nothing of this sort takes place in the above example. It would be more correct to say that conduct is *sometimes* determined by an *interest,* that is, by a deliberate and conscious aim; and sometimes by an *impulse,* that is, by a feeling (call it an association if you think fit) which has no ulterior end, the act or forbearance becoming an end in itself.

The attempt, again, to *enumerate* motives, that is, human desires and aversions, seems to me to be in its very conception an error. Motives are innumerable: there is nothing whatever which may not become an object of desire or of dislike by association. If may be desirable to distinguish by peculiar notice the motives which are strongest and of most frequent operation; but Mr. Bentham has not even done this. In his list of motives, though he includes sympathy, he omits conscience, or the feeling of duty: one would never imagine from reading him that any human being ever did an act merely because it is right, or abstained from it merely because it is wrong. In this Mr. Bentham differs widely from Hartley, who, although he considers the moral sentiments to be wholly the result of association, does not therefore deny them a place in his system, but includes the feelings of "the moral sense" as one of the six classes into which he divides pleasures and pains. In Mr. Bentham's own mind, deeply imbued as it was with the "greatest-happiness principle," this motive was probably so blended with that of sympathy as to be undistinguishable from it; but he should have recollected that those who acknowledge another standard of right and wrong than happiness, or who have never reflected on the subject at all, have often very strong feelings of moral obligation; and whether a person's standard be happiness or any thing else, his attachment to his standard is not necessarily in proportion to his benevolence. Persons of weak sympathies have often a strong feeling of justice; and others, again, with the feelings of benevolence in considerable strength, have scarcely any consciousness of moral obligation at all.

It is scarcely necessary to point out that the habitual omission of so important a spring of action, in an enumeration professing to be complete, must tend to create a habit of overlooking the same phenomenon, and, consequently, making no allowance for it, in other moral speculations. It is difficult to imagine any more fruitful source of gross error; though one would be apt to suppose the oversight an impossible one, without this evidence of its having been committed by one of the greatest thinkers our species has produced. How can we suppose him to be alive to the existence and force of the motive in particular cases, who omits it in a deliberate and comprehensive enumeration of all the influences by which human conduct is governed?

In laying down as a philosophical axiom, that men's actions are always obedient to their interests, Mr. Bentham did no more than dress up the very trivial proposition, that all persons do what they feel themselves most disposed to do, in terms which appeared to him more precise, and better suited to the purposes of philosophy than those more familiar expressions. He by no means intended by this assertion to impute universal self-ishness to mankind, for he reckoned the motive of sympathy as an *interest*, and would have included conscience under the same appellation, if that motive had found any place in his philosophy, as a distinct principle from benevolence. He distinguished two kinds of interests, the self-regarding and the social; in vulgar discourse the name is restricted to the former kind alone.

But there cannot be a greater mistake than to suppose that, because we may ourselves be perfectly *conscious* of an ambiguity in our language, that ambiguity therefore has no effect in perverting our modes of thought. I am persuaded, from experience, that this habit of speaking of all the feelings which govern mankind under the name of *interests*, is almost always in point of fact connected with a tendency to consider *interest* in the vulgar sense, that is, purely self-regarding interest, as exercising, by the very constitution of human nature, a far more exclusive and paramount control over human actions than it really does exercise. Such, certainly, was the tendency of Mr. Bentham's own opinions. Habitually, and throughout his works, the moment he has shown that a man's *selfish* interest would prompt him to a particular course of action, he lays it down without further parley that the man's interest lies that way; and, by sliding insensibly from the vulgar sense of the word into the philosophical, and from the philosophical back into the vulgar, the conclusion which is always brought out is that the man will act as the selfish interest prompts. The extent to which Mr. Bentham was a believer in the predominance of the selfish principle in human nature, may be seen from the sweeping terms in which, in his Book of Fallacies, he expressly lays down that predominance as a philosophical axiom.

"In *every* human breast (rare and short-lived ebullitions, the result of some extraordinarily strong stimulus or excitement, excepted) self-regarding interest is predominant over social interest; each person's own individual interest over the interests of all other persons taken together." Pp. 392-3.

In another passage of the same work (p. 363) he says, "Taking the whole of life together, there exists not, *nor ever can exist*, that human being in whose instance any public interest he can have had will not, in so far as depends upon himself, have been sacrificed to his own personal interest. Towards the advancement of the public interest, all that the most public-spirited (which is as much as to say the most virtuous) of men can do, is to do what depends upon himself toward bringing the public interest, that is, his own personal share in the public interest, to a state as nearly approaching to coincidence, and on as few occasions amounting to a state of repugnance, as possible, with his private interests."

By the promulgation of such views of human nature, and by a general tone of thought and expression perfectly in harmony with them, I conceive Mr. Bentham's writings to have done and to be doing very serious evil. It is by such things that the more enthusiastic and generous minds are prejudiced against all his other speculations, and against the very attempt to make ethics and politics a subject of precise and philosophical thinking—which attempt, indeed, if it were necessarily connected with such views, would be still more pernicious than the vague and flashy declamation for which it is proposed as a substitute. The effect is still worse on the minds of those who are not shocked and repelled by this tone of thinking, for on them it must be perverting to their whole moral nature. It is difficult to form the conception of a tendency more inconsistent with all rational hope of good for the human species, than that which must be impressed by such doctrines upon any mind in which they find acceptance.

There are, there have been, many human beings in whom the motives of patriotism or of benevolence have been permanent steady principles of action, superior to any ordinary, and in not a few instances, to any possible, temptations of personal interest. There are, and have been, multitudes in whom the motive of conscience or moral obligation has been thus paramount. There is nothing in the constitution of human nature to forbid its being so in all mankind. Until it is so, the race will never enjoy one-tenth part of the happiness which our nature is susceptible of. I regard any considerable increase of human happiness, through mere changes in outward circumstances, unaccompanied by changes in the state of the desires, as hopeless; not to mention that, while the desires are circumscribed in self, there can be no adequate motive for exertions tending to modify to good ends even those external circumstances. No man's individual share of any public good which he can hope to realize by his efforts, is an equivalent for the sacrifice of his ease, and of the personal objects which he might attain by another course of conduct. The balance can be turned in favor of virtuous exertion, only by the interest of *feeling* or by that of *conscience,* those "social interests," the necessary subordination of which to "self-regarding" is so lightly assumed.

But the power of any one to realize in himself the state of mind without which his own enjoyment of life can be but poor and scanty, and on which all our hopes of happiness or moral perfection to the species must rest, depends entirely upon his having faith in the actual existence of such feelings and dispositions in others, and in their possibility for himself. It is for those in whom the feelings of virtue are weak, that ethical writing is chiefly needful, and its proper office is to strengthen those feelings. But to be qualified for this task, it is necessary, first to have, and next to show, in every sentence and in every line, a firm unwavering confidence in man's capability of virtue. It is by a sort of sympathetic contagion, or inspiration, that a noble mind assimilates other minds to itself, and no one was ever inspired by one whose own inspiration was not sufficient to give him faith in the possibility of making others feel what *he* feels.

Upon those who *need* to be strengthened and upheld by a really inspired moralist—such a moralist as Socrates, as Plato, or (speaking humanly and not theologically) as Christ, the effect of such writings as Mr. Bentham's, if they be read and believed and their spirit imbibed, must either be hopeless despondency and gloom, or a reckless giving themselves up to a life of that miserable self-seeking, which they are there taught to regard as inherent in their original and unalterable nature.

Mr. Bentham's speculations on politics in the narrow sense, that is, on the theory of government, are distinguished by his usual characteristic, that of beginning at the beginning. He places before himself man in society without a government, and considering what sort of government it would be advisable to construct, finds that the most expedient would be a representative democracy. Whatever may be the value of this conclusion, the mode in which it is arrived at appears to me to be fallacious; for it assumes that mankind are alike in all times and all places, that they have the same wants and are exposed to the same evils, and that if the same institutions do not suit them, it is only because in the more backward stages of improvement, they have not wisdom to see what institutions are most for their good. How to invest certain servants of the people with the power necessary for the protection of person and property, with the greatest possible facility to the people of changing the depositories of that power, when they think it is abused—such is the only problem in social organization which Mr. Bentham has proposed to himself. Yet this is but a part of the real problem. It never seems to have occurred to him to regard political institutions in a higher light, as the principal means of the social education of a people. Had he done so, he would have seen that the same institutions will no more suit two nations in different stages of civilization, than the same lessons will suit children of different ages. As the degree of civilization already attained varies, so does the kind of social influence necessary for carrying the community forward to the next stage of its progress. For a tribe of North American Indians, improvement means taming down their proud and solitary self-dependence; for a body of emancipated Negroes, it means accustoming them to be self-dependent, instead of being merely obedient to orders; for our semibarbarous ancestors, it would have meant, softening them; for a race of enervated Asiatics, it would mean hardening them. How can the same social organization be fitted for producing so many contrary effects?

The prevailing error of Mr. Bentham's views of human nature appears to me to be this: he supposes mankind to be swayed by only a part of the inducements which really actuate them, but of that part he imagines them to be much cooler and more thoughtful calculators than they really are. He has, I think, been, to a certain extent, misled in the theory of politics by supposing that the submission of the mass of mankind to an established government is mainly owing to a reasoning perception of the necessity of legal protection, and of the common interest of all in a prompt and zealous obedience to the law. He was not, I am persuaded, aware, how very much of the really wonderful acquiescence of mankind in any government which they find established, is the effect of mere habit and imagination, and therefore depends upon the preservation of something like continuity of existence in the institutions, and identity in their outward forms; cannot transfer itself easily to new institutions, even though in themselves preferable, and is greatly shaken when there occurs any thing like a break in the line of historical duration, any thing which can be termed the end of the old constitution and the beginning of a new one.

The constitutional writers of our own country, anterior to Mr. Bentham, had carried feelings of this kind to the height of a superstition; they never considered what was best adapted to their own times, but only what had existed in former times, even in times that had long gone by. It is not very many years since such were the principal grounds on which parliamentary reform itself was defended. Mr. Bentham has done much service in discrediting, as he has done completely, this school of politicians, and exposing the absurd sacrifice of present ends to antiquated means; but he has, I think, himself fallen into a contrary error. The very fact that a certain set of political institutions already exist, have long existed, and have become associated with all the historical recollections of a people, is in itself, as far as it goes, a property which adapts them to that people, and gives them a great advantage over any new institutions in obtaining that ready and willing resignation to what has once been decided by lawful authority, which alone renders possible those innumerable compromises between adverse interests and expectations, without which no government could be carried on for a year, and with difficulty even for a week. Of the perception of this important truth, scarcely a trace is visible in Mr. Bentham's writings.

It is impossible, however, to contest to Mr. Bentham, on this subject or on any other which he has touched, the merit, and it is very great, of having brought forward into notice one of the faces of the truth, and a highly important one. Whether on government, on morals, or on any of the other topics on which his speculations are comparatively imperfect, they are still highly instructive and valuable to any one who is capable of supplying the remainder of the truth; they are calculated to mislead only by the pretension which they invariably set up of being the whole truth, a complete theory and philosophy of the subject. Mr. Bentham was more a thinker than a reader; he seldom compared his ideas with those of other philosophers, and was by no means aware how many thoughts had existed in other minds which his doctrines did not afford the means either to refute or to appreciate.

Mill's
Excerpt from a letter to
Henry Jones

As to the sentence you quote from my "Utilitarianism"; when I said that the general happiness is a good to the aggregate of all persons I did not mean that every human being's happiness is a good to every other human being; though I think, in a good state of society & education it would be so. I merely meant in this particular sentence to argue that since A's happiness is a good, B's a good, C's a good, &c., the sum of all these goods must be a good.

Notes and Glossary

This list contains foreign words and phrases not included in *Webster's Seventh New Collegiate Dictionary*, as well as notes on historical figures and events mentioned in the text. Suggestions for additional entries are welcome.

Ad misercordium, **appeal to:**   an appeal "to pity."

Akbar (the Great):   (1542–1605) third Mogul emperor of India, noted for his wise and tolerant reign.

Albigeois: the Albigensians (or Cathars), a group of Christians embracing a version of the Manichaean heresy in southern France during the 11th–13th centuries; the object of a crusade by Innocent III (1161–1216).

Alcibiades: (450–404 B.C.) Greek statesman and general famous for his beauty, brilliance, courage, extravagance, self-indulgence, and unscrupulousness; a friend of Socrates (q.v.).

Alexander (the Great):   (356–323 B.C.) son of King Phillip of Macedonia, tutee of Aristotle, and conqueror of much of Asia and the Near East.

Anabaptists: any of a number of reformist Christian sects stressing the need for adult baptism; many were persecuted in Europe and fled to the United States in the eighteenth century.

Apologia: Plato's dialogue ("The Apology"), in which Socrates defends his teaching against the charge that it is impious and corrupts the youth.

Argumentum ab inconvenienti: an argument against construing an unclear law in a way that would render it unnecessarily burdensome.

Arians: Christians who hold the heretical belief that Christ is not of the same substance as God, a doctrine first made famous by Arius (c. 250–336).

Arnold of Brescia: (c. 1100–1154) ecclesiastic rebel who held that clergy should possess no material goods and that Christians should confess to one another rather than to a priest; hanged by order of Pope Adrian IV.

Bain, Alexander: (1818–1903) Scottish Utilitarian and early contributor to *The Westminster Review;* best known for his work in physiological psychology; author of *John Stuart Mill: A Criticism, with Personal Recollections* (1882) and *Emotions and the Will* (1859).

271

Barnwell, George: Protagonist of *The History of George Barnwell* (1731) or *The London Merchant,* a domestic tragedy in prose by Lillo.

Beccaria: (1738–1794) Italian legal theorist whose *On Crimes and Punishments* (1764) influenced Bentham.

Big-endians vs. Little-endians: In Jonathan Swift's *Gulliver's Travels* (1726), the Big-endians are a group of political dissidents who break their eggs at the larger end, while the Emperor of Lilliput demands that his subjects break them at the smaller end. Swift's discussion satirizes English suppression of Roman Catholics.

Burlamaqui, Jean Jacques: (1694–1749) Swiss jurist who wrote *Principles of Natural Law* (1747) and *Principles of Political Law* (1751); strong proponent of natural law.

Calvin, John: (1509–1564) French Protestant reformer whose *Institutes of the Christian Religion* (1536) is the basis of much Presbyterian and Reformed theology.

Carlyle, Thomas: (1795–1881) Scottish writer and social critic; a close friend of J. S. Mill and an early contributor to *The Westminster Review*; his later views diverged markedly from Mill's.

Catherine II: (1729–1796) German princess who became Empress of Russia after disposing of her ineffectual husband, Peter III.

Charlemagne: (768–814) Charles the Great, King of the Franks and Holy Roman Emperor; noted for his just and effective rule.

Cicero: (106–43 B.C.) Roman orator, politician, and philosopher; proponent of Stoic ethics.

Clive, Robert: (1725–1774) early functionary of the East India Company; defeated the army of the Nawbab of Bengal at the Battle of Plassey in 1757.

Coke, Sir Edward (Lord Coke):   (1552–1634) English jurist whose *Reports* and *Institutes* constitute an influential statement of English Common Law (q.v.).

Commission *de lunatico*:   a warrant declaring a person to be insane and subject to commitment.

Common Law: the ancient unwritten law of England, deriving its authority from usage and customs of immemorial antiquity, rather than explicit statutes.

Comte, Auguste: (1798–1857) French philosopher and social theorist; one of the founders of sociology. His "Positivism," which he sometimes described as a "secular religion," intrigued Mill, though Comte's vision of a tightly controlled, highly hierarchic society repelled him.

Constantine I (The Great): (280–337) Roman emperor whose conversion to Christianity was an important factor in its successful dissemination.

de Tocqueville: (see *Tocqueville*).

Delegatus non potest delegare: "the delegate may not further delegate what has been delegated to him."

Deorum injuriae Diis curae: "Leave offenses against the gods to the care of the gods"; a quotation from Tacitus.

Dumplers: another name for the Dunkards or Brethren, an Anabaptist group that came to America in the 18th century to escape religious persecution in Europe.

East India Directors and Proprietors: the executives of the East India Company, a corporation that ruled India for much of the 18th and 19th centuries; both James Mill and John Stuart Mill were officers of the company, which was finally dissolved in 1858.

Entsagen: the renunciation of self; a philosophical doctrine that Carlyle (q.v.) borrowed from Novalis (q.v.).

Epicurus: (341–270 B.C.) Greek philosopher who established a community, called "The Garden," in Athens and advocated a life of maximum pleasure; Epicurus emphasized the importance of peace of mind and ridding oneself of desires that go beyond what is necessary and natural, but his critics often ignored this.

Fiat Justitia, ruat coelum: "Do justice, though the heavens fall."

Fra Dolcino: (d. 1307) Italian heretic and member of the Apostolic Brothers; preached against private property and led a peasant rebellion in Piedmont; tortured and burned at the stake during a Crusade declared by Clement V.

Goethean and Fichtean period: the period in German intellectual history during which the philosopher Johann Fichte (1762–1814) and the literary giant Wilhelm von Goethe (1749–1832) were active; Kant and Hegel wrote during this period.

Grotius, Hugo: (1583–1645) Dutch legal theorist and pioneer of natural law theory; his *On the Law of War and Peace* (1625) earned him the title of "Father of International Law."

Hastings, Warren: (1732–1814) First Governor-General of India (1773–1784); impeached for extortion after his return to England; prosecuted by Edmund Burke but acquitted.

Helots: serfs of ancient Sparta, prone to rebellion because of their harsh treatment.

Humboldt, Wilhelm von: (1767–1835) German philosopher and linguist whose *The Limits of State Power* (1792) argued that state power should be limited to protection of citizens' lives and property; his work was a strong influence on Mill's *On Liberty* (1859).

Hussites: followers of the Moravian reformer Jan Hus, executed as a heretic in 1418; Hus preached against clerical excess and advocated the study of scripture by the laity.

"I maestri di color che sanno": "the master of those who know"; Dante's characterization of Aristotle in *The Divine Comedy*.

Idée mère: literally, "mother idea"; the original concept.

Impey, Sir Elijah: (1732–1809) Chief Justice of Bengal, impeached with Warren Hastings (q.v.) and also acquitted.

Inductive school: a system of ethics, like Utilitarianism, holding that moral principles are grounded in observation and experience and cannot be known *a priori*.

Intuitive school: a system of ethics, like Kant's, holding that moral principles can be known *a priori*.

Johnson, Samuel: (1709–1784) English author and lexicographer, celebrated for his wit and memorialized in Boswell's *Life of Johnson* (1791).

Kant, Immanuel: (1724–1804) German Idealist whose ethical theory, put forward in the *Foundations of the Metaphysics of Morals* (1785) and the *Critique of Practical Reason* (1788), offers (*pace* Mill) a non-consequentialist rival to Utilitarianism.

Knox, John: (c. 1505–1572) Scottish priest who became a Protestant reformer and founded the Presbyterian Church.

Lex talionis: the "law of retaliation," appearing in Hammurabi's Code (c. 1780 B.C.) and in the Bible as "eye for eye, tooth for tooth" (Exodus 21:24; but compare Matthew 5:38-39).

Locke, John: (1632–1704) the foremost English philosopher of his age; his *Two Treatises on Government* and his *Essay Concerning Human Understanding* had a great impact on 18th-century political and philosophical developments.

Locrians: citizens of an ancient Greek colony in southern Italy, famous for their harsh laws.

Lollards: members of a heretical Christian sect that originated in England in the 1380s and was strongly influenced by the teachings of John Wycliffe (c. 1320?–1384).

Lord Coke: (see *Coke*).

Luther, Martin: (1483–1546) German monk who began the Protestant Reformation; Professor of philosophy and then theology at the University of Wittenberg; founder of Lutheranism.

Lycurgus: Greek warrior, perhaps legendary; often referred to as "the Father of Sparta."

Maine Law: a law passed in the state of Maine in 1851 banning the manufacture and sale of liquor in that state.

Marcus Aurelius: (121–180) Roman Emperor famous for his exposition of Stoicism (q.v.) in his *Meditations*.

Mill's British India: in 1817 James Mill published the first full history of British rule in India; despite its severe criticisms of this rule, the book earned Mill a position as an official of the East India Company, where for 17 years he worked to better conditions in India.

Montesquieu, Baron de: (1689–1755) French legal theorist whose writings, especially *On the Spirit of the Laws* (1748), had a significant impact on the framers of the American Constitution.

Nisi prius **advocate:** an advocate before an assizes court.

Novalis: pen name of Friedrich Leopold, Baron von Hardenberg (1772–1801); early German Romantic poet; introduced Carlyle (q.v.) to Kant's philosophy.

Odium theologicum: hatred of those with different religious beliefs.

Os sacrum: the large heavy bone at the base of the spine.

Owen, Robert: (1771–1858) Welsh socialist; pioneer in cooperative factories; established "Owenite" communities in Britain (New Lenark, built with financial backing by Bentham) and America (New Harmony, Indiana).

Pericles: (490–429 B.C.) Athenian statesman who combined many classical virtues of private life with an exemplary career as a politician.

Plato: (c. 427–347 B.C.) Greek philosopher; disciple of Socrates and teacher of Aristotle; founded a school (the Academy) in Athens and wrote the most influential dialogues in the history of philosophy.

Pleonexia: "greed."

Pourétre embesoignèes: "to be taken by force."

Pro re natâ: literally, "for the thing born"; to meet an emergency.

Pro tanto: "to that extent."

Protagoras (of Abdera):   (c. 490–c. 420 B.C.) Greek Sophist (q.v.) most famous for his relativist assertion that "man is the measure of all things."

Roturiers: commoners in France who leased land from those of noble descent.

Rousseau, Jean-Jacques: (1712–1778) French political philosopher often invoked by the more democratic elements in the French revolution.

Savonarola, Girolamo: (1452–1498) Italian Dominican reformer whose fervent sermons against corruption in the Church and his political activities led to his condemnation to death by hanging on charges of heresy and treason.

Sepoy Insurrection (also known as the "Great Mutiny" and the "Revolt of 1857"):   A year-long insurrection that began with a mutiny of Indian soldiers (Sepoys) in the British Indian Army; it led to the dissolution of the British East Indian Company, direct rule of India by Great Britain, and the end of the Mogul Empire.

Sic volo sic jubeo: "thus I will, thus I command."

Socrates: (470–399 B.C.) Athenian philosopher; the teacher of Plato, who made Socrates the protagonist of many of his dialogues; Socrates' political associations and teaching methods led to his trial on vague charges of impiety and corruption of the youth, and Socrates accepted his death sentence rather than abandoning Athens.

Socratici viri: "the men of Socrates," i.e., the disciples of Socrates.

Sophists: itinerant Greek teachers in the time of Plato who often gave instruction in rhetoric and taught their students how to make the worse appear the better case.

Spencer, Herbert: (1820–1903) English philosopher and social theorist who attempted to apply Darwin's theory of evolution to ethics and the social sciences; his *Social Statics, or the Conditions Essential to Human Happiness* (1851) is a defense of individual liberty exemplifying this attempt.

Stanley, Henry: (1827–1903) third Lord of Alderley; diplomat, writer, traveler, civil servant, and orientalist; converted to Islam and was buried on his estate by the Imam of the Turkish Embassy in London.

Sterling, John: (1806–1844) British essayist and poet; founder of a literary club that included J. S. Mill, Carlyle, and Tennyson; his posthumously published *Essays and Tales* (1845) contrasts Christian and pagan virtues.

Stoicism: a philosophical system founded by Zeno of Citium (333–264 B.C.); its ethical teachings stressed the virtues of self-sufficiency and control, urged the abandonment of emotions such as fear and distress, and taught that evils over which one has no control are only apparent and should be accepted with equanimity; later Stoics include the slave Epictetus and the emperor Marcus Aurelius.

Sui generis: "a class of its own; unique."

Themis: in Greek mythology, a titaness, the daughter of Gaea and Uranus.

"Things in themselves": Kant's term for objects as they really are as opposed to objects as they appear to us.

Tocqueville, Alexis de: (1805–1859) French statesman and historian whose *Democracy in America* (1835–1840) convinced Mill that a democracy could become a "tyranny of the majority."

Transcendentalism: an American philosophical movement, led by Emerson and Thoreau, with its roots in post-Kantian Idealism.

Vaudois: (also called the "Waldensians" or the "Poor Men") a heretical group that followed the teachings of the lay preacher Peter Waldo of Lyons; excommunicated in 1184, they were subjected to religious persecution well into the 19th century.

Velitis jubeatis: "would we accept, would we command"; a phrase used in asking a Roman assembly if it accepted a proposal.

Violenti non fit injuria: "there is no injury to a willing party."

Voltaire: (1694–1778) French philosopher and satirist, famous for his *Candide, or All for the Best* (1759) and his *Philosophical Dictionary* (1764).

Bibliography

Bentham

Bentham wrote a great deal but published relatively little. During his lifetime much of his work was known only in the French redactions published by his Swiss admirer, Étienne Dumont. After Bentham's death, John Bowring produced an 11-volume edition of *The Works of Jeremy Bentham*, including much previously unpublished material and English versions of Dumont's redactions. A fuller and more accurate edition of Bentham's *Works* is being prepared by the Bentham Project at University College London, and many volumes are already in print. The Bentham Project also publishes the *Journal of Bentham Studies* (formerly *The Bentham Newsletter*) and maintains an informative web site (http://www.ucl.ac.uk/Bentham-Project), which includes views of Bentham's "auto-icon."

Mill

Mill's major works include the following:
A System of Logic (1843)
Essays on Some Unsettled Questions of Political Economy (1844)
Principles of Political Economy (1848)
On Liberty (1859)
Considerations on Representative Government (1860)
Utilitarianism (1863)
Examination of Sir William Hamilton's Philosophy (1865)
The Subjection of Women (1869)
Autobiography (1873)

Mill's *Collected Works* have been published (in 33 vols, 1963–1991) by Toronto University Press. *The Mill Newsletter* (1965–1989) is no more, but *Utilitas* (supported by the International Society for Utilitarian Studies) continues to publish articles on Mill and Bentham, as well as on contemporary developments in utilitarian theory.

Works on Utilitarianism and Works Cited

Albee, Ernest. *A History of English Utilitarianism*. London: Swan Sonnenschein, 1902.

Amis, Kingsley. *Lucky Jim.* London: Victor Gollancz, 1953.

Aristotle. *Nicomachean Ethics.* Translated by Martin Ostwald. Indianapolis and New York: Bobbs Merrill, 1962.

Atkinson, Charles Milner. *Jeremy Bentham, His Life and Work.* Westport, CT.: Greenwood Press, 1970. Originally published in 1905.

Austin, John. *Lectures on Jurisprudence.* 2 vols. 4th ed. London: John Murray, 1873.

Bayles, Michael, ed. *Contemporary Utilitarianism.* New York: Doubleday, 1968.

Bergström, Lars. *The Alternatives and Consequences of Actions.* Stockholm: Almqvist & Wiksell, 1966.

Brandt, Richard B. *Ethical Theory.* Englewood Cliffs, N.J., Prentice-Hall, 1959.

―――. "Toward a Credible Form of Utilitarianism." In *Morality and the Language of Conduct,* edited by H. N. Casteñeda and G. Nakhnikian. Detroit: Wayne State University Press, 1963.

―――. *A Theory of the Good and the Right.* Oxford: Oxford University Press, 1979.

Davidson, William L. *Political Thought in England: The Utilitarians from Bentham to Mill.* Oxford: Oxford University Press, 1915.

Edgeworth, Francis Ysidro. *New and Old Methods of Ethics.* Oxford: James Parker, 1877.

―――. *Mathematical Psychics: An Essay on the Application of Mathematics to the Moral Sciences.* London: C. Kegan Paul,1881.

Gibbard, Allan. "Rule Utilitarianism: Merely an Illusory Alternative?" *Australasian Journal of Philosophy* 43 (1965): 211–220.

Gorovitz, Samuel, ed. *Utilitarianism: with Critical Essays.* Indianapolis: Bobbs-Merrill, 1971.

Halévy, Elie. *The Growth of Philosophic Radicalism.* Clifton, N.J.: Augustus M. Kelly, 1972. [Originally published in 1904.]

Jeffrey, Richard C. *The Logic of Decision.* 2d ed. Chicago: University of Chicago Press, 1983.

Lyons, David. *Forms and Limits of Utilitarianism.* Oxford: Oxford University Press, 1965.

―――. *In the Interest of the Governed: A Study in Bentham's Philosophy of Utility and Law.* Oxford: Oxford University Press, 1973.

The Mill Newsletter, vols. 1–23 (1965–1989).

Miller, Harlan B. and William H. Williams, eds.*The Limits of Utilitarianism.* Minneapolis: University of Minnesota Press, 1982.

Moore, G. E. *Principia Ethica.* Cambridge: Cambridge University Press, 1903.

Nesbitt, George L. *Benthamite Reviewing: The First Twelve Years of The Westminster Review 1824–1836.* New York: Columbia University Press, 1934.

Nozick, Robert. *Anarchy, State, and Utopia.* New York: Basic Books, 1974.

Packe, Michael St. John. *The Life of John Stuart Mill.* London: Martin Secker & Warburg, 1954.

Parekh, Bhikhu, ed. *Bentham's Political Thought.* London: Croom Helm, 1973.

Ramsey, Frank Plumpton. *The Foundations of Mathematics and other Logical Essays.* New York: Humanities Press, 1950.

Rawls, John. "Two Concepts of Rules." *Philosophical Review* 64 (1955): 3–32.

———. *A Theory of Justice.* Cambridge: Harvard University Press, 1971.

Runes, Dagobert D. *Pictorial History of Philosophy.* New York: Philosophical Library, 1959.

Scheffler, Samuel, ed. *Consequentialism and Its Critics.* Oxford: Oxford University Press, 1988.

Schneewind, J. B., ed. *Mill: A Collection of Critical Essays.* Garden City, N.J.: Anchor Books, 1968.

Sen, Amartya. *On Economic Inequality.* Oxford: Oxford University Press, 1973.

Sen, Amartya and Bernard Williams, eds. *Utilitarianism and Beyond.* Cambridge: Cambridge University Press, 1982.

Sidgwick, Henry. *The Methods of Ethics.* 7th ed. London and New York: Macmillan, 1907.

Smart, J.J.C. and Bernard Williams. *Utilitarianism: For & Against.* Cambridge: Cambridge University Press, 1973.

Steintrager, James. *Bentham.* Ithaca, N.Y.: Cornell University Press, 1977.

Stephen, Leslie. *The English Utilitarians.* London: Duckworth, 1900.

Stillinger, Jack. *The Early Draft of John Stuart Mill's Autobiography.* Urbana: University of Illinois Press, 1961.

———, ed. *John Stuart Mill: Autobiography and Other Writings.* Boston: Houghton Mifflin, 1969.

Temkin, Larry. *Inequality.* Oxford: Oxford University Press, 1993.

Thomson, Judith. "Goodness and Utilitarianism" (Presidential Address), *Proceedings & Addresses of the American Philosophical Association* 67:2 (1993): 145–159.

Utilitas: A Journal of Utilitarian Studies (1989–).